Buried Histories

Critical Human Rights

Series Editors

Scott Straus ❧ Tyrell Haberkorn
Steve J. Stern, **Editor Emeritus**

Books in the series **Critical Human Rights** emphasize research that opens new ways to think about and understand human rights. The series values in particular empirically grounded and intellectually open research that eschews simplified accounts of human rights events and processes.

Across the Indonesian archipelago during the long months of 1965–66, supporters of the Communist Party of Indonesia (PKI) were hunted down, arrested, detained, tortured, and killed. For decades, the killings were shrouded in silence. In *Buried Histories*, John Roosa combines oral history and fine-grained archival research to elucidate how the killings were systematic and planned from the top of the military dictatorship. Careful attention to the subjectivity of both perpetrators and victims illuminates both the series of social and political transformations that led to mass violence in Indonesia during the Cold War and the difficulty of redressing it decades later.

Buried Histories

*The Anticommunist Massacres
of 1965–1966 in Indonesia*

John Roosa

The University of Wisconsin Press

The University of Wisconsin Press
728 State Street, Suite 443
Madison, Wisconsin 53706
uwpress.wisc.edu

Gray's Inn House, 127 Clerkenwell Road
London EC1R 5DB, United Kingdom
eurospanbookstore.com

Copyright © 2020
The Board of Regents of the University of Wisconsin System
All rights reserved. Except in the case of brief quotations embedded in critical articles and reviews, no
    part of this publication may be reproduced, stored in a retrieval system, transmitted in any format
    or by any means—digital, electronic, mechanical, photocopying, recording, or otherwise—or
    conveyed via the Internet or a website without written permission of the University of Wisconsin
    Press. Rights inquiries should be directed to rights@uwpress.wisc.edu.

Printed in the United States of America

This book may be available in a digital edition.

Library of Congress Cataloging-in-Publication Data

Names: Roosa, John, author.
Title: Buried histories: the anticommunist massacres of 1965-1966 in Indonesia / John Roosa.
Other titles: Critical human rights.
Description: Madison, Wisconsin: The University of Wisconsin Press, [2020]
        | Series: Critical human rights | Includes bibliographical references and index.
Identifiers: LCCN 2019041277 | ISBN 9780299327309 (cloth)
Subjects: LCSH: Political atrocities—Indonesia. | Targeted killing—Indonesia. | Death squads—
    Indonesia. | Anti-communist movements—Indonesia. | Indonesia—History—Coup d'état, 1965.
Classification: LCC DS644.32 .R655 2020 | DDC 959.803/5—dc23
LC record available at https://lccn.loc.gov/2019041277

ISBN 9780299327347 (paperback)

For **Ayu**
for blessing many wounded springtimes

Contents

List of Illustrations ix
Acknowledgments xi
Abbreviations xv

Introduction 3

1. Unarmed Fortresses: The Army and the PKI's Rival Struggles for Hegemony during Guided Democracy 28

2. Mental Operations: The Army's Propaganda after October 1, 1965 57

3. Tortured Words: Interrogations and the Production of Truth 85

4. Surprise Attacks: The Destruction of the PKI in Surakarta 116

5. Vanishing Points: Disappearances in Bali 147

6. Invisible Worlds: The Kapal Massacre in Bali 179

7. Dead Labor: Disappearances in Sumatra 209

Conclusions 241

Afterlives 254

Notes 267
Bibliography 319
Index 341

Illustrations

Maps

Provinces and regional army commands of Indonesia in 1965	2
Surakarta and its environs in 1965	121
Bali in 1965	153
Sumatra in 1965	222

Figures

Still image from *The Look of Silence* (2014) showing the grave of Ramli	13
"Separation," a painting by Misbach Tamrin, 2007	19
Sukarno and Aidit at Senayan Stadium, Jakarta, May 23, 1965	29
Sukarno, ca. 1946	37
D. N. Aidit, June 1963	44
Suharto being sworn in as army commander, October 16, 1965	58
The mob attack on Res Publica University, Jakarta, October 12, 1965	66
Front page of the army's newspaper, *Berita Yudha*, November 19, 1965	72
The graves of eleven PKI leaders at Ngalihan, Central Java, ca. 1960	82

ix

The door to the former Infico Film Studio, Jakarta, 2011	86
Drawing by Gumelar of a torture session in Jakarta	95
Diagram of the September 30th Movement drawn by military prosecutors	110
Ceremony at the Bacem Bridge, 2005	117
Pak Bronto, Surakarta, 2012	129
An army truck, Surakarta, late October 1965	136
The ruins of stores owned by Sino-Indonesians after a riot, Surakarta, late October 1965	140
The *lontar* written by I Gusti Nyoman Gede, December 1965	148
A group of the PNI's Tameng militia, Bali, ca. late 1965	161
Statues in honor of I Gusti Nyoman Gede and his Legong group, Bedulu, Bali	178
The cremation grounds of Kapal village, 2012	180
I Gde Puger and Ida Ayu Rai Parmini, Denpasar, Bali, ca. 1960	190
The office of the Legal Department of Kodam IX, Denpasar, Bali, 2012	205
Drawing of the Railway Workers' Union Hall near Manggarai Station, Jakarta	210
The PKI's thirty-fifth anniversary celebration, held in the Railway Workers' Union Hall, May 1955	212
An aerial view of the oil refineries in Palembang, Sumatra, ca. 1930	218
Art installation by Semsar Siahaan, Jakarta, 1994	242
A session of the national symposium, Jakarta, April 18, 2016	255
Sukar standing next to a plaque marking the mass grave near the village of Plumbon, Semarang, Central Java	266

Acknowledgments

Much of the research on which this book is based was a collaborative effort with my colleagues at the Indonesian Institute of Social History (Institut Sejarah Sosial Indonesia, ISSI) in Jakarta who have been committed to unburying the history of the events of 1965–66: Razif, Muhammad Fauzi, Grace Leksana, Yayan Wiludiharto, Taat Ujianto, Anom Astika, Rini Pratsnawati, Alit Ambara, and Hilmar Farid. I have been fortunate to work closely over many years with two master oral interviewers at the Institute: Rinto Tri Hasworo and Erlijna. I am grateful to the many people who have supported the Institute's work over the years, especially Irwan Firdaus, Yudi Priyanti, and Agung Putri.

I am particularly proud of ISSI's work in 2010 in fighting the government's banning of the Indonesian translation of my earlier book *Pretext for Mass Murder*. ISSI petitioned the Constitutional Court to have the 1963 law on book banning declared unconstitutional, and my colleagues drew upon their rich knowledge of history to present a comprehensive and convincing case before the court. The court's decision, in October 2010, to strike down the law was a landmark victory for the right of freedom of expression in Indonesia.

My desire to study the events of 1965–66 began in the mid-1990s when I visited Jakarta for the first time and entered into a social circle of former political prisoners who had been involved in the cultural organization Lekra before 1965: Pramoedya Ananta Toer, Oey Hay Djoen, and Joebaar Ajoeb. I also spent a lot of time conversing with Joesoef Isak, who had been a journalist before 1965. Upon his release from prison in 1979, he helped set up the publishing house Hasta Mitra with Pramoedya and Hasjim Rachman to publish the many manuscripts that Pramoedya had written while being held in the Buru Island labor camp. I frequently met another former Lekra member and

Buru Island alumnus, Hersri Setiawan, once he moved back to Jakarta from his exile in the Netherlands. These five men were my teachers and my friends, from whom I learned much about writing history and surviving the worst experiences that this world can offer.

Political imprisonment was not just of historical interest to me while in Jakarta at that time. In 1996, my brother-in-law, Anom Astika, was arrested with other leaders of the People's Democratic Party and charged with political crimes. They were young people, all in their twenties. When visiting him in Cipinang Prison in Jakarta in 1997–98, I was able to meet political prisoners from earlier cases. During the weekly visiting hours, all the political prisoners and their relatives freely mingled in one pavilion. There, I conversed with three men who had spent more than thirty years in prison for their involvement in the September 30th Movement: Abdul Latief, Bungkus, and Asep Suryaman. In the wake of the collapse of the Suharto dictatorship, in May 1998, all of the political prisoners in Cipinang Prison were released. I kept in close touch with Asep, visiting him in his home in Tasikmalaya and meeting him in Jakarta whenever he came to the city.

I learned much from socializing with other former political prisoners in Jakarta, including Putu Oka Sukanta, Martin Aleida, Tedjobayu Sudjojono, Hardoyo, Amarzan Loebis, and Gumelar Demokrasno, and in Bali, I Wayan Santa, Prayitno, Ngurah Jenawi, and I Wayan Natar. All of these former political prisoners were survivors of the massacres of 1965–66—the fortunate ones who happened not to be taken out and executed—and survivors of the malnutrition and disease that claimed the lives of so many other prisoners.

A constant source of inspiration was Ade Rostina Sitompul, whose humanitarian work began in 1965 when her older brother, Djoni Sitompul, an editor of the daily newspaper *Warta Bhakti*, became a political prisoner. She worked tirelessly to arrange deliveries of food, medicine, and clothes to him and his fellow inmates—supplies that meant the difference between life and death. She continued that work for political prisoners from East Timor and Papua all the way up to the late 1990s.

I want to thank Jaya Laksana, Ciptapura, Roro Sawita, and the late Agus Januraka, who helped the research in Bali. I have learned from historians and human rights activists in Indonesia: Asvi Warman Adam, Yunantyo Adi, Rukardi Achmadi, Bonnie Triyana, Kamala Chandrakirana, Karlina Supelli, Stanley Adi Prasetyo, Baskara Wardaya, Wasis Sasmito, and Al Muiz Liddinillah. I thank Bunga Siagian for corresponding with me about her father.

At the University of British Columbia, I would like to thank the Department of History heads who have facilitated my research and teaching over the years: David Breen, the late Danny Vickers, Anne Gorsuch, Tina Loo, and Eagle Glassheim. I would also like to thank all my colleagues in the department; the department administrator, Jocelyn Smith; the librarian, Keith Bunnell; and colleagues in other departments: Jim Glassman, Thomas Hunter, Kai Ostwald, and Abidin Kusno (now at York University). Erin Baines and Pilar Riaño-Alcalá have led an inspiring international project on Transformative Memory at UBC. I am indebted to my students who have assisted the research: Teilhard Paradela, Edgar Liao, Genevieve Cruz, Daniel Carkner, and Jason Salim. Nila Ayu Utami and Abigail White played crucial roles in the final stages of preparing the manuscript. Thanks to the students of my 2018 graduate writing seminar who commented on one of the chapters. I am grateful to Eric Leinberger of the UBC Cartography Lab for creating the maps.

Gwen Walker and Tyrell Haberkorn have been sagacious and patient editors.

A small part of the research was funded by a SSHRC grant in 2007 for a project titled "Memories of Mass Violence." Chapter 3 incorporates some passages from my article "The Truths of Torture: Victims' Memories and State Histories in Indonesia," *Indonesia* no. 85 (April 2008).

I thank fellow academics scattered around the world: Michael Bodden, close by at the University of Victoria; Ben White, Ratna Saptari, Gerry van Klinken, Uğur Ümit Üngör, and Henk Schulte Nordholt in the Netherlands; Joshua Oppenheimer in Britain; Akihisa Matsuno, Aiko Kurasawa, and Brad Horton in Japan; Joseph Nevins, Jeffrey Winters, Geoffrey Robinson, Robert Lemelson, Mary McCoy, Brad Simpson, Siddharth Chandra, Rudolf Mrázek, Charley Sullivan, Bernd Schaefer, Mary Zurbuchen, and Margaret Scott in the United States; Douglas Kammen and Taomo Zhou in Singapore; Dag Yngvesson in Malaysia; Robert Cribb, Siauw Tiong Djin, Katherine McGregor, Jess Melvin, Adrian Vickers, Mark Aarons, and Vannessa Hearman in Australia. I am immensely indebted, as always, to Alfred McCoy at the University of Wisconsin–Madison. I have been saddened by the passing of three Indonesianists in recent years who I had hoped would read this book: Benedict Anderson, Mary Steedly, and Jeff Hadler.

It is still difficult to accept the death of my father-in-law, I Gusti Ngurah Oka, a professor of the Indonesian language, in 2006 as a result of the poor medical care in a hospital in Malang. He was a healthy and fun-loving man who should have lived for many more years. I am grateful for the countless acts of kindness by Ibu Non Oka, a pillar of strength during tumultuous times.

I would not have been able to write about death if I had not been living with someone who is so full of life. Ayu Ratih is a shining exemplar of biophilia, attending daily to the well-being of all manner of plants and animals, including the strange creatures found within the species *Homo sapiens*. She has been with me every step of the way. Both of us would like a world for our son, Tossan, that is nothing like the past and the present described in this book.

Abbreviations

AB	*Angkatan Bersenjata*
ANRI	Arsip Nasional Republik Indonesia (National Archives of the Republic of Indonesia)
Baperki	Badan Permusjawaratan Kewarganegaraan Indonesia (Consultative Body of Indonesian Citizenship)
BKS	Badan Kerja Sama (Bodies of Cooperation)
BPS	Badan Pendukung Sukarnoism (Body for Promoting Sukarnoism)
BTI	Barisan Tani Indonesia (Indonesian Peasants Front)
BY	*Berita Yudha*
CDB	Comite Daerah Besar (Provincial Committee)
CGMI	Consentrasi Gerakan Mahasiswa Indonesia (Indonesian Student Movement Center)
CPM	Corps Polisi Militer (Military Police)
Dekon	Deklarasi Ekonomi (Economic Declaration)
FFC	Fact Finding Commission
FSAB	Forum Silaturahmi Anak Bangsa (Friendship Forum of the Nation's Children)
Gerwani	Gerakan Wanita Indonesia (Indonesian Women's Movement)
GMNI	Gerakan Mahasiswa Nasional Indonesia (National Student Movement of Indonesia)
HSI	Himpunan Sarjana Indonesia (Association of Indonesian Scholars)
IPKI	Ikatan Pendukung Kemerdekaan Indonesia (League of Supporters of Indonesian Independence)
IPPI	Ikatan Pemuda Pelajar Indonesia (Indonesian Association of Youths and Students)

IPT	International People's Tribunal (The Hague)
KAMI	Kesatuan Aksi Mahasiswa Indonesia (Indonesian Student Action Front)
KAP-Gestapu	Kesatuan Aksi Pengganyangan Gestapu (Action Front for the Crushing of the September 30th Movement)
KAPPI	Kesatuan Aksi Pemuda Pelajar Indonesia (Indonesian Youth and Student Action Front)
KOKAP	Badan Koordinasi Kesatuan Aksi Pengganjangan Kontrev Gestapu (Coordinating Body for Unifying the Actions to Crush the Counterrevolutionary September 30th Movement)
KOTI	Komando Operasi Tertinggi (Supreme Operations Command)
Lekra	Lembaga Kebudayaan Rakjat (Institute for People's Culture)
Lemhanas	Lembaga Pertahanan Nasional (National Resilience Institute)
MKTBP	Metode Kombinasi Tiga Bentuk Perjuangan (Method for Combining the Three Forms of Struggle)
NU	Nahdlatul Ulama (Revival of the Ulama)
Partindo	Partai Indonesia (Indonesian Party)
PDI-P	Indonesian Partai Demokrasi Indonesia-Perjuangan (Indonesian Democratic Party of Struggle)
Perbum	Persatuan Buruh Minyak (Oil Workers Union)
Pesindo	Pemuda Sosialis Indonesia (Socialist Youth of Indonesia)
PGRI	Persatuan Guru Republik Indonesia (Teachers Union of the Republic of Indonesia)
PKI	Partai Komunis Indonesia (Communist Party of Indonesia)
PNI	Partai Nasionalis Indonesia (Indonesian National Party)
PRRI	Pemerintahan Revolusioner Republik Indonesia (Revolutionary Government of the Republic of Indonesia)
PSI	Partai Sosialis Indonesia (Socialist Party of Indonesia)
PUSRI	Pabrik Pupuk Sriwijaya (Sriwijaya Fertilizer Factory)
PWI	Persatuan Wartawan Indonesia (Indonesian Journalists' Association)
RPKAD	Resimen Para Komando Angkatan Darat (Army Paracommando Regiment)
RRI	Radio Republik Indonesia (Radio of the Republic of Indonesia)
Sarbupri	Sarekat Buruh Perkebunan Republik Indonesia (Plantation Workers Union of the Republic of Indonesia)
SBKA	Serikat Buruh Kereta Api (Railway Workers Union)
SBKB	Serikat Buruh Kendaaran Bermotor (Motorized Transport Workers Union)

SBKP	Serikat Buruh Kapal dan Pelabuhan (Ship Workers and Dockworkers Union)
SBPP	Serikat Buruh Pekerja Pelabuhan (Dock Workers Union)
SEATO	Southeast Asia Treaty Organization
SI	*Suara Indonesia*
SOBSI	Sentral Organisasi Buruh Seluruh Indonesia (Central Organization of Indonesian Workers)
TT	Tentara dan Territorium (Troop and Area Command)
UI	University of Indonesia
VSTP	Vereeniging van Spoor en Tramweg-Personeel (Union of Rail and Tramway Personnel)
WPC	World Peace Council
YPKP	Yayasan Penelitian Korban Pembunuhan 1965–66 (Research Foundation for the Victims of the 1965–66 Killings)

Buried Histories

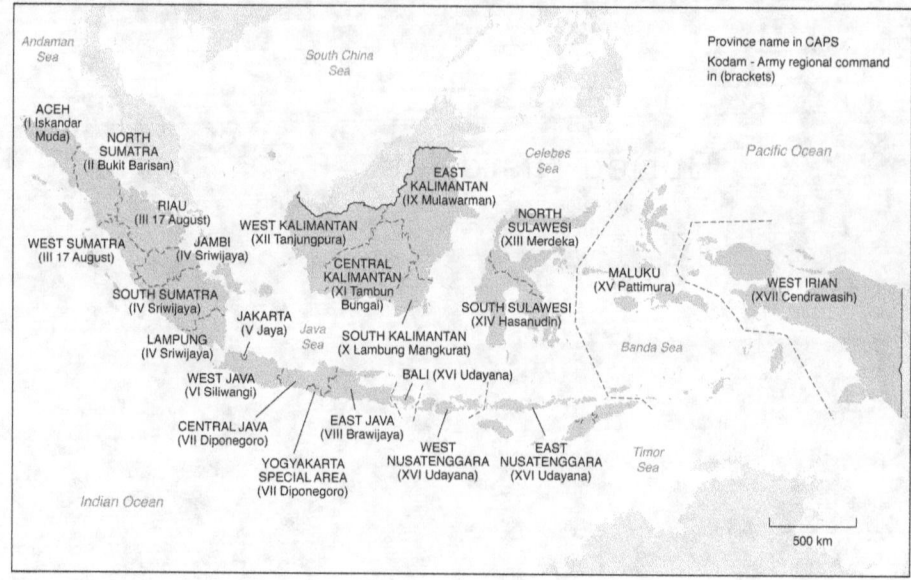

Provinces and regional army commands of Indonesia in 1965

Introduction

In early March 1966, Ibnu Santoro, a graduate of the University of Wisconsin–Madison, was removed from an army detention camp in the city of Yogyakarta, trucked with twenty other captives to a desolate forest off a backcountry road, and shot point-blank in the back of the head. He was buried in a mass grave with the other captives—all accused of being supporters of the Partai Komunis Indonesia (PKI, Communist Party of Indonesia). A guard on the truck returned to Yogyakarta secretly carrying a piece of paper that contained a list of the names of the twenty-one victims and a rough, hand-drawn map that showed where they had been buried. The location was on a hillside in the regency of Wonosobo, some forty miles away in Central Java. If not for this compassionate guard, acting on his own accord, this massacre would have remained undocumented, like countless other massacres in Indonesia. Ibnu Santoro's relatives never knew what had happened to him until the guard's document became public in 1999. Santoro's wife had spent years searching the prisons of Java for him, encountering nothing but blank stares and walls of silence from the world of officialdom.

By virtue of the guard's piece of paper, the mass grave was located and exhumed thirty-four years later. The Suharto dictatorship that had come to power through the mass killings of 1965–66 collapsed in 1998. With the political elite in chaos, the victims of that dictatorship had a new freedom to organize. One group of former political prisoners formed an organization to document the mass killings and decided in 2000 that the Wonosobo mass grave in which Ibnu Santoro lay would be the first one to be exhumed. Not only did they have the guard's document as evidence, but they had the testimony of a man who had been a prisoner in the town of Wonosobo at that time (because of a criminal case). He and several other prisoners had been forced by army personnel to dig the mass grave and bury the victims. He remembered the exact location. Local government officials and community leaders, after lengthy negotiations, allowed the exhumation. Forensic specialists brought in from Jakarta uncovered twenty-six skeletons. Only six of them could be identified. One of them was Ibnu Santoro's.[1]

Ibnu Santoro was teaching economics in 1965 at Gadjah Mada University, which was one of the largest and most prestigious universities in the country at that time. He, like many of his fellow instructors, supported the PKI-affiliated organizations on campus, such as the one for university students, though his support could not have been extensive. He had spent most of the preceding six years in the United States. The limited support he offered seems to have been at least partly motivated by self-preservation. The PKI was leading campaigns against everything American at the time—Hollywood films, the Peace Corps, the libraries of the US Information Agency—and he would have been a prime target as a Ford Foundation–funded graduate of an American university. Such nuances were lost after October 1, 1965, when the university systematically dismissed professors and expelled students who had been in some way connected with these PKI organizations. Many among the thousands of students and instructors dismissed from the university were detained by the army.[2] One of the army's main detention sites in Yogyakarta was the US Information Agency's library, called the Thomas Jefferson Library, which had been closed down because of protests in August 1964.[3] Some among those detained were, like Ibnu Santoro, taken out at night and summarily executed. They disappeared. One of the ways his family was able to identify his skeleton at the exhumation in 2000 was by the bits of Levi-Strauss blue jeans found next to it. He had been wearing the jeans that he had brought back from Madison.

I first learned of the name Ibnu Santoro from the reporting on the exhumation in 2000, but I learned that he was from the same university at which I had earned my doctorate only when I watched the documentary film *Shadow Play* (2002), which contained an interview with Ibnu Santoro's younger brother and showed scenes of the ceremony for his reburial.[4] I had by that time interviewed many former political prisoners and their relatives, but none had a connection to my alma mater. I wondered how he had come to study in Madison and who he met there and what he thought about the place. My own interest in Indonesia had begun in Madison, where I had the opportunity to befriend Indonesian students and take courses on Southeast Asian history in the 1990s.

By chance, many years later, I learned more about Ibnu Santoro's time in Madison. Arthur Ray, a colleague of mine at the University of British Columbia, mentioned to me that he had been a graduate student in Madison in the early 1960s and had become friends with a group of Indonesian students who frequently visited the house of L. Reed Tripp, a professor of economics. I asked him if he remembered someone named Ibnu Santoro. He did, and he put me in touch with the late professor's son, Jon Tripp, who knew him better. Ibnu Santoro had been a student of Tripp's and had become very close to the family. Professor Tripp had worked in Yogyakarta, Indonesia, in 1957–59 as the director of a Ford Foundation project to develop the economics department at Gadjah Mada University.[5] He had become an aficionado of Javanese gamelan music and had an entire set of the instruments shipped to Madison.[6] Jon Tripp wrote in an email:

> Ibnu began as a graduate student under Dad's guidance when we returned from Indonesia in 1959. In those days there were perhaps 15 or 20 Indonesian students at the University of Wisconsin, and our home became a meeting place for these students, typically on Sunday afternoon, extending into the evening. We would cook Indonesian food and the students would sing folk songs from home. On occasion, we would play the gamelan instruments. The university held an international student exposition once a year and we would participate with the Indonesian students, setting up a trade-show type of booth with Indonesian statues, fabrics, puppets, and photographs.

Charismatic and gregarious, Ibnu Santoro made a lasting impression on the Tripps, more so than any of the other Indonesian students gathering at their home. This young man from Central Java had no trouble fitting into Midwestern society.

> Ibnu was a cut above the rest, having a very engaging personality and a great sense of humor. He spoke American English right down to slang words. He and Dad would sit at the dining room table and debate for hours about politics, government, economics, democracy and communism. I was a pretty good chess player back in those days and I remember Ibnu as the only one of Dad's students who I could never beat at chess. He went with us on the family vacation up to the National Forest, camping in northern Wisconsin. He was very much a member of our extended family. Our Mom virtually adopted him.

He was killed only about one year after finishing his graduate studies in Madison and returning to Yogyakarta to teach economics. The Tripp family heard some years later that Ibnu Santoro had been killed, but they were not informed of the precise circumstances. I told Jon Tripp of the *Shadow Play* film. After watching it, he wrote back that he had been profoundly moved upon seeing the younger brother speaking on screen because he looked so much like Ibnu Santoro. He found it "devastating" to learn how Ibnu Santoro died: "The sense of waste is overwhelming."[7]

The killing of hundreds of thousands of people in Indonesia in 1965–66, as the army under Major General Suharto was taking power from President Sukarno, remains a mysterious event. All historians acknowledge that the mass killing occurred, that Suharto's army and various groups of civilians killed people connected with the PKI, but have difficulty documenting any single death. Thousands of massacres must have taken place, but only one has been thoroughly investigated—the Wonosobo massacre—and many unanswered questions remain even about that one: Who decided that those twenty-six men should be executed? Who decided that Ibnu Santoro should be executed? If only twenty-one individuals were in the truck, where did the additional five victims come from? Which army troops carried out the executions? Why did they truck them to that particular faraway location?

The mass killing has been understood in the abstract, as one big event, divorced from the many small, individual events that constituted it. Books on the history of Indonesia describe the event with a level of generality and imprecision that seems incongruous with the significance of it. There is no extensive literature of fine-grained monographs and research articles that can supply a solid evidentiary basis for analyses of the nationwide patterns in the killing. No truth commission has been formed to conduct an investigation and hold public hearings. Indonesian government documents, especially those of the army, have not been declassified. The event has been nebulous, like some distant galaxy about which our knowledge extends little beyond the fact that it exists.

Without detailed knowledge, scholars have been confused over the most basic questions: Who were the perpetrators—the army, civilian militias, or ordinary villagers? Which group was most responsible for the killing? What were their motives? What were their methods? How were the killings organized? Who were the victims—communists or ordinary people killed for nonpolitical reasons? Did the victims resist? If they did not resist, why did they not resist? Precisely where and when were the killings? When did they start and when did they stop in different areas? Why was there killing in one village, district, or province and not in another? Calculating the number of deaths has been pure guesswork, which is why the number I mentioned above—"hundreds of thousands"—is intentionally imprecise.

Historians have been trapped in a hermeneutic circle: without a clear understanding of the event as a whole, they have been unable to grasp the significance of information from a particular locality, and with little information from particular localities they have been unable to construct a model of the event as a whole. Was the execution of truckloads of detainees in remote areas, as in the Wonosobo massacre, the typical form of killing in Indonesia? Was it even typical for Central Java? Given that no one has firm answers to these questions, it has been an interpretive free-for-all, with many people venturing a model of the whole based on a limited range of evidence. Some scholars have drawn grand conclusions from a single anecdote. It has been difficult to even determine what information from documents and oral interviews should be counted as evidence and what should be discounted as myth.

Consider the problems in interpreting what one would expect to be the most important primary source on the killings: the official Fact Finding Commission (FFC) report issued on January 10, 1966. President Sukarno formed the commission with the mandate to "gather the facts and data" about the "number of victims, the causes, and other matters, that would be useful in the resolution and handling of the serious conditions." The commission's nine members included five ministers in his cabinet, a representative of the army, and representatives from three noncommunist political parties. The head was Sukarno's interior minister, Soemarno, who was a major general in the army. The nine members broke up into small groups and fanned out across the country, visiting four provinces over a ten-day period (from December 27 to January 6) where the killings were believed to have been extensive (North Sumatra, Central Java, East Java, and Bali).[8]

The FFC report contained three parts: the prologue to the event (*proloog*), the event itself (*peristiwa*), and the epilogue (*epiloog*). It was a tripartite structure that neatly corresponds to the definition of a narrative as a story with a sense of coherency across a beginning, middle, and end. Instead of reporting on the facts that they had found, the commissioners constructed a grand narrative that they could have written from their offices in Jakarta. Their narrative blamed the victims for having provoked the massacres. The prologue was a long period before October 1, 1965, during which the PKI's militancy had antagonized all noncommunists. Many years of aggressive behavior on the part of the PKI had made the party widely hated. The central event in the middle of the FFC narrative was the September 30th Movement, for which the PKI was allegedly responsible. During this short-lived revolt, which began on October 1, 1965, six army generals in Jakarta (and six other people besides) were murdered by the Movement and a new government led by a Revolutionary Council was proclaimed over the radio. The FFC presented the violence against the PKI after October 1, 1965, as a logical, natural response to the Movement and the preceding years of aggressiveness: "the masses" (*massa*) rampaged in revenge. The violence was the epilogue to the story; it was "an explosive eruption of emotion." The army, with its limited resources, was unable to stop the fury of "the masses." If one were to follow the commission's report, one would believe that the killings of 1965–66 represented a case of spontaneous violence and popular vengeance.

But one suspects something is amiss with this narrative. One sentence contradicts it by mentioning the involvement of state officials in disappearances: "there were executions of September 30th Movement individuals by government agencies that were not officially announced to their family members." If the killings were committed by the *massa* running amok, how did state officials become responsible for executing people? The FFC commissioners provided no details but did offer a blanket justification for these secret, extrajudicial executions: "such executions can be considered normal in security operations done in the context of suppressing a rebellion." Still, the commissioners were worried about this kind of killing. Not making an "official announcement" made the executions appear as "wild" (*liar*) actions. State officials were operating no differently from the wild *massa*.[9]

One discovers, upon investigating the FFC's behind-the-scenes procedures, that the army high command controlled the workings of the commission and determined the composition of the final report. The grand narrative about wild and violent civilians was the one that the army wished to present to the public. The US ambassador, who was in close touch with the army high command, noted after the commission had been formed that the army would arrange for it to die a "natural death."[10] The generals would not openly defy Sukarno's order to investigate the killings; instead, they would quietly strangle it, preventing the commissioners from learning the specifics of the massacres and disappearances. The commissioners, when visiting the regions, stayed for a short time and were allowed to speak only to army and police officials. The one commissioner who was loyal to Sukarno avoided his army minders while visiting Bali by sneaking out of his hotel through the kitchen, with the help of the cooks, to make his own inquiries.[11] The generals on the commission ensured that the final report reflected the army's propaganda line. Sukarno realized that the report was baseless and did not release it for publication. His only statement to the press about it concerned its finding on the number of deaths. The report's arbitrarily determined estimate was 78,500. Sukarno, either carelessly misreading the number or intentionally inflating it, announced that the number was 87,000.[12]

This particular primary source turns out to be evidence not of the killings but of the army's disavowal of its own role in the killings. The fact that the army did not want to acknowledge that it had any responsibility for the killings provides us with one clue as to why there has been so little evidence of them.

Army officers have discouraged and suppressed public discussion of the killings, and when they have been forced to discuss them, as with the Fact Finding Commission report, they have kept matters vague. Their default explanation has been that anonymous, unidentified "masses" did the killing and that there was no point in bringing up painful memories. General Suharto's army dictatorship stayed in power for thirty-two years and enforced a general silence on the killings.

On the rare occasions when the Suharto regime mentioned the killings, it did not delve into the specifics. The regime neither denied that the killings occurred nor composed its own history of the killings. It simply avoided discussing them. There was no official version of history when it came to the killings. The regime routinely celebrated the "crushing" and "destruction" of the PKI but did not mention that anyone was killed in the process. The violence was glossed over amid the praise for the elimination of the PKI from the body politic, as if that had been achieved without bloodshed. The Suharto regime's first book justifying the repression of the PKI was written by two state officials, Nugroho Notosusanto and Ismail Saleh. The book, published in English in 1968, admitted in passing that killings had occurred and then followed the FFC report in presenting them as the result of spontaneous violence. Local conflicts "exploded into communal clashes resulting in bloodbaths."[13] Details as to where and when these bloodbaths took place and the identities of the perpetrators and victims went unmentioned. Clashes happened. People died.

One finds the same evasiveness in the six-volume canonical history text issued by Suharto's Education Ministry, *Indonesian National History*, which covered the history of the archipelago from ancient times to the present. One of the editors of this mammoth project was Nugroho Notosusanto, the coauthor of the regime's 1968 book on the September 30th Movement. He was a professor of history at the University of Indonesia in Jakarta and held the titular rank of brigadier general. *Indonesian National History* served as the authoritative source for all writers composing textbooks to be used in the schools. Notosusanto decided that one sentence was sufficient to describe the killings: "Only in East Java and Bali arose the chaos of abductions and killings, which were successfully brought to order again."[14] This oddly phrased sentence suggests that communists and anticommunists killed one another, for a brief time, in just two provinces, and then the army stepped in to bring peace. Notosusanto ignored the FFC report, which had acknowledged that Central Java and North Sumatra were also provinces where the death toll was high. The history textbooks used in the schools did not include even this vague and inaccurate description of the mass killing. Still today, school children do not learn about the killings from their history textbooks. The only lessons about the events of 1965 that they learn are that the PKI masterminded the September 30th Movement and that it was an evil organization.

It is revealing that those responsible for the massacres have tended not to reveal themselves. When pressed, the army has made a policy of claiming that the civilians committed the killings, while the civilians have tended to claim that they were merely following orders from the army. The British American journalist John Hughes, while uncritically reproducing the army's disavowals of responsibility, noticed when talking to Javanese militiamen in 1966 that they did not forthrightly proclaim themselves as the ones responsible: they were reluctant "to admit that they themselves took part in any killings."[15] Few have stepped forward to clearly claim authorship of these massacres. When young radical activists in the mid-1990s accused the army of having organized the mass killing of 1965–66, the army responded, out of habit, by putting the blame on civilians. The Islamic organization Nahdlatul Ulama (NU), which had worked with the army to carry out the massacres, especially in East Java, did not like being assigned sole blame and published a book in 1996 to prove that the NU and its militia, Banser, had strictly followed the army's lead.[16] The army and the civilian militias have routinely shifted blame onto each other, while keeping the story about the killings hopelessly vague.

On the odd occasion when perpetrators have spoken about the killings, they have usually justified their actions as a matter of self-defense. They have claimed that the PKI had started a revolt and was preparing to massacre all its enemies. It was a time of "kill or be killed" (*membunuh atau dibunuh*).[17] The NU book of 1996 justified the killings in this way, as self-defense against a violent uprising. It was a war (*perang*), and the victims were combatants. But the book's brief descriptions of the killings are about massacres of prisoners. For instance, the book mentions that Banser, following the orders of an army officer in one district in East Java, rounded up six thousand individuals and then held them in a field like a herd of sheep. Every night thirty or forty of the prisoners were driven into a nearby forest and executed. Nearly all of the PKI supporters "had already resigned themselves to being butchered [*disembelih*] by Banser," and those few who tried to run away were tracked down and killed.[18] In other districts, the local army commanders routinely sent batches of detainees to the NU militia with written orders for the detainees to be executed.[19] It is an odd sort of war that involves the killing only of unarmed, defenseless prisoners. In wishing to prove that the NU always operated under the command of the army, the authors revealed the state's dirty secrets.

In excusing or justifying the massacres, the perpetrators have had trouble keeping their story straight. The claim of self-defense is inconsistent with other claims by other anticommunists. The Notosusanto and Saleh book of 1968, for instance, did not justify the killings in the name of self-defense; they presented the killings as an expression of popular vengeance against the PKI for having killed six generals, attempting a coup, and antagonizing many other people over the preceding years. The mass murder, in their view, was an immediate, uncontrollable reaction to past events, not a reaction to an ongoing armed insurrection. The FFC presented the popular vengeance story but then also portrayed the PKI as having been engaged in a "rebellion."

If it were actually a time of war, then one would expect much greater openness on the part of the anticommunists to describe their war stories, in the manner of the Indonesian nationalists who were proud of their armed resistance to the Dutch in the late 1940s. Notosusanto himself had been a part of that resistance and wrote much about it.[20] Since it is difficult to construe executions of tied-up prisoners as noble and courageous deeds, those acts have usually been left untold and unheralded. The bloodshed involved in the victory over the PKI does not have a thousand fathers; it is, like a defeat, an orphan.

Some viewers of Joshua Oppenheimer's documentary *The Act of Killing* (2012) have mistakenly concluded that perpetrators have made a practice of flaunting their bloody deeds. The flamboyant protagonist, Anwar Congo, a midlevel mafia boss in Medan, the capital of North Sumatra, seems to have no qualms in admitting what he did. In front of the camera, he and fellow gangsters reenact executions and brag about their ruthlessness. The army dropped off batches of tied-up prisoners at the headquarters of the youth organization Pemuda Pancasila, and the organization's members, Anwar among them, strangled the prisoners to death on a terrace in the back of the building. They carried out the corpses in sacks, loaded them into a truck, drove down the street, and then threw them off a bridge into the Deli River. "It was beautiful, like parachutes floating down," comments Anwar while at the bridge reenacting the method for disposing of the corpses. Anwar and his friends also speak in front of the cameras of a local TV talk show in Medan.[21] Slavoj Žižek assumes from these scenes in the film that brazenness is the norm in Indonesia: "After their victory, their terrible acts were not relegated to the status of the 'dirty secret'; on the contrary, Anwar and his friends boast openly about the details of their massacres." Indonesia is a society, Žižek imagines, that revels in sadism: "what kind of society publicly celebrates a monstrous orgy of torture and killing decades after it took place, not by justifying it as an extraordinary, necessary crime for the public good but as an ordinary, acceptable pleasurable activity?"[22] The answer to this rhetorical question is certainly not Indonesian society.

Žižek missed the many other scenes in the film that contextualize Anwar's boasting. Anwar moves through a series of reenactments precisely because he cannot find one that provides a convincing justification for the executions. He is haunted by having watched the faces of people as he choked them to death. His boasting and his dancing the cha-cha at the execution site turn out to be methods for repressing the constant torment of his memories. Watching the Suharto regime's vulgar propaganda film that demonizes the communists calms his nerves; it reassures him that his murders were justified. But that film is not enough. In making his own film with Oppenheimer, he is seeking stronger medicine for his nightmares. His grand finale for the film is a scene at a waterfall where the spirits of the victims thank him while placing medals around his neck for saving them from their miserable lives as communists. Female dancers sway like angels around them to the song of "Born Free." Even that over-the-top, ultra-kitsch performance is still not strong enough to make Anwar feel at peace with his past. After having staged all the self-aggrandizing scenes, he revisits the terrace where he and others killed the detainees in the building that he had earlier described, seemingly with pride, as "the office of blood." He is overcome by shame and admits his strangulations of defenseless prisoners were "wrong" (*salah*). They cannot be represented on film in a way that makes them appear acceptable or heroic.

One observes in *The Act of Killing* that the people who are in touch with public opinion and national-level politics urge Anwar not to proceed with the film. Anwar's horizons do not extend beyond his hometown of Medan, where he is part of a powerful gang that runs profitable protection rackets and enjoys the patronage of the governor. Those familiar with the world outside Medan know that many Indonesians would be shocked to see a candid discussion of the dirty secrets. His old friend Adi, who visits Medan from Jakarta, cautions him that a film about the executions they committed would make them look worse than the communists. A fellow gang member who holds a position in a government ministry in Jakarta stops the filming of one scene and urges the killers to appear less vicious. A journalist allied with the gang disingenuously claims to have known nothing about the killings at the time. It is clear from the film that Anwar's brazenness is not shared by all perpetrators. Anwar is an exceptional case—a perpetrator whose provincialism and complicated combination of immense vanity and severe inner torment temporarily blind him to the reasons why his acts of violence were meant to remain a dirty secret.

Oppenheimer has commented in an interview that his film about the executioners (*algojo*) exposes the repressed reality of the "destruction of the PKI" that is celebrated in the official history.

Still image from *The Look of Silence* (2014) showing the grave of Ramli, a young activist in the plantation workers' union in North Sumatra who was brutally murdered in late 1965. In the film, Ramli's younger brother, Adi Rukun (shown walking away from the grave with their mother, Rohani), courageously demands answers from the killers. Photo by Joshua Oppenheimer / Final Cut for Real.

I think at least in hindsight it's clear to me the reason I focused on the *algojo* [as opposed to higher-ranking commanders] is because they are haunted, they're struggling with these horrifying images of killing, strangling, cutting off heads. And they have the need to candy-coat these rotten images with the glorious rhetoric of the official history. The official history, of course, does not speak about the killing of hundreds of thousands or millions of people; it's silent on that. . . . When you hear the *algojo* boast about what they've done, the brutal details of slaughtering defenceless civilians, as though it was some kind of glorious, victorious, patriotic thing to do, it gives the lie to the official history.[23]

The executioners in Oppenheimer's subsequent film, *The Look of Silence* (2014), are similarly haunted by their memories and struggling to narrate their killings as noble deeds. Amir Hasan, living in the plantation belt outside the city of Medan, reenacts before the camera how he hacked tied-up prisoners to death by a river bank and threw the bodies into the river. The army delivered the prisoners to him for execution. He was nothing but a butcher of humans, a labor-saving device for overstretched army troops engaged in an ambitious project to remove tens of thousands of unionized plantation workers from the society. Hasan, in later years, wrote and illustrated a personal scrapbook about his experiences in which he tried to recast his role as that of a heroic warrior. Oppenheimer, in an article with his coauthor, Uwemedimo, described the text: "Clichéd invocations of massacre as 'heroic' and 'historic' frame the killing as part of an epochal battle against an enemy of mythic proportions."[24] Hasan halfway knew that the heroic framing was false; he declined to publish his book for wider circulation. At the end of the film, his widow and sons refuse to admit, even as Oppenheimer is holding a copy of the book, that he had been involved in the killings.

Anwar's and Hasan's on-screen performances should be contrasted with that of another civilian perpetrator who appeared on screen. *Kick Andy*, a popular weekly TV talk show broadcast throughout the country, devoted one of its weekly one-hour shows in 2006 to the events of 1965–66. The host, whose name is Andy Noya, interviewed an executioner in the TV studio in front of a live audience. The executioner used a pseudonym and wore a strange wooden mask with a nose that stuck straight out like a needle. He neither boasted of being a hero nor displayed inner torment. He frankly described how army troops arrived in his village in Central Java and asked him to help them identify PKI members in his area and recruit other youths to serve as "butchers of humans" (*tukang jagal manusia*). His neighbors, friends, and even an uncle were among the eighty-six captives he executed. (He did not explain how he kept track of the exact number of victims.) This faceless person on the TV screen disavowed responsibility for the killings, saying that he was just "acting under orders" and "serving the state" and carrying out "official duties." Neither boastful nor remorseful, he presented himself as an individual without agency. It was as if he were trying to exemplify Arendt's idea of "the banality of evil." One wonders, however, about the emotional life of the person behind the mask and the history of those events in his village beyond what was recounted in that brief, formal interchange in a TV studio.[25]

This episode of the *Kick Andy* talk show demonstrates how a unilateral, army-directed slaughter of unarmed civilians can remain masked and unrecognized. The show placed the perpetrator's story about executing captives within a broader story about a civil war. "It became common," the narrator at the beginning of the show explained, "for people to denounce, arrest and kill each other." The premise was that communists killed anticommunists and vice versa in one massive, chaotic fratricide. Everyone was both victim and perpetrator. A photographer interviewed on the program recalled how he accompanied military personnel in Central Java who told him that the corpses he saw were those of people who had been killed by the PKI. He spoke about Indonesians "killing each other."[26] If anyone was to be blamed, the show's narrator affirmed, it was the PKI because it had "masterminded the September 30th Movement that gave birth to a national tragedy." A TV talk show that dared to broach the taboo subject of the killings dared not disturb the old myths about it.

This book delves into the details of the massacres by drawing upon oral interviews with perpetrators, bystanders, and victims. The aim is to unearth the history of the massacres through the personal stories of individual Indonesians. Only by attending to the specifics of how the massacres were organized can one construct a well-founded analysis. One conclusion from the case studies in this book is that the army-organized killing of detainees was the most typical form of killing. The cases already mentioned—the Wonosobo massacre in Central Java, the NU "butchering" in East Java, and the executions by Anwar Congo and Amir Hasan in North Sumatra—were not anomalies. They were the norm. Those accused of being PKI supporters were taken into custody and held for varying lengths of time, and then select groups were taken out at night by the truckload and executed. Their bodies were either buried in mass graves or thrown into rivers. The state did not take responsibility for these executions, and many relatives of the victims were left uncertain as to what had happened to their loved ones. The events usually called "mass killings" can also be called "mass disappearances."

The silence on the massacres, while not absolute, has been pervasive enough to inhibit a clear recognition of their horror. Scholars, until recently, were unable to grasp the main method by which people were killed. The first scholarly book exclusively devoted to the subject of the "mass killings" was not published until 1990, and that was an edited collection of various documents and essays rather than a single-authored monograph. The editor, Robert Cribb, noted in his introductory essay that "detailed information on who was killed, where, when, why and by whom, however, is so patchy that most conclusions have to be strongly qualified as provisional."[27] Of the eleven chapters in the book, only one was written by a scholar who drew upon original, primary-source information.[28] Some of the other chapters analyzed the context of the killings or synthesized secondary-source information. Still other chapters were translations of Indonesian-language documents, and some of those documents presented the army's propaganda line that the killings were committed by mobs of enraged civilians. The book contained nothing about areas outside Java and Bali. This laudable, pioneering effort revealed the many limitations to the knowledge scholars had of the event.

The basic question on categorizing the violence has been difficult to answer. As Cribb noted in a later essay, "the most intractable difficulty" for historians has been the determination of "the relative importance of army initiative and local tension."[29] Most historians specializing in Indonesia have recognized that the killing involved both spontaneous and bureaucratic violence, that the event lies somewhere on the spectrum between bottom-up, communal violence and top-down, well-organized state violence. Historians have debated where on the spectrum it should be placed. Without detailed accounts of the massacres from a variety of regions, a rough consensus among scholars has been impossible to achieve.

Many Indonesian historians have characterized the violence as being on the bottom-up, communal side of the spectrum. They have emphasized the role of the anticommunist organizations and downplayed the role of the army. In their view, civilian militias and frenzied mobs were primarily responsible for the killing in all provinces of the country. For instance, a large-scale research project funded by the government and directed by the senior historian Taufik Abdullah proceeded on the premise that one need study only local tensions within the civil society to understand the killings.[30] The research project began after the fall of the Suharto regime and involved historians from many different regions of the country. Abdullah and his colleagues published a volume in 2012 on the killings and subtitled it "Local Conflicts." The actions of the army high command in Jakarta and regional army commanders were deemed irrelevant and left unexamined. This "local conflicts" paradigm builds upon the Suharto regime's own characterization of the violence and the work of earlier scholars. The well-known anthropologist Clifford Geertz, who conducted fieldwork in Java and Bali in the 1950s and 1960s, believed that local conflicts caused the killings and that the army intervened to stop civilians from killing one another.[31]

Christian Gerlach has attempted to move beyond analyses that emphasize one end or the other of the spectrum. His book surveying various cases of large-scale violence around the world, *Extremely Violent Societies* (2010), opens with a seventy-five-page chapter on the 1965–66 killings in Indonesia. Not being a specialist on Indonesian history, he draws entirely on European-language sources, especially the reports from the foreign embassies in Jakarta. His conclusion is that the killings were the result of a "coalition" between the army, anticommunist organizations, and ordinary civilians. There was a messy combination of organized state violence, semiorganized violence by militias, and chaotic mob violence. Gerlach places the killings of 1965–66 on all points on the spectrum. Still, his analysis winds up following the "local conflicts" paradigm. He downplays the role of the army, claiming that it was responsible only for encouraging civilians to kill. The fact that so many communists were killed is supposedly a testament to the tremendous energy that those civilians, on their own, dedicated to the task.[32]

More recent writings based on a better grasp of Indonesian history and Indonesian-language sources have settled this long-standing controversy over whether to emphasize the spontaneous or the bureaucratic aspects of the violence. It is now clear that the primary responsibility for the killings lies with Suharto's army. Jess Melvin's careful analysis of the killings in Aceh knocked down one pillar of the "local conflicts" paradigm.[33] Aceh, the province on the northern tip of the island of Sumatra, had always been held up as the clearest example of civilian-led violence. Gerlach, following earlier historians, attributed the killings in Aceh to "Muslim radicals" who killed "without official help."[34] Melvin's 2018 book convincingly demonstrates the exact opposite: the army initiated and organized the killings there. Melvin drew upon newly discovered army documents and many oral interviews with a wide range of Acehnese. The army commander for the province toured the army posts in early October, personally issued instructions for PKI supporters to be killed, and carefully monitored the progress of the campaign. That the older literature could be mistaken over such a fundamental aspect of the killing in Aceh—a large province with about two million people in 1965—is indicative of the lack of empirical information and the success of the army in camouflaging its role.

An important finding in Melvin's research is that there were two phases to the killing in Aceh. In the first phase, the army and its allied civilian militias grabbed PKI supporters from their homes and offices, killed them in the streets, and left their corpses there for others to see. Melvin calls this phase "public killings." In response, many PKI supporters sought protection by placing themselves in the custody of the police and army. The second phase involved the killing of these people who were in custody. Many more people were killed in this second phase since the "mechanics of mass murder," as she terms it, were different. Instead of gangs hunting down and attacking selected individuals, as in the first phase, the killers massacred large groups of people all at once; detainees were taken away by the truckload to be executed and then buried in mass graves or dumped down hillsides. The army kept track of the death toll for the first phase. It counted 1,941 PKI supporters killed.[35] Army documentation of the death toll for the second phase has not been found. An army commander told the US consulate in Medan that six thousand PKI supporters had been killed in Aceh, which would mean that four thousand were killed in the second phase. Melvin suspects that the total death toll for the second phase is higher, closer to eight thousand.[36] Melvin has achieved a breakthrough in the historiography of the killings by attending to the precise chronology of events and the methods of execution.

While Melvin burrowed down and studied one province, another historian of Indonesia, Geoffrey Robinson, has adopted a bird's-eye view of the entire country and brought in the international context of the 1965–66 killings. His book *The Killing Season*, also published in 2018, is a masterful synthesis of the existing literature. It rejects the "local conflicts" paradigm and asserts that the violence cannot be "understood without recognizing the pivotal role of the army leadership in provoking, facilitating, and organizing it." The civilian militias "would never have committed acts of violence of such great scope or duration" without "army organization, training, logistical assistance, authorization, and encouragement." Whatever violence the civilian anticommunists committed on their own was of secondary importance; it did not—and could not—result in such a high death toll.[37]

An important contribution of Robinson's book is to distinguish between the different levels of the army hierarchy. In emphasizing "army leadership" over the anti-PKI violence, the book points to the different roles of "the center" and "the regional commanders." The variations in the timing and severity of the violence in different provinces can be explained largely by the "political postures, strategies, and capacities of the different regional commanders as they sought to implement central directives."[38] A point often lost in the older discussions over whether to emphasize the army or the civilians was that the army itself was divided. Some of the regional commanders were not eager to organize a slaughter of the PKI supporters, while others, like the one in Aceh that Melvin studied, were eager. They had different "political postures." Suharto's group of officers in Jakarta ordered that the PKI be "crushed," but how that "crushing" was to be done and how many people would have to killed before it was judged to be complete were matters usually left to the regional commanders to decide. The variation in the timing and extent of the killing was not determined solely by the severity of the preexisting conflicts in the civil society, as was assumed by the "local conflicts" paradigm.

Robinson's book is a general overview in both spatial and temporal terms. Although the title of the book references a "killing season" in 1965–66, there are only two chapters on the massacres themselves. Those chapters demonstrate the disconnect between preexisting social conflicts and the killing and clarify the army's role in mobilizing civilians to carry out the killing, providing them a license to kill along with "guns, trucks, and hit lists."[39] The other chapters address the events before October 1965, the international assistance provided to Suharto's army so that it could destroy the PKI, the long-term incarceration of political prisoners, and the legacies of the violence. Covering the history of the entire country over many decades, the book does not provide in-depth studies of the massacres in any one region.

"Separation," a painting by Misbach Tamrin, 2007. The painting depicts a story that Tamrin heard from a fellow political prisoner. The man was being held with his father when army soldiers arrived with a list of names of prisoners to be taken out and put on a truck. He heard his father's name called and knew that meant that his father was to be executed. He hugged his father tightly and cried on his shoulder before being forever separated from him.

Both Melvin's and Robinson's books focus on proving that the army was primarily responsible for a nationwide, coordinated campaign of mass killings. Such a focus has been necessary given the army's persistent disavowal of its responsibility, from the FFC report on, and the widespread acceptance of that disavowal, even among scholars of Indonesian history. Their books provide a clear refutation of the "local conflicts" paradigm. The centrality of the army in carrying out a politically motivated mass murder seems impossible to deny. Both books mark a clear advance over earlier works, Melvin's by marshalling new empirical data on one province and Robinson's by refining the analysis of the national pattern.

This book covers the middle ground between Melvin and Robinson's books: it both analyzes the national-level pattern of the violence and presents case studies of four regions. Taking the responsibility of the army for granted, it is able to explore a range of topics that have been only lightly touched upon in the existing literature. The killing of the PKI supporters was largely organized by the army's Territorial Command, which had been constructed in the late 1950s and early 1960s to counter the PKI. Chapter 1 describes the history of the Territorial Command and the army's rivalry with the PKI for hegemony over the civil society and the state. Chapter 2 presents a comprehensive and detailed account of the army's anticommunist propaganda campaign in late 1965. The basic facts of that campaign are well known; this chapter reveals lesser-known details of the campaign and proposes a more precise analytical framework for understanding its effects. Chapter 3 does the same for the topic of torture, bringing out new information about the army's practice of it and sharpening our analytical grasp of its effects.

Taken together, chapters 2 and 3 represent an attempt to answer a question that the existing literature has not clearly posed: How could the perpetrators, both the army personnel and their civilian militias, misconstrue unarmed civilians as armed combatants who presented a mortal threat? These two chapters address the "delusional reality" of the perpetrators that Jacques Semelin has shown to be an enabling factor behind the commission of atrocities. The chapters explore what he calls the "social imaginary" of the perpetrators.[40] The army created an environment in which many civilians came to believe, against all other evidence, that they were living in a time of war.

Chapters 4–7 are case studies of four regions: the city of Surakarta and its environs in Central Java; the island of Bali; and two provinces on the island of Sumatra, South Sumatra and Riau. These regional case studies are meant to bring out the variation in the relationships among four different kinds of actors: the army high command in Jakarta, the regional army commanders, the non-communist political parties, and the PKI. The massacres in each region are understood as being outcomes of these relationships. The different case studies illustrate the differences in the logistics for organizing the massacres, what Melvin calls the "mechanics of mass murder."

Each chapter that presents a regional case study contains a section on the pre-1965 history of that region. This section is not designed to show, in the manner of the "local conflicts" paradigm, how the killings were natural outcomes of preexisting tensions between the PKI and other parties. The purpose of the section is exactly the opposite: to show how unnatural and unexpected the killings were. Indonesian politics had been tumultuous since the 1940s, with many wars and riots. But it is facile to position the 1965–66 massacres as just one more episode within a long, continuous history of violence. The mass execution of prisoners was not common practice before 1965.[41] It was a particularly atrocious kind of violence that Indonesians of that time found to be shocking. The decisions taken by army officers in different parts of the country to execute prisoners en masse were decisions that could have easily not been taken. Some army officers did not allow the killing of prisoners. The decisions to carry out massacres were contingent upon events during the repression of the PKI.

Another purpose of the sections on the historical background is to describe the experiences of the people who became the victims. These sections roughly describe their subjectivity as they approached the events of 1965–66. In writing the history of a human rights violation, especially one that has been so poorly understood, it is easy to become preoccupied with proving that the violation occurred. Historians are tempted to write prosecutorial briefs or human rights reports that follow the investigatory paradigm of "who did what to whom?"[42] I have tried to place the history of the massacres within the broader cultural, intellectual, economic, military, and political history of Indonesia. The tragic character of the killings cannot be grasped without some understanding of the pre-1965 lives of the victims. My aim has been that of a typical historian: to represent how people experienced past events, even the event of their deaths.

All the chapters in the book help answer a question that has not been addressed at any length in the existing literature, especially those works that follow the model of a human rights report: How could the supporters of the PKI wind up in such a vulnerable position and become victimized in such large numbers? What were they thinking and doing at the time that they were being attacked? How could such a large organization—the largest communist party in the world outside the USSR and China—be demolished so quickly, with so little resistance? Much more needs to be written to provide fuller answers to these questions. This book is meant to be a start.

The greatest difficulty I have faced in writing this book has been the choice of case studies. Having decided to write in-depth, personalized histories of specific locales, I could not cover every province of the country. Indonesia is the fourth largest country in the world and is currently divided into thirty-four provinces. Had I decided to cover the entire country, my research and writing would have consumed even more time and this book would have become a multivolume work. Ultimately, I decided to include case studies of four regions that could reveal something about the national pattern. I chose the Surakarta area, the colonial-era Surakarta Residency, because it was where the PKI had roots going back to the 1920s and enjoyed its strongest base of support. The PKI controlled the city and several of the surrounding regencies. Revealing how PKI supporters were massacred there would reveal how they could have been massacred anywhere in the country. I chose the province of Bali because it was the opposite of Surakarta: the PKI had become popular only in the early 1960s and was not the most powerful party there by 1965. Its supporters had extensive ties of kinship and friendship with the noncommunists. The massacres there seemed especially gratuitous. I chose Riau and South Sumatra to bring out the working-class experiences with the violence. Java was the demographic center of Indonesia, but Sumatra, with its rubber plantations, coal mines, and oil wells, was the economic center. The two provinces of Riau and South Sumatra were the major oil-producing areas of Indonesia, and the PKI's trade union for oil workers was powerful in both. The two provinces, neglected in the literature on the 1965–66 killings, make a good contrast: relatively few PKI supporters were killed in Riau, while many thousands were killed in South Sumatra.

I did not write case studies of two provinces that probably accounted for most of the deaths: North Sumatra and East Java. This neglect is partly a result of the vicissitudes of the oral history project in which I was involved. I did not feel that the oral interviews my colleagues and I conducted in East Java were as compelling as those we conducted in other provinces. In North Sumatra, we had trouble arranging the research and wound up not conducting any interviews. Fortunately, other researchers have been writing about the massacres in these two provinces.[43] Also, the two films of Joshua Oppenheimer (*The Act of Killing* and *The Look of Silence*) elucidate the manner in which the massacres were organized in North Sumatra. The research on the two provinces indicates that the militias, while playing a large role in carrying out the killing, had the same basic modus operandi as militias in other provinces. I do not think the inclusion of North Sumatra and East Java would have altered my conclusions.

Most of the chapters of this book are largely based on oral history interviews that I and my colleagues at the Indonesian Institute of Social History conducted. We began interviewing former political prisoners and their families in 2000. Within five years we had interviewed nearly four hundred people in Java (West, Central, and East Java), Jakarta, Bali, South Sumatra, Central Sulawesi, and East Kalimantan.[44] Given that the total number of victims of the massacres and detentions must have been in excess of one million, this was a small, unrepresentative sample. Indeed, the unknown scale of the disaster as a whole makes it impossible to determine what a representative sample would be. These life-history interviews are not used here for quantitative purposes.

This book is a sequel to my earlier book *Pretext for Mass Murder*, which is about a single event: the September 30th Movement. Suharto's army used that event as the justification for the mass murder of the supporters of the communist movement. *Buried Histories* is about the mass murder itself. One does not have to have read *Pretext for Mass Murder* to follow the stories in this book. When I began the oral history research in 2000, I focused on neither the September 30th Movement nor the mass murder. I focused on the post-1965 experiences of the political prisoners and their families. The result of that research was a coedited, Indonesian-language volume of essays published in 2004, *Tahun yang Tak Pernah Berakhir* (The Year That Never Ended). These three books constitute a trilogy on the events of 1965–66.

Each chapter in this book has two purposes: to present new empirical information, especially on how the massacres were carried out; and to propose an analytical framework for how the events of 1965–66 should be studied. For instance, the first chapter presents new information on the PKI's strategy up to September 1965, drawing upon recently published memoirs and internal party documents. It also advances a particular kind of Gramscian interpretation of the PKI's struggle for hegemony. Each chapter weaves together storytelling and argument-making, or what can also be called narrative and analysis. These two strands are interdependent: the analysis is often about how to tell the story, elaborating on issues such as the depiction of the characters (e.g., the extent of their agency) and the causal connections between the events; likewise, the storytelling is often designed to make an argument.[45] When composing the concluding chapter, I decided to separate the two strands. The chapter titled "Conclusions" presents the analytical conclusions of the book, while the chapter titled "Afterlives" presents a closing story about recent efforts to both open up and close down public discussions about the massacres.

Historians have struggled with the question of how to apply the term "genocide" to the mass murder of 1965–66. The answer to the question depends on one's definition of the term. If one strictly follows the definition of the 1948 UN Convention, then the mass murder of 1965–66 would not be considered a genocide. The victims were targeted because of their affiliation with a political group. The UN Convention does not include political groups in its listing of the four protected groups: national, ethnic, racial, and religious groups. One can, however, interpret the meaning of those four categories in a looser way. Cribb has suggested that the PKI was a kind of "national group." It was "an alternative nation within the state," and the mass killings "arose from fundamental conflicts over the national character."[46] Melvin has suggested that the PKI was a kind of "religious group."[47] The perpetrators, when calling for Indonesians to support the destruction of the PKI, accused the communists of being atheists. The victims were targeted for their lack of religion. If one interprets the meaning of group identity in a more expansive way, one can assert that the mass killings of 1965–66 can be categorized as a genocide according to the terms of the UN Convention.

Another way to handle this conundrum is to add a modifier to the term "genocide." While arguing that the event can be called a genocide, Cribb also calls it a political genocide.[48] The man who coined the term "genocide" and cowrote the first draft of the UN Convention, Raphael Lemkin, included political groups in the list of groups to be protected. It was removed by the UN commissions that drafted the subsequent versions. Using the term "political genocide" is a way of acknowledging that the event was indeed a genocide—that the perpetrators clearly intended to destroy (and succeeded in destroying) the collective existence of a group of people they called "the PKI"—while also acknowledging that the event does not precisely fit the terms of the UN Convention. The term "political genocide" is much like the term "cultural genocide." Both refer to Lemkin's original conception of the term "genocide" and both implicitly critique the UN Convention's narrower definition.[49]

Another option is to use the term "politicide." One of the first uses of this term was in a 1988 article by Barbara Harff and Ted Gurr, where it was defined as a genocide inflicted upon political groups. It was meant to be understood "in precisely the same way" as a genocide.[50] The authors coined the term because of the exclusion of political groups from the text of the UN Convention. One possible disadvantage of this term is that it can be misconstrued as part of a larger idiosyncratic lexicon of -cides: ethnocide (or ethnicide), democide, gendercide, ecocide, and so on. In one of her later writings, Harff has defined "politicide" as "political mass murder" without reference to Lemkin's and the UN Convention's concern for the destruction of a group.[51]

Many scholars in the humanities and social sciences who study genocide have defined the term in a much more expansive way than the UN Convention. It has been characteristic of the scholarly study of genocide, since its origins in the 1950s, to consider the text of the UN Convention as limited or faulty.[52] Historians, sociologists, anthropologists, and other scholars have come up with their own definitions to guide their research. While the UN and the International Criminal Court have been bound by the terms of the 1948 UN Convention, scholars have felt free to innovate. Alexander Hinton, for instance, an advocate of "critical genocide studies," has proposed that genocide be thought of as "the more or less coordinated attempt to destroy a dehumanized and excluded group of people because of who they are."[53] His definition does not limit the types of groups whose destruction would be entitled to the label "genocide."

I do not think that any of these terms—"genocide" according to the UN Convention, "genocide" according to scholars, "political genocide," "politicide"—is more accurate or correct than the others as a descriptor of the mass murder of 1965–66. The choice depends upon one's purposes. As a researcher, I have found it helpful to compare the Indonesian case with the full range of other cases covered by the scholarly field of genocide studies. When I do use the term "genocide" in this book, it should be understood in the way that Hinton defines it. The usefulness of the genocide studies literature can be illustrated by considering the following generic description of genocide proposed by the historian A. Dirk Moses: "Genocides are generally driven by traumatic interpretations of past events in which, for various reasons, a group is constructed as disloyal and threatening and held collectively guilty and then collectively punished, deported or destroyed pre-emptively to prevent the feared annihilation of the state. Despite the threatening activities of some of its members, though, these communities were loyal."[54]

The Indonesian mass murder of 1965–66 fits this description exactly. The September 30th Movement was interpreted by the army as a traumatic event, and everyone belonging to the PKI was held to be collectively responsible for it. All of the PKI supporters were deemed to be traitors to Indonesia, and their very existence was treated as an ongoing threat to the stability of the state. To be constructed as disloyal in this way came as a shock to the PKI supporters, who had been positioning themselves for years as more patriotic than anyone else. Many of them had participated in the nationalist struggle for independence. They could be killed in such large numbers because they were unarmed civilians loyal to the state and were not prepared to resist.

However much the Indonesian case may fit within the field of genocide studies, the term "genocide" remains problematic: it will always be tethered to the UN Convention, where it is defined as a matter of protecting the right of a group to exist as a group. Some legal scholars have viewed the entire project of guaranteeing group rights as mistaken and have suggested that greater priority be given to the international law on crimes against humanity.[55] Scott Straus has noted that many policymakers over the past twenty years have adopted the term "mass atrocity" to encompass the complete range of crimes covered by the laws on genocide, crimes against humanity, and war crimes. The basic crime common to all cases is, as Straus puts it, "large-scale, systematic violence against civilian populations."[56]

The emphasis in this book is on the fact that the violence against civilians in 1965–66 took the form of disappearances. The Indonesian government signed the UN's International Convention for the Protection of All Persons from Enforced Disappearance in 2010 but has yet to ratify it. At this point, the Indonesian government should be able to acknowledge that many people were victims of enforced disappearance in 1965–66. It should also assist the relatives as they seek to find more information about what happened to the victims and where the remains are located.

The genocide or mass atrocity in Indonesia in 1965–66 can be categorized as a case of anticommunist violence. During the decades between the Russian Revolution of 1917 and the collapse of the USSR in 1990, communists in many regions of the world were persecuted, imprisoned, and killed. Violence against communists was nothing unusual. Communist states, such as the Democratic Republic of Vietnam, were ruthlessly attacked by anticommunist states. The PKI itself was repressed several times before 1965. Anticommunist writers, such as the editors of *The Black Book of Communism* (1997), have emphasized (and often exaggerated) the mass atrocities committed by communist states and parties.[57] One could, however, easily compile a rival "black book" about the mass atrocities committed in the name of anticommunism. Within such a book, the mass murder of 1965–66 in Indonesia would occupy a prominent place.

Some of the anticommunists in Indonesia who participated in the campaign of 1965–66 have had second thoughts. They have recognized that the mass execution of people who had already been taken captive was inexcusable. A well-known Jesuit scholar in Jakarta, Franz Magnis-Suseno, who was part of a Catholic anticommunist youth group in Central Java in 1965–66, has been advocating a humanitarian perspective beyond the simple communist-versus-anticommunist lens: "that the PKI was a hated and feared enemy cannot justify the systematic killing and destruction of millions of people who had been attracted to the PKI."[58] A Muslim scholar who led the NU in the 1980s–90s, Abdurrahman Wahid, apologized to the victims in 2000 when he was president of the country.[59] Younger members of the NU, such as M. Imam Aziz, have also adopted a humanitarian perspective and condemned the mass murder as a human rights violation.[60]

The permanent elimination of the PKI through massacres and disappearances in 1965–66 became an inspiration for anticommunists elsewhere in the world. It became a model to emulate, an example of what could be accomplished. The CIA was "extremely proud" and recommended it "as a model for future operations."[61] Both General Augusto Pinochet in Chile and the military junta in Argentina were aware of the Indonesian precedent when they aspired to eliminate the left movements in their countries in the 1970s by using the same tactics of disappearing large numbers of detainees. Prior to Pinochet's coup in 1973, some of the leftists who were targeted received fliers on their doorsteps on which were written the words "*Djakarta se acerca*": Jakarta is coming.[62]

1

Unarmed Fortresses

The Army and the PKI's Rival Struggles for Hegemony during Guided Democracy

For D. N. Aidit, it was a moment of triumph. He was standing in front of an auditorium full of uniformed officers at the army's Staff College in Bandung on June 29, 1963. Officers who believed that he was an incorrigible traitor, someone more loyal to the Soviet Union than to Indonesia, were now sitting in rows and politely listening to him expound on the principles of patriotism. The Staff College was the army's think tank where officers were not so secretly plotting strategies to counter the PKI.[1] The directors of the college did not want Aidit to speak there, but they had no choice in the matter. Aidit had become a high-level official; he was a coordinating minister in the president's cabinet and the deputy head of the People's Consultative Assembly. He was the head of a political party whose militant millions supported the commander in chief of the military, President Sukarno. By virtue of the alliance between the PKI and Sukarno, Aidit had a license to enter the corridors of military power. The army that had been serving as the fortress of anticommunism had been compelled to lower the drawbridge and welcome the enemy inside its inner sanctum as a guest of honor.

Aidit took full advantage of the moment. He unleashed a charm offensive, praising the army as "anti-fascist, democratic, anti-imperialist and socialist."[2] Refusing to dredge up past conflicts, he did not complain about being jailed for several days by an army colonel on trumped-up charges three years earlier or rebuke the officers who had repressed the PKI at various times over the

Sukarno (*right*) and Dipa Nusantara Aidit, the head of the PKI, at Senayan Stadium, Jakarta, May 23, 1965, on the occasion of the party's forty-fifth anniversary celebration. Photo by Associated Press.

previous fifteen years. Instead, he emphasized a "long tradition of unity" between the party and the army.[3] He recalled the cooperation between "the people" and "the military" during the armed struggle against the Dutch in the second half of the 1940s. He did not mention the army's attack on the PKI in 1948, which claimed the lives of hundreds of party members and prompted Aidit himself to move into hiding for nearly two years. He emphasized what they had in common: they were both loyal servants of President Sukarno. Both institutions supported Guided Democracy, the president's improvised, one-man polity that began in 1959. Both treated his Political Manifesto (*Manifesto Politik*, abbreviated as Manipol) as a sacred text. They also had a common enemy: imperialism. Aidit insisted that the army had to work with the PKI to defend the country against foreign threats, especially the Southeast Asia Treaty Organization (SEATO), a US-led military alliance that included three neighboring anticommunist states: Australia, Thailand, and the Philippines.

The army generals pretended, for the sake of the stability of Guided Democracy, to be amiable allies of the PKI. In reality, both the army and the PKI supported Sukarno as a shield against the other. Sukarno's untrammeled presidential powers temporarily fulfilled the agendas of both institutions: it helped the PKI recruit more members without being repressed by the army and it helped the army by halting the PKI's path to power through the ballot box. Sukarno's polity was a strange and unstable structure precisely because it was riven by an ongoing tension between the two large institutions that propped it up. While presenting themselves as loyal followers of Sukarno, both the army and the PKI promoted an anxiety about people who were "two-faced" (*kepala dua*), people who pretended to be loyal to Sukarno while secretly conspiring to undermine him. Neither clearly denounced the other, opting instead to emphasize the unity of all pro-Sukarnoist forces. The enmity between the army high command and the PKI leadership, while well known among those familiar with national-level politics, was left to insinuation, implication, and indirection in public discourse.

The PKI leaders never spoke about the army as their enemy. All the way up to the start of the army's murderous campaign in October 1965, they habitually referred to the army as "an armed peasantry." It was, as Aidit stated at the Staff College in 1963, an institution that "serves the People, struggles for the People, and consists of the People." Aidit spoke again at the Staff College in July 1964, and he repeated those words, explaining that any conflicts between the PKI and the military only reflected "contradictions within the People itself, since the military is an inseparable part of the People."[4] The PKI was in conflict with individual anticommunist officers, not with the army as an institution. For its part, the army did not demonize the PKI. Even in the months before October 1, 1965, the army's newspapers did not run stories that clearly criticized the PKI. One had to be an expert at reading between the lines to discern the criticisms. Sukarno's condemnations of a "phobia of communists" (*Komunisto-fobi*) kept the anticommunists quiet. Aidit reminded army officers of the president's antipathy toward *Komunisto-fobi* in his speeches at the army's Staff College.

Seventeen months after Aidit's last speech at the Staff College in July 1964, officers of "the armed peasantry" secretly executed him in a village in Central Java and buried his corpse in an unmarked grave. Around the same time, in Jakarta, army officers captured and killed three senior Politburo leaders: Njoto, Lukman, and Sakirman. These three men, like Aidit, disappeared without a trace, and the location of their bodies remains unknown.

This chapter is about the army's gradual rise to power during the years of Sukarno's Guided Democracy (1959–65) and its often disguised struggles with the PKI, especially its struggle to control the media. Both the army and the PKI became much more powerful forces during those years. The army seized greater political and economic power, turning itself into a state within a state, and the PKI, enjoying Sukarno's protection, recruited many more members into the party and its front organizations. The complex, many-sided configuration of political conflict during the years of parliamentary democracy (1950–59) became reduced under Guided Democracy to a two-sided conflict between the army and the PKI. Political parties either sided with the PKI or with the anticommunist army officers or, as in the case of the largest party, the Partai Nasional Indonesia (PNI, Indonesian National Party), split between a pro-PKI faction and an anti-PKI faction.

The struggle between the army and the PKI during the Guided Democracy years can be understood as a case of what the Italian communist Antonio Gramsci (1891–1937) called a "war of position." Both the army and the PKI endeavored to occupy key sites in the state and civil society. Gramsci likened such a "war of position" to protracted siege warfare that involved digging trenches, placing troops at strategic sites, denying supplies to the other side, and securing supplies for one's own side. Gramsci's military metaphor for political contestation was particularly salient after the trench warfare of World War I. Contemplating the reasons for the rise of fascism while a political prisoner from 1926 until his painful death in 1937, Gramsci argued that Italy and other Western European countries, as "modern democracies," consisted of "massive structures" and "complexes of associations in civil society." For a communist party to seize state power in a country where state power rested more upon consent than coercion, it had to occupy "the 'trenches' and the permanent fortifications of the front in the war of position." It had to gain consent for its own authority and acquire a hegemonic influence over a nation's political and cultural life.[5] This "war of position" was distinct from the "war of maneuver," which involved lighting strikes that breeched the enemy's lines and opened up spaces that allowed one's troops "to rush in and obtain a definitive (strategic) victory."[6] General strikes or mass insurrections were examples, for Gramsci, of a war of maneuver.

Aidit and the other PKI leaders were not familiar with Gramsci's writings. They may not have even known his name. But the party's practice from 1951 to 1965 can be described as Gramscian.[7] In responding to the contingent circumstances of postcolonial Indonesian politics, the PKI independently forged a strategy that happened to resemble what Gramsci had articulated in his *Prison Notebooks*. Robert Cribb, a historian of Indonesia, has noted that the PKI had an "indigenous" and "distinctive" interpretation of Marxism that placed an emphasis on "the preservation and spread of Marxist-Leninist ideas rather than on direct revolutionary action."[8] Aidit and his fellow youths who took over the party in early 1951 did not support the proposal of some militants to wage an armed struggle against the "bourgeois" nationalists. They insisted the party move into the open and take advantage of the democratic rights of the newly independent state. The mass arrests of thousands of party members in August 1951 did not provoke them to change that strategy. Their ability to free the prisoners and to reassert the PKI's legal status after several months convinced them of the correctness of the parliamentary path.[9]

Postcolonial Indonesia was a modern state in which political competition operated in many of the same ways that it did in Western Europe, with class conflict being waged over a common national identity. The PKI competed with noncommunists and anticommunists for leadership positions in the media, public-sector companies, local government administrations, universities, trade unions, artists' associations, veterans' associations, and so on. Political parties did not just contest elections. Virtually every association in the civil society and department of the state bureaucracy became a site of struggle. It was a largely nonviolent competition that all sides claimed was in service of a common struggle against external threats.

Not every aspect of the PKI's practice can be understood as Gramscian. Indonesia was a postcolonial country, unlike the imperialist Europe of Gramsci's time. The PKI was preoccupied with taking state power in Indonesia in the interests of a worldwide struggle against imperialism.[10] Even after Indonesia had gained independence, the most significant contradiction for the PKI was a global one between the imperial powers, such as the United States and Britain, and the nations that had been or still were their colonies. In this respect, the PKI was similar to all other Indonesian nationalist organizations. The first sentence of the nation-state's 1945 Constitution called for imperialism "to be eliminated from the face of the earth." The PKI leaned toward China in the Sino-Soviet split in the early 1960s precisely because it supported the idea of an ongoing international struggle against imperialism rather than peaceful coexistence. Aidit and the other party leaders understood their efforts to gain greater state power within Indonesia to be just one part of a global war.

The PKI saw itself during Guided Democracy as struggling to establish a "proletarian hegemony" (*hegemoni proletariat*) in the country through a "peaceful offensive."[11] The party occupied many positions within the state: its members were representatives in parliament, civil servants in the administration, mayors of cities, and even members of the president's cabinet. Upon gaining such positions of authority, the party saw itself as bringing about a "revolution from above." At the same time, the party maintained mass organizations of workers and peasants that wielded much influence in factories, urban neighborhoods, villages, and universities. Such organizations were the bases for a "revolution from below." It was the task of the party leaders to harmonize these revolutions from above and below.[12]

In "integrating communists in large numbers with state institutions" and "practicing *direct contact*" with noncommunists (as when Aidit spoke before the army's Staff College), the communists tried to cultivate a reputation for themselves as being hard-working, intelligent, incorruptible, and responsible. The PKI leaders routinely insisted that communists be "of high character and cultured" (*berwatak dan berkebudayaan*) and "know everything about something and something about everything." They maintained a strict code of ethics that banned drinking alcohol, taking drugs, gambling, and philandering. They knew they could not gain moral authority and outperform the noncommunists on the basis of militancy and sloganeering alone. The cadre had to be able win arguments, persuade people, and set examples of good behavior.[13]

The unique conditions of Indonesian society and politics allowed the PKI to attract millions of supporters and become the largest communist party in the world outside the Soviet Union and China. By 1965, the party was not the most dominant force within the heterogeneous environment of Indonesian politics—no party was—but it was growing at such a rate that many observers believed that it could be in a position to take state power at some point in the future. Even allowing for a large measure of exaggeration in its claimed numbers of party members (3.5 million in 1965) and members of front organizations (23.5 million), it was still a large organization. The party saw itself in early 1965 as being very close to achieving a hegemonic position.[14]

It is symptomatic of the Eurocentric blinders of the voluminous literature on Gramsci's ideas since the 1960s that the PKI has not been discussed in relation to them. Marxists who have analyzed Gramscian strategies have not seen the relevance of the PKI's experience.[15] If they had, they would have been compelled to address a lacuna in their writings: the question of military power. Amid the constant employment of military metaphors in Gramscian discourse, the very real strategic question of how a left-wing movement should relate to the military has been almost entirely ignored. Gramsci's heirs have emphasized the need for a left movement to build a hegemonic presence for itself in the society; they have not written about what should be done about the military power of the state while doing that.[16] Gramsci himself was not explicit on the matter. The assumption of Gramscians seems to have been that questions of military power will be automatically solved once hegemony is achieved. The fact that the PKI was still vulnerable to military repression, even after achieving such remarkable success through a Gramscian struggle for hegemony, demonstrates the unavoidable importance of focusing on military strategy.[17]

The PKI's strategy for dealing with the military drew on the experience of the Comintern: it was to burrow within the military and organize the troops. Among the twenty-one conditions devised by Lenin for a communist party to gain admission into the Comintern in 1920 was a condition that concerned the military: "The duty of propagating communist ideas includes the special obligation of forceful and systematic propaganda in the army."[18] The Comintern's Sixth World Congress in 1928 approved a document, *Instruction on Work within the Armed Forces*, that demanded that each communist party organize a special clandestine section that would organize soldiers in a "strictly conspiratorial" manner. The document chastised communists who thought a secret section of the party would contradict the party's mass organizing: "All too often this work is looked upon as something mystical and criminal, something that is outside of regular party work, and even called military espionage or conspiracy."[19] The Comintern insisted that such work was necessary so that a party could protect itself from military repression and prepare the ground for an eventual insurrection. As Trotsky noted in his *History of the Russian Revolution*, the success of the October 1917 revolution depended upon the fact that the Bolsheviks "had won over the garrison of the capital before the moment of open insurrection." He concluded that "the first" and "the most important" task of every insurrection was "to bring the troops over to its side."[20]

The PKI leader, Musso, who spent many years in the Soviet Union in the 1920s and 1930s, was thinking about the PKI's influence in the army when devising his new strategy for the party in 1948. He returned to Indonesia in the midst of the armed struggle against the Dutch and hoped to reorganize the party. He called for the communists to stop working within other political parties (for instance, the Labor Party and the Socialist Party) and openly appear before the public as communists. By camouflaging itself, the party had protected itself against repression (which had been constant from 1927 to 1945), but it could not organize military personnel while obscuring its identity. Musso's strategy, called the "New Road," complained that soldiers were confused about which political party to support: "in practice, the workers and peasants who are armed don't have a clear position on the PKI, such that a sympathy with communism can't be spread among the soldiers."[21] After independence was attained, in late 1949, the PKI continued to work hard at attracting military personnel. It provided moral and material support for every military operation, such as the fight against the rebellion by the Pemerintahan Revolusioner Republik Indonesia (PRRI, Revolutionary Government of the Republic of Indonesia) and Permesta in 1957–58, and it maintained a clandestine group of activists to contact military personnel.

Sukarno

Sukarno's Guided Democracy, from 1959 to 1965, was a strange polity that has often been misunderstood. By appearances, Sukarno was a dictator: the legislative and judicial branches were wholly subordinate to him. The law of the land was determined by his decrees. In reality, Sukarno was a balancer of the existing political forces rather than a master of them. He did not fully control the institution with the preponderance of armed power, the army, nor did he fully control a political party that mobilized large numbers of civilians. The three big political parties, the PNI, NU, and the PKI, operated independently of him. He controlled which parties could exist—he banned Masjumi and the Socialist Party in 1960—but he was not in charge of any single party. The Indonesian political scene, with its complicated mélange of old aristocratic families, wealthy merchants, Islamic organizations, and fiery populists, was entirely different from the postrevolution, one-party state of the People's Republic of China, which had been Sukarno's inspiration for Guided Democracy.[22] His grand titles, such as the Great Leader of the Revolution, were compensations for his lack of a solid institutional base.

Guided Democracy was Sukarno's response to two serious crises in the late 1950s: the CIA-backed PRRI/Permesta Revolt of 1957-58, which threatened to break up the country; and the deadlock in the Constitutional Assembly that pitted the Islamic parties (Masjumi and NU) against the secular parties (PNI and PKI). Sukarno had never been a fan of parliamentary democracy—what he habitually called "free fight liberalism"—but he had been unable, as a president in a prime ministerial system, to impose a different kind of paradigm until the events of the late 1950s generated a widespread sense of an emergency. The combination of internal and external threats made many Indonesians feel that their impoverished, fledgling nation-state could collapse. In Sukarno's view, the parliamentary system was incapable of producing a state cohesive enough to overcome the existential threats the country faced.

When Sukarno stood on the steps of the presidential palace on July 5, 1959, and announced the end of parliamentary democracy, he did so with the consent of the army and most of the major political parties, including the PKI.[23] Many politicians were willing to temporarily suspend electoral democracy at that time and assent to Sukarno's experimentation with an untrammeled presidency. He voided the Provisional Constitution of 1950 and reinstated the hastily drafted Constitution of 1945, which provided for a strong presidency. It was an entirely extralegal move—as president he had no authority to decide what the constitution would be—but at that confusing and chaotic time, much of the political elite was willing to grant him that authority. Even the PKI, which had been doing well in the elections, thought it better to support the "revolutionary" Sukarno than to side with the anti-Sukarno parties led by the "counterrevolutionary" Masjumi, a virulently anticommunist party whose supporters had just massacred PKI members in Sumatra during the PRRI rebellion.[24]

To overcome the various fissiparous tendencies in the nation-state, Sukarno chose to emphasize issues around which all Indonesians could unite, regardless of their differing political ideologies and class interests. He called it "returning to the rails of the Revolution," recapturing the spirit of the August 1945 Revolution, when (supposedly) all Indonesians had been perfectly united. His first major campaign as president was to pressure the Dutch to cede sovereignty over West New Guinea to Indonesia. The mass mobilization and threats of military action ultimately paid off in 1962 when the Dutch handed the territory over to the United Nations, which then handed it over to Indonesia the following year. Soon after that campaign ended, Sukarno started a new one: Confrontation. He declared in July 1963 that the formation of Malaysia was an imperialist plot against Indonesia. Malaya, independent since 1957, merged with Singapore and the two British colonies on the island of Borneo—Sabah and Sarawak—to create the new state of Malaysia in 1963. He was determined that Sabah and Sarawak, sharing a land border with Indonesia, should not become part of a rival nation-state. A rebel group inside those territories was willing to work with Indonesia and keep their legal status in dispute. Sukarno placed troops on the border with Malaysia and threatened to invade.

Sukarno was uniquely able to play this role as the living symbol of the unity of the nation, the one individual who embodied the whole, largely because of his history of speaking over the radio. It was the radio that offered the promise of uniting a sprawling archipelagic nation, and it was Sukarno who had been the voice of Indonesian nationalism on the radio. He had become the auditory icon of the nation during the Japanese occupation from 1942 to 1945. The Dutch had silenced him for years by holding him captive in internal exile, but the Japanese put him behind a microphone and gave him an audience of millions. The Japanese placed speakers in public squares throughout the country to deliver their propaganda. When the Dutch returned to reconquer Indonesia, they often felt that they were facing a ghostlike enemy that survived on the airwaves even after the guerrilla fighters had been driven out of an area. One Dutch official referred to Indonesia as a "microphone republic."[25] Sukarno's disembodied voice on the radio provided a sense of the new national collectivity.

Sukarno, ca. 1946. Photo from Getty Images.

After the Dutch withdrew in 1950, it was an annual ritual for many Indonesians to gather around a radio and listen to Sukarno's Independence Day speeches. Sukarno took to the airwaves every year on August 17 to deliver a lengthy speech informing Indonesians of the state of the nation, telling Indonesians where they had been, where they were, and where they were going. He was both the historian of the nation tracing its past and its visionary prophet leading it into the future. There were about one million radio sets in the country by 1965—about one for every twenty households.[26] Many of the households that owned radios let them become public property on Independence Day and invited neighbors to listen. Government offices in more remote areas set up loudspeakers for communal listening. Soldiers listened together in their quarters.

Sukarno put on an elaborate and dramatic performance every August 17, employing the full range of his oratorical skills, alternatingly humorous, instructive, exhortive, and censorious. His pitch varied from a gentle whisper to a thunderous roar. He would stretch syllables out and repeat phrases for dramatic effect. His vocabulary included neologisms of his own invention and words from multiple European languages and regional languages of Indonesia. Just about every Indonesian recognized his French catchphrase, "*l'exploitation de l'homme par l'homme.*"

When delivering his monologue, standing in front of a crowded clutch of microphones, he felt as though he shared a mystical unity with the Indonesian people. He did not call himself "the tongue of the people"—he did not claim to speak *for* the people. He called himself "*the extension* of the tongue of the people." He was some kind of supplementary device that helped the people verbalize their own inchoate hopes and desires. The people spoke through him. The people out there listening to his voice over the radio were already inside him or attached to him, just as he was already part of them. In his Independence Day speech of 1963, he explained that his monologue was actually a dialogue: "A direct back-and-forth conversation between me and the People, between my Ego and my Alter-Ego. A back-and-forth conversation between Sukarno-the-Man and Sukarno-the-People." The distinction between himself and the People became erased: "A back-and-forth conversation between two comrades who are actually One!"[27]

Guided Democracy was premised on this political theology in which Sukarno was the unique individual who contained the nation within himself. The PKI, in an internal document of 1965, wrote that "the history of Sukarno's politics has been the history of Indonesian politics."[28] He magically transcended all particularities of religion, ideology, ethnicity, and class and stood for pure Indonesianness. Such abstraction made it difficult for him to decisively intervene on the side of any one political group. The rough game of power politics continued largely outside his control. As his passionate rhetoric of anti-imperialism floated on radio waves through the atmosphere, the army created facts on the ground and warrened the country's internal administration from end to end with soldiers.

An Army of Occupation

Senior army officers supported Sukarno's Guided Democracy. Indeed, they pushed hard for it. As Daniel Lev observed, they were "the main driving force" behind it.[29] One reason they liked it was that it promised to check the growth of the PKI. Nearly all of the senior army officers were anti-communists, and they were alarmed by the PKI's successes in the 1955 elections for the national parliament and the 1957 elections for provincial parliaments and regency administrations. The PKI was the fourth largest party in the country and the dominant party in many areas of Java, where the majority of Indonesians lived. Guided Democracy, by canceling elections, blocked the PKI's ascent to state power by the ballot.

The top army officers had acquired an antipathy for the PKI during their service for the Dutch colonial army (up to 1941), the Japanese army of occupation (1942–45), or the Indonesian army during the armed struggle against the Dutch (1946–49). The Dutch arrested thousands of communists in the late 1920s and kept them in internal exile throughout the 1930s. The Japanese took over where the Dutch had left off, imprisoning and killing all the communists they could find. The Indonesian national army resumed the repression in 1948 after the PKI involved itself in a rebellion in Madiun, a city in East Java. The most influential army officer after independence was the Dutch-trained General Abdul Haris Nasution, who had led the attack on the PKI after the Madiun incident. He made no secret of his hatred for the PKI and ensured in the 1950s that only anticommunists were promoted to senior positions in the army. He was, as the headline of a *New York Times* profile of him in 1959 put it, "An Indonesian Reds Hate."[30]

Nasution's anticommunism, like that of many of his fellow officers, was partly rooted in his evaluation of Indonesia's national interests in the global context of the Cold War. While Nasution agreed with Sukarno's policy of dealing with both blocs and even led missions to the USSR to obtain weapons, he was convinced that Indonesia had to side with what he called "the West." The West had a much larger market in which to sell the country's exports and more capital to invest in the country's businesses. Moreover, the West's military alliance of SEATO, formed in 1954, included three neighboring countries. The USSR and China were weaker and further away. Indonesia, he argued, "lies in the middle of the Western defense line, in the middle of SEATO countries, where this power controls the connections by sea and air, such that there will always be pressure on us, especially since Indonesia is located in a crossroads and has strategic raw materials (most importantly oil for which Indonesia was the only supplier for the war in Southeast Asia and the Western Pacific)."[31]

Until 1957, the army had divided the country into seven Tentara dan Territorium (TT, Troop and Area Commands). Nasution, the main architect of this TT system, designed it so that the army could engage in "territorial warfare": if a foreign military were to invade, troops could move throughout the countryside and rely on the civilian population for food and supplies, as they did during the struggle against the Dutch from 1946 to 1949.[32] Nasution borrowed the term "territorial warfare" from writings about the Yugoslavian resistance to the German army of occupation during World War II.[33] He assumed that any invading military would be armed with superior weaponry. The Indonesian army, lacking machine guns, mortars, and tanks, would have to resist the invaders with guerrilla warfare tactics until it was strong enough to organize a large-scale offensive with conventional warfare tactics.³⁴ The troops stationed in these seven TT had expansive and uncodified powers over the society, but they did not deeply penetrate the society. The troops were concentrated in a limited number of cities and bases, where they prepared themselves to defend the country against attacks by foreign powers.

Once the PRRI/Permesta revolt broke out in 1957, Nasution and the army high command decided that a drastic overhaul of the seven TT commands was necessary. The revolt had been led by several TT commanders. When one commander went over to the side of the rebels, he took a large chunk of the country with him. For instance, the rebel commander of TT VII, headquartered on the island of Sulawesi, was in charge of the entire eastern half of the country. To reduce the power of the TT commanders, the army brass in Jakarta increased the number of regional commands from seven to sixteen, roughly halving the geographical area covered by each. This redrawing of the army's map was accompanied by a name change: each of the sixteen new commands was called a Kodam, an abbreviation for Komando Daerah Militer, or Military Area Command.

The army generals had an even more ambitious agenda beyond reorganizing the army's internal chain of command: they were also thinking about expanding the army's power over the civil society. The generals added a new function to the existing "territorial warfare" structure: control of the civilian population. The army's new term was "territorial management" (*pembinaan wilajah*).³⁵ The army tentatively began the restructuring in 1957 and completed most of it during the first four years of Guided Democracy, from 1959 to 1963. It was during these years that the Indonesian army turned itself into an army of occupation, capable of intervening in all aspects of civilian governance and economic life. One purpose of the new "territorial management" doctrine was to monitor and influence the political activities of civilians. To achieve stability, the army thought it necessary to control the thoughts of the civilians; the purpose of the territorial structure, from the Kodams down, was to "mentally secure" the people and "prevent mental unrest," as the Kodam commander for West Java, Ibrahim Adjie, put it in 1963.³⁶

In place of the seven TT commands, a new structure was developed that closely paralleled every level of the civil administration, from the province down to the village. The sixteen new Kodams were meant to roughly correspond to the twenty provinces. The Kodams sat at the top of an extensive pyramid: each Kodam contained two or more Korems and each Korem contained five or so Kodims, and each Kodim contained dozens of Koramils. Contingents of troops were stationed at every level. In some regions, the army went further and stationed individual noncommissioned officers (*bintara*) at the village level, naming them Babinsa. The entire structure, with each level nested under the others in a neat hierarchy, was called the Territorial Command. The general principle was that army officers would be full partners of the civilian administrators, such that every official, from the provincial governors to the village heads, would have to consult their counterparts in the army when making decisions. The governors would be shadowed by the Kodam commanders; mayors of cities would be shadowed by the Korem commanders; the *bupatis*, the civilian administrators in charge of the regencies, would be shadowed by the Kodim commanders, and so on. Given that the army officers held the guns and troops, it was not an equal relationship; civilians almost always had to defer to them.

By building its own bureaucracy and firmly latching it onto the civilian bureaucracy, the army mangled the lines of jurisdictional authority within the state. The army was free to intervene in the work of all other state officials while remaining outside the control of any other department. Nothing in the Constitution of 1945 (or the provisional one of 1950) provided for the army to play such a role. The powers of the Territorial Command were not defined by law. About a third of the army's troops were stationed in it, shadowing and duplicating the work of civil administrators and policemen. In the army's logic, the task of "managing" Indonesian society was a necessary corollary of the army's duty to defend the society from external attacks. By preventing internal revolts, the army saw itself as preventing opportunities for foreign militaries to intervene within Indonesia. The army erased the distinction between domestic and foreign just as it erased the distinction between civil and military.

The formation of the Territorial Command entailed a fundamental change in the Indonesian state. Under the cover of martial law, which began in 1957, the army built a state within a state. Sukarno ended martial law in 1963, but the Territorial Command lived on as a perdurable feature of the Indonesian state. The army embedded itself deeply inside the state in a way that has few parallels elsewhere in the world.[37] In most countries with military-dominated states, the military officers occupy positions in the civilian administration rather than set up a parallel, wholly military bureaucracy. Other army-dominated states in Asia, such as Pakistan and Myanmar, do not have equivalents of the Territorial Command.[38]

Sukarno, ever indifferent to bureaucratic procedures and the rule of law, allowed the army to build the Territorial Command. He imagined that he was leading a revolution and believed all the branches and agencies of the state would need to function in absolute harmony as a single organism. He agreed with the army's erasure of the dichotomy between civilian and military. A revolutionary state, he argued, could be judged only by "revolutionary standards," not by the standards found in textbooks written by "bald-headed professors from Oxford or Cornell."[39] He incorporated the army officers of the Territorial Command within his strange "Four-as-One" (Catur Tunggal) councils for local governance. At every level of the bureaucracy from the province down to the subdistrict, four officials—the civilian administrator, army officer, police officer, and prosecutor—were supposed to meet as a group and make decisions as a collective.

For Sukarno, the purposes of the Territorial Command were to prevent revolts from starting and to suppress revolts that had already started. That is how Nasution and other army officers advertised it to him. When speaking among themselves and with officials from the US and other Western countries, the generals emphasized its anticommunist purposes. The army's 1962 classified manual on "territorial warfare and management" identified "international communism" as an "antagonistic element" to Indonesia's nationalism.[40] The army wished to thwart the PKI's organizing efforts in the villages and urban neighborhoods. As the Rand Corporation's expert on Indonesian politics, Guy Pauker, put it, "the underlying political motive" of the Territorial Command was "to compete with the Communist Party of Indonesia for control of the country."[41] The army followed its own version of a Gramscian strategy.

Starting in the late 1950s, the army created its own mass organizations, which mirrored those controlled by the PKI. They were called by the generic name Badan Kerja Sama (BKS, Bodies of Cooperation). There were BKS for workers, artists, Islamic scholars, and so on. An activist in the Catholic youth group in the early 1960s recalled that the BKS were "wholly initiated by the Army" and "were intentionally formed to mobilize forces to confront the PKI." That activist, Cosmas Batubara, acknowledged that supporters of the Catholic Party looked to the army to protect them. He routinely met army officers at Nasution's Defense Ministry offices to discuss strategies for countering the PKI.[42] The civilians who were opposed to the PKI, whether for reasons of religion, ideology, or economic interests, viewed the army as a fortress to which they could retreat for safety.

In 1963, the army began a Civic Action program that involved army personnel in economic development projects. The US military, with its experience in South Vietnam and Latin America, advised and supervised the Civic Action program. Pauker worked as an adviser on Civic Action, as did the US military attaché in Jakarta, George Benson. Their key contact in the army was Colonel Suwarto, the deputy head of the Staff College in Bandung.[43]

The PKI's Strategy of Burrowing Within

The PKI leaders knew that the Territorial Command was meant to strangle the party but did not campaign for its abolition. Since their overall strategy for dealing with the army since the early 1950s was to covertly burrow within its ranks, they did not perceive the spreading of army troops within the society to be an inherent threat. As their enemy built fortifications all around them, the PKI leaders rested content, believing that at some point in the future the party itself would control those fortifications.[44] The Territorial Command actually presented the party with an opportunity: by placing soldiers within the civil society rather than isolating them in the barracks, the army made them available to be more easily influenced by the PKI. Moreover, the supreme commander of the military, Sukarno, was a close ally. It seemed he would never countenance those fortifications being used for an attack on the PKI.

The party followed a strategy that it called Metode Kombinasi Tiga Bentuk Perjuangan (MKTBP, Method for Combining the Three Forms of Struggle). An internal party document of May 1965 explained that the Three Forms of Struggle referred to the three sectors of the society that were to be mobilized: (1) peasants in the villages, (2) workers in the cities, and (3) soldiers in the military.[45] The party did not publicly discuss that third group. Indeed, the entire paradigm of the MKTBP was not explicitly discussed in public. The work of mobilizing soldiers was clandestine. The published party literature could not, for obvious reasons, acknowledge that the party was contacting and influencing military personnel. The most detailed scholarly works about the PKI's history have been based on the public record and have not mentioned the MKTBP strategy.[46]

The neglect of MKTBP has led to a misperception of the party as engaged in a struggle for hegemony only within the civil society. Actually, its struggle for hegemony extended to the military; soldiers were considered as important as workers and peasants. This inclusion of soldiers in the party's strategy for organizing its forces represented a creative and distinct approach to the problem of confronting the coercive power of the state. While the PKI operated as a legal party contesting elections, it also burrowed within the military.

Aidit occasionally mentioned the term "MKTBP" in his speeches. But he mentioned it only in reference to the struggle against the Dutch in the second half of the 1940s. His standard line was that the PKI had failed to lead the nationalist armed struggle because it did not correctly combine the three forms of struggle. In a lecture in 1963, for instance, he stated, "The guerrilla war at that time would have been more successful and achieve victory if we had

D. N. Aidit, June 1963. He was only forty-two when he was secretly executed by the army in Central Java in late November 1965. Photo from Getty Images / Terence Spencer.

implemented MKTBP, that is, guerrilla struggles in the villages, revolutionary actions in the cities by workers, especially transport workers, and better and more intensive work within the enemies' armed forces."[47] Aidit's public use of the term made it seem that it had only historical significance. After independence, the party kept the term "MKTBP" but changed the meaning. It no longer referred to military strategy (guerrilla warfare, urban insurrection, and winning over enemy troops). It referred to the social groups to be mobilized by the party. The PKI did not see the Indonesian armed forces as enemy forces. Party work within the military, while clandestine, was much the same as the party's work with peasants and workers.[48]

One way that Aidit expressed the new postindependence meaning of MKTBP can be found in a speech he gave in 1964. Unless one is familiar with the party's terminology, one will not notice the reference to MKTBP: "we must combine the three forms of struggle if we are to win the Indonesian revolution, namely, the struggle among the peasants, the struggle among the workers in the towns, and the struggle to integrate the apparatus of the state with the revolutionary struggle of the people."[49] Aidit did not mention the effort to recruit supporters within the military. Instead, he spoke of the more general idea of the party winning over supporters in the "apparatus of the state."[50]

It is true that the PKI had a much broader agenda to mobilize state officials, not just military personnel. One sector of "the apparatus of the state" that PKI supporters entered in large numbers was the National Front, a body that Sukarno established in December 1959 for mobilizing support for the Irian campaign and, more broadly, for his new Guided Democracy regime. It was not a powerful or well-funded bureaucratic body. Most political parties did not attach much importance to it. But the PKI, always ready to seize upon any chance to integrate itself into the state, fought hard to occupy the positions in it.[51] Like the army's Territorial Command, the National Front paralleled the civilian bureaucracy: it had a hierarchy of members from the national to the village level. Sukarno raised the prominence of the National Front in 1963 when he added its members at every level of the bureaucracy to his Four-in-One Councils (Catur Tunggal). Those councils were renamed Five-in-One Councils (Panca Tunggal), allowing the National Front members, who were often PKI supporters, to feel equal to the other officials on the councils: the civilian administrator, army officer, police officer, and prosecutor.[52]

It is impossible to determine whether the number of army personnel supporting the PKI increased during Guided Democracy. At the very least, the PKI was able to solidify its already existing base of support. During the military campaigns in those years, the party did its best to prove that it was more patriotic, reliable, and self-sacrificing than any other political party. PKI members volunteered in large numbers to serve as auxiliaries and provided the army with intelligence information, manual labor, and material supplies.[53] They had the chance to work closely with army personnel during the suppression of the Darul Islam revolt and the PRRI-Permesta revolt, the takeover of Papua, and the preparations for war with Malaysia. They presented themselves as the most militant and consistent defenders of Sukarnoist principles — principles that the army itself had pledged to uphold. The party was proud that Aidit, as a minister in Sukarno's cabinet and vice-head of the legislature, was able to deliver lectures in front of the various schools of all four branches of the armed forces (army, navy, air force, and police) from 1962 to 1964.[54]

In all his speeches, not just those in front of military personnel, Aidit did not denounce army generals as enemies of the people. He did not claim they were reactionaries working for imperialist powers. Aidit explained the party line when speaking in Beijing in 1963. He insisted the Indonesian armed forces were not "reactionary": "It can be seen from their inception that they have been anti-fascist, democratic and anti-imperialist in character. The duty of the PKI is, therefore, to closely unite the people and the armed forces, so that in any crisis the armed forces, or their greater part, will stand firmly on the side of the people and revolution, as was demonstrated in the struggle against the counter-revolutionary PRRI-Permesta clique, which not long ago was fought and defeated by the Indonesian people."[55]

To keep track of the anticommunist officers and to cultivate supporters within the military, Aidit set up what was called the Special Bureau.[56] In Jakarta, about five experienced party loyalists worked undercover, meeting military personnel, collecting intelligence, and discussing party policies with them. They maintained a secret network of party members who would do the same work in the various provinces. Information from this network was funneled up to Aidit so that he could stay apprised of what was going on inside the military. Up to October 1965, he believed that the PKI was in a fairly secure position, that "the greater part" of the military did not side with the anticommunist officers. While PKI leaders knew that the army generals wished to attack the party, they believed that such an attack would not inflict significant damage even if it did occur. A former PKI leader, Oei Hay Djoen, told me that the general belief among the leaders was that any army general who attempted to attack the party would be stymied by party supporters within the army itself and by the air force, navy, and police.[57]

Even the Indonesia watchers in the US intelligence agencies did not expect that the army generals would be willing to carry out a thoroughgoing mass murder of communists. A joint assessment in September 1965 by analysts from the CIA, NSA, Defense Department, and State Department opined that, in the event of the death of Sukarno, "the military would probably be reluctant to risk civil war to initiate a roll back of the Communists."[58] The PKI's war of position, which included burrowing within the military, seemed to have been a remarkable success.

The Media as a Terrain of Struggle

During the Guided Democracy period, there were many dozens of Indonesian-language daily newspapers. Just about every political party and religious group published its own newspaper, and every city was served by at least several local papers. By 1964, there was, as David Hill has commented, "an amazingly resilient press industry which could then boast 609 daily, weekly or magazine-style publications with a total circulation per edition of 5,561,000."[59]

It was not until the 1980s that the press runs were again consistently as large as that.

Despite the size and diversity of the press, there was a great deal of state regimentation. After promulgating Guided Democracy in 1959, Sukarno started "guiding" the press. All newspaper owners and editors had to sign a loyalty oath, pledging "to support and defend" the government's nineteen principles, such as Indonesian Socialism and the Political Manifesto. The editors of two of the largest national newspapers, *Abadi* and *Pedoman*, refused to sign since they were affiliated with political parties—Masjumi and the Partai Sosialis Indonesia (PSI, Socialist Party of Indonesia), respectively—that Sukarno had banned. Sukarno ordered the closure of those two newspapers. The journalists of Masjumi and the PSI lost control of the Persatuan Wartawan Indonesia (PWI, Indonesian Journalists' Association) to Sukarno loyalists in 1961. A key figure in the PWI thereafter was the editor of *Warta Bhakti* (formerly *Sin Po*), Karim Daeng Patombong, who went by a shortened form of his name, Karim DP.

Sukarno banned more newspapers in early 1965 as part of a crackdown on the Badan Pendukung Sukarnoism (BPS, Body for Promoting Sukarnoism). The organization was led by anticommunists who wished to woo Sukarno away from the PKI by claiming to be more faithful to his teachings than the PKI. The head of the organization, Adam Malik, had once been a journalist, and the vice-head was a senior journalist, B. M. Diah, who had founded the leading newspaper, *Merdeka*, in 1945. The PKI's press published unremitting attacks on the BPS, calling it an effort to "kill Sukarnoism with Sukarnoism." The party alleged, with some reason, that the enemies of Guided Democracy were masking themselves as the finest supporters of it.[60] Sukarno eventually decided to side with the PKI on this issue and treat the BPS as "counterrevolutionary." He banned the BPS and twenty-one newspapers that had a connection with it.

Sukarno's banning of a large number of anticommunist newspapers in early 1965 greatly worried the army high command, since it resulted in the press becoming dominated by the left-wing newspapers *Harian Rakjat* and *Warta Bhakti*. The army decided at that time to start publishing its own daily newspapers. The first issue of *Berita Yudha* hit the stands on February 9, 1965, and *Angkatan Bersenjata* came out a month later, on March 15. At the same time, Nasution's Defense Ministry and the army, headed by General Ahmad Yani, encouraged anticommunist civilian groups to form new newspapers to replace the ones that had been banned.[61] *Kompas*, which later became the paper of record during the Suharto years, began publishing on June 28 with backing from an elite group of Catholics who were committed anticommunists. The key figure behind the formation of *Kompas* was Frans Seda, the minister of plantations. General Yani approached him with the suggestion that the Catholics publish a paper to help counter the PKI.[62]

Sukarno was not the only one who censored the press, and anticommunists were not the only victims during Guided Democracy. The army had extensive, unchecked powers over the press during the period of martial law, from 1957 to 1963. Army commanders throughout the country had blanket authority to arrest journalists and close down newspapers in the name of state stability at a time of war. The army tended to focus its repression on the left-wing press. Sales of *Harian Rakjat* were frequently banned in a number of provinces.[63] Pramoedya Ananta Toer, the most prominent writer associated with Lekra, the PKI-affiliated cultural organization, was imprisoned by the army in 1960 for nine months without charge for publishing a book about the history of Chinese Indonesians.[64] Even after martial law was withdrawn in 1963, the army retained informal powers to intervene in the press. It intervened not just by censoring the press but also by patronizing it. Army officers controlled large, unaudited budgets, largely derived from their own efforts at self-financing. Their patronage could make the difference between survival and bankruptcy for many newspapers.[65]

Communists and anticommunists waged an intense struggle for control of the national news agency, Antara, which functioned like an Indonesian version of the Associated Press. It provided news and photographs to newspapers about events that their own journalists could not cover. Unlike AP, it was a semi-official body; it was funded by the state even as it was managed by a self-governing foundation (*yayasan*). Different factions jostled for the top positions. One of its main editors was Djawoto, a close, trusted political associate of Sukarno's from their work together in the nationalist movement in the late 1920s. The anticommunist faction within Antara believed Djawoto was overly supportive of the PKI and arranged for him to be dismissed from his job as chief editor in May 1962. The director of Antara who dismissed him, Pengulu Lubis, was aligned with the Murba party, whose head, Adam Malik, had founded Antara in 1937. Once Djawoto was fired, Sukarno immediately intervened and declared that from then on Antara would function under direct presidential control.[66] Djawoto was reinstated. It was the second time within two years that Djawoto had prevailed over the anticommunists: he had won the election for the head of the Indonesian Journalists' Association (PWI) the year before.[67]

The life history of the journalist Joesoef Isak illustrates the way in which the PKI gained influence in the media. He was from an elite family in West

Sumatra and was educated in Dutch-language schools. Isak began his career in the 1950s with the newspaper *Merdeka* and was close to the PSI journalists who saw themselves as the country's intellectual elite. He became attracted to the PKI by meeting Njoto, a Politburo member who was cultured and intelligent in the ways that a PSI intellectual could appreciate: he played Western classical music and spoke knowledgeably about world literature. Isak liked the idea of being part of a mass movement rather than a small clique, especially when that mass movement was just as internationalist and cosmopolitan as his little clique. He approached the PKI general secretary, Sudisman, and offered to join the party, but Sudisman told him that he would be more valuable by continuing to appear as unaffiliated. He could occupy positions of leadership in journalists' associations without provoking resistance from the anticommunists. Isak replaced Djawoto as head of the Asia-Africa Journalists Association in 1964 and wore the mask of a noncommunist, even while he covertly received regular briefings on the PKI's analysis of current events.[68]

The media of the Guided Democracy years can be seen as an arena in the struggle between the communists and the anticommunists. It was a key terrain for the Gramscian "war of position," a gradual, nonviolent struggle to attain leadership in the institutions of the civil society and the state. The communists had achieved many strategic positions by 1965. Their own newspaper, *Harian Rakjat*, had the second highest circulation in the country, and the paper with the highest circulation, *Warta Bhakti*, was an ally. Sukarno had closed down influential anticommunist papers in 1960 and early 1965. The journalists' association was under the control of an ally (the editor of *Warta Bhakti*), as was the Asia-Africa Journalists Association. The state news agency, Antara, was under the direct control of Sukarno, who ensured that left-wing journalists were allowed to work there.

Since the PKI's ideas were so close to Sukarno's, they acquired the appearance of common sense. An information minister of Suharto's in the late 1970s referred to this fact when training the staff of the ministry. Lieutenant General Ali Moertopo let his staff know that they were still trying to undo the effects of the Sukarno years: "Indonesians had been influenced by communism as a system of thought for so long that it had come to seem that it was the Indonesian way of thinking."[69] Moertopo's formulation was inaccurate—Sukarno's ideas were the ones that had defined "the Indonesian way of thinking"—but he alluded to the reality that the PKI's ideas had become nearly indistinguishable from Sukarno's.

Even as the PKI gained greater influence by piggybacking on Sukarno, the anticommunists remained powerful forces in the media. Many economic, political, military, and cultural elites were anticommunist, and they patronized newspapers that reflected their perspectives. Because of Sukarno's disapproval of *Komunisto-fobi*, they could not be militant in their denunciations of the PKI, but they could still undermine the party by criticizing specific policies and individuals. The PKI frequently promoted noncommunist allies and covert party supporters, such as Joesoef Isak, precisely because party members faced so much resistance inside official and semi-official institutions.

The Army's Takeover of the Media

It was entirely predictable that the September 30th Movement, in launching its putsch against the army high command, would take over the main station of the state radio, a seven-story building just kitty-corner to the presidential palace. An army officer who played a minor role in the Movement, Brigadier General Supardjo, noted in his postmortem analysis (written while he was in hiding in 1966) that the Movement should have made better use of the radio: "If that had been done, its effectiveness would have been equal to dozens of divisions." Radio, as Suparjdo understood it, was equivalent to a large number of army troops.[70] The Movement announced over the radio that it had unmasked a conspiracy of right-wing generals who were plotting on overthrowing Sukarno. Its first broadcast justified its action against "The Generals' Council" as a defense of Sukarno and all of his "progressive revolutionary" principles.

On October 1 the "war of position" over the media changed into what Gramsci would have called "a war of maneuver." The troops were in motion and targeting enemy command centers. It was such a lopsided war, however, that one must use caution in employing the term "war" to describe it. One side did not fight. The Movement triggered the "war" by killing six army generals and taking over the RRI station, but then it collapsed within hours. It did not resist as the army advanced and seized positions. Major General Suharto's troops occupied the radio station of RRI around 7 p.m. The Movement's partisans had left hours earlier, and the takeover was effortless.[71] The head of the army's information department, Brigadier General Ibnu Subroto, calmly strode into the building and read out a prepared statement on air that claimed that the Movement was "counterrevolutionary."[72]

At the same time, the army began taking control of all the newspapers. The army commander of Jakarta issued an order at 6 p.m. on October 1, instructing his men to occupy the premises of all printing presses and to protect the offices of the two newspapers published by the army. Most editors shut down their papers on the night of October 1 and did not publish an October 2 edition. A contingent of soldiers knocked on the door of the PKI's paper, *Harian Rakjat*, that night, but the editors insisted on receiving a written order and went ahead with publishing the October 2 edition that they had already prepared. They even had time to publish a Sunday, October 3, edition that, as was customary for Sunday editions of Indonesian papers, focused on cultural issues. It carried a short story, several poems, a musical score for the song "Crush the Three City Devils," and the news that the party's Ikatan Pemuda Pelajar Indonesia (IPPI, Indonesian Association of Youths and Students) demanded that the Minister of Education and Culture be "retooled." That October 3 issue was the paper's last issue.[73]

A team of army officers spent the days from October 2 to October 5 determining which papers were to be given permits to publish. Those that were permitted to continue were ones that had been anticommunist and were willing to cooperate with the army in printing its propaganda. *Kompas*, for instance, resumed publishing on October 6. It placed a notice about its new publishing license on the first page and asked for the readers' understanding for the absence of issues over the previous four days. It also pledged the support of all its employees for the military's campaign to "completely eradicate the counterrevolutionary September 30th Movement."[74] The editors of the papers in Jakarta that were granted licenses to publish were summoned to the army's press office on October 7 to be informed of their tasks within the campaign against the PKI.[75]

The army was able to seize total control of the press after October 1 because it had already been involved in regimenting the press, especially since the start of martial law in 1957. The post–October 1 level of control was unprecedented, but it was possible on the basis of the army's already existing interventions into the media. The two army generals most responsible for controlling the press were Brigadier General Ibnu Subroto, Kepala Pusat Penerangan Angkatan Darat (head of the Army's Information Center) and editor of *Berita Yudha*; and Brigadier General Sugandhi Kartosubroto, the head of the information section of the Ministry of Defense and editor of *Angkatan Bersenjata*. They determined which papers would publish and which would perish. Even as they wielded absolute power over the press, they were not publicity seekers. They did not become well-known public figures.[76]

Subroto and Sugandhi saw Antara as an especially strategic site since it was the official news agency for the country. They alleged that Antara was a "nest of September 30th Movement elements."[77] They sent a senior officer, Lieutenant Colonel Noor Nasution, to occupy the Antara office on October 8 and begin screening the journalists who worked there. One of his first victims was the editor in chief, Soeroto, who had allegedly told Antara journalists at an editorial meeting that the September 30th Movement had been "just an ordinary event" (*peristiwa biasa sadja*)—a remark that accurately reflected Sukarno's perspective on the event.[78] Within a week, the army had taken away twenty-six employees of Antara.[79] Dozens more Antara journalists were arrested over the following weeks. Members of the workers union at Antara were targeted.[80] In total, about one hundred journalists, 30 percent of Antara's staff, were fired and/or imprisoned.[81]

One of the editors taken away was Ibu Rusiyati, who was vice head of the national news desk. She recalled the circumstances of her arrest:

> On October 15, 1965, the Antara office building was surrounded by military troops from the Jakarta regional army command [*Kodam Jaya*]. Twenty-six employees were arrested by calling out their names one-by-one and gathering them in the editorial room. Those called to be arrested included the editor in chief, Soeroto, and others who were heads and vice heads of the desks covering national, foreign, and economic news. Arrested with them was a woman from the administrative side of the office, Tini, who was a typist. There were just two women arrested, Tini and me.[82]

Similar scenes were repeated at newspaper offices throughout the country. Even well-known, high-circulation papers were forced to close their doors. In Indonesia's second-largest city, Surabaya, the popular newspaper *Trompet Masyarakat* was shuttered, and its journalists were summoned for interrogations.[83] In Bandung, the paper *Warta Bandung* suffered the same fate. Soldiers from the Kodam brought the banning order to the paper's office on October 10.[84] Altogether, the army closed down a total of 163 newspapers in the days after October 1.[85] It was not just the PKI papers that were targeted. The large-circulation newspaper published by the PNI, *Suluh Indonesia*, which had begun publishing in 1953, was also forced to close.

Subroto and Sugandhi purged the journalists' association, PWI. The head of it, Karim DP, was frequently condemned in the army newspapers in early October. Forced out as head of the PWI, he was replaced by H. Mahbub Djunaedi, the editor of the NU newspaper, *Duta Masyarakat*.[86] If that were not enough, he was imprisoned without charge, and his house in Jakarta was destroyed by a mob.[87] He was accused of having conspired with other PWI members to support the September 30th Movement.[88] At a hastily organized "extraordinary conference" held over three days in early November, the organization confirmed the expulsion of the left-wing journalists and chose new leaders.[89] No organization was too small to escape the army's attention.

The Senat Corps Mahasiswa Publisistik (Senate of the Journalism Students) removed Karim DP as its honorary head and replaced him with none other than Brigadier General Soegandhi himself.[90]

With an increased role for the army press after the Movement, Soegandhi's newspaper, *Angkatan Bersenjata*, started recruiting more journalists and holding training sessions for them. General Nasution spoke at one of the training sessions in December, informing the newcomers that the key task of a journalist was to "guarantee harmony between the military and the society."[91]

Conclusion

When the PKI decided to support Sukarno's Guided Democracy in 1959, some party members were skeptical. It seemed unwise for the party to abandon its phenomenal progress on the parliamentary path and to opt instead for an autocracy. The party leaders assured the membership that the party could continue to grow in a different environment, even in the absence of elections. Under Sukarno's protection, it could more freely recruit members and organize more people into its myriad front organizations. The argument seemed plausible enough: the benefits of Sukarno's protection were immediately obvious. The PKI was able to convene its Sixth Party Congress only four months after the start of Guided Democracy because Sukarno held the army in check. Sukarno appeared at the closing ceremony of the Congress and made sure the audience members understood that he was their protector. He started his speech by recounting how he had summoned the Jakarta army commander to the palace for coffee some months earlier and had ordered him to guarantee that the PKI's Congress could safely proceed.

His speech at the PKI's congress in 1959 was prophetically titled. He referred to a Javanese proverb as a nod of recognition to his audience, who were mostly Javanese. The original version of the proverb was "Neither a relative nor a sibling, I will share in the loss if you die." It was used among Javanese to refer to close friendships. Sukarno could have stuck to that original version of the proverb: he had not been close to the PKI and had even attacked it in 1948, but he had harbored a grudging admiration for its sacrifices to the nationalist cause since the 1920s. To mark the warming of his relationship to the PKI with the start of Guided Democracy, he reworded the proverb: "A relative and a sibling, I will be the one to feel the loss if you die." He declared that he was a brother to the PKI, not just a friend. The party members applauded wildly when hearing Sukarno address them as brothers. It was an honor for the party to have won over the most important leader of the nation. Still, the reference to a possible death haunted this particular expression of solidarity.[92]

Six years later, Sukarno addressed a sports stadium full of PKI supporters who had assembled to commemorate the party's forty-fifth anniversary. It was May 1965. He reaffirmed his kinship with them. Immediately after stepping up to the podium, he engaged in some playful banter with Aidit, whom he affectionately called by the nickname Dit, as if he were a younger brother, and insisted Aidit stand next to him: "C'mon, let's have our photograph taken together." Sukarno mocked the "imperialist countries," saying that they did not need spies sneaking around to know that he was closely allied with the communists: "I am happy to show myself here in front of the public of the whole world." Continuing the chitchat, he asked Aidit to explain the meaning of his name, Dipa Nusantara. Aidit had given the name to himself as a sign of his commitment to nationalism sometime in the 1940s. He explained that Dipa meant "fortress" (*benteng*). Thus, Dipa Nusantara meant Fortress of the Archipelago.

After displaying his fondness for Aidit, Sukarno explained his political strategy of allying with the PKI and "unifying all progressive revolutionary forces" in the country: "who can deny that the PKI is not a great part of this Indonesian Revolution?" The PKI had grown into such a massive organization, Sukarno contended, because it had been so "consistent" in its commitment to "progressive revolutionary" principles. The stadium roared with applause as he repeated the Javanese proverb that he had coined in 1959: "A relative and a sibling, I will be the one to feel the loss if you die."[93]

Neither Sukarno nor Aidit could have predicted that the PKI would soon die, that the army would just five months later start slaughtering the party's supporters, including many of those who had been in the stadium that day. There was no sign of an impending genocide in the months prior to October 1965. Sukarno's mass mobilization of people against external enemies had provoked great anxiety about internal enemies, about Indonesians who were secretly working with foreigners to sabotage Sukarno. Tensions ran high, with rumors of an impending coup against Sukarno and proposals by the PKI to organize civilian militias into a full-fledged Fifth Force of the armed forces. But it was not obvious to anyone that these tensions would lead to a unilateral slaughter of PKI supporters.

The army did not issue open threats to destroy the PKI during the years of Guided Democracy. Both Sukarno and Aidit had enough sources of information from inside the army to know that some generals were hoping to attack the PKI. Nasution and Yani routinely assured Western leaders in confidence that the army had contingency plans and would never allow the PKI to take power. Yani told an Australian officer, Colonel East, who was attending the army's Staff College in Bandung in 1964, that the army had plans to crush the PKI that would be implemented "when the time was ripe." East concluded that Yani was not simply telling him what he wished to hear. The army really was capable of "crushing" the PKI. Colonel East had frequent conversations with Colonel Suwarto at the college and at the swimming pool and tennis courts of the colonial-era country club Bumi Sangkuriang. From a reading of the diary that East kept while at the school, the military analyst Robert Lowry wrote that East had "observed that the Army was strongly entrenched and very influential throughout the whole country and should be in a position to combat effectively any attempted communist takeover."[94]

The PKI leaders, when facing the army's trenches of the Territorial Command, which blanketed the country with a network of Kodams, Korems, and Kodims, should have been worried. The book-length history of the party written in May 1965 did not mention the Territorial Command. The authors saw the Guided Democracy period as a time that had been wholly beneficial for the party: "the *peaceful offensive* of the communists spread to the enemies' walls of power."[95] They should have added that the enemies' walls had spread further and risen higher during that same time. Given its strategy of burrowing within, the PKI did not see the walls of the Kodams, Korems, and Kodims to be those of the enemy. The party assumed that a good portion of the army personnel were supportive of the party and that one day they would take over the fortress of the Territorial Command and use it for their own purposes.

The September 30th Movement was Aidit's way of using military troops to sneak inside the opponent's fortress and remove the top commanders. This classic tactic in a war of maneuver turned out to be misjudged. Aidit overestimated the power of the party's supporters inside the military. The top commanders were killed, but then other generals immediately stepped into their place and held the fortress for the anticommunists. Those generals had the power to reject Sukarno's appointee, General Pranoto, who could have protected the party. The troops who had supported the PKI were confused and paralyzed by the quick turning of the tables and did nothing further. The sole surviving member of the PKI's core group of leaders, the general secretary Sudisman, acknowledged in 1967 that he and his fellow party leaders had been overly confident in their assessment of the party's strength. They had not imagined that the army would develop the fierce determination and logistical ability needed to destroy such a large and popular organization: "at the height of its power, the PKI forgot to be vigilant, forgot that the imperialists and the reactionaries here at home could be consumed by a rage to strike."[96]

Decades later, with the benefit of hindsight, another one of the few surviving party leaders, Siswoyo, a Central Committee member, lamented that the party had not fully registered the dangers posed by the rising power of the army during Guided Democracy. He criticized the strategy of organizing military personnel, as licensed under MKTBP. The party leaders had failed to appreciate the grip that the anticommunists had on the army and the powerful pressure of the internal chain of command, which made the many party supporters inside the army virtually useless in a time of crisis.[97] Siswoyo opined that MKTBP—the strategy that called for the party to organize workers, peasants, and soldiers—was based on the idea that organizing soldiers was as important as organizing workers and peasants, even though soldiers did not have the same kind of independence. Soldiers were entirely caught in a "bourgeois institution." The PKI did not have its own army; it had only secret contacts with some soldiers who were inside an army commanded by anticommunists. The party could not rely upon them in the same way it could rely upon workers and peasants. Regardless of Siswoyo's reservations about MKTBP, one should recognize that the strategy was the PKI's original and creative attempt to neutralize the coercive power of the state so that the party could struggle for hegemony over the civil society and the state.

The Movement, to the surprise of the PKI, provided the anticommunist generals with the pretext for which they had been waiting. Sukarno's protection of the PKI proved as effective as the Maginot Line. The troops poured out of the fortress of the Territorial Command, overran the many trenches that the party had painstakingly dug over the previous years, and drowned the "peaceful offensive" of unarmed communists in blood.

2

Mental Operations

The Army's Propaganda after October 1, 1965

As he stood in front of a crowd of journalists inside the state's grand palace, President Sukarno knew he was losing control of the army. He was swearing in Major General Suharto as army commander—a position that he did not want him to have. A little over two weeks earlier, on October 1, 1965, he had appointed a different general to be the army commander. When faced with resistance from Suharto and other army brass, he came up with a vague, unworkable arrangement one day later that made the two generals co-commanders. Suharto was supposed to be something like an assistant in charge of "restoring order" while the other general, Pranoto, was supposed to be the overall commander.[1] By dropping Pranoto and elevating Suharto as the sole commander on October 16, he was implicitly announcing that he, as commander in chief, no longer controlled the army. But he could not admit that to the journalists. He hoped they would see the image of Suharto taking an oath in the palace, like a Javanese knight of a bygone age pledging his fealty before his sultan, as evidence that the army was still solidly behind him. Suharto obliged and played the role expected of him in a performance of mutual dissimulation.

Immediately after the ceremony, Sukarno launched into a speech: "I want to laugh, my friends. Do you know why I want to laugh? Since the September 30 incident, the foreign press, especially from the imperialist countries—the radio, TV, nonsensical gossip columns and such—say that *the Republic of Indonesia is collapsing*." He repeatedly broke into English to address the foreign

Suharto being sworn in as army commander, October 16, 1965, at the presidential palace, Jakarta. Photo from the National Library of Indonesia.

correspondents in attendance and laughed at the absurdity of the idea that "*Soekarno has been overthrown.*" He assured everyone that he was still in power and that the army remained "an instrument of the Revolution." His laughter was meant to break the tension in the room and make it seem like the political crisis that had been raging since October 1 was just a minor squabble that would be quickly resolved. To make light of the situation, he cited an advertising slogan certain to resonate with foreign journalists who spent long hours drinking whiskey in hotel bars: "*And the real fact is,* in the words of Johnny Walker, *we are still going strong, we are still going strong!*"[2]

At this early stage of the crisis, Sukarno believed that he could regain control over the army. For six years he had singlehandedly ruled the country. He was President for Life, Great Leader of the Indonesian Revolution, and the Extension of the Tongue of the People. The legislature that had awarded him those grandiose titles was his echo chamber. The judiciary consisting of career bureaucrats was entirely beholden to him. The newspapers had been competing with one another to prove their loyalty. By law, they were required to run daily columns on "The Teachings of Bung Karno." Since becoming a leader of the anticolonial nationalist movement in the late 1920s, he had acquired a larger-than-life status as a man who had made world history, like Gandhi and Nehru in India, by overturning European imperial rule. He had stood up in court in 1930 and, in a speech titled "Indonesia Accuses," condemned Dutch rule with the élan of Zola. He had proclaimed national independence with Mohammad Hatta in 1945 and had been the sole president of the Republic ever since. He had convened the Asian-African Conference in 1955 and spoken at the first Non-Aligned Conference in Belgrade in 1961. He was no ordinary mortal for Indonesians; he was the icon of their nation who made them proud by challenging the Western-dominated world order. Suharto, twenty years his junior, was a drab, unremarkable, barely literate career officer from a small village in Central Java.

Suharto had been able to veto the Pranoto appointment because he had a solid phalanx of army generals behind him. The army brass, after losing six of its top generals at the hands of the September 30th Movement, was determined to steer its own course and reject a commander known to be close to the president. Sukarno had to relent. The generals did not just control the preponderance of armed force within the state—more than the air force, navy, and police—they had total control over the media. With that control, the generals whipped up a hysteria over the September 30th Movement in direct defiance of Sukarno's demand for calm. At the swearing-in ceremony on October 16 and in just about every public address in late 1965, Sukarno called for everyone to "keep your head" and not to run around "like a chicken with its head cut off." He explained that the country had been through many crises before—such as the PRRI revolt and the Darul Islam revolt—and claimed that this was just one more crisis to be overcome. Indeed, in comparison to the earlier crises, this one was minor. Sukarno described the September 30th Movement as another "ripple in the ocean of the Indonesian Revolution": it was a relatively small-scale event that could be easily resolved. He urged people not to "burn down the house to kill a rat." He condemned the made-up stories in the media about PKI atrocities, but he could not admit, without ruining the image of unity, that Suharto's generals were the ones subverting his policy. He blamed journalists and unnamed officials but not the generals who were most responsible for the wild, incendiary propaganda.[3]

The US ambassador, Marshall Green, just a few days before Suharto's swearing-in ceremony, noticed the dualism within the Indonesian state: "we are actually dealing with two governments rather than one. One is headed by Sukarno and the other consists of the Army leadership." The army was proceeding with its own agenda outside Sukarno's control: "Sukarno obviously does not approve of the Army action but at the moment lacks power to stop anti-PKI campaign."[4] Green and his CIA station chief, B. Hugh Tovar, had worried in the early days of the October crisis that the generals would capitulate to Sukarno and not take full advantage of the crisis. But by the time of the swearing-in ceremony, they were confident that Suharto was stubbornly defying the president and leading the campaign to destroy the PKI.[5]

The army generals, over the preceding six years of Guided Democracy, had developed the art of appearing to be loyal while covertly undermining Sukarno. They wore the masks of faithful Sukarnoists. They continued the practice after October 1 such that all of the anti-PKI propaganda came wrapped with the most fervent declarations of loyalty to Sukarno. The elimination of the PKI, the press claimed, was needed to better fulfill Sukarno's ideals. Sukarno admitted in a speech one week after the swearing-in ceremony that he felt that some officials were not following his orders even when they were telling him to his face that they were absolutely faithful: "Sometimes, just recently, I get the impression that the expressions of loyalty are only words. It's not with all officials, just some individuals." Sukarno ordered his officials to promote an atmosphere of calm: "I've strongly ordered: don't stoke the flames, don't fan people's prejudices."[6] But the army's propaganda was fanning prejudice against the PKI every day, and Sukarno could not stop it. He could not even bring himself to name the people responsible, much less dismiss them from their posts.[7]

The army's total power over the media after October 1 meant that it was able to cut off Sukarno's connection to the public. Sukarno's speeches were selectively quoted in the reports on the radio and in the newspapers—something he complained about to his top officials.[8] He could not go out of the palace and address mass rallies because of security concerns, even as the army itself mobilized crowds to rampage through the streets. The army's Territorial Command, which had troops stationed in every part of the country, became the de facto state. Sukarno was left to communicate with others through face-to-face meetings and gatherings in the presidential palace. With both the media and the streets under the control of the army, the Extension of the Tongue of the People was effectively mute, his tongue cut off like Philomelo of Greek mythology, left to pantomime futile protestations as the army proceeded to slander and slaughter his most steadfast supporters.

After the army generals had taken control of the media and sidelined Sukarno, they issued a steady stream of fake news that was meant to justify a violent attack on PKI supporters. The propaganda campaign was the product of thoughtful strategizing and hard work; it took much imagination to invent the false stories and much labor to spread them. The army generals carried out the campaign as they did any military operation—with definite predetermined protocols. They pinpointed the PKI as the sole institution responsible for the September 30th Movement, glossing over the participation of military personnel. They avoided direct appeals for the murder of communists. Instead, they called for "crushing the PKI," terminology that could be interpreted as calling for the suppression of the PKI as an organization rather than the killing of its supporters. They always made the "crushing" look as if it were being led by civilian organizations while the army was merely conforming itself to the wishes of public opinion. They were careful to present all of the army's actions as being in accordance with President Sukarno's instructions and to exclude any mention of the massacres the army was organizing.[9]

A special aide to the attorney general, Adnan Buyung Nasution, explained the public relations protocols to the US embassy in meetings on October 15 and 19: "Nasution said that the Army had already executed many Communists but this fact must be very closely held." He was "shocked" to hear Radio Malaysia refer to such executions. The secrecy was necessary to prevent Sukarno from learning how far the Army was going in destroying the PKI in contravention to his orders. The embassy official noted, "While Sukarno would probably hear reports to this effect, it was very important that he not be able to cite particular sources such as foreign radio and press reports." Nasution claimed to represent "moderates" who were cleverly taking advantage of the moment to help the army kill communists before Sukarno could stop them.[10]

Suharto's army officers created a "delusional reality," to use Jacques Semelin's term.[11] The steady stream of news stories in the newspapers and over the airwaves created the impression of a massive, ongoing, nationwide crisis and depicted those affiliated with the left movement as dangerous traitors secretly plotting more murders, similar to the executions of the six army generals in Jakarta on October 1. The media built an alternative universe unmoored from the reality on the ground where PKI supporters were not waging war or even resisting arrest. It encouraged people to believe in events that never happened and to perceive dangers that did not exist. It made violence against everyone affiliated with the PKI appear necessary and even laudable.

The army's media campaign was important for directly shaping public opinion; newspapers and radio broadcasts reached millions of people. The indirect effects of the media campaign, however, were perhaps just as important given that many Indonesians did not have regular access to newspapers and radio. The propaganda shaped the views of elite groups around the country who then relayed these views to the nonreading and nonradio-listening public. Political, economic, and cultural elites repeated the themes of the propaganda within their respective social spheres.[12]

The army used its own personnel to spread the propaganda. One of the army's terms for its psychological warfare campaign was *"operasi mental"* — mental operation. A common name for its propaganda detachments was Tim Penerangan Operasi Mental (Mental Operation Information Team). Such teams toured the countryside after October 1965 wielding megaphones.[13]

Soldiers addressed crowds of villagers and lectured them on the evilness of the PKI. The aim was to bring the stories that appeared in the newspapers directly to the illiterate masses. In East Java, the army's Kodam had what it called a "mental management" program (*bina mental*).[14] The Territorial Command positioned itself as the controller of the thoughts of Indonesian citizens.

The army's propaganda was an essential part of the violence against the left movement. Without the steady, daily barrage of misinformation, Sukarno and his many supporters could have prevented the September 30th Movement from being treated as such a major crisis and could have limited the murderous campaign against PKI supporters. The propaganda gave the people collaborating with the army a sense of confidence in the correctness of the killings. For the broader public who were bystanders, it encouraged passive acquiescence; they could believe that the PKI was a real danger and that the army had good reasons for attacking it. If alternative news sources had existed, it is unlikely that the bystanders would have been so passive. Apart from the explicit justifications for the violence, the propaganda provided euphemistic language that made it appear acceptable. Some impersonal entity, "the PKI," was being "crushed" and "destroyed." Radio listeners and newspaper readers did not encounter the suffering of the victims and the reality of the army's atrocities.

The propaganda was essential to enable the army to carry out the violence, but it was not the means by which the violence was carried out. The army did not use the newspapers and radios to mobilize people for specific acts of violence. The hate propaganda of the Indonesian media did not include explicit instructions to murder. The violence was largely organized through face-to-face meetings and oral communications between the army and civilian organizations (see chapters 4–7). When army commanders began the repression in a particular city or district, they held private meetings and public rallies with civilians at which they explained the need for the repression and the plan of action. The stories in the media helped to reinforce the army commanders' claims, giving them a sense of objective truth. The stories, by themselves, did not cause people to murder communists. The murders in Aceh began before the media campaign, and there were few murders in West Java even though the people there were exposed to the same propaganda. The propaganda was not an engine powering the machine of death. Rather, it was a lubricant that allowed the machine to move forward, week after week, month after month.

When considering the relationship between the media and mass violence, one should not focus exclusively on the *effects* of the media on the society. Even in the case of the 1994 Rwandan genocide, when Hutu extremists broadcast explicit calls for the murder of Tutsis, the propaganda was not a significant cause of the violence. Hutus did not function as remotely activated automatons, moving out of their houses and killing Tutsis because the Milles Collines radio station told them to do so. The hate propaganda, as Scott Strauss has argued, played a supporting role but did not directly cause the violence: it "emboldened hard-liners and reinforced face-to-face mobilization, which helped those who advocated violence assert dominance and carry out the genocide."[15] The same can be said about the Indonesian case.

The anti-PKI propaganda in Indonesia that began in early October 1965 can be viewed not just in terms of its effects on the public. It can also be viewed as an expression of the subjectivity of the perpetrators, as a window into the ways that they were speaking among themselves about their actions. Nearly all the myths that one finds in post-1965 perpetrator memory can be found in the army propaganda of that time. The army's press, in its lies, exaggerations, and silences, helped to construct a certain way of understanding the violence for both military and civilian perpetrators. While the newspapers and radio did not report on the massacres, they did express the genocidal intent of the people carrying out the massacres. Semelin has described the role of the media in many genocides as the elaboration of an "*imaginaire* of destruction" that can serve as a "common binding agent" among the perpetrators and bystanders and a discourse that can "allay individuals' anxiety" about killing.[16]

The army propaganda will be analyzed here in terms of four themes:

1. *Collective guilt.* The propaganda made the millions of people affiliated with the PKI appear collectively responsible for the September 30th Movement, a brief, small-scale, clandestinely organized action.
2. *Dehumanization.* The propaganda dehumanized PKI supporters by depicting them as savage beasts that needed to be eliminated from the country.
3. *Ongoing threats.* The propaganda claimed that PKI supporters presented a mortal threat to all noncommunists. The September 30th Movement, instead of a quickly suppressed flare-up among a small number of military personnel, was portrayed as a never-ending, generalized revolt that intended to commit mass murder. A military operation against PKI civilians was treated as a war against armed combatants.
4. *Past threats.* The propaganda distorted the historical record to present the PKI as an incorrigible, violence-prone group that was a traitor to the Indonesian nation, a group that had repeatedly proven itself to be incapable of living in peace with noncommunists.

In what follows, these four themes will be discussed at greater length. The main sources are the army's two daily newspapers, *Berita Yudha* and *Angkatan Bersenjata*. Both papers wrote original material and printed news stories from the Antara news agency, which functioned as another outlet of army propaganda once it was under the control of Lieutenant Colonel Noor Nasution.

Privately owned newspapers, such as *Kompas*, generated very little original material about the September 30th Movement and the crackdown on the PKI. They tended to follow the army's lead on these issues by republishing articles from Antara and the army's newspapers. The state radio station, RRI, also tended to report the same news from army sources.[17] The shortwave broadcasts beamed into Indonesia from American, British, Australian, and Malaysian state-run radio stations relayed the army's propaganda too but do not appear to have had a significant listenership within Indonesia.[18]

Collective Guilt

During the first few days after October 1, the army newspapers pointed out that the left-wing newspapers, such as the Communist Party's *Harian Rakjat*, had expressed support for the Movement. They did not allege that the PKI had organized the Movement. The first mention of the PKI as the mastermind came on October 5 when the army newspapers reported on the newly formed Kesatuan Aksi Mengganjang Gerakan Kontra Revolusi 30 September (Action Front to Crush the September 30 Counter-Revolutionary Movement), which issued a statement claiming that the PKI had been the "puppet master" (*dalang*) of the September 30th Movement.[19] The Action Front held a rally in downtown Jakarta on October 4 to demand the banning of the PKI and all its affiliated organizations and the "cleansing" of their members from state institutions.[20] Helping to generate an atmosphere of crisis, it held a second rally on October 8 to reiterate its demands. The front-page banner headline of *Berita Yudha* was "The society can't wait any longer: it is urgent for the President to immediately ban the PKI and its mass organizations." *Angkatan Bersenjata* carried a similar banner headline: "A mass action of half a million from 46 political parties and organizations demand the banning of the PKI."[21] The figure of a half-million demonstrators was, of course, heavily inflated.

Since the Action Front, or KAP-Gestapu as it was later known, was largely a creature of the army, the reporting on it had the quality of a ventriloquist's act. The key officer in charge of mobilizing the anticommunist civilians was Brigadier General Sutjipto, the head of the "political section" of the Komando Operasi Tertinggi (KOTI, Supreme Operations Command). He already had close connections with anticommunist figures in Jakarta and was able to summon them for a meeting at his office on October 2, less than twenty-four hours after the Movement had collapsed. Sutjipto, like his fellow generals, had decided at that early stage to blame the PKI. Sutjipto negotiated an alliance between public figures from various religious and political organizations and helped them announce the new organization on October 4. The leaders were two civilians, Subchan ZE, a thirty-four-year-old active in the Muslim organization NU, and Harry Tjan Silalahi, a thirty-one-year-old Chinese Indonesian active in the Catholic Party. They were the middlemen who linked the youths mobilized for the street demonstrations, the senior leaders of their respective religious organizations, and the army generals like Sutjipto.[22]

At the time of the calls for banning the PKI in early October, the army newspapers had not presented evidence of either the PKI's leading role in the Movement or the participation of large numbers of PKI members. The available evidence indicated only that the party had *supported* the Movement. *Harian Rakjat* had expressed support in its October 2 issue, and some members of the PKI-affiliated organizations for youths and women were among the civilians taking part in the Movement in Jakarta on October 1. Those facts did not prove that the PKI had been the puppet master, but the army adduced them as proof anyway. The *Angkatan Bersenjata* editorial on October 6, for instance, jumped from the evidence of PKI "being involved" to the conclusion that the PKI had "masterminded" the Movement, asserting that "the evidence speaks for itself."[23] The army placed a lot of weight on a public statement made by a PKI leader, Anwar Sanusi, on September 30: "the situation in the nation's capital is heavily pregnant"—a statement that puns in Indonesian since the word for "the nation's capital" (*ibu kota*) is literally "mother city." The army interpreted this ambiguous, metaphorical statement as proof of the PKI's culpability. The Movement was the PKI's baby.[24]

The calls for banning the PKI were accompanied by mob attacks on PKI offices. On the morning of the Action Front's second rally, on October 8, a crowd of youths burned down the PKI's national headquarters in Jakarta. The army newspapers celebrated the attack. One headline blared, "The rage of the people is uncontrollable."[25] The army depicted this premeditated attack as a spontaneous response to a provocation from PKI supporters. Supposedly, some youths waiting at a bus stop in front of the building were mocked by people inside the PKI's compound for chanting pro-Sukarno slogans. Those youths retaliated, and people in the neighborhood joined in: "spontaneously the people who were there attacked the building" and burned it down.[26] *Angkatan Bersenjata* contradicted *Berita Yudha*'s account and claimed the communists set fire to the buildings themselves to destroy incriminating evidence.[27] A US journalist who witnessed the attack noticed that the army had cordoned off the streets around the building and protected the demonstrators as they "smashed the interior to pieces, then torched the building."[28]

Mobs with a license to destroy roamed Jakarta's streets over the following days, attacking the offices of organizations affiliated with the PKI, such as

The mob attack on Res Publica University, Jakarta, October 12, 1965. The Sino-Indonesian organization Baperki established the university in 1958 as Baperki University. The name was changed to Res Publica University in 1963, in reference to a 1959 speech by Sukarno about "res publica." Photo from Getty Images.

Sentral Organisasi Buruh Seluruh Indonesia (SOBSI, Central Organization of Indonesian Workers), Gerakan Wanita Indonesia (Gerwani, Indonesian Women's Movement), and Pemuda Rakjat (People's Youth).[29] The mobs also attacked the homes of PKI leaders, such as Aidit, Njoto, Lukman, and Njono, and the homes of prominent public figures, such as the newspaper editor Karim DP and the writer Pramoedya Ananta Toer.[30] Bookstores selling PKI literature were wrecked.[31] Since the mobs had army protection, the police dared not interfere. The mobs did not rampage mindlessly. They knew which addresses to target and headed straight for them. The army newspapers praised the meticulousness by which they went about destroying and ransacking buildings. The mob that ranged widely over the city on October 10, for instance, conducted itself "in a very orderly and smooth manner" even as it was "full of spontaneity."[32] The army mobilized mobs in other cities as well for identical actions.[33]

A major target in Jakarta was Res Publica University, which had been founded by the Sino-Indonesian organization Badan Permusjawaratan Kewarganegaraan Indonesia (Baperki, Consultative Body of Indonesian Citizenship) in 1958. It consisted of several buildings in the Grogol neighborhood and had an enrollment of about six thousand students, many of them non-Chinese.[34] Syarief Thayeb, the minister of higher education and research and a brigadier general in the army, ordered the closing of fourteen universities on October 11; Res Publica was number one on the list.[35] The mob that besieged Res Publica the day after claimed to be enforcing Thayeb's order. That order did not have the approval of Thayeb's superior, the coordinating minister for education, Priyono. The fact that the rector of the university was Utami Suryadarma, a friend of Priyono's and the wife of a national hero, the founder of the Indonesian Air Force, provided no protection from the army onslaught.[36]

Following the standard protocol for reporting on mob attacks, the army newspapers blamed the victims for provoking the attack. The newspapers condemned the Res Publica students guarding the building for "arrogantly defying the masses of the People [*massa Rakjat*]" and throwing rocks and even firing bullets into the crowd of demonstrators. The demonstrators were supposedly provoked into rushing inside and battling the students. Once inside, they built a bonfire in the university's courtyard, throwing books, administrative records, and brand-new laboratory equipment into it. The army account depicted the vandalism as methodical: the demonstrators, "the masses," ensured that Sukarno's books and his photographs were spared the flames. The book burners also spared "many PKI publications and foreign magazines" so that they could be turned over to the army.[37] Eventually, they set fire to all the buildings and blocked the fire trucks until the whole campus had burned to the ground. This brazen act of arson of a well-respected university shocked many middle-class Jakartans. While celebrating the attack, the army disavowed responsibility for the fire, contending that PKI elements had infiltrated the demonstration.[38] The minister of higher education and research, Thayeb, claimed that the students guarding Res Publica were PKI supporters and had set the fire themselves.[39]

A leader of the Res Publica student senate has written his own account of how the attack was carried out. Some of the students at Res Publica were members of Catholic and Muslim anticommunist organizations and had attended meetings with army officers in the days before the attack. They informed the other Res Publica students that the campus was on the army's list of targets. The students started living on the campus, hoping to defend it. On the day of the attack, the army gave marching orders to a mob of demonstrators gathered at the University of Indonesia campus across town in Salemba. The students at the Res Publica campus learned that the attack was coming from journalists who arrived at the campus by car from Salemba before the mob did. A platoon of army soldiers also arrived before the mob, apparently sent by Sukarnoist officers wanting to protect the students from the mob. The platoon herded the students to a corner of the campus to keep them out of harm's way as the mob invaded.[40]

The mobs invading and ransacking buildings around the country were under instructions to confiscate documents and turn them over to the army. When the newspapers reported on the attacks, they usually noted that documents had been seized. The newspapers soon became filled with sensational stories about secret documents being discovered that proved that the PKI had masterminded the Movement. The army still felt it had to prove that the PKI had masterminded the Movement though it was already punishing it for the crime. Many headlines contained the phrases "the facts speak," "the evidence speaks," and "the documents speak." Most of the articles in this vein did not describe the contents of the documents. They simply stated that documents had been found: "Documents again seized from a Gestapu kingpin," "Evidence is stronger that the PKI indeed masterminded the September 30th Movement."[41] A document found in the small town of Ciamis supposedly revealed that the PKI had ordered university students to overthrow Sukarno and treat PNI members as enemies.[42]

News about secret documents came from all over the country, giving the impression that the PKI's plans for the Movement had been shared widely among party members, even down to the village level. In the army propaganda over the course of October and November, the Movement assumed monstrous proportions. It was not a clandestine action carried out by a limited number of military personnel in Jakarta and Central Java. Rather, it was the start of a mass revolt. The PKI, it was alleged, had prepared elaborate plans for carrying out violent actions all over the country. It was a vast conspiracy involving millions of people that had somehow gone undetected. The propaganda suggested that the Movement, if it had not been suppressed, would have led to mass killings. The PKI supporters had been fully prepared for carrying out mass killings.

The newspapers were full of stories about hit lists, so-called black lists (*daftar hitam*), being found among the confiscated documents. From a document found at the home of a Pemuda Rakjat member, it was revealed that the PKI had put the leader of the NU, Idham Chalid, on a list of people to be killed.[43] PKI members in every locality had supposedly prepared lists of people marked for execution. On the southern coast of Java, in the city of Cilacap, a hit list was discovered in late October. The PKI in Pati, a town in Central Java, was planning on killing twenty-five people. In North Sumatra, an army colonel reported that the PKI had plans to behead no fewer than fifteen thousand people. In East Kalimantan, the PKI had put the names of three hundred people on a hit list. An extraordinarily detailed "black list" was found in the small town of Garut in West Java; it contained hundreds of names of the individuals to be killed, the time they were to be killed, and the method to be used when killing them.[44] It became standard practice of the army's Territorial Command in late 1965 to tell noncommunists that their names had been found on PKI hit lists.

By late October, the rumors were running as wild as the imagination of the army's psy-war specialists. PKI chapters had supposedly had gone to great lengths to prepare the massacres. In Jakarta, the PKI's youth organization had collected thirty thousand one-rupiah notes to distribute as some kind of coded message to its members. In the Central Java town of Delanggu, where there was a large burlap cloth factory, the army claimed that the PKI had formed a "4P Movement" to take over the factory. The PKI sent coded messages to its members, ordering them to either kidnap, murder, loot, or burn—words that begin with the letter P in Indonesian (*pentjulikan, pembunuhan, perampokan, pembakaran*). The PKI used the code word "red pill" to refer to guns donated by "a foreign country," implying the People's Republic of China. In Bondowoso, the PKI used a particular brand of cigarette, "4669," to send coded messages, with the numbers symbolizing different actions. It also marked houses with various objects, like coins and chili peppers, to indicate which houses should be attacked.[45] The PKI had organized a secret army with specialized squads named Black Cat Troops and Black Dog Troops that would carry out the mass murder.[46] A document found in Tandjungsari, a village in West Java, revealed that the PKI had a special squad called the Black Button Troops that consisted of attractive Gerwani women who would seduce anticommunist men and convince them to follow the PKI.[47]

Many articles reported that the PKI had stockpiled weapons. In the immediate aftermath of the Movement, there was a legitimate concern that the Movement had distributed weapons to civilians. Some of the early reports about finding thirteen guns in the Tanjung Priok area or thirty guns in the Kebayoran Baru neighborhood were plausible.[48] Even the early reports that were false, such as the finding of guns in PKI headquarters and one hundred Chinese-made hand grenades near the Jakarta dockyard, were still within the realm of possibility.[49] By early November, however, the stories became outlandish. The PKI was said to have a plan to import fifty thousand guns through Manado, on the northern tip of the archipelago. A PKI detainee in a small town in West Java confessed that the PKI planned to import fifteen thousand guns.[50] PKI supporters in villages had secretly marked underground stashes of guns.[51]

To bury all the people that the PKI planned on murdering, the party supposedly had the remarkable foresight to order its members to dig mass graves beforehand. The army encouraged people to imagine that the PKI had prepared thousands of *lubang* (pits, holes, ditches) to function like the one at Lubang Buaya, the Crocodile Hole, into which the Movement had dumped the corpses of the seven army officers. Stories of *lubang* digging started appearing in the press on October 8. Many *lubang* were said to be found near houses of PKI members in a Jakarta neighborhood. They had been dug just the night before the Movement erupted and were meant "for the burial of bodies after having been tortured just like the seven national heroes."[52] In the "Daily Brief Notes" section of *Berita Yudha* on October 11, a reporter claimed, "In a number of places around the capital city one also finds large pits that were made by the September 30th Movement."[53] A couple weeks later, the army reported on pits that had been dug in a village near Bogor on orders from a local peasant union leader. Around the pits, each six feet long and four and a half feet wide, were posted signs that read "Long live the PKI."[54] This propaganda about *lubang* had a great impact. People in villages and towns all over the country began to see every hole in the ground as having been dug for an insidious purpose.

Because of the army's propaganda, the September 30th Movement was transformed from a coup attempt that involved a limited number of people into a social revolt involving millions of people. Indonesians were led to assume that every PKI member and sympathizer had some foreknowledge of the Movement and had been prepared to murder noncommunists in their locality. Having an affiliation to the party, no matter how tenuous, meant complicity in a brutal, treasonous action and became sufficient justification for summary execution.

One can find an exposition of this perverse logic of collective punishment in a training manual used during the years of the Suharto regime at the state's school for ideological regimentation, the Lembaga Pertahanan Nasional (Lemhanas, National Resilience Institute). Military officers, government officials, businessmen, and religious leaders were required to attend courses there and to learn the official line about a variety of issues. One of the manuals used in the courses was *Basic Materials on the September 30th Movement/PKI and Its Destruction*, first issued in 1968 and reissued multiple times in later years. It was a semiclassified document, marked for "limited" (*terbatas*) circulation. It was written in a question-answer format, with the answers containing the official line that the learners could repeat if they were ever asked the same questions by journalists or ordinary citizens. The training manual posed the question: "Was every member of the PKI necessarily involved in the September 30th Movement/PKI?" The answer was: "All members of the PKI can be considered as involved in the September 30th Movement, either directly or indirectly (every person is obligated to report to the authorities if the person knows about a crime that will take place and also according to the PKI's organizing principle that a decision of the party leaders is binding on all members)."[55] The sentence's ungrammatical structure, reproduced in this translation, makes the reasoning slightly difficult to follow. The claim is that all PKI members knew about the Movement beforehand and were thus guilty, at the very least, of not reporting a crime. At the same time, Lemhanas wished to argue that they were guilty even if they did not know about the Movement beforehand. Being a member of the party made one responsible for the actions of the party leaders. Lemhanas revealed the legal reasoning of collective punishment: if the party leaders committed a crime, then all the members of the party and even members of affiliated organizations were guilty of the crime.

Dehumanization

The army propaganda presented PKI supporters as traitors to the nation (*pengkhianat*) and dangerous murderers. It also presented them as subhumans and nonhumans. PKI supporters were depicted as "barbarians" (*orang biadab*) and "savage animals" (*hewan ganas*). They were murderers who took pleasure in murdering. They were people who found torture to be an aphrodisiac. They were atheists who had lost all sense of right and wrong. The events at Lubang Buaya were presented as the inevitable results of the cultural values of the entire left-wing movement in Indonesia. By dehumanizing PKI supporters, the army encouraged violence against them. The newspapers ran headlines declaring that PKI supporters had lost "the right to live in Indonesia." The people killing the PKI could rest assured that they were not killing other people; rather, they were killing savage creatures that happened to have assumed human form.

One of the army generals in charge of the propaganda, Sugandhi, decided within a week to sexualize the violence against his fellow generals at Lubang Buaya. It was not enough to report that the generals were murdered; he felt it necessary to concoct a story about the generals having been murdered by sex-crazed women. A short article in *Angkatan Bersenjata* on October 9 titled "Here is Gestapu" asserted that Gerwani women, in order to humiliate the army officers, "fondled the genitals of the victims while exposing their own genitals before proceeding to kill the victims with all manner of tortures and cruelties."[56] Two days later, a similar article meant to demonstrate, as the headline put it, "the savagery of Gestapu" added to the storyline by claiming that the "handsome and dashing" Lieutenant Tendean became "a lewd plaything

Front page of the army's newspaper, *Berita Yudha*, November 19, 1965. The lead headline quotes a statement by the army commander for West Java, Major General Ibrahim Adjie: "The PKI and its mass organizations no longer have the right to continue to exist." The teenaged girl in the photo at the bottom is absurdly alleged to be the killer of the army commander, General Yani.

for the evil women of Gerwani."[57] Neither of the two articles cited sources for these claims.

Sugandhi's paper resumed this theme in early November with stories from detainees. A twenty-two-year-old man named Memed was said to have been part of the team that kidnapped Yani and brought him to Lubang Buaya, where about thirty Gerwani women were screaming "Kill Yani." The women sang the nationalist song "The Blood of the People," which contains the line "The People shall be the judge." The army propaganda quoted Memed as saying that the women "tortured and ridiculed Yani who no longer had any strength left."[58] More details were added in the next day's issue. Another detainee, this one being held in Cirebon, was quoted as saying that the Gerwani women, as they attacked the generals, sang "Gendjer Gendjer," an innocent folk song about women picking and cooking vegetables written by a musician affiliated with Lekra.[59] The following day more details appeared. A detainee from Jakarta, a fifteen-year-old girl named Jamilah, said that she and the other women were given small knives and razor blades (*silet*) to stab and slice the bodies of the generals.[60] This story about sadistic Gerwani women was further embellished in the newspaper *Api*, which was established by Brigadier General Sukendro in early October as a venue for the most scurrilous and sensationalist anti-PKI propaganda. *Api* alleged that about one hundred Gerwani women had wielded razor blades and had repeatedly sliced the genitalia of the generals.

Sukarno was infuriated by these absurd stories, especially those in *Api*, and his outburst at a cabinet meeting on November 6 appears to have put a temporary halt to them. He directly addressed Suharto at the meeting:

> Now look here, Harto [Suharto], look here, I've formed, I have this impression [*oordeel*], that just doesn't make sense: a penis cut by a thousand razor blades. And it's not just me. I asked Leimena [Deputy Prime Minister], he's a doctor, and I asked Bandrio [Subandrio]—he used to work as a surgeon, a professional. Azis [Minister of Light Industry], Marno [Interior Minister], they're all doctors. Maybe, maybe, weapons were distributed. If it is said that weapons were given out OK, one person gets a razor blade, one gets a knife, and the others get a machete. OK, a machete or a dagger, that makes sense, handing those out. But handing out razor blades, razor blades, razor blades, razor blades. Really, that makes no sense at all.[61]

Sukarno harped on this issue: "Does it make sense for the genitals of man to be cut by a hundred razor blades? . . . But this is what is reported in the newspapers! These journalists are fools! Do they think we're stupid? What's the point of this? To whip up hatred! Does it make sense? No! I mean, is that reasonable, a penis cut up by 100 Gillette blades?"[62]

On the same day as Sukarno's rant at the cabinet meeting, Sukarno's minister of information, Achmadi, ordered *Api* to cease publishing a daily edition; it was permitted to publish only a weekly edition. Just three weeks later, Achmadi closed down the weekly edition after finding that *Api* had not stopped its irresponsible reporting.[63] Sukarno was able to remove the most extremist paper from circulation, but he could not ban the official army newspapers and Antara.[64] With the journalists of those institutions, he tried persuasion.

To celebrate Antara's twenty-eighth anniversary, he hosted a reception on Sunday, December 12, at the presidential palace in Bogor. The army officers who had been purging Antara, Ibnu Subroto and Nur Nasution, attended, along with the journalists they still employed. A number of other Indonesian and foreign journalists were also present. Sukarno was in a defiant and didactic mood. He reminded the Antara journalists that they worked for him, that he was the Great Leader of the Revolution, and that they had better "upgrade" themselves to understand his ideas. He lectured them on Marxism, the meaning of revolution, and even the spelling of the Dutch term *militaire junta*, which an Antara journalist had misspelled as *militaire juncta*. To counter the anti-PKI line of their army bosses, he insisted that "from the very start, the Indonesian Revolution has been leftist" and that he himself was "a Marxist." Then he upbraided them for their fictional stories about the killing of the generals at Lubang Buaya, pointedly referring to Antara's reports about Jamilah and the razor blades. He told them about the autopsy report on the generals and explained the meaning of the Latin term for such a report: "OK journalists, I'm going to check your knowledge. Do you know what a *visum et repertum* is? It's a statement, it's the result of a doctor's investigation. If a person has been murdered, for instance, the corpse is taken to a doctor and the doctor writes up a *visum et repertum*, and he writes it as a sworn legal document that can be used in court." Sukarno informed them that the *visum et repertum* of the seven officers killed at Lubang Buaya revealed that they had not been castrated: "And this *visum et repertum* wasn't written by just one doctor; it was written by a team of doctors who examined the corpses. There wasn't one of them who had been castrated. My god, my god, my god. In the newspapers it was said they were cut off, some said with razor blades. My God,[65] you journalists are spreading news that isn't true! You're not confirming the news first. So I'm asking you, where are you getting this news from?" Sukarno, feeling as if he were facing a collection of dunces, expressed himself as bluntly as possible. He ordered the journalists to print the following sentence word for word in the next day's edition: "According to the *visum et repertum* prepared by the doctors, none of the victims at Lubang Buaya had been castrated." Ibnu Subroto's *Berita Yudha* obliged and published the statement on the front page under the headline "Once Again Sukarno Scolds Journalists."[66] It had run only one article on the theme of Gerwani's castrating nymphomaniacs, and even that was an article based on *Angkatan Bersenjata*'s reporting.[67] Sugandhi's newspaper, having specialized in the theme, refused to publish Sukarno's statement. *Angkatan Bersenjata* merely reported that Sukarno had called upon journalists to "write what is true." It did not mention that he had denounced the Lubang Buaya stories for not being true.[68] Sugandhi signaled that he was not going to follow Sukarno's orders even as his newspaper was still justifying the anti-PKI campaign in the name of upholding Sukarno's authority.

Angkatan Bersenjata and Antara refused to quietly disregard the scolding. They retaliated. The very day after Sukarno's lecture, they took the Lubang Buaya story to a new outlandish and pornographic extreme. *Angkatan Bersenjata* published an Antara article on December 13 about a seventeen-year-old girl being held by the army in Bandung who claimed that she had received military training at Lubang Buaya with two hundred other Gerwani women and four hundred PKI men in the weeks before October 1. Instead of military training, they had held nonstop orgies. The women were "assigned the task every day, noon and night, to dance stark naked" in front of the men. They danced "The Dance of Fragrant Flowers" (a name invented by the army's psychological warfare specialists) and afterward they fell into extended sessions of "free sex," with each woman "having to serve three or four men."[69] *Angkatan Bersenjata* disregarded Sukarno's explicit instructions and invented even more absurd stories.

The newspaper also twisted his words. Sukarno stated on December 17, in front of journalists gathered in the presidential palace, that those people killing in the name of suppressing the September 30th Movement should be shot. It was a bold and candid statement condemning the mass murders, and he demanded the journalists print it: "Hey journalists, write this all down, write it."

> I am not just going to punish those who were directly involved in the Gestok or Gestapu, but everyone who acts outside the law, those who are turning our revolution to the right, those too we will punish. Because there are many people now, as I said before, who are taking justice into their own hands and carrying out killings against people who were not actually involved in a direct way with Gestok or Gestapu—killing them and doing other things as well. I have already ordered that such people too will be punished, sternly punished. If necessary, they should even be shot.[70]

The next day *Angkatan Bersenjata* quoted him as saying that the people involved in the September 30th Movement should be shot. That was the exact opposite of what he meant.[71]

By mid-December, army propagandists, especially those at Antara and *Angkatan Bersenjata*, had constructed a story about Gerwani women joyously dancing and fornicating, castrating the generals with razor blades, inflicting death by a thousand cuts, inciting a fifteen-year-old girl to serve as the "lead executioner," all the while Untung, a leader of the September 30th Movement, watched, "laughing out loud."[72] The story was based on so-called confessions of several scared and vulnerable captives. The teenaged girls such as Jamilah, as later research has suggested, were coerced into saying what their army captors wanted them to say.[73] The army, when using textbook psychological warfare tactics, may not have expected their absurd story to persist past the moment of crisis. But persist it did. It became the official version of history during the Suharto years. A scene of naked dancing women stuffing corpses down a well stands at the center of the bas relief lining the Sacred Pancasila Monument built in 1969. A scene of frenzied women screaming and slicing the generals with razor blades is a climactic scene in the official film released in 1984 about the September 30th Movement.[74]

The army's stories about PKI supporters at Lubang Buaya were meant to characterize the moral character of everyone affiliated to the party. All over the country ordinary PKI members were supposedly committing similar atrocities or preparing to commit them. A group of Pemuda Rakjat youths killed fourteen children and threw them into a graveyard for dogs. Four corpses were found in a canal with their eyes missing. One man, following "the teachings of the PKI," killed his elderly father and his own children because they were members of a rival political party. Bloody hammers and eye gouging instruments were found in the homes of PKI members. The wife and children of an army officer in Central Java were chopped into little pieces.[75] And so on.

Stories about eye gouging became one of the staples of army propaganda. The PKI had supposedly planned to grotesquely mutilate the bodies of its victims. The fact that one of the corpses of the generals was missing its eyes helped spur this story. A headline of October 7 declared that the generals' "eyes had been gouged out and their faces smashed beyond recognition."[76] The army did not care that the eyes had fallen out because the body had been sitting in water for several days.[77] *Berita Yudha* published a photograph on October 13 of a knife used to make incisions on rubber trees. It was a common tool in a country that was one of the largest producers of rubber in the world. The accompanying text explained that, while it looked like a rubber tapper's knife, it was actually an instrument that the PKI had custom designed and manufactured in large quantities for the sole purpose of gouging out eyes. It had been found on a "Pemuda Rakjat kingpin" in Jakarta. To make the story seem more convincing, the text included a guide on how to use it to gouge out eyes, beginning with instructions on the proper position: "hold the knife horizontal in your right hand."[78] Soon more stories appeared. A similar tool had been discovered in the small town of Garut. The governor of West Java announced that a whole crate of these eye gougers had been found in a neighborhood of Bandung, not far from his residence.[79]

The army propaganda asserted that the moral depravity of PKI supporters, seemingly proved by all these atrocity stories, was a result of their atheism. The allegation was that the communists had rejected religion and had thereby lost a commitment to moral behavior. No longer understanding the difference between right and wrong, they were no longer human; they had surrendered to the base animal instincts of sex and violence. They were amoral beasts. A banner headline on October 11, citing Sukarno out of context, proclaimed, "People who do not believe in God are not human." Other headlines declared: "Not believing in God makes one the prey of Satan" and "Humans who don't believe in God are more savage than animals." The army commander leading the massacres in Aceh and North Sumatra, Major General Mokoginta, announced at a rally of Christians in Medan that "God does not allow people who are anti-God to live in a country of those who believe in God."[80] Suharto, when meeting a delegation of Christians, said much the same thing: "The September 30th Movement was clearly anti-God, so we have to crush it and not allow even one little bit of it to live in our country which is based on Pancasila."[81]

Because communists had become savage animals, they had to be hunted down and eliminated in the same way villagers killed man-eating tigers that came out of the forest. The army newspapers ran many headlines about how the PKI supporters had lost any right to live in Indonesia and had to be completely eliminated. The army commander for West Java proclaimed, "The PKI and its mass organizations no longer have the right to keep living." The army commander for Central Java declared, "Gestapu must be made to disappear from Indonesian soil." Nasution announced, "We must completely wipe out Gestapu-PKI; there is no place for them on Indonesian soil." The commander of the Navy, Martadinata, insisted, "There is no place for the traitors of the nation." The banner across the topmost part of *Angkatan Bersenjata*'s front page on December 13 read, "There is no place for the Gestapu-PKI traitors on Indonesian soil." The headline summarizing a statement by Suharto succinctly expressed the spirit behind his genocide: "Gestapu does not have a right to live in Indonesia."[82]

Ongoing Threats

The army's propaganda exaggerated the threat that the PKI posed by depicting the party as being engaged in a massive social revolt that intended to kill off all of the party's rivals, even those at the village level. The September 30th Movement lasted less than a day in Jakarta. It lasted only three days in some cities in Central Java. But the army's propaganda pretended that the September 30th Movement had never ended. Throughout the repression of the PKI, the party was accused of committing violence and plotting to commit more violence. The propaganda helped generate an atmosphere of "kill or be killed." A headline of late November blared: "The supporters and hidden defenders of the September 30th Movement are still around: they are still trying to defend themselves and continue their counter-revolution."[83]

Stories about PKI violence in Central Java became common after the army's paracommandos entered that province on October 17. The left movement there rarely resisted the assault, but the army newspapers depicted it as the aggressor. The army was supposedly defending the society against a violent offensive that the PKI had begun on October 1. A headline of late October announced, "Central Java is in a state of war: Gestapu is increasing its terror, burnings, kidnappings, and robberies."[84] This storyline had to ignore the fact that Central Java, according to the army's own newspapers, had been quiet before the paracommandos entered on October 17 and began violent attacks on communist supporters on October 21. Anderson and McVey, writing in 1966, stressed this point: "three weeks elapsed in which no violence or trace of civil war occurred."[85] PKI members were not on the offensive; they were trying to "desperately roll with the punches" and "appease the Army by going about their business as normally as possible."[86] But in the army's propaganda, they were wildly rampaging across the province and massacring people. Reports of late October and early November claimed that the PKI had killed six people in Solo, seventy-seven in Boyolali, fifty-eight in Klaten, and an unknown number in Prambanan.[87] It is not clear that any of these massacres, or "carnivals of death" (*pesta maut*), as one newspaper colorfully put it, ever occurred. There were no follow-up investigations.

Every act of violence committed by the army in Central Java was presented as an act of self-defense. When the army killed fifty members of Pemuda Rakjat, it was only after they had attacked a peaceful gathering of noncommunists. To compound the image of Pemuda Rakjat's depravity, the army claimed that the gathering was a funeral for the people who had been recently slaughtered by the PKI. When the army "crushed alive" (*diganjang hidup2*) 341 PKI supporters, it was because they were civilians who had transformed themselves into "combat troops" (*pasukan tempur*) and had begun attacking police posts. Sometimes the army disclaimed responsibility even for killing in self-defense: PKI rank-and-file members themselves were said to have killed local party leaders after realizing they had been cheated and deceived.[88]

PKI supporters were alleged to have massacred large numbers of people in a small village on the remote east coast of Java, in Banyuwangi, on October 18. The newspapers reported in early November that the army had found three mass graves containing sixty-two bodies in the hamlet (*dusun*) of Cemetuk.[89] The Antara report, based on information relayed to Jakarta by an army major, is hard to believe. Allegedly, a group of NU members was heading home through Cemetuk when it encountered a roadblock. The NU members descended from their trucks and started walking. A group of PKI supporters pretended to be noncommunists and offered to put them up for the night in their homes. Gerwani women acted like hospitable hosts. Then the NU members, while eating snacks that had been graciously provided, suddenly keeled over and died. It was a trap. The PKI supporters had poisoned their food. However improbable this story was, it became a fact in the literature on the 1965–66 events and became categorized as a massacre committed by the PKI. The Suharto regime erected a monument in Cemetuk in 1994, modeling it on the monument at Lubang Buaya. The place is now known as "the second Lubang Buaya."[90]

Extensive oral interviews conducted decades later by university students reveal a very different story. Three truckloads of NU supporters in Banyuwangi raided a village named Karangasem that was thought to be a PKI stronghold. When the villagers ably defended themselves, the NU attackers fled helter-skelter. Some of them followed a path that happened to lead them to Cemetuk, which was not a PKI stronghold. The villagers of Cemetuk, assuming they were going to be attacked by this mob of strangers carrying weapons, assembled to defend themselves. They slaughtered the NU supporters who entered their village and buried their bodies. Two days later, when news arrived from stragglers who had escaped the massacre, the army command for the area sent troops to Cemetuk to massacre its residents.[91] The army propaganda did not report on this second massacre of the villagers, opting instead to report only on the first one and to report on it as if it had been unprovoked.

Stories about mass poisoning like the one in Cemetuk were fairly common in the army propaganda of late 1965, as they were in many other propaganda campaigns elsewhere in the world. The Indonesian army newspapers claimed that members of the PKI's youth wing were caught redhanded just before they were going to poison wells in Surabaya. A PKI member in detention confessed that he had been given poison by his superiors in the party and told to dump it into the main pumping station in Jakarta. The residents of the country's two largest cities were meant to feel grateful to the army for saving their lives.[92]

Past Threats

The army propaganda of late 1965 contextualized the September 30th Movement to make it appear part of a pattern of PKI subversion. The Movement was not an anomalous event; it expressed the true nature of an organization that was committed to causing violence and mayhem. The army recast the history of the PKI as the story of an incessant quest to seize state power through bloodshed. Within only four days of the outbreak of the Movement, *Berita Yudha* was reminding its readers of the Madiun Revolt of 1948. One of the front-page headlines, on the day the bodies of the generals were being buried in the Heroes' Cemetery, was: "The memory of Madiun cannot be forgotten."[93]

For army generals and other anticommunists in Indonesia, that revolt had always been understood as a traitorous action by the PKI, a stab in the back of the nationalist movement that was then fighting the Dutch military. They had cultivated a memory of the revolt as a time when the PKI massacred noncommunists in Central and East Java. The September 30th Movement became known in army propaganda as "the second Madiun." The two events became yoked: "Madiun and Gestapu had the same mode of operation and the same mastermind." In both, the PKI committed "barbaric killings."[94] One banner headline called for the total destruction of the PKI "so that there will never be a third Madiun."[95]

From the post-1965 propaganda, one would think that armed partisans of the PKI had launched a rebellion in Madiun against the national leaders, Sukarno and Hatta, and then started slaughtering people they viewed as enemies, such as devout Muslims. The PKI allegedly went on the offensive simply because it wanted to seize state power. The noncommunists were innocent angels while the PKI was grotesquely evil. An army colonel explained in early November, "We've known the character of the PKI since Madiun."[96] Another officer quoted in the press recalled that he had witnessed the "barbarism" of the communists when he was being held as a prisoner in Madiun in November 1948: "The PKI gangs of Madiun shot the prisoners without following standard procedure. Instead, just as a prisoner came out of the door of the prison, he was shot."[97] As the army was organizing executions of prisoners in late 1965, it was describing the victims as "barbarians" for executing prisoners seventeen years before. The 1965 violence was considered a belated act of justice for crimes from 1948. A newspaper article claimed that "the PKI was never cleared in court after the Madiun Revolt."[98]

This definition of "the Madiun Revolt" as an atrocity by "the PKI" grossly distorts what was a complicated series of events. As Benedict Anderson, an expert on that period, noted, "Serious atrocities were committed by both sides in the Madiun Affair of 1948, in a situation of national emergency and huge social and economic tensions."[99] An assorted collection of left-wing militiamen, soldiers, and policemen seized the local government of Madiun on September 19, 1948, because they believed they were going to be attacked. They were not acting on orders from the PKI leaders. Once these left-wing groups took the city, the PKI leaders supported them but did not control them. The party was still too inchoate. It did not want a national-level revolt at that time and did not attempt to organize similar actions elsewhere in Java. The initial action on September 18 resulted in only two deaths, and it was followed by two weeks of negotiations during which only sporadic violence took place. The widespread violence began only after Sukarno and Hatta sent their troops to Madiun on September 30. To save themselves from the onslaught, the left-wing groups fled the city and moved into the countryside. It was then, while they were on the run in October and November, desperate for food and shelter, that they became involved in fighting villagers, such as those loyal to the Muslim organization Masjumi, which was helping the army track down and capture them.[100]

While the army and Masjumi in later years spoke only about the victims on their side, the left-wing side suffered many casualties as well. Indeed, it was the losing side. The army imprisoned about thirty-five thousand people in Central and East Java and summarily executed some of them, including eleven of the top PKI leaders in the village of Ngalihan, outside the city of Solo, on December 19. Among those eleven was Amir Sjarifoeddin, who had, as of only eleven months earlier, been the minister of defense.[101] Another massacre was organized in the town of Magetan, just to the west of Madiun, around the same time. The anticommunists tied together dozens of prisoners with rope, marched them out of prison, and executed them in mass graves, as the townspeople looked on and a cameraman snapped photographs.[102] The anticommunists have cultivated a social memory that depicts the communists as heartless butchers and diggers of mass graves even though the documentation, both written and visual, clearly shows that the anticommunists played such roles.[103]

A comprehensive reckoning of the late 1940s would also have to include the massacres committed by Indonesian militias against Sino-Indonesians and Eurasians in Java who were suspected of collaborating with the Dutch.[104] After independence was achieved, many nationalists were willing to forgive

The graves of eleven PKI leaders executed by the army in 1948 in the village of Ngalihan, ca. 1960. The PKI exhumed their corpses and buried them in individual graves in 1950. Party members regularly tended the graves until 1965. Photo from Oey Hay Djoen Collection, Indonesian Institute of Social History.

the atrocities committed during the period of the armed struggle against the Dutch, even those the Dutch had committed against Indonesians, because they were aware that no side had survived the war with clean hands. The Indonesian government neither compiled documentation on the Dutch atrocities nor demanded reparations after the Dutch forces withdrew in 1950. The general attitude of nationalists was to focus on building the new nation-state. Sukarno and the PNI quickly forgave the PKI for the Madiun Affair and worked with the party in the legislature in the early 1950s. But the Masjumi and NU continued to hold a grudge against the PKI, and they were given the chance to fully air their grievances after October 1965. With army encouragement, they started publishing a large amount of literature about the Madiun Revolt that presented the PKI as some uniquely barbaric and evil force in Indonesian society.[105]

Conclusion

The army's propagandists, led by Sugandhi and Ibnu Subroto, generated many obviously absurd stories. What organization intending to launch a revolt orders its members to first exhaust themselves in the hard work of digging mass graves? Is not that a task that can wait? Have any rebels in human history laboriously prepared methods for the disposal of corpses beforehand? Even the innermost core of the September 30th Movement at Lubang Buaya had not dug a mass grave beforehand and was unprepared to handle the corpses of the six army generals. The Movement improvised and used an already existing well. How could the PKI send the message to dig holes to millions of party members without any information leaking out? Magically, no one else in the country learned of their secret plans. The army intelligence chief killed by the September 30th Movement, General Parman, had spies at the PKI headquarters and received reports from army personnel stationed all over the country. How could he not know about such widely shared information? How could a party possess such an amazingly cohesive organization and develop such intricate plans for a revolt, even tackling the problem of corpse disposal, and then collapse in complete disarray once attacked by the army? How did militant die-hards, all primed for savagery, suddenly turn passive and offer no resistance once the army started rounding them up? The storyline does not make sense.

It is impossible to determine how much the public believed the army's propaganda at that time. At least some of the stories, such as the stories about the orgies at Lubang Buaya, must have been greeted with the same incredulity with which Sukarno greeted them. Before October 1, the PKI had a reputation for puritanism and stern discipline. It was the only political party that strictly policed its members' conduct and enforced rules against "womanizing," conspicuous consumption, and corruption. Perhaps even those people who joined the army's campaign of violence against the PKI understood that many of the stories in the propaganda were false and were meant only to slander the communists. It was possible to disbelieve particular stories while still believing in the general story about the PKI being an insidious foe that needed to be eliminated.[106]

This kind of logic was expressed by the *New York Times* journalist Seymour Topping, when writing in August 1966 about the "staggering mass slaughter of Communists." He endorsed the general story that the perpetrators told him: the massacres had been "reprisals" committed "in retaliation" for the September 30th Movement. He did not see the perpetrators as criminals who should be condemned in the way that the US had been condemning mass murderers in communist states. Indonesians supposedly had a tradition of "running amok." But Topping did not believe their claim that they had been in mortal danger: "Many of the Indonesians who participated in the killings justify their acts by saying, 'It was them or us.'" The evidence they offered of being in danger consisted of the stories they had heard from army officers or read in army-controlled newspapers. The perpetrators' memories were filled with suspicions, rumors, and apprehensions—not stories of pitched battles in which they had to defend themselves against armed gangs of PKI supporters:

> In most Indonesian cities and big towns, one is told that mass graves were dug by the Communists before September 30 to receive the victims of an impending coup d'état. It is said that lists were seized in Communist party files naming army officers, religious leaders, foreign missionaries and local officials who were to be executed. Boxes of eye pluckers to be used in the torture of prisoners are also said to have been found in the possession of Communists. Most experienced observers believe that the stories have been spun out of a need to rationalize the mass killings. There is no substantial evidence that the Communists had large supplies of weapons or were planning a mass nationwide uprising to seize total power in the near future.[107]

A NU leader, Salahuddin Wahid, writing in 2000, reassured the members of his organization that they had nothing to feel guilty about, even if the PKI had not really been a mortal threat: "the atmosphere of the time was like a war, if one did not kill, one would be killed." The wording is revealing. He wrote it was "like a war" (*seperti perang*), not that it was a war. He mentioned that his family feared for their lives because they had seen their names on a hit list found in the house of a PKI leader. He acknowledged that the list may have been fake: "Now we can say that the list may not necessarily have been true and maybe the names weren't meant to be intended victims. But living in the atmosphere of that time, it was entirely normal for us to believe that the list was authentic."[108] Wahid did not pursue the implications of that admission. If the list was not authentic, then who created it and for what purpose? If the army had concocted the list, then would not that suggest that the army was trying to deceive his family? And would not the NU members have to feel some measure of guilt for allowing themselves to be deceived?

Salahuddin Wahid was writing in 2000 to counter his older brother, the better-known and broader-minded NU leader and then president of Indonesia, Abdurrahman Wahid, who had just apologized to the victims of the 1965–66 terror. It was a brief apology on a TV talk show. But it unleashed a storm of criticism from military officers and other NU leaders.[109] All the elements of the old propaganda line were reasserted with a vengeance after the elder Wahid's apology: the PKI had begun a civil war with the aim of slaughtering noncommunists, the violence against the party was committed in self-defense, both sides suffered, the PKI just happened to be the losing side, and so on. A war that never happened remained the ever-reliable alibi for denying the mass atrocity that did happen.

3

Tortured Words

Interrogations and the Production of Truth

The Old Kebayoran Road cuts a long and straight north-south line through the labyrinthine welter of Jakarta's narrow streets and alleys. It is hard to imagine these days, as the cars creep inch by inch through the congested traffic, that this area was on the sparsely inhabited western fringes of the city back in 1965. With inexpensive land and quiet surroundings, the Old Kebayoran neighborhood was then a perfect site for a film studio. Some of Indonesia's best script writers, directors, and actors made feature-length films here at a studio called the Indonesian Film Company, or Infico for short. The building is undistinguished now and is easy to miss. It appears from the street as a narrow, generic single-story house. It is just another building crammed up against others in a steady procession of sliding steel gates and concrete walls. The high-ceilinged, warehouse-like studio, where stage sets were once constructed and dramatic scenes of love and loss enacted, lies in the back hidden from sight.

The Infico studio was a modest operation, as was the entire film industry in Indonesia at that time. Indeed, it barely deserves to be called an industry. All of the equipment, from the cameras to the film processing chemicals, had to be imported, and there were few businesses that could afford the high prices. Filmmakers struggled just to get the basic supplies. It is remarkable how many high-quality films were made during the 1950s and early 1960s in spite of the severe material constraints. One of the country's most prolific and prominent filmmakers was Bachtiar Siagian, who had helped establish Infico.

The door to the former Infico Film Studio, Jakarta, 2011. Photo by John Roosa

He served as the head of the film department of the PKI-affiliated cultural organization Lekra, and some of the people he hired were from Lekra. It was perhaps through the PKI's facilitation that Infico was able to obtain some of its film stock from the Soviet Union.

Suharto's army, seeing the Infico building as a nest of the PKI in October 1965, confiscated it and arrested many of the artists, including Siagian. The building was one of many properties in the country stolen outright by the army during the anti-PKI repression. Once in possession of such a spacious studio, the army officers set their imaginations to work on how they could redesign it for their own purposes. They turned the studio into an interrogation center, with cages made from wooden planks and chicken wire covering the floor space. The building was turned over to Satgas Intel (an intelligence taskforce), which brought political prisoners there from detention camps and prisons from around Jakarta and temporarily held them for weeks or months while they were being interrogated. It was the army's way of centralizing information extracted from the prisoners. The relative isolation of the building, which had made the location suitable for a film studio, also made it suitable for an interrogation center: there were few people outside to hear the screaming.

Torture was standard operating procedure during the interrogation sessions. The studio where people once performed tender, romantic scenes before cameras was now the site of secret, in-camera scenes of sadism in which docile bodies were beaten, shocked, and burned. Fictional scenes brought to life in the studio were replaced by real-life scenes that left prisoners permanently disabled. The all-too-real tortures were carried out as part of the army's enactment of a fictional story—a story about a vast underground communist conspiracy organizing an armed revolt. The interrogators asked prisoners about their roles in this made-up conspiracy and discovered what they wished to discover. The propaganda line in the army press found confirmation in this former film studio, as interrogators forced prisoners to admit to all sorts of nefarious deeds. The building was the army's secluded laboratory for a strange alchemy that combined equal measures of myth and pain to produce official truths.

When a colleague of mine in Jakarta discovered the Infico-Satgas Intel building in 2009 after a long search, it was being used as an all-purpose warehouse.[1] The wire cages had been removed to create an empty space that contained old cars, boxes of industrial chemicals, and a hobbyist's collection of large remote-controlled model airplanes. It had not been renovated since the army stopped using it as a torture center sometime in the 1980s. It was run down, dank, and dusty. The older neighbors recalled hearing the screams of the detainees many years ago and still considered the place to be spooky (*angker*). There were no signs of the violence that had once taken place there except for some words etched into a wall close to the floor near a corner. They must have been made by a prisoner, scratching the concrete with some small shard of metal. The words were hard to make out amid the flaking, but one word was clear: *zalim*, meaning cruel and oppressive.

I first visited the building in 2011. The etching in the wall had been scraped smooth and painted over. Even that single elusive trace of the horror that had taken place here had been erased. The studio's interior had white walls and bright lights and looked clean and cheery. It was being used by a kung fu club, and the floor on which rows of wire cages had once confined the sick and suffering, with their scabs and bedbug bites, was covered by a brand-new shiny red mat. The martial arts enthusiasts avoided inflicting pain on each other and fell onto the cushioning of the mat. Anyone coming into the building now, seeing men and women improving their physical health by pushing their bodies through the delicate, elaborate dance-like moves of kung fu, would think that the stories of torture in this building must be imagined, like stories in a movie.

Torture and Fantasy

As Suharto's army began arresting civilians en masse in October 1965, it created a new bureaucratic structure to conduct interrogations of the detainees. The Supreme Operations Command, KOTI, ordered in mid-October the formation of a Central Interrogation Team in Jakarta (Teperpu) and a Regional Interrogation Team (Teperda) for each one of the provinces. The army was preparing to imprison many people and was concerned about an "efficient" way to process them outside the regular judiciary.[2] A subsequent order from Suharto on October 29 detailed the objectives and functions of these new teams. They were tasked with passing on relevant information obtained from interrogations to army officers of the Territorial Command to help them defeat the September 30th Movement. They were also tasked with classifying the detainees according to the seriousness of their involvement in the Movement.[3] An order of November 12 elaborated on the classification system that was to be used. Detainees were to be classified as either A prisoners, "definitely involved in a direct way"; B prisoners, "definitely involved in an indirect way"; or C prisoners, "having found indications or strong suspicions of being involved directly or indirectly."[4] The members of these Interrogation Teams became all-powerful, functioning simultaneously as detectives, prosecutors, and judges. They decided the fates of many of the hundreds of thousands of detainees.

On paper, the process seemed rational enough: individuals were arrested, interrogated, classified, and then either kept imprisoned or set free. In practice, the process was a wild witch hunt. The September 30th Movement had been a small-scale, clandestine movement that involved very few people. The leaders—the men who planned and organized it—numbered about ten, even going by the Suharto regime's own official history. The army set itself the impossible task of finding connections between the Movement and hundreds of thousands of people from all over the country. Connections were established using that vague category of "indirectly involved" (*terlibat tidak langsung*). The very fact that one was a member of the PKI or one of its mass organizations or an organization that agreed with the PKI on many issues (such as the Sukarnoist political party, Partai Indonesia [Partindo, Indonesian Party]), was sufficient proof of one's "involvement" in the Movement.

The interrogations were not only meant to discover links to a fetishized past event; they were also meant to uncover links to an ongoing mythical event: the PKI's armed revolt. The propaganda line at the time was that the PKI was in the middle of a massive insurrection. In spreading that made-up story, army personnel inevitably wound up having to behave as if it were true. The interrogators set about finding actionable intelligence, believing they were involved in a counterinsurgency campaign. Who was leading the revolt? What was their plan? Who were the double agents? Where were the weapons? Where were the hideouts? A detainee was invariably asked to explain his or her position in the party and to name the names of other supporters of the party. The detainees were interrogated as though they were enemy soldiers, possessing information that was crucial for determining the war's outcome.

When interviewing former political prisoners, I was struck by how many reported that they had been tortured. Former political prisoners from a great variety of provinces reported that torture was standard operating procedure during the interrogations.[5] Torture appears to have been practiced more frequently in some districts and some military units than in others.[6] Not enough data are available, or will ever be available, to establish precisely the total number of torture victims. Given that about 1.5 million people were detained in relation to the September 30th Movement, it is safe to assume that hundreds of thousands of people were tortured. The prevalence of the practice can be inferred from the fact that former political prisoners who returned unharmed from the interrogation rooms often had to explain to their fellow prisoners how it was possible for them to have been spared. Prisoners suspected anyone whose body was unscathed of having agreed to collaborate with the interrogators.

In terms of the number of victims, this was one of the worst cases of torture in human history. It is puzzling that it has not been recognized as such. The scholarly literature on torture rarely mentions the Indonesian case.[7] The lack of source material may have resulted in this neglect. Amnesty International mentioned in its pioneering *Report on Torture* (1973) that it had "comparatively few first-hand accounts" from Indonesia in its files.[8] It was able to collect many more accounts of torture from other countries, such as Greece and Argentina. The cases that have been better documented have attracted more scholarly attention. Moreover, there has not been a single poignant autobiographical book written by a victim of the torture in Indonesia similar to the now-iconic books by Henri Alleg, Jean Améry, and Jacobo Timerman.[9]

A person from outside Indonesia, on being informed that the Suharto regime tortured prisoners on such a massive scale in the 1960s, might react with indifference. There is often a tendency to expect torture and all kinds of other atrocities in so-called underdeveloped, Third World countries. But one should not ascribe the extensive use of torture to presumed primitive, premodern conditions in the country. The Indonesian interrogators used torture for the same reasons that the French in Algeria, the US in Vietnam, US-trained militaries in Latin America, and the Greek military used it during that same decade. It was considered a necessary part of counterinsurgency warfare—a kind of warfare in which information about the identity and location of the insurgents was all-important.[10]

My argument about torture in Indonesia is that it worked to confirm the regime's fantasy that there was an insurgency to counter. The army's propaganda became the army's own understanding of what it was doing as an institution. As the stories of the PKI insurgency circulated, army personnel found it difficult to separate accurate intelligence from their own propaganda. The army forced prisoners during interrogations to speak in accordance with the premises of that fantasy: that the PKI had launched a nationwide armed revolt and all members of the PKI were participants in that revolt. The army became convinced it was waging a war of counterinsurgency, even if it did not face any significant resistance. The feedback loop was complete as the army used the information from the interrogations as evidence of the insurgency to be presented to the public. Since late 1965, army publications have routinely cited interrogation reports as evidence of the official version of events, as if torture chambers produced unimpeachable truths.

Critiquing Critiques of Torture

The critique of torture here pertains to its ability to generate and sustain a fantasy world. This is different from the usual kind of critique, which contends that it produces false and unreliable information. That critique is usually expressed by the statement "torture does not work." The argument here is that torture does work: it works to reaffirm the preexisting narrative that the torturers have before they enter the interrogation rooms. To develop an effective critique of torture, one must move beyond the platitudinous assertion that torture produces false information.

The fact that the infliction of "bodily torment and pain for the drawing out of the truth" (to use the second-century Roman jurist Ulpian's definition of interrogation) can also produce untruths has never been an effective argument against torture.[11] Aristotle noted that "those under compulsion are as likely to give false evidence as true."[12] Legal scholars of ancient Rome admitted that evidence obtained through torture was "weak and dangerous, and inimical to the truth," as the sixth-century *Digest of Justinian* put it, yet they remained wedded to the practice, believing that it "ought not to be rejected as absolutely unworthy."[13] The legal systems in Europe from the thirteenth to eighteenth centuries, when the paradigm of "the law of proof" was in force, employed judicial torture despite an awareness of its tendency to produce false information. As John Langbein has pointed out, "The law of torture survived into the eighteenth century, not because its defects had been concealed, but rather in spite of their having been long revealed."[14] The Spanish Inquisition in colonial Peru, as Irene Silverblatt notes, "employed torture to get to the truth while, at the same time, doubting the truth of the confessions obtained by torture."[15] When Beccaria argued in 1764 that "torture is not a fit means of discovering the truth," he was not saying anything that was not already recognized.[16] Many states have remained committed to torture because they have remained committed to the belief that it can yield valuable information, even if sometimes it does not.

Liberal political theorists, otherwise concerned with personal dignity and liberty, have tended to endorse torture during interrogations (what can be called interrogational torture) in the belief that it can be useful in obtaining information that is vital to public safety. Jeremy Bentham, the inventor of the Panopticon, the prison design that Foucault's *Discipline and Punish* made so well known, endorsed interrogational torture in the early 1800s even as he opposed corporal punishments for convicts (what can be called penal torture). In certain circumstances, Bentham argued, the information obtained through torture is of greater social utility than the well-being of the individual being tortured. If a detainee has information that could save the lives of "100 innocent persons," then the state should employ torture "to extract the requisite information."[17] Bentham was one of the first theorists to outline the hypothetical "ticking bomb" scenario to justify interrogational torture.[18]

Liberal political theory since Bentham has frequently returned to the same reasoning.[19] The premise seems valid since torturers can always cite cases in which torture led to correct intelligence and therefore claim that the unsuccessful cases were worth the gamble. Advocates of torture have tended to accept the claim that their technique for discovering the truth is fallible. Their reasoning proceeds from the premise that torture *can* produce reliable information; it does not always "work," but it sometimes does and thus should be permissible, however morally repugnant it is. Nothing in modern liberal political theory about ethics, rights, human dignity, democracy, and abhorrence of cruelty mandates an absolute ban on torture; indeed, precisely those principles can be used to justify it.[20]

One way to argue against the advocates of torture is to claim that torturers do not care about finding the truth. Elaine Scarry has argued that the purported objective of interrogational torture, gaining information, is just a pretense, an enabling fiction. The actual goal is to punish the person suspected of having committed a crime and to restore the confidence of state officials whose power had been undermined by the commission of the crime. From this perspective, interrogational torture should be considered a form of penal torture. She argues that torture is "the production of a fantastic illusion of power." For states that feel their power threatened, it is "a grotesque piece of compensatory drama."[21] For Scarry, the infliction of pain on a captive, docile body provides a virtual reality in which the torturers see another person's pain as proof of their power, even when their power in the world outside the interrogation room is in crisis. She contends that interrogational torture, ostensibly intended to discover information, is actually "terroristic torture" intended to punish the victim and instill fear in the society.[22] The performative element of interrogational torture—the acting out of absolute power over a helpless body—is not its surplus but its raison d'être. Scarry believes that interrogators are indifferent to the information they receive, that the verbal exchanges between the interrogator and the captive mean nothing. In her analysis, the only part of the interrogation that has meaning is the nonverbal, physical actions of bodies.

While Scarry's argument is valid for many cases of interrogational torture, it is incomplete. A torturer's search for information should not be entirely dismissed as a "false motive syndrome."[23] The Indonesian case indicates that interrogators can be very attentive to the verbal information elicited from battered bodies. Simply by positioning the verbal information from the captives as the ostensible goal of the interrogations, the torturers had to consider at least some of that information as valid even when they sensed that they were only generating an echo chamber. They persisted in using the words muttered from bruised and bleeding mouths as valuable intelligence. They even touted the transcripts of the torture sessions in public as evidence of the regime's truth claims about the PKI. Interrogational torture should not be collapsed into the category of penal torture.

A point that Scarry overlooks is that the power the torturers feel derives not just from the infliction of pain; it also derives from being able to impose their own peculiar understanding of reality upon other people. They insist on hearing words that confirm their symbolic construction of the world. The torture room becomes the locus for the reaffirmation of the state's official truths. When they receive new, unexpected information from the prisoners, they trust the validity of the verbal exchanges in the torture chamber even more. They feel that they are engaging in a dialogue and coming to understand their enemies better.[24] The stories constructed during the verbal exchanges of the torture sessions wind up circulating for years far outside the confines of the interrogation room walls, sustaining the fantasies of power behind the original faith in torture's efficacy.[25] Scarry's analysis is so preoccupied with the "world-destroying" effects of torture for the victims that she misses what could be called the "world-creating" effects for the perpetrators or, more precisely, the fantasy-world-creating effects.[26]

When states decide to practice torture, they create their own frame of reference for determining truth and falsity. Torture represents an effort to turn a preexisting fantasy world into reality; its value becomes self-confirming. By practicing torture, state officials are implicitly admitting that they have abandoned any attempt to subject their strategies to an evaluation outside their internal feedback loop. Their search for truth inevitably pulls them ever deeper into self-delusion. Interrogational torture is the opposite of what it claims to be: it is not the extraction of information but the imposition of information.

Scholars studying the Argentinean junta, in power from 1976 to 1983, have developed this kind of critique of torture. Lindsey Dubois has argued that the junta's torturers used "their victims to confirm and act out their worldview" and to create them "as terrorists."[27] The junta believed that it faced a vast insurgency that threatened all that was civilized, good, and Christian, and its secret torture sessions produced information that confirmed that belief. During the years the junta was in power, the official representation of events had its supporters in the society: "People who were abducted 'must have been involved in something,' it was said (and is still said); or 'the military knows what it's doing.'"[28] The junta presented the repression of the left-wing forces as part of an effort to establish the rule of law and human rights in the country.[29] The torture began with the belief that terrorists were everywhere and needed to be uprooted. Mark Osiel has noted, "The officers were indeed fighting ghosts in their minds, something of their own imagination. There is often an irreducibly imaginative element in the construction of an enemy. 'The enemy' is often, at least in part, a social and intellectual 'fiction,' the by-product of a particular theory about how the world is divvied up and constituted into 'friendly' and 'unfriendly' forces."[30]

The Suharto regime, unlike the Argentinian junta, lasted for a long time—thirty-two years. Its success owed nothing to the information gathered through torture. State officials succeeded in staying in power in spite of their torture-fueled delusions about their enemies. The consequence of that success was that their delusions became institutionalized as official knowledge, taught in schools and repeated in the popular media until they became transformed into common sense.

Logistics of the Illogical

The prisoner about to be tortured would be led into the interrogation room and ordered to sit in front of a desk facing the interrogator. Typically, a muscleman known as a "punching specialist" (*tukang pukul*) stood in the room, ready to move into action at the interrogator's signal. Sometimes the interrogator himself doubled as the *tukang pukul*. The questions would begin. What is your name? What is your address? What was your position in the PKI? Where were you on September 30? What was your role in the September 30th Movement? Who else do you know in the PKI?

The interrogator would usually work from an informant's report about the prisoner's identity—the information the army had that had led the army to arrest the person in the first place—and then demand that the prisoner admit that the information in the report was correct. The prisoners, realizing that their categorization would determine the duration of the detention, if not their life or death, would usually respond by claiming that they had little or no connection to the PKI. Some claimed they had been gullible followers, unwittingly caught up in what friends and neighbors were doing.

Ahmad, a former prisoner from a village near Magelang in Central Java, recalled being forced to admit under torture to being a PKI member. He had joined the "Non-Central Faction" of the schoolteacher's union, Persatuan Guru Republik Indonesia (PGRI), when it split in early 1965. Suharto's army classified that faction of the union as a PKI organization and rounded up as many members as it could find, whether they were PKI supporters or not. Ahmad happened to have been a local leader of the PNI. The police took him from his classroom while he was teaching one morning in late December 1965. The police were rounding up all the suspected PKI members in his neighborhood (*kelurahan*) that day. Once gathered together, the captives were trucked to the capital city of the *kabupaten* (regency). Since the prison in the city was already full, they were deposited in a former orphanage that had been turned into a detention camp. Some days after his arrival, Ahmad was escorted to one the rooms set aside for interrogations.

> I was called around seven in the evening for the interrogation. They were from the military, two of them, one who typed and another who asked questions.
> "So you're a PKI member, right?"
> "No. I'm a member of PGRI."
> "Wrong! You're PKI. Just admit it—here on the document you're already down as PKI."

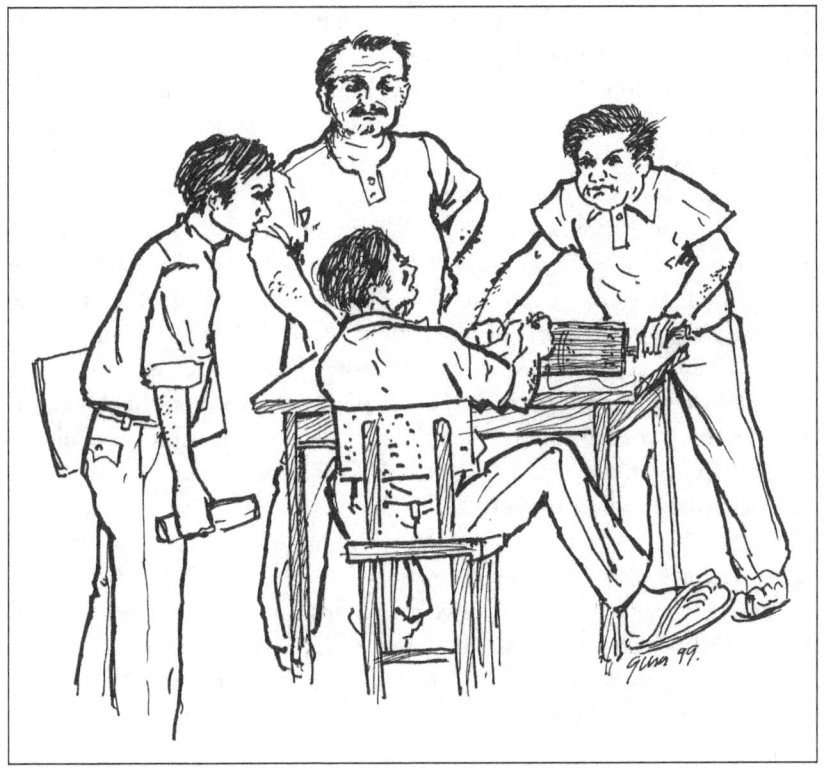

Drawing of a torture session in Jakarta. Gumelar, a former political prisoner who had been affiliated with Lekra, made the drawing in 1999 to represent the time he was tortured in 1968 in an army command post.

"But I'm not PKI. I'm PGRI, a member of PGRI."
Then I was hit, electroshocked, hit again, all the while I was naked.[31]

Ahmad recalled being hit with a rustic, homemade instrument similar to a medieval flail: "They hit me with, oh, what was that called? It was, umm, cow testicles that had been dried rock hard and wrapped in wire. At the end of it they attached a piece of tin. If you were hit with that you'd definitely bleed." By about one in the morning, he had had enough of the torture: "Yeah, finally, finally I just admitted it so that I wouldn't get hit anymore. It was because of the electroshocks and the beatings." Ahmad's identity was thus confirmed for the interrogators. He himself admitted to being a PKI member. It became an official fact entered in the records. The torture in that detention camp in Magelang was standard operating procedure: "There wasn't anyone who didn't cry and there wasn't anyone who could just stay quiet. Definitely, they would scream in pain from the beating."

The interrogators in Indonesia targeted the body of the prisoner, employing simple ancient methods. They did not use the techniques of psychological torture that the CIA developed in the 1950s and applied most recently in Guantanamo and Abu Ghraib. The torture in Indonesia was a purely physical torture. In a cruel application of E. F. Schumacher's principle of appropriate technology, they used tools that were ready to hand. Everyday objects of the office became instruments of pain. One of the favorite techniques was to place a table leg on the toes of the prisoner and then sit on the table, bouncing up and down for better effect. A leg from a disassembled wooden chair became a handy billy club. A pen became a knife to puncture the skin. A lit clove cigarette became a means to burn the skin. A more exotic instrument could be obtained free from the local fish market: the barbed tail of a stingray. A former political prisoner who has written a dictionary about all matters related to the anticommunist repression noted that whipping with the stingray tail was called "giving the tail."[32]

The military's most sophisticated torture instrument was a hand-cranked generator placed on a desk to deliver electroshocks. Its component parts could be assembled from materials found in a junkyard. The shock was delivered by metal rings placed on the prisoner's thumbs or toes. Electroshock was called "putting on the rings" in the euphemistic language of the interrogators.[33] If nothing else was available, punches and kicks would do.

Krisnayana, a former worker at the Jatinegara railway station in Jakarta, described the damage punches, kicks, and beatings with wood planks could do.[34] He was a night watchman at the station in the early morning hours of October 11 and was stopped by the police for violating curfew. The police suspected that he was a member of the Serikat Buruh Kereta Api (SBKA, Railway Workers Union), and that he had a connection with the September 30th Movement. He remembered the initial questioning in the street proceeded somewhat like this:

> "Where were you when the September 30th Movement happened?"
> "I was at home."
> "Did you hear its announcements?"
> "I didn't hear anything because I've never had a radio of any sort."
> They kept insisting that I must have known that I needed a letter authorizing night duty and that I must have known about the September 30th Movement.

The police let him go and told him to come to the nearby police station later in the afternoon. He voluntarily came back, expecting to be released once they discovered he was just a harmless, low-paid menial laborer with three years of elementary school education from a village in Central Java. Instead, they kept him in the station's holding cells for about three weeks. One night at around 1:00 a.m. the police took him out of his cell and interrogated him for several hours. While insisting that he admit he was a union leader and a participant in the Movement, they hit him with rifle butts, burned his skin with lit cigarettes, and threw hot coffee on him.

> "Who abducted the generals and where were you?"
> I kept saying I didn't know. Even the bench I had been sitting on was smashed up in order to get the wood to destroy my body. They hit me with a teak board about one meter long.

The police hit him all over the trunk of his body until he was coughing up blood: "It was only then that they stopped." He was carried back to his cell unconscious. About four days later, the police interrogated him once again, going over all the same questions. He signed the transcript even though he disagreed with it since he knew the beating would resume if he did not sign. In November 1965 he was transferred to the Kodim for East Jakarta, where he was interrogated yet again: "You kidnapped the generals, right? You were out that night. Don't play stupid; you were the head of the local PKI chapter." The interrogator put metal rings on his thumbs and electroshocked him to force him to confess and sign yet another statement. By the time he was released, after seven years of detention without charge, his lungs and spine had been permanently damaged. He suffered from chest pains in later years as he worked odd jobs in the neighborhood, everything from carrying baggage at the Jatinegara railway station to pedaling a bicycle rickshaw to hawking fried bananas on the street.

A former political prisoner in Rembang, Central Java, recalled that torture was routine in the prison where he was detained. Kasmin, from a penniless family of day laborers, attended six years of school and then, by virtue of his high grades, entered a teacher's training program in the 1950s when the newly independent government, desperate to raise literacy rates, provided funding for people intending to become teachers.[35] He received a monthly paycheck from the government to be trained as a teacher. As soon as he graduated, in 1958, the Ministry of Education sent him to teach in a small, remote village in the hills with a salary that just covered the cost of his food. Having grown up shoeless and shirtless in the wars of the 1940s, he was a proletarian who strongly identified with the PKI. He volunteered to serve as a village-level leader for the party. In October 1965, he was required to report to the police station every day at the nearest town, Sluke. When he showed up at the police station on November 9, the police ordered him to stay. They trucked him to the town of Lasem and then to the prison in Rembang, where thousands of men from all around the *kabupaten* were being held. Fifty men were squeezed into cells meant for only five.

> Kasmin: After we were being held in the prison, the interrogations started. They were done by the Teperda. What I heard and saw was a treatment by the state officials that wasn't at all humane.
> Interviewer: Can you describe it?
> Kasmin: The thing was that each time a prisoner was called from the prison to go to the place of the interrogation, he would definitely return unable to walk. It was because of all the inhumane beatings. Some came back with their ears ripped, because there was one policeman who was famous; he was named, if not mistaken, oh, I forget, Lan . . . Lan . . . Das . . . Darlan or what was it? He was a policeman. Kasilan, that was his name! He was on the interrogation team and was famous for having a thing for ears. If a prisoner was assigned him as the interrogator, he had no hope of coming out with his ears intact.
> Interviewer: What would he do?
> Kasmin: Bite them, always. Intentionally bite the ears.

When it came Kasmin's turn for an interrogation, he was fortunate enough not be assigned to the ear-biter Kasilan. The interrogator turned out to be a decent man: "I returned to the prison uninjured. Once I got back inside the prison a lot of my friends started getting suspicious: 'What's going on? How is it possible for you to come back in one piece?' Because most of my friends' bodies were badly hurt."

Although detainees in West Java do not appear to have been tortured as often as those in neighboring Jakarta and Central Java, some were tortured there, too. Tubagus Suryaatmadja, a member of the PKI's provincial leadership committee for West Java, was tortured when he refused to admit that the PKI had planned a revolt. He was arrested on October 29, 1965, in Serang, a city in the regency of Banten, and imprisoned in the military police headquarters there. A few days after his arrest, he was interrogated by three men—a captain, a lieutenant, and a corporal. As he recalls in his unpublished memoir:

> The first questions were about my identity, my name, address, occupation, position in the Party. Then there were questions about the Party's program, both the short-term and long-term goals of the Party. I answered those questions smoothly and thoroughly. After going through that general questioning, they moved onto specific questions about the plan of the PKI

in Banten to do what the PKI did in Jakarta. Their accusation was that the PKI in Banten already had a plan to seize state power through violence and kidnap and kill all the top state officials in the regency. Of course, I strongly rejected the accusation and said there was no such plan. That made the interrogator furious. The interrogation switched from the mouth to the hands and feet: I was tortured with punches and kicks from all three interrogators until I was unconscious. I only came to when I was back in my cell.[36]

The next week, when he was brought to the interrogation room again, he was told to sign the typed-up interrogation report. Having been tortured over his refusal to admit that the PKI had a plan to take over Banten, he was surprised to discover that the report contained nothing about the issue. His interrogators did not insist that he admit the truth of their accusation. He found the report's contents unobjectionable and signed it.

The interrogators usually typed up a report that purported to represent the words of the prisoner. They then demanded that the prisoner sign it. The signature was supposed to signify the prisoner's uncoerced assent to the report's contents. Prisoners who refused to sign could face further torture. Tan Swie Ling, imprisoned in late 1966 in Jakarta, was tortured under such circumstances. The interrogators shredded the flesh on his back with a stingray tail until he signed a report in which he admitted to knowing all about the PKI's secret underground network.[37] When he was brought before a military court months later as a witness in the case of Sudisman, a PKI Politburo leader, he was asked to repeat in public the information in the interrogation report. He refused and shocked the court by stating that his signature reflected only his desire not to be tortured to death. The judges, prosecutors, and audience were taken aback since no other witness had been willing to admit that he had been tortured for fear of being tortured again.[38] An observer of the Sudisman trial in 1967, Benedict Anderson recalled that, of all the witnesses who testified at the trial, he was most impressed by Tan Swie Ling, who was "straightforward, brave, respectful, and never once willing to surrender to the court."[39]

Suppressing a Mythical Insurgency

The army's interrogation methods were predicated on the idea that the PKI was covertly organizing an armed insurrection. To defeat the PKI, the interrogators believed that they had to arrest and interrogate as many party supporters as possible. Prisoners were forced to reveal the names and locations of other people who supported the party. The interrogators then dispatched teams of soldiers to search for those individuals. They grabbed them from their homes or workplaces, brought them into the interrogation room, and repeated the same line of questioning on them. The former political prisoners, in describing the process, used a metaphor from the railroads: one train car is put on the tracks, another is added behind it, and another, and so on.

The army interrogators, believing that the PKI was engaged in an insurgency, asked many prisoners about where weapons were stored. In October 1965, Ibu Sarbinatun was eighteen years old and newly married to a man who was a member of the PKI's provincial committee for Central Java. She and her husband were detained and interrogated. Both were badly tortured in Surakarta while being accused of storing large quantities of rifles from China to be used to arm the people and overthrow the government. Ibu Sarbinatun was also accused of being a participant in the killing of the six army generals in Jakarta on October 1. After repeated interrogation sessions during which she had been kicked and sexually assaulted, she finally gave up: "'Enough! Whatever you want, go ahead. Write down whatever you want. I'll sign it.' And that was it. I signed the report."[40]

Bhaskoro, a former adjutant to the commander of the military police in Palembang, Sumatra, narrated a story about the time when his detachment was sent on a wild goose chase looking for Chinese-made weapons.[41] It was around March 1966. His superior officers had come to believe, on the basis of interrogations of detainees, that the PKI in Palembang had squirreled away a massive shipment of weapons from China that had been intended for use by the September 30th Movement: "After reading the interrogation transcripts, we realized—we *imagined*—that the information was correct. That's what was in the transcripts, right?" The weapons were supposedly buried off a road outside the city: "I was ordered to join the operation—I was directly under the command of Loho [a military police officer]—that was at a plantation near Kilometer 29, to look for a pile of weapons from Beijing." The soldiers spent several weeks looking for the weapons there: "it turned out that we didn't find a single one." The operation wasted much time and energy.

It also cost lives. In the course of the hunt for PKI weapons in Palembang, the army, according to Bhaskoro, interrogated and tortured two civilians and two of its own personnel. One of them was an acquaintance of his who had been posted to a Kodim in the Lampung area. He was a private by the name of Nurjanjo. Having been the trainer for a women's civil militia that was being organized for the purposes of Confrontation against Malaysia, he was accused of giving military training to the PKI-affiliated women's organization, Gerwani, and arranging weapons for them. He was interrogated for many hours and tortured to death: "The cruelty was such that, my goodness, Nurjanjo was barely recognizable. The torture was nonstop." Bhaskoro was assigned the task of burying him and the three others. One of the civilians killed had been the owner of the plantation at which the weapons had been allegedly stored.

Furious and futile hunts for weapons also cost lives in Central Java. Ahmad, the teacher detained in Magelang, recounted the story of how his friend had been tortured to death:

> There was a friend of mine from Pakis, a fellow named Citro, who was beaten from seven in the evening to six in the morning and finally died. They just kept kicking him. They had some kind of evidence that he had hidden a tank with a mounted cannon. That was funny [*lucu*] [*laughing*]. Now if it was a toy tank, that would be possible, or a cigarette lighter. But a tank—that was the accusation, that he had hidden a tank so that it could be used in a revolt—I mean that is really funny [*laughing*].

The absurdity of the story temporarily overwhelmed Ahmad's grief, and he laughed while speaking about a sadistic killing.

In torturing prisoners, the army repeatedly sabotaged its own campaign against the PKI. As commentators on torture have noted for more than two thousand years, torture measures a person's ability to withstand pain, not the importance of the information the person may have or the extent of the person's criminal culpability.[42] In the Indonesian case, those who were the least committed to the PKI, who had the least amount of information to provide, admitted to all sorts of lies: to being top-ranking PKI leaders, to hiding weapons, and to knowing the location of important party leaders. Meanwhile, the PKI members who were the most committed to the party were the ones better able to withstand the torture.

One torture victim I interviewed had been a high-level clandestine activist in the PKI. He had been a member of the Special Bureau, which was responsible for contacting military officers. He appears in my book *Pretext for Mass Murder* under the pseudonym Hasan. His real name was Asep Suryaman (1926–2009). He joined the party in the late 1940s and spent six years in China in the 1950s, becoming a committed Maoist in the process. He wholeheartedly believed in the inevitability of a worldwide communist revolution through armed struggle. In an autobiographical essay he gave me, he described how he was tortured in a military building in Jakarta:

> In the interrogations, I kept insisting that I was a building contractor, not a PKI activist or sympathizer. I was able to withstand the torture. I was

hit, my toenail was smashed [by placing it underneath a table leg] by a policewoman interrogating me, I was stabbed in the face with a pen. Still today I'm partly deaf in my right ear because of the pummeling from the interrogators. I was interrogated six times, each time with violence, but I stuck to my story. A lot of my friends in the prison also corroborated my story.[43]

Since the interrogators found no incriminating information about him, they did not classify him as a high-priority prisoner. Torture operated according to the logic of an ordeal: his ability to withstand the torture was a sign of his innocence. The PKI's underground party network inside and outside the prison, deciding that he was an especially valuable activist whose identity had not yet been uncovered, raised money so that he could bribe an interrogator and gain his freedom. In November 1966, he was released from prison. He joined the underground network and tried, unsuccessfully, to organize a real armed insurgency in South Blitar in East Java in late 1967 as a response to the state repression of a nonexistent one.

The Second Wave of Mass Detentions: 1968

With the complete collapse of the PKI in the face of army repression in late 1965 and early 1966, the few surviving PKI leaders had to devise a new strategy. Sudisman, as the highest-ranking leader still alive, took up the task of composing a document that could explain what had gone wrong and what direction the party should take. His "Self-Criticism" document of September 1966 was widely circulated among party loyalists, even those inside the prisons. With the parliamentary path violently shut down, he announced that the PKI would turn to a peasant-based armed struggle along the lines of the Chinese revolution. Given that the party had neither weapons nor territory of its own, the new strategy was extraordinarily ambitious. Before Sudisman could even begin to implement it, he was captured in his hideout—a small, inconspicuous house in West Jakarta owned by Tan Swie Ling—in December 1966.

Once Sudisman was captured, the remaining party leaders, such as Oloan Hutapea, began the desperate attempt to organize an armed struggle. They urged party members who had not been imprisoned to move to one of the most inaccessible places on Java—South Blitar—where there were hardly any paved roads and government officials. Many party members refused to go there, believing that it would be impossible to turn that area into a liberated zone.[44] Even if it was a remote corner of Java, it was still on Java—a small, densely populated island. By the end of 1967, about a couple hundred party supporters had gathered there undetected by the army. Some deserters from the military brought guns, but most of the people there had been civilians and arrived there without weapons. South Blitar became more of a safe haven for people fleeing army repression than a base for a Maoist armed struggle.[45]

The Kodam in East Java caught wind of something suspicious going on in South Blitar in early 1968 and soon discovered that PKI members had congregated there. The army launched a full-scale invasion of the area in April 1968, bringing in about five thousand soldiers and three thousand militiamen. The PKI members were quickly overwhelmed. Oloan Hutapea and other leaders were captured and immediately executed.[46] Many of the local inhabitants were considered complicit and were arrested and massacred in large numbers. Asep Suryaman, fleeing the area just before the army's invasion, was one of the few survivors.

The discovery of the base in South Blitar prompted the Suharto regime to think that the PKI was secretly organizing clandestine cells all over the country. The regime was spooked. It responded by ordering a second wave of mass arrests to root out what it called the "Night PKI." The usual suspects were rounded up yet again; people who had been arrested back in 1965–66 and then released were brought back in for questioning. People who had not even been considered important enough to arrest before were arrested. All those considered harmless before were treated as though they were actually dangerous PKI "kingpins" in disguise. The army became paranoid, seeing threats everywhere. In 1968 thousands of people throughout the country who had little or no connection to the PKI were arrested, interrogated, tortured, and then imprisoned without charge. East Java, the province in which South Blitar is located, was intensively scoured by the army in the search for the hidden PKI.[47]

A fairly typical story is Jatiman's.[48] He had been a guard since 1958 at the main prison in Surabaya, Kalisosok, and had patiently worked his way up the ladder, earning promotions and raises. He was an active member of the prison employees' union and felt comfortable in his career. The government had provided him a house right across the street from the front of the prison. Then he was unexpectedly arrested.

> On October 17, 1968, when I was working at the prison, on official duties, in my uniform, I was called to the security section. It turned out there was

an army officer there, from the Banteng Raiders unit. He said, "OK, sir, you've been asked to provide some information to the Kodim. Later, once it's done, then you can come back here."

Nine other prison guards were taken into custody that day and trucked over to the Kodim. Jatiman was called into the interrogation room around midnight and discovered that his crime was being a union activist. He had been overly close to the other trade unionists of industrial Surabaya who filled the cells of the prison after October 1965. Someone had reported him as a clandestine supporter of the PKI:

In the interrogation I was asked, "So you're a member of the union?"
    And I said, "Yes."
    "Do you pay dues?"
    "Yes, but they're deducted from my salary by the payroll department."
    The questions went on like that and then escalated to: "Are you a member of the PKI?" I said no. Now this was something they kept harping on and eventually I was ordered to take off my clothes. Yeah, I was just sitting there in my underpants. I sat with the back of the chair in front of me. My arms were resting on the top of the chair back. I was looking around right and left and noticed someone bring in some wire and I thought, whoa, what's going on here? All of a sudden, I was given an electroshock. They put the clips on my ears, one on the left, one on the right. I was told to confess: "You're a PKI member!"

All the while the cables from a hand-cranked generator were attached to his ears, the interrogators punched and kicked his body until his back was covered in blood. He finally just said "yes, yes, yes" to whatever they asked. On the basis of his interrogation, he was deemed guilty of being a PKI member and classified as a B prisoner. He was kept at the Kodim for about three months, transferred to the military prison in the Koblen neighborhood of Surabaya, and then imprisoned in Kalisosok prison, where he used to work as a guard. He was shipped off to Buru Island in September 1969. From the truck that took him out of Kalisosok, he waved good-bye to his family standing in front of their house across the street from the prison gate:

My goodness, just imagine, how emotional it was for me. I felt awful. I mean, this was where I had worked and then it became a source of suffering for me and my family. I was being separated from my family. Before I had a house provided by the government in front of the prison and my family was standing there. You can picture for yourself how I felt.

When interviewed in 2000 and 2001, Jatiman was still suffering from the torture that had damaged his nervous system. He had dizzy spells, pinched nerves, and numbness in certain parts of his body.

Ruswanto, a PKI activist, was captured in Surabaya at about the same time as Jatiman.[49] Unlike Jatiman, he had been a fairly important figure in the PKI. In 1965 he was twenty-five years old, working at the provincial office of the party's youth group, the Pemuda Rakjat, in Surabaya. By luck, he managed to evade capture by assuming a new identity as a rice merchant in the Wonokromo bazaar. He put the past behind him and fully embraced his new life: he married a woman who had nothing to do with the party and bought a house. The date disaster struck sticks in his mind: September 7, 1968. Soldiers from the Korem banged on his front door as he and his wife were sleeping. They knocked him down with a blow of a rifle butt to his face and dragged him through the street to an awaiting jeep. He realized that some of his comrades who had been caught in this dragnet must have named him and showed the intelligence agents the way to his house. As soon as he was brought in for interrogation, the army demanded he start naming names. The place of the interrogation was a large house that the Korem had confiscated from a Chinese-Indonesian man, Dr. Chang. Ruswanto recognized the house since he had often been in that neighborhood.

> I was ordered to point out my friends. That night I told them I didn't know anyone and if I told them the names of all the shopkeepers in the bazaar at Wonokromo I might be wrong because I didn't know them all. I just knew the rice sellers. I was beaten to a pulp. I was hit with fists, wood, rattan, and then the worst was the electric shock. That made me really groggy, to the point that I nearly mentioned someone's name, but I was still able to retain my composure. I gave them names of friends who were already dead.

Ruswanto managed to survive repeated interrogations over three days without betraying his comrades. He was classified as an A prisoner and kept imprisoned in Kalisosok. He was released in 1979 before the government put him on trial.

The army organized mass roundups of suspects all over the country in 1968. One of the victims in Bali was Taran, a young man who had been involved in agitations for land reform before 1965. He was arrested in late 1965 and then released in 1967. After enjoying only a year outside, he was arrested again in 1968 and accused of being a key member of an underground PKI network.

> They had already come up with a scenario, a whole storyline. I was accused of being part of the "Night PKI," and the story had all been planned out:

the leader here was so-and-so, and the members were so-and-so. So, I was slotted in as a leader. There they were, grouping people into what they called "trios" [three-person cells]. I had never heard of these "trios" before.[50]

Taran was laughing as he recalled the procedures of the interrogators. They presumed that the PKI had organized a tight cell structure, but since they could not obtain enough information from the prisoners to confirm that presumption, they forced the prisoners to admit it. They read the silence of the prisoners as evidence of their guilt: "We were called 'GTM,' Gerakan Tutup Mulut [Closed Mouth Movement]. If we didn't want to answer their questions, they'd say, 'Oh, you must have already been instructed to be in the GTM. . . . Who would confess if he operates clandestinely; after all, their name is the Night PKI.'" Torture was used to force each prisoner to sign the interrogation transcript that had already been drawn up: "So they created the scenario. Then if we didn't want to sign the transcript, well, you know what would happen: the cow testicles—that was a tool for torture. They were quite heavy. Then there was stingray tail—that was also a tool for torture."

Putu Oka, a Balinese writer who was member of Lekra before 1965, wrote in his novel *Merajut Harkat* (1999) about the interrogations that he had experienced or knew about as a political prisoner. He was arrested in 1968 in Jakarta. He described in detail what was, in his experience, a typical interrogation. The main character of the novel, Mawa, is punched, burned, and kicked while the interrogator demands he confess to being a PKI member and working for the clandestine network. He refuses to identify the names of his comrades and declines the rewards offered for his collaboration.[51]

Satgas Intel

The Infico film studio in Jakarta described at the start of this chapter was turned into an interrogation center in 1968. Carmel Budiardjo begins her autobiographical account of her three years as a political prisoner by recounting how the army drove her in a jeep to Satgas Intel after arresting her at her home on September 3, 1968. She had not been taken into custody before though both her husband and her fifteen-year-old daughter, a member of the PKI-affiliated group for high school students, Ikatan Pemuda Pelajar Indonesia (IPPI, Indonesian Association of Youths and Students), had been jailed for relatively short stints.

I fell silent and glanced out the back of the vehicle at the streets as they receded into the gathering darkness. We had now turned onto the main thoroughfare to Kebayoran.[52]

Before the jeep reached the building, she was ordered to cover her eyes so she could not identify its exact location. Once she realized that that she was being taken to a secret location, she panicked: "The shock was too great and I became hysterical. This had never happened to me before and I couldn't stop screaming." The jeep stopped, and the soldiers led her to the front gate:

Someone pulled my blindfold off and I found myself being taken through a huge, darkened shed with a very high ceiling. . . . Some days later I realized that I had once visited this place. It was a film studio owned by a progressive film company.[53]

Over the following days in this makeshift prison camp, she learned that the place had been set up as "the army's central intelligence unit, Satgas-Pusat, which was in charge of the huge new influx of detainees rounded up when a communist base had been discovered in Blitar, East Java."[54] She was part of the first batches of prisoners to be confined there. Workmen were still renovating some of the rooms so that the building could serve the army's purposes as a place of torture and incarceration.

The questions that were posed to her in the interrogation sessions were about her connections to other people in the party. The lead interrogator, a man named Atjep, was trying to identify everyone in the PKI's clandestine network. Most of the detainees were tortured during their interrogations.

My stay there was a period of perpetual fear and anxiety, of hearing about the arrival of new detainees at all times of the day and night, of hearing them being tortured and seeing them immediately after their sessions with the torturers, covered in blood or with other signs of physical abuse.[55]

The commander of the camp was an officer named Bonar, who delighted in ruling over the prisoners as an all-powerful lord. He had, she wrote, "the most ghastly face I have ever seen in the flesh. He was dark with a long-shaped face, unkempt hair, bulging eyes that were full of menace." He walked with a swagger, pummeled prisoners on the slightest pretext, and regularly pulled out his pistol and threatened to shoot them.[56]

Carmel Budiardjo was originally from Britain. She had married an Indonesian man, Budiardjo, in 1950 and had decided to spend the rest of her life in

Jakarta. She became an Indonesian citizen and raised two children there. The British government eventually learned of her imprisonment and decided that it would continue to recognize her as a British citizen. Gaining her freedom after three brutal years of imprisonment, she returned to London and founded a nongovernmental organization named Tapol, meaning "political prisoner" (*tahanan politik*), and established herself as the most well-informed resource person on Indonesia for human rights organizations in Europe. Amnesty International's pioneering *Report on Torture* (1973) relied on information from her for the section on Indonesia. The report stated: "The gravest allegations of torture relate to interrogations by the Central Satgas Unit in Kebayoran Lama on the outskirts of Jakarta."[57]

The first ex–political prisoner I interviewed who had been held in Satgas Intel was Partono.[58] He had been a colonel in the army's legal department in 1965, working under Brigadier General Sutoyo Siswomiharjo, the army's attorney general who had been killed by the September 30th Movement. Partono helped prepare the cases in the Extraordinary Military Court (Mahmillub) against the Movement's participants.[59] He had been so trusted by the Suharto regime that he was sent to work in the Indonesian embassy in the United States as an attaché in 1968. Soon after arriving in Washington, DC, he was recalled to Jakarta. Somehow, the army came to suspect him of having helped the PKI. He was arrested immediately upon disembarking from the airplane and was taken to Satgas Intel for about four months of interrogations. He described the place as a hell on earth. He was punched in the head so many times he was left deaf in one ear. The interrogators attached wires to his body and delivered electric shocks as they demanded he admit that he was a covert agent of the PKI. He developed a kidney stone from being denied water and was left to suffer the pain without any medical treatment. His thin mattress was covered in bedbugs and he never had a restful night of sleep. And then there were the screams and groans of the other prisoners, day and night.

The only full-time resident of the torture center was a political prisoner, Dr. Ashar Munandar, who was kept there from 1969 to 1978.[60] He had been a highly respected doctor in Jakarta, teaching medicine at the University of Indonesia and heading up the PKI-affiliated organization for intellectuals, Himpunan Sarjana Indonesia (HSI, Association of Indonesian Scholars). Carmel Budiardjo, as an economist, had also been a member of HSI. At the time of the September 30th Movement, Munandar was traveling in Eastern Europe. He had attended a conference of the Soviet-backed World Federation of Scientific Workers in Budapest. He was arrested soon after his return to Jakarta in late 1965. Classified as a B prisoner, he was sent to the labor camp on Buru Island in 1969. Being from an elite family meant that his relatives had connections inside the military powerful enough to rescind his exile to faraway Buru; he was shipped back to Jakarta immediately after arriving at Buru. His relatives, however, were not powerful enough to have him released from confinement altogether.

Munandar, once back in Jakarta, was placed in Satgas Intel so that the torture victims could receive some basic medical treatment. He could do nothing for one man who had lost hearing in both his ears due to the beatings. At first, his room for treating patients was located right next to the interrogation room. Unable to tolerate the sound of the screams, he insisted that it be moved further away. Some of the victims he treated were military personnel who had been purged in the 1970s on suspicion of being connected to the PKI. One of his cellmates was a soldier who had been involved in capturing him in late 1965.

Making the Interrogation Transcripts Public

The army conducted interrogations of PKI detainees in secret, in places like Satgas Intel, where prisoners' screams of pain could not be heard by many other people. The interrogators wrote the transcripts (Berita Acara Pemeriksaan or Proses Verbaal) as rough paraphrases of their verbal exchanges with the detainees. The transcripts were not verbatim accounts of what was said during the interrogations. The interrogators were like playwrights composing a dialogue between characters, and they could, whenever they wished, put words into the detainees' mouths. They could also force the detainees to sign the document they had composed as a sign of their uncoerced assent to its contents. The army then extracted these interrogation transcripts from the secret torture chambers in which they were composed and brandished them in public as solid evidence.

The army's practice of making the interrogation reports public began in late 1965. The army's Information Department issued a document in November 1965 that cited the transcripts of the interrogations of Colonel Latief and Lieutenant Colonel Untung, two officers who had participated in the September 30th Movement, as proof of the PKI's leadership of the Movement.[61] They had supposedly confessed while under interrogation to having acted on orders from the PKI. I have a copy of the transcript of Latief's interrogation held on October 25, 1965.[62] According to the transcript, Latief admitted to being a "sympathizer" of the PKI who was willing to accept orders from the party. He unequivocally stated that the PKI "planned the kidnapping" of the generals and that he was a mere "implementer" of the party's plan.[63] He

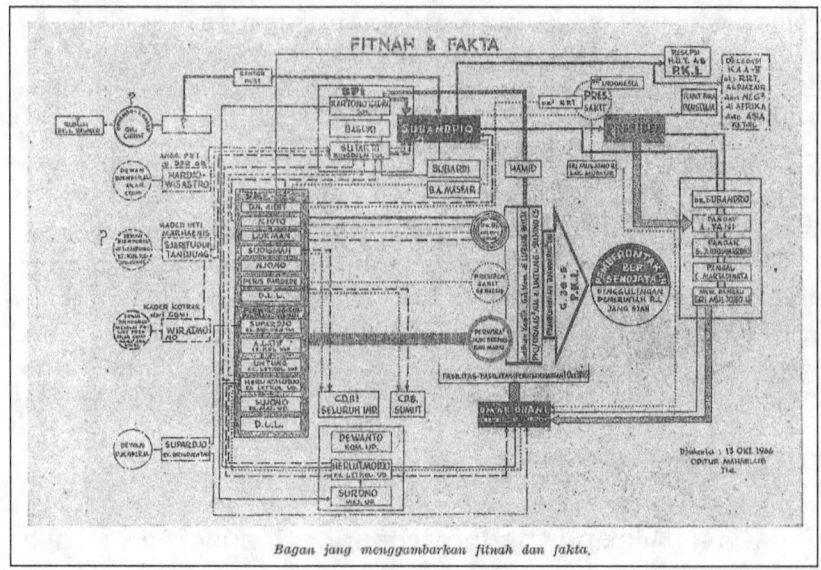

Diagram of the September 30th Movement drawn by military prosecutors after interrogating prisoners. Its profusion of arbitrarily drawn lines and boxes illustrates the madness of the military bureaucracy that carried out the anti-PKI witch hunt. Source: Lt. Col. Ali Said and Lt. Col. Durmawel Ahmad, *Sangkur Adil, Pengupas Fitnah Chianat* (Jakarta: Ethika, 1967).

confessed to having been "more loyal to the party's orders" than to those of his own superior officer.[64]

When Latief was brought to trial in 1978, after thirteen years of captivity, he claimed that he was barely conscious during that interrogation. Military Police officers came to Salemba Prison when he was still suffering from the wounds inflicted during his capture two weeks earlier. The soldiers who raided his hiding place on October 11 had badly damaged both his legs while capturing him.[65] His interrogation took place while he was lying prostrate on a table, doped up on painkillers, immobile with both his legs in casts, and starving from not having been given enough food for days. During the twelve-hour interrogation, from 3 p.m. to 3 a.m., he occasionally passed out. At his 1978 trial, he admitted to having put his signature on the transcript so that the interrogation would end: "I hoped that once I recovered or was in a condition to be interrogated again I could correct it."[66]

He was interrogated again, in late December 1965, and he corrected the claims in the first interrogation transcript.[67] His story completely changed. He denied that he had any affiliation to the PKI and insisted that the PKI had not led the Movement. The Suharto regime's publications never cited or even mentioned this second interrogation transcript.

The Suharto regime's first official, comprehensive account of the Movement, the Notosusanto and Saleh book of 1968, is filled with notes referencing interrogation reports.[68] The authors pretended that these interrogation reports were unimpeachable sources; indeed, they were more reliable than the statements individuals made in public. Consider how the two authors handled the statements of Njono, a PKI Politburo member and trade union leader who was the first person put on trial in a special military court for those accused of involvement in the Movement.[69] The authors noted that Njono, while on the stand at his trial in February 1966, rejected the contents of his interrogation report. They broached the question of torture: "Could one argue that Njono had been forced to confess in the first investigation, or that he had been coerced?"[70] They immediately dismissed that possibility out of hand: "He had enough time to give his information calmly and clearly." To clinch their case, they pointed to his signature: "The minutes of the investigation were read back to him before he signed them."[71] Notosusanto and Saleh even claimed that Njono had committed a crime by rejecting his interrogation report: "it was an attempt to substitute true information with false information."[72]

Once Notosusanto and Saleh concluded that Njono's interrogation report was true and his public statements false, they studied his personality to explain his motives: "Why did he give such clear information during the preliminary investigation?"[73] They moved into his unconscious mind: "Njono himself may not have been aware or conscious of the reasons for his confession." The army knew Njono's mind better than he did. After all, the army's psychologist conducted a "psycho-test" on him and concluded that he was "cooperative," "understood instructions well and could adapt himself to new situations," and "was not a stupid person."[74] But his behavior at his public trial showed a different side to his character; he was "very explosive and aggressive in trying to defend the Party." He lied at the trial because "of his ambition, and his strong primitive lurge [sic, urges] which were not properly channeled."[75] Notosusanto and Saleh's psychological conjectures were premised on the assumption that the interrogation reports were unimpeachable evidence.

Notosusanto and Saleh also cited the interrogation report of another PKI Politburo member, Sakirman. They did not mention that Sakirman disappeared while in military custody; he was, one presumes, secretly executed in late 1965, like three other key party leaders—Aidit, Lukman, and Njoto. Perhaps Sakirman's execution occurred after Notosusanto and Saleh published their book, though it is unlikely; other prisoners would have encountered him in detention camps in 1967–68. Whether his execution occurred before or after, it indicates the absurdity of a book that relies on secret testimonies of people the military held under the threat of summary execution.

The interrogation reports acquired a life of their own. They wound up traveling halfway around the world. The CIA, in Langley, Virginia, decided to help the Indonesian army make its case against the PKI by assigning one of its agents, Helen-Louise Hunter, the task of writing an analysis of the September 30th Movement. Indonesian army officers, presumably Notosusanto and Saleh, provided a large number of the interrogation reports to the CIA, which then had them translated into English for Hunter to consult. (Hunter did not know Indonesian; she was chosen for her expertise in analyzing military coups.) The CIA published her analysis of the Movement, *Indonesia—1965: The Coup That Backfired* (1968), without identifying her as the author.[76] She wrote an appendix meant to justify the use of the interrogation reports as evidence. Her main argument was that the claims in the reports were similar; different individuals, interrogated separately, made the same claims. The claims, however, were not similar. Even for the same individual (such as Latief), the interrogation transcripts were not consistent. Besides, whatever similarities existed can just as easily be attributed to the uniformity of the interrogators' storyline that was forced upon the prisoners.

Some anticommunist writers who were close to the army officers and wanted to help them make their case against the PKI also picked up the interrogation transcripts as evidence. The Dutch journalist Antonie C. Dake and the Canadian political scientist Victor Fic used the interrogation reports as primary sources for their studies. For decades, Dake touted the interrogation transcript of Sukarno's adjutant, Bambang Widjanarko, as the single most important document pertaining to the September 30th Movement, even when Widjanarko himself, once released from captivity and able to write for himself, did not endorse the statements attributed to him in the transcript.[77]

Conclusion

The turning of a film studio into a torture center is emblematic of the cultural destruction brought about by the Suharto regime. The films that had been produced at that studio, such as those by Bachtiar Siagian, were left to rot. Of the thirteen or so films Siagian wrote and directed between 1955 and 1965, only one survives, *Violetta* (1962).[78] Siagian himself was left to rot in Jakarta's prisons and the forced labor camp on Buru Island. Once released from captivity in 1979, he earned some money by ghostwriting screenplays.[79] He was blacklisted, like all the other Lekra artists, and could not legally work in the film industry.

The noncommunist filmmakers, even as their rivals from Lekra were put out of commission after 1965 and funding was more easily available, failed to develop the film industry any further. The Suharto regime forbade representations of social conflict within Indonesia while simultaneously allowing Hollywood films, many of them about intensely violent social conflict elsewhere in the world, to flood the market. Suharto handed the sole license to import foreign films to his half brother, Probosutedjo, who earned a fortune from his monopolistic power. One of the most populous countries on Earth did not produce a single film over a thirty-two-year period that attracted a significant international audience.[80] High-quality films were few and far between. Two of the best directors during the New Order period, Ami Priyono and Sjumandjaja, had been trained as filmmakers in the Soviet Union during the Sukarno years.

When the Suharto regime decided in the early 1980s to make a propaganda film about the September 30th Movement, it drew upon the artistic talents of Jakarta's filmmakers and actors. The director who agreed to follow the instructions of the army's storytellers was Arifin C. Noer. He became complicit in purveying the army's lies. His film presents the communists as torturers and Gerwani women as wild sadists. The film's climatic scene—screaming, frenetic women slicing the bodies of the captive generals with razor blades—was lifted straight from the army's psywar propaganda of late 1965. The Lubang Buaya Monument contains a display with life-size mannequins called the Torturing Veranda. The communists, in the regime's imaginary, were the perpetrators of torture, not the victims of it.

Once the Suharto regime collapsed, in 1998, its defenders were on the defensive as many Indonesians expressed a dislike of the film's vulgarity and demonstrated an interest in hearing from the victims who had been silenced for decades. The defenders returned to the transcripts of the interrogations in their search for incontrovertible proof of the unmitigated villainy of the PKI. The products of secret torture chambers were brought out before the public once again and presented as evidence. The head of the army's information department, Brigadier General Ratyono, vowed in 2003 to publish all the interrogation reports of the PKI leaders. He stated that the reports would convince any doubters of the correctness of the army's version.[81] So far, none has been published, perhaps because the army officers have realized the problems with them. The interrogators have found their champion in the journalist Aco Manafe, who published a book in 2007 celebrating their work as if it had nothing to do with torture. He upheld their version of events, as if many historians had not already proved it to be false.[82]

Torture became standard operating procedure in the army after its widespread use in the 1965–68 period against an enemy that did not fight back. When Suharto's generals faced real armed insurgencies in later years, their use of torture proved counterproductive, provoking widespread hatred of their rule while producing little reliable intelligence. In Papua, East Timor, and Aceh, the army used torture as part of its counterinsurgency campaigns against movements for national independence.[83]

The military did not hesitate to use torture on its own personnel. Officers understood in later years that they could curry favor with their superiors by claiming to have discovered a hidden PKI conspiracy within the ranks and then suppressing it. I interviewed Utomo, a former navy officer in East Java, who was arrested along with dozens of others in 1974 and accused of having supplied arms to the PKI in South Blitar six years earlier.[84] The men were tortured to force them to confess to the crime with which they were charged. The navy later acquitted these men, but not before they had spent three years in prison and had suffered from torture. Before the interview, I noticed Utomo walked with a limp. As he explained how he had been tortured, I understood why: the interrogators had placed a table leg on his toes and sat on the table, crushing the bones.

In Bandung, West Java, I interviewed a man who had been a captain in the air force until October 1970, when he was accused of being a secret member of the PKI.[85] At work on the airbase one day, he was handed a written order to report to the office of legal affairs. Once he reported to the office after his day's work was done, he was thrown into a jeep and taken outside of town to an air force building in the hillside resort area of Lembang, where no one could hear his screams. He was set upon by interrogators and their *tukang pukul*: "I was punched and kicked all over. Their main objective was to get me to admit that I really was a member of the communist party." Eventually he admitted to being a PKI member and signed a transcript of the interrogation: "Yeah, I just signed it. Instead of dying for no purpose. If I died my family would suffer. What was important was not to get hit any more." He was first classified as B-2, later reclassified as B-1, and imprisoned without trial for eight years. More than three decades later, he still suffers from the torture inflicted that night. "I was suddenly kicked in the back. I didn't see it coming. Until today I'm crippled because my spinal cord became pinched. It still hurts. I wear a corset every day; if I don't, I'm not strong enough to get around." He claimed he was only one among dozens of air force personnel framed on false charges that year.

I interviewed this former air force captain in a small, cramped house that also accommodated his acupuncture practice, from which he barely earned a subsistence. His expulsion from the military and his stigmatization as "PKI" resulted in a drastic fall in economic status and security. While he related his story, his wife sat near him, listening. She added when he was finished that they were content despite all the suffering. "We live in a neighborhood named Suka Senang [Happy], on a street named Senang Hati [Happy Heart], just off the main street named Jalan Pahlawan [Heroes Avenue]." Then she broke down sobbing, wordlessly contradicting the words she had just uttered.

4

Surprise Attacks

The Destruction of the PKI in Surakarta

By the banks of the Solo River, under the shade of a wide, four-lane bridge, elderly men and women sit in their finest batik clothes listening to the dulcet tones of a Javanese gamelan orchestra. It is a bright morning in the city of Surakarta in 2005. Hundreds of men and women have come from all over the city and its outskirts to remember those who were executed at this place in 1965–66. Here, prisoners were brought in trucks under the cover of darkness to the middle of the bridge, shot one by one, and then pushed into the flowing water below. The bridge that army soldiers used back then as an aerial execution ground no longer exists, but one of its massive brick-and-concrete pillars still stands in the river like some hulking ruin from an ancient fortress. For some unknown reason it was not demolished when the bridge was torn down and a new steel girder bridge erected next to it. The decrepit, reddish-brown pillar, overgrown here and there with vegetation, stands as a marker of the exact location of the executions.

The ceremony at the Bacem Bridge begins with speeches of welcome, thanks, and introductions. One of the speeches is delivered by a former political prisoner. He describes how he witnessed his fellow prisoners in the Surakarta Kodim being taken out in batches every night and never being heard from again. He kept a count as best he could of the number of men disappeared from the Kodim: 144. From conversations with the Kodim staff, he heard they had been killed at the Bacem Bridge and that the killing had left pools of blood that the soldiers had trouble cleaning off the girders.

Ceremony at the Bacem Bridge, 2005. Photo by Ayu Ratih.

An elderly man who lives near the river also stands up to speak before the microphone. He recalls how the people in his neighborhood heard the sounds of gunshots every night from the bridge and found corpses lying in the water the next morning, having washed ashore or become stuck on some detritus instead of floating with the current northward to the distant Java Sea. Soldiers ordered the residents who were up in the first light of dawn to use poles to push the corpses into the current, before the bridge was crowded with commuters who would be shocked to see the traces of their nocturnal labors. The river served as the waters of forgetfulness. Years later, when the new bridge was erected, the dredging machines unearthed skeletons of victims whose bodies had sunk to the riverbed.

Those attending the memorial ceremony are the survivors of that time of terror in Surakarta. They do not know if their relatives and friends who disappeared in 1965–66 were among those who lost their lives here at the Bacem Bridge or somewhere else in this part of Central Java. They have gathered to commemorate all the victims of the massacres in and around Surakarta. Their ceremony is for the unknown victim, a kind of ephemeral equivalent of a Tomb of the Unknown Soldier. It is being held in 2005 — a commemorative year that works well in terms of both the decennial periodization of the Gregorian calendar (four decades) and the eight-year periods of the Javanese calendar (five *windu*).

A small homemade raft of banana tree trunks attached to five small model ships floats downstream. The ships carry letters written by the victims' relatives. One of the handwritten letters reads:

> Dad, it's me, your daughter who has come here
> with Simbok, your wife, and your grandchildren.
> We've come here to express our love for you.
>
> Dad, I hope your soul
> Is received by the side of the Lord.
> We, your children and grandchildren,
> Will continue your struggle.

The relatives of the missing and murdered climb up to the pedestrian walkway on the edge of the new bridge and scatter fragrant flower petals over the river. It is a tradition in Java and Bali, called *larung*, to set offerings afloat on a body of water. The letters and flower petals are the offerings of the survivors.

The dumping of bodies from the Bacem Bridge has been memorialized in Indonesian fictional literature. It is described in the short story "Gray Night," published in 1970 by the writer Martin Aleida.[1] The story is about a Sumatran man, named Kamaluddin Armada, who arrives in Surakarta and walks to a nearby village to meet his fiancée. They had met in Jakarta and had kept in touch through love letters after she returned to her village. He is informed by a local official whom he happens to meet on the path that his fiancée and her entire family have recently been massacred. His fiancée's father had been a communist leader in the area. The official tells Armada: "He was killed on Bacan and thrown into the river like a dead chicken." (The name of the bridge appears in the story as Bacan rather than Bacem.) Some weeks later, a mob burned down the family's house and killed his fiancée, her mother, and her siblings: "They were also disappeared into the river." The man, heartbroken and despondent, walks to the bridge that night. He tosses her last letter into the river and then stabs himself with a knife. The story ends with the image of him falling into the river.

> Finally, all his strength was gone as the soul that had enlivened his body flew away to who knows where. He was no longer Kamaluddin Armada. He was just a dead body, crumpled at the waist, its stomach touching its thighs, curling over the railing of the bridge, and falling with a splash into the current of the Solo River.

The story is loosely based on Aleida's real-life experience as a writer from Sumatra who married a woman from the Surakarta area. Her father disappeared from a place of detention. She and Martin believed, from the stories circulating in the city at the time, that he had been executed at the Bacem Bridge. They made a practice in later years of going to the bridge to scatter flowers into the river.[2] It turns out that the *larung* ceremony in 2005 was just a collective and open form of a ritual that has been quietly practiced for many years by individuals, on their own, without public knowledge.

The relatives of the victims, in coming to the banks of the Solo River in 2005, transform, for just one moment, a place that had been defiled with needless suffering and terror into a place of beauty and auspiciousness. As the gentle melodies of the gamelan fill the air, the flower petals and letters float downstream. Two men wade into the middle of the river and release a large bucketful of young catfish, symbols of good fortune and regeneration. Other men on the shore release doves from their cages and turn their heads skyward to watch them fly away.[3]

Prior to October 1965, it would have seemed impossible for the supporters of the PKI in Surakarta to end up as corpses floating down the river.[4] The PKI was the dominant political party in the city and most of the surrounding districts. Surakarta had been the heartland of the PKI from its early years in the 1920s. If one draws a line around Surakarta and the adjacent three regencies (*kabupaten*) to the south and west—Sukoharjo, Klaten, and Boyolali—one delimits an area where being a communist had become a perfectly normal matter by the 1950s. In the country's first elections for the parliament, in 1955, the PKI won this area by a landslide. The PKI gained support not just from workers and peasants. It had also won over a good section of the middle class and even some members of the lesser aristocracy. Many village heads, mayors, city council members, school teachers, and shopkeepers were PKI members. In the city of Surakarta proper, the PKI won more than twice as many votes as the second-place finisher, the PNI. It was the same story in Sukoharjo and in the populous regency of Klaten. In Boyolali, the PKI won twice as many votes as the second- and third-place finishers combined.

To understand how the PKI could be defeated at the national level by the Indonesian army in 1965–66, one should begin with a case study of Surakarta. It was where the PKI was at its strongest. The party had long-standing roots there and enjoyed support from the majority of the population. If the PKI could be defeated in Surakarta, then it could be defeated anywhere. One finds in Surakarta that a crucial factor in the army's victory was its ability to take the PKI supporters by surprise. The party's very success over the preceding years had led many of its supporters to believe they were perfectly safe. They did not see the army as an enemy, much less an enemy that would adopt a policy of disappearing detainees and dumping their corpses into the Solo River.

Surprise is a powerful weapon, one that cannot, by its very nature, appear in a military's lists of its troops and guns. It belongs to the contingencies of history. The victory of the army over the PKI in Surakarta was not preordained. The key to the army's victory was something that could not have been foreseen by either the PKI or the army high command. The PKI, taken by surprise, was paralyzed and did not resist. The PKI was not, of course, a rival army that could array itself in battle formation. But it did have some supporters within the Indonesian army who were armed and had many unarmed civilians who could have attempted to resist in nonviolent ways. The military theorist Edward Luttwak has argued that surprise, for a military, is "not merely one advantage among many." It is not comparable to other advantages, such as superior firepower. Achieving the element of surprise results in "*the suspension, if only brief, if only partial, of the entire predicament of strategy.*" Against an enemy that does not react, "the conduct of war becomes mere administration."[5]

The Making of a Red City

To understand how the PKI became the dominant party in this region, one must go back to the second half of the nineteenth century. Surakarta became a vibrant city of commerce at that time. Lying in the middle of a large contiguous stretch of flat land, it became the site of the production of agricultural commodities. Bankers, plantation owners, and merchants congregated in the city amid a sea of waged workers and peasants. The commercialization of Java under Dutch colonialism was nowhere more pronounced than in the fertile, densely cultivated land around Surakarta. On this plain between the towering volcanoes of Central Java, peasants grew sugarcane and, at harvest time, delivered the cut stalks to steam-powered sugar mills. The first railway line in the Dutch East Indies was built from 1867 to 1873 to connect the sugar fields and mills of the Surakarta area to the port of Semarang to the north.

The men and women living amid the rail lines could see they were connected to a much larger world and that world was being constantly revolutionized by new technologies. They could also see great disparities of wealth. Surakarta was the capital city of the Surakarta Residency, which was a nominally independent state, much like a princely state in British India. The two royal dynasties maintained by the Dutch as the joint rulers of the Residency earned the funds for their glittering palaces and obsequious armies of servants by leasing out their land for commercial purposes.[6] The trappings of feudalism were dependent upon the international market. Communism, with its

Surakarta and its environs in 1965

denunciations of colonialism, capitalism, and feudalism, made sense to many people in the Surakarta area, especially when it also extolled solidarity with people across the globe, on the other ends of the railway and steamship lines.

The ideas of communism entered Surakarta on the same rail lines by which the sugar was carried out. The workers at nearly every link in the commodity chain became unionized in the 1910–20s, from the factory workers who made the sugar to the railway workers who transported it to Semarang, the stevedores who loaded it onto the steamships, and the sailors who carried it to foreign markets.[7] The railway workers union, founded in 1908, was one of the first unions in the Dutch East Indies. It was initially led by Dutch and mixed-race workers. In 1914 it came under the control of the Dutch socialist Henk Sneevliet, who recruited lower-wage Indonesian workers and built the union into a radical mass organization.[8] The workers picked up the union's publications from headquarters in Semarang and distributed them in towns all along the railway lines. The precocious Javanese teenager Semaoen, who would later become a key leader of the PKI, was the editor of the union's Indonesian-language newspaper, *Si Tetap* (The Steadfast One), starting in 1916.[9]

The socialists in the East Indies, rooted in the trade unions, were also active in an organization of urban merchants called the Sarekat Islam (Islamic Association), which had been established in Surakarta in 1911. Its founders were Javanese batik cloth traders concerned that Chinese merchants were receiving preferential treatment from the colonial state. The Sarekat Islam grew into a mass organization in the 1910s as merchants and Islamic preachers of the urban bazaars set up chapters in towns all over Java. As it grew, its agenda expanded well beyond its original mercantile and ethnocentric concerns. The Sarekat Islam came to represent those categorized under colonial law as "the natives" (*inlander*). Its educated leaders thought of themselves as messengers, conveying the grievances of the illiterate masses to the Dutch officials. The socialists of the railway union, such as Semaoen, led the Sarekat Islam chapter in Semarang in the late 1910s. Given that their chapter was large and able to produce its own newspaper (*Sinar Djawa*, later renamed *Sinar Hindia*), the socialists greatly influenced the character of the whole organization.[10]

The PKI grew out of the Indies Social Democratic Association (ISDV), founded by Sneevliet in 1914. Reading the news reports from the wire services and hearing stories from people who had been in Europe, the socialists and trade unionists in the Indies were inspired by the Russian Revolution and the formation of the Communist International in Moscow. At its seventh congress, in Batavia, on May 23, 1920, the ISDV changed its name to the Communist Party of Indonesia (PKI). It was the first communist party in Asia.[11]

Communism began in the Indies in the form of an anticolonial Islamic movement. The communists of the early 1920s retained the strategy they had been following in the 1910s when they called themselves socialists: they built up a left-wing bloc within the Sarekat Islam. This was a particularly effective strategy in Surakarta, where some Muslim scholars upheld a theology of Islam that called for supporting the poor and oppressed. One scholar who articulated a synthesis of Islam and communism was Haji Misbach (1876–1926), the son of a wealthy batik trader who grew up in Kauman, the neighborhood of Surakarta that the royal families reserved for Muslim scholars. He helped organize peasants and workers in the Surakarta area in the 1910s. As the founding editor of the newspaper *Islam Bergerak* (Islam in Motion), he served as the spokesperson for villagers who carried out a six-month-long campaign in 1919 against corvée labor. Islam, as Misbach imagined it, was an identity that could unite a great variety of classes, from the poor peasants in the villages to wealthy cloth traders in the city, in a common struggle against colonial exploitation.[12]

The presence of the communists inside the Sarekat Islam prompted a split within the organization in 1923 between a "white" faction, consisting of the anticommunists, and a "red" faction. Haji Misbach joined the "red" faction. The Dutch, taking advantage of the split, cracked down on the communists and exiled Misbach to Papua in 1924. The experienced activist and prolific writer Mas Marco Kartodikromo (1890–1932) arrived in Surakarta in 1924 to replace him. The relentless repression from the Dutch police combined with the attacks from the right-wing Muslims made organizing almost impossible. Misbach's disciples Ahmad Dasuki and Haroen Rasjid were in and out of prison, punished for their incendiary writings and statements at public meetings.

Some communists became desperate in the face of the repression and decided to launch a rebellion along the lines of the Bolshevik revolution in Russia. Other PKI leaders and activists opposed such a strategy, believing the party did not have enough mass support to attempt a revolt. The revolt began in the West Javanese region of Banten in November 1926. Ultimately, only the chapters in Batavia and West Sumatra followed Banten's lead and staged revolts in late 1926 to early 1927.[13] The revolts were quickly defeated. The troops of the colonial state, most of them *inlander* themselves, faithfully followed the orders of their superior officers. The Dutch banned the PKI and rounded up about 13,000 people and sent 1,300 of them to a prison camp called Boven Digoel in the middle of the jungle on the island of Papua.[14]

PKI activism in Surakarta was thoroughly decimated in 1927 as it was everywhere else in the archipelago. Party leaders already in custody in Surakarta before the revolt, such as Mas Marco Kartodikromo, Ahmad Dasuki, and

Haroen Rasjid, were shipped out to Boven Digoel in chains.[15] Those communists who were not captured went underground and sustained a spirit of resistance by reading and circulating the writings of the Boven Digoel prisoners.[16] Surakarta thereafter appeared quiet. It was a region where the feudalism of the two royal houses and the colonialism of the Dutch officials faced little overt opposition, even during the immiseration of the economic depression of the 1930s. The left-wing movement remained largely inactive during the Japanese occupation from 1942 to 1945.[17]

The communists reappeared with a vengeance in Surakarta as soon as the Japanese occupation collapsed in August 1945. They had to contend with many rivals but quickly became a powerful force by virtue of their base in the unions for workers and peasants. Misbach's followers Ahmad Dasuki and Haroen Rasjid returned to Surakarta in late 1945 and picked up where they had left off eighteen years before. As "Digoelists," they were hometown heroes. They claimed veto power over the officials the Republic of Indonesia appointed to govern the Surakarta Residency. Using the PKI's militia, Dasuki arranged the kidnapping of the Republic's Resident and Vice-Resident for Surakarta in November 1946. Dasuki became Resident for about one week and then allowed Sukarno to appoint a new Resident. In those chaotic times when there were many violations of the Republic's chain of command, his action went unpunished, and a compromise was reached.[18]

The PKI's position in Surakarta became stronger when the minister of defense, Amir Sjarifoeddin, appointed a communist, Wikana, as the military governor for the Surakarta Residency in August 1947. Wikana, a leader of the Pemuda Sosialis Indonesia (Pesindo, Socialist Youth of Indonesia), used his position to support the left-wing militias as they were being incorporated into the national army and to introduce courses on Political Education (Pendidikan Politik, known as *pepolit*) for all the troops. A veteran PKI leader from the 1920s in Surakarta, Alimin, worked closely with Wikana in implementing these policies.[19]

The rising strength of the PKI in Surakarta from 1945 to 1947 alarmed the economic elites and the right-wing Muslims who had opposed Misbach's liberation theology since the 1920s. The anticommunists gained outside backing when four battalions of troops from West Java, under the command of the staunch anticommunist Colonel Abdul Haris Nasution, arrived in February 1948. The existing tensions between left-wing and right-wing groups were exacerbated. The vice president, Mohammad Hatta, began a "rationalization" program designed to purge the left-wing troops, such as the militias that Amir Sjarifoeddin had just incorporated into the regular army. The commander of the troops based in Surakarta, Colonel Sutarto, rejected Hatta's "rationalization" program and implemented his own program, which was the exact opposite; he started purging the troops in his Division IV who refused to accept the left's Political Education courses.[20]

The conflicts within the Republic's army in 1948 were occurring at the same time as a massive strike by plantation and factory workers. That strike, led by the PKI, clearly posed a distinction between what was called at the time "bourgeois nationalism" and "proletarian nationalism." It provoked many Indonesians in the area into making a choice as to which side they wished to support. The strike was centered in the town of Delanggu, about eight miles to the southwest of Surakarta. Some 1,500 workers at the burlap sack factory went on strike in April 1948 and were joined by about eight thousand more workers at the seven plantations that produced hibiscus bush stalks and cotton, the raw material for the factory. The factory and the plantations had been nationalized by the Republican government two years earlier.[21] The humble burlap sacks were crucial to the Republic's economy: they were used for the packaging of other commodities, such as tobacco, sugar, and coffee. Sukarno, Hatta, and the other nationalist leaders saw the resolution of the strike as a matter of some urgency, but the negotiations dragged on for months.[22]

Outside the negotiations, the rhetoric was heated. The noncommunists accused the communists of organizing the strike for political purposes and of sabotaging the war effort against the Dutch. The communists insisted that the strike was necessary as a simple matter of survival for the workers, who had been receiving less than subsistence wages for years even as the managers of the factory and the plantations lived quite comfortably. The main demand of the workers was that they receive rations of rice and cotton cloth so that they could properly feed and clothe themselves and their families. Since the Japanese occupation, many of the working poor had resorted to eating roots and leaves and using the factory's burlap sacks for clothing. Given that the workers alternated between working and fighting on the front lines north of the city, the strikers contended that improvements in the living standards for workers meant improvements in the fighting strength of the national army.

The union leading the strike, Sarekat Buruh Perkebunan Republik Indonesia (Sarbupri, Plantation Workers Union of the Republic of Indonesia), chose Delanggu to be the site of its national congress in February 1948. The head of the Sarbupri chapter in Delanggu was Asep Suryaman. He had been the head foreman (*kepala sinder*) at the Delanggu plantation during the Japanese occupation and had become radicalized by his knowledge of the workers' suffering. He joined the PKI in 1946 as part of his new life as a union organizer.[23]

Throughout the months of the strike, from April to July 1948, the social identities of "left" and "right" became more solidified. The right-wing Islamic party, Masjumi, used its militia, Hizbullah, to attack the strikers. It relied on officers in the West Javanese troops for protection. Sarbupri and the PKI relied on the troops of Colonel Sutarto's Division IV for protection. The two sides engaged in street fights.[24] An unidentified assassin gunned down Colonel Sutarto on July 2 as he emerged from his car in front of his house. The brazen murder of such a high-level officer who had been openly supporting the left-wing political movement raised tensions in the city to new heights.[25]

The central government, seeing that the strike could not be broken, capitulated and agreed to the union's main demands on July 16. It was an important victory for Sarbupri and the PKI, but they had little chance to celebrate. They were in the middle of a wider struggle for control of the streets and the armed forces in the Surakarta Residency. After the assassination of Colonel Sutarto, left-wing and right-wing troops engaged in nearly constant skirmishes, kidnapping and killing one another. The surviving officers in Sutarto's Division IV continued to resist Hatta's orders to demobilize. Sukarno declared a state of emergency in the Residency on September 15 and appointed an anticommunist, Colonel Gatot Subroto, to be the military governor, replacing Wikana.

The conflicts in the Surakarta Residency affected other regions of Java under the control of the Republic. Left-wing troops took over the city of Madiun in East Java on September 18 in response to the events in Surakarta. They were hoping to establish a stronghold against Hatta's "rationalization" program and the attacks by right-wing troops. Sukarno and Hatta construed this takeover of a single city as the start of a full-scale armed uprising by the PKI. They ordered the mass arrests of all left-wing troops and PKI members. The leaders of the PKI had not ordered the action in Madiun and were unprepared to challenge the Republican government. About thirty-five thousand suspected leftists were imprisoned from September to December 1948 in the areas of Central and East Java under Republican control.

Sukarno and Hatta carried out the purge of the PKI after the Madiun uprising to curry favor with the United States. The Cold War had begun, and US diplomats had made it clear that the PKI's growing strength was preventing the US from supporting the Republic of Indonesia. The Dutch recolonization campaign was bankrolled by the US, and it was obvious to everyone involved that the US had the power to call it off. The US was so pleased by the Republic's attack on the PKI that it forced the Dutch to negotiate a withdrawal of its troops and allow the Republic to become independent. The US could feel confident that independent Indonesia would be in the hands of anticommunists. The anticommunists in Indonesia learned an important lesson from that experience: if they attacked the PKI, they would receive a reward from the US. Sukarno and Hatta's murderous repression of the PKI after the Madiun uprising may have brought Indonesian nationalism into the good graces of the US, but it built a formidable wall of blood in Java between left-wing and right-wing nationalists.

Even after the anticommunist violence of late 1948, the PKI in the Surakarta area remained immensely popular because of its service to the nationalist struggle since the 1920s and its empowerment of workers and peasants, as with the Delanggu strike. Its popularity was proved by the results of the 1955 election for the national parliament. The PKI won a majority of the votes in the city and in three of the six regencies that had been part of the erstwhile Surakarta Residency. The party did even better in the 1957 elections for the provincial parliaments and regency-level administrations. In Central Java as a whole, the PKI was the top vote-getter, beating the PNI, which had won the 1955 elections.

The 1957 elections changed the city government in Surakarta. The PKI, having won the majority of seats on the city council (seventeen out of thirty), replaced the mayor, a supporter of the Muslim organization Muhammadiyah who had been appointed by the government, with Utomo Ramelan, a descendant of a prominent aristocratic family. Ramelan's father had been the chief of police of Surakarta, and his siblings were accomplished and well educated. Utomo Ramelan's older brother, Utoyo, had earned a law degree in Leiden and was a founding father of the Republic's Foreign Affairs Ministry. Another older brother, Utaryo, was a doctor. His older sister, Utami, was married to the founding father of the Republic's air force, Suryadi Suryadarma.[26]

The PKI did not adopt radical policies when running the city. Ramelan's administration, which lasted until October 1965, did not expropriate property or persecute the wealthy. The noncommunists, such as the wealthy batik producers and merchants of the Laweyan neighborhood, remained powerful forces; they had money and musclemen. The PKI continued to face much resistance. Ramelan worked within the limitations of his office to use the little discretionary spending he had to fund projects for public welfare.[27]

During Guided Democracy, the cultural life of Surakarta was deeply influenced by the communist movement. Many artists in the city, such as the highly skilled performers of *wayang orang* (wayang plays acted out by people rather than puppets) at the main theater downtown, Sriwedari, were party members. In the villages, Lekra organized the troupes performing *ketoprak*, a genre of Javanese folk theater involving music and comedy.[28] Lekra held its first national conference in 1959 in Solo, and the attendees could feel as if the city were theirs: trade unionists greeted them at the railway station, red flags flew in the streets, President Sukarno spoke at the opening ceremony, and the city residents flocked to attend the performances.[29]

The PKI could become popular in the Surakarta area because it represented the two rich traditions of the region: Islamic communism and youth (*pemuda*) activism. The party cannot be understood in the formulaic, doctrinaire terms of Leninism and Stalinism. It was tied to the culture of the Central Javanese workers and peasants who organized themselves against colonialism from the 1910s to the 1940s. Surakarta's postindependence PKI was a continuation of the egalitarian culture fostered in the earlier decades. Ahmad Dasuki and Haroen Rasjid, the disciples of Haji Misbach, who synthesized Islam and communism, were still prominent leaders of the PKI. Dasuki represented the PKI at the Constitutional Assembly (1956–59), where he denounced the anticommunist Muslims for betraying the true meaning of Islam. Rasjid's wife was a key leader of the PKI-affiliated women's association, Gerwani, in Surakarta. The *pemuda* activists of the 1940s did not have as much interest in religion as the earlier generation of communists, but they shared the same commitment to a more egalitarian society.[30]

The September 30th Movement in Surakarta

The September 30th Movement was not a nationwide movement. It hardly deserves to be called a "movement" since it involved so few people and lasted for such a short time. Its core action was a putsch of the army high command in the capital city. There was, however, one area outside Jakarta where many army personnel held actions in support of the Movement: Central Java. The army's Kodam for the province, named Diponegoro, was the Kodam most heavily affected by the Movement.[31] An army report of December 1965 estimated that "at least 30% of the troops in the Diponegoro Kodam involved themselves in the September 30th Movement or sympathized with it."[32] Colonels in the provincial capital, Semarang, kidnapped the Kodam commander and took over the radio station, while officers in other large cities, such as Yogyakarta, Surakarta, and Salatiga, took similar actions on October 1. In Surakarta, junior officers kidnapped the head of the Kodim, his chief of staff, and the commander of the Sixth Brigade. They also occupied the RRI station in the city and read out announcements in support of the Movement.

The extensive involvement of Diponegoro personnel led some early observers to believe that the Movement should be understood as an action led by a group of Central Javanese officers, some of whom, such as Lieutenant Colonel Untung, happened to be stationed in Jakarta. Untung had been based in Surakarta prior to his transfer to Jakarta in early 1965. These observers

Pak Bronto, Surakarta, 2012. Photo by John Roosa.

suggested that the masterminds of the Movement were not located in Jakarta; rather, they were located in Central Java. Anderson and McVey, writing in early 1966, believed that "the effective core" of the Movement was a group of officers at the Diponegoro Division headquarters in Semarang.[33]

It is by now clear that the masterminds of the Movement were in Jakarta; they were the men in the PKI's clandestine Special Bureau whose task had been to maintain contact with military officers sympathetic to the party.[34] The fact that so many Central Javanese officers and soldiers were involved in the Movement was simply a result of the PKI having more supporters in the Diponegoro command than elsewhere. The PKI's powerful presence in the civil society of the province since the 1920s had influenced many army personnel there.

To understand how the Movement was organized in Surakarta, I spoke with a former sergeant who took part in it.[35] Pak Bronto was a sergeant major in the army's Sixth Brigade, which was headquartered at Fort Vastenburg, an eighteenth-century garrison right in the center of Surakarta. When I met him in the city in 2012, he was eighty-three years old and held himself with the erect posture of a young soldier, despite a lifetime of crushing poverty punctuated by fourteen brutal years of imprisonment. His early childhood had been comfortable enough. His father, a German immigrant, owned a fleet of three-wheeled taxis in Yogyakarta. But then disaster struck in 1942. His father fled the invading Japanese troops and was never heard from again. His Javanese mother and her relatives raised Bronto on their own, with what little they had, in the nearby town of Delanggu. He recalls the time of the Japanese occupation as one of constant hunger and fear. Since he looked a little like a European, he was worried the Japanese would assume he was Dutch and imprison him. Once the Japanese surrendered and independence was proclaimed in 1945, he joined a gang of other barefoot youths called Laskar Kere (Militia of the Poor).

Some members of his militia eventually became incorporated into the regular Indonesian army. Bronto recalled that at the start of the armed struggle, his political knowledge was rudimentary. All he and his friends understood was that they were fighting the foreigners, the "whites" (*londo*). A "political commissar" who accompanied his brigade in 1947–48 provided them with an education about all the big -isms: imperialism, nationalism, capitalism, and communism. The battalion commander, Major Sudigdo, facilitated this *pepolit* (political education): "It was in the Digdo Battalion that we started talking about politics." It was an education for which he felt forever grateful.

The discussions with the political commissar prompted Bronto to support the PKI. He felt he could better make sense of the events he was witnessing. A key event that made him a PKI supporter was the workers' strike in Delanggu: "What most stands out in my experience of that time was the 1948 strike of workers at the burlap sack factory in Delanggu. It was then and there that I became an activist, when I could identify who is a friend and who is an enemy." He could see that some of his fellow nationalists were not on the side of the poor workers and peasants.

The Digdo Battalion is the key to understanding the PKI's relationship with left-wing army personnel. Bronto was in a twelve-man squad commanded by Untung, the man who would become the nominal leader of the September 30th Movement in 1965. Bronto remembered Untung as a selfless leader: "When there was fighting, he wasn't in the back, he fought from the front." Untung looked after the lower-ranking soldiers under his command and never demanded special treatment: "We ate and slept together." It appears that Untung became politicized in the same way as Bronto in the Digdo Battalion in the late 1940s.[36] The two of them were good friends with Suradi, who would later play a prominent role in the Movement as well.[37]

Bronto and his fellow soldiers in the Digdo Battalion were nearly barred from being readmitted to the army after independence. The Madiun uprising in September 1948 had resulted in a general purge of all left-wing troops, and the Digdo Battalion was already well known for its alliance with the PKI. Bronto explained that the commander for the Surakarta area, Brigadier

General Slamat Riyadi, agreed to readmit the soldiers from the battalion. Riyadi, all of twenty-one years old, did not share the intense anticommunism of his superior officers.[38] Still, to play it safe, the members of the battalion, such as Untung, slightly changed their names on the army's rolls when readmitted to avoid being easily detected in any future purge.

Bronto's story about the Digdo Battalion has been confirmed by Siswoyo, who was a PKI leader in Surakarta in the late 1940s. Siswoyo has written in his memoir about the PKI's close relationship with that battalion. When Gatot Subroto started attacking communists in Surakarta after the uprising in Madiun, the left-wing militias in the city moved to Sukoharjo and joined the Digdo Battalion. PKI leaders contemplated using the battalion and its militias to attack Gatot Subroto's troops and exact revenge for the Ngalihan massacre. Siswoyo recalls in his memoir that they ultimately decided not to attack in the interests of national unity. Meanwhile, senior PKI leaders like Alimin trekked to a remote part of Wonogiri to be protected by the Digdo Battalion.[39]

Siswoyo also confirms that the PKI provided a political education to the troops of the Digdo Battalion. A PKI leader in Surakarta of Alimin's generation, "Suhadi alias Pak Karto," lived with the battalion for some time and served as a "political adviser" to Major Sudigdo. I wrote about Pak Karto in *Pretext for Mass Murder* largely on the basis of information from Asep Suryaman. Pak Karto was the head of what later became the party's Special Bureau, maintaining a network of PKI supporters among military personnel. Siswoyo's memoir provides new details about his career. Pak Karto led the underground PKI in Surakarta after the 1926–27 revolts and then led a PKI front organization after August 1945. At the PKI's Fourth National Congress, in Surakarta, in January 1947, Pak Karto was chosen to be the head of the Surakarta chapter.[40]

Bronto, in the interview with me, expressed great respect for Pak Karto. He recalled that Pak Karto would discreetly hold discussions with the soldiers in the 1950s about topics such as guerrilla warfare in communist China. One of the texts they read was an Indonesian translation of the book *China Shakes the World* (1949), by the American journalist Jack Belden. Pak Karto emphasized the need for soldiers to eschew the practices of stealing from the civilian population and profiting from smuggling. They needed to serve people and win the support of the poorest members of society. With his ascetic lifestyle and calm demeanor, he served as the party's wise old man. Bronto thought of him as a "Marxist shaman" (*dukun Marxis*).[41]

Pak Karto passed away in 1964 (according to Siswoyo). The person put in charge of military affairs as his replacement was not a wise old man; it was a former *pemuda* activist, Sjam. In Surakarta itself, there was also a changing of the guard. The new head of the Special Bureau for the Surakarta area was Joseph Rabidi, who was a young schoolteacher without much military experience.[42]

According to Bronto, the Special Bureau organized the September 30th Movement in Surakarta. Bronto attended a secret meeting on September 28 at which a Special Bureau member informed a small group of army personnel that there would be an action in Jakarta soon and that they should be ready to support it: "At the briefing there were only several of us [army personnel], but we had a pyramid system, so the news spread." The Special Bureau did not provide a detailed plan of action. The instructions were brief and vague. The army personnel were told that they needed to seize Surakarta, issue a statement supporting the Revolutionary Council, and then wait for further instructions to be broadcast over the radio.

Bronto did not know all the other PKI supporters within the army in Surakarta. They had never met as a group before. The pro-PKI officers always had rough ideas of the political leanings of other officers, but they were not always certain which ones were in contact with the party. Only the Special Bureau had full knowledge of all the military personnel with whom it was in contact. Once ordered to stage an action, these soldiers and officers discussed what they should do. The Special Bureau had brought them together and then left them to determine the specific plan of action.

Bronto and the other officers formed what they called "the Committee." Within this Committee, discussions were carried on as if all the attendees were equals. Their military rank did not matter, and decisions were made by consensus. Meeting in the early morning hours of October 1, they had to choose who would appear in public as the leader of their group. That role did not automatically fall to the highest-ranking officer among them. While laughing, Bronto recalled that their first choice, Captain Sukarno, declined, claiming that he had diarrhea—a condition that had probably been caused by nervousness. After further discussion, they chose Major Iskander, who just so happened to be in town. Iskander had been transferred to the Kodam for North Sumatra and had already taken up residence there. He had come back to Surakarta for a short rest and relaxation break. He agreed to serve as the nominal head of their group in Surakarta even though he was not the one who had brought them together—the Special Bureau had done that—and did have any power over them—the collective membership of the Committee was in charge.

The Committee broke up into different teams to kidnap the key army commanders in Surakarta. Bronto explained: "We came and told them that there had been a change of the leadership in Jakarta and then we arrested them."[43] He recalled that their top priorities were to capture the commander of the Sixth Brigade and the Kodim commander. These officers were not selected because they were believed to be right-wingers. They were selected purely for strategic purposes: they were the ones who commanded the most troops in the city. The Movement wanted to control the city, and to do so it had to neutralize the officers in charge of the preponderance of troops. The Movement also kidnapped the chief of staff of the Kodim. None of the three officers put up a fight when being taken into custody: "They knew what would happen if they resisted, so there wasn't any resistance."[44]

Once the Committee had these officers in custody, another team was sent to carry the statement to the RRI station. Bronto was on this team: "It wasn't anything strange. We came to the RRI station. We knew all the people who worked there very well. It was at seven o'clock, just after the news aired. The announcer said, 'Yono [Lieutenant Suyono] wants to say something, go ahead please.' The microphone was just turned over to him. The reports that came out in the newspapers later claimed we forced our way in and occupied the station. Those reports weren't true at all." The Committee's statement proclaimed that Major Iskander was the head of the Movement in Surakarta.

The Committee members heard the Movement's first broadcast from Jakarta around the same time. It was relayed from RRI Jakarta to RRI stations around the country, including the station in Surakarta. It was only then that they learned that Untung was the leader of the Movement. Many members of the Committee knew Untung personally. Bronto had known him from the late 1940s and had attended the send-off ceremony held in Surakarta before Untung moved to Jakarta to command a battalion of the presidential guard. They had not been told at the briefing on September 28 that Untung would lead the Movement and they had not been contacted beforehand by Untung himself. Upon hearing their close friend named over the radio as the leader of the Movement in Jakarta, they became particularly determined to support it.[45]

On the morning of October 1, Bronto and his comrades in the Committee felt triumphant. Their action had gone according to plan. But as the day wore on, they became worried: "After we had captured the commanders and made the announcement, we didn't know what the next step was. We were all confused, waiting for the decision from Jakarta." Bronto noted that it was normal for troops to be waiting for orders, but this case was different. They had taken orders from a civilian as part of a political action: "If we take a village, we know what to do afterwards. There is an army procedure to follow. We already know it. It's automatic. But we were in control of Surakarta. So what were we supposed to do?" Without any further orders from the Special Bureau and without any established military procedure to follow, the only conclusion the

Committee could reach was that, at the very least, they needed to ensure there was no bloodshed in the city.

For its part, the PKI in Surakarta did not mobilize civilians to come out into the streets to support the action of the "progressive revolutionary" officers on October 1. The only action the PKI took was to make a radio announcement in the evening. The city's mayor, Utomo Ramelan, issued a statement supporting the Movement. It was read out around 6:00 p.m. over the RRI station in Surakarta. The statement was also signed by the secretary of the local National Front, who was also a leader of Lekra in Surakarta.[46]

The members of the Committee knew that the Movement was failing once RRI in Jakarta was taken over on the evening of October 1. The mutineers in Semarang, like those in Jakarta, went into hiding on the night of October 1. But Bronto and his comrades did not want to call off their action until they were certain that it had no chance of being revived. Surakarta could still be used as a rear base for continuing the Movement. They kept waiting for further instructions. Their contacts in the Special Bureau were just as confused as they were. The PKI in Surakarta remained quiet and did not take any further action. On October 3, the Committee, after not hearing anything more from the people in the Special Bureau who ordered them to stage the action, decided to call it off and release the captives. Bronto and his fellow officers in Surakarta did not end the Movement because they were attacked. They simply quit. There had been no bloodshed, and the captives had not been harmed.

The three army commanders, once released, did not set about arresting those who had joined the Movement. Bronto recalled that the commanders were uncertain of their authority and were wary about provoking a conflict in a city where the majority of people were PKI supporters. They too were confused about what to do. Even the detachment of Resimen Para Komando Angkatan Darat (RPKAD, Army Paracommando Regiment), with a base just on the western edge of Surakarta, in Kartasuro, did nothing. Surakarta was tense but remained calm for three weeks after the Committee called off the Movement. The army's own documents of the time note that there was no fighting in Surakarta in early October.[47]

One reason for the relative peace was the fact that the Diponegoro commander, Suryosumpeno, did not have enough troops to send to Surakarta. Many of his battalions were stationed in Sumatra and Kalimantan as part of the Confrontation against Malaysia. The Movement in Surakarta had taken control of three battalions of the Sixth Brigade. It seemed that at least three battalions would be needed to retake Surakarta, and Suryosumpeno did not have three battalions to spare.[48] He followed a policy of reconciliation: he met the commanding officers of the Sixth Brigade in Surakarta on October 8 and obtained a pledge of unity.⁴⁹ An army report about Central Java from sometime in November 1965 admitted that the army had not actively repressed the Movement during the first three weeks of October: "there was still an air of hesitation, especially when considering the reality of what had happened and what was being done by the local Military Units."⁵⁰

Bronto and his comrades, after quitting, expected that at least some of them would be punished some way or another, either discharged or sentenced to prison terms, but only after a lengthy process of investigations and political negotiations. There had been previous mutinies in the military. Only seven months earlier, in March 1965, seven hundred junior naval officers had staged a mutiny in Surabaya against what they called the "right-wing" policies of the navy commander, Vice Admiral Martadinata. Even though Sukarno did not dismiss Martadinata as the mutineers demanded, he did not treat the mutineers as dangerous traitors. Only a minority were punished, and the only punishment was a transfer to a different unit.⁵¹

The tentative peace in Surakarta was broken by the arrival of paracommandos from Jakarta. They entered Surakarta on October 22 and began mass arrests and mass killings. Their commander, Colonel Sarwo Edhie, had already arranged for the three battalions of the Sixth Brigade to be sent out of the city; Battalion K was put on a train for Jakarta on the night of October 23, and Battalion M was put on a train on October 25. From Jakarta, they were quickly shipped to West Kalimantan.⁵² Sent far away, the three battalions could not protect the PKI supporters as they were being massacred.

Bronto angrily recalled the entry of the paracommandos: "If those people had been normal, if they hadn't wanted anyone to be victimized, there would have been negotiations and nothing violent would have happened in Surakarta." Bronto noted that the three battalions of the Sixth Brigade let the paracommandos into the city without a fight: "They were passive!" With the collapse of the Movement, the officers had looked for guidance from President Sukarno, and his orders were to stay calm. The paracommandos under Colonel Sarwo Edhie seemed to be coming to Central Java with Sukarno's blessing. Bronto thought that the Surakarta troops, especially the battalions of the Sixth Brigade, would have fought to the death if they had understood what was at stake: "If the left-wing troops had been prepared, really prepared to resist, there would not have been a flood of blood, there would have been a sea of blood. It was, after all, Surakarta. Imagine, we had three battalions in Surakarta, definitely. And we would have been helped by the mass organizations of the PKI."

Bronto, part of the intelligence unit within the Sixth Brigade, stayed in the city. The Corps Polisi Militer (CPM, Military Police) summoned him sometime in November. He does not remember the exact date. He claims he went

An army truck, Surakarta, late October 1965. Don North, a Canadian journalist working for US news agencies, reported from Surakarta on November 5 that the army was bringing in "suspects by the truckload." The truck in this photo appears to be carrying civilian allies, not prisoners. Photo by Don North.

of his own free will, driving a jeep to the CPM headquarters, surrendering his gun, and submitting himself for questioning. Captain Sukarno, the one who declined to be the leader of the Movement in Surakarta due to diarrhea, and another captain and two sergeants of the Sixth Brigade allowed themselves to be arrested without a fight on October 29.[53] The paracommandos, facing no resistance from the pro-PKI troops who had been involved in the Movement, turned their attention to rounding up the civilians of the PKI who had played no role in the Movement.

Aidit, the head of the PKI, was somewhere in the area. When the Movement in Jakarta collapsed on the night of October 1, Aidit flew to Central Java in an air force plane. He landed in Yogyakarta and then secretly traveled around the province over the following weeks, apparently spending much of his time in and around Surakarta, where the party had many supporters who could hide him. He was eventually captured on November 22 in the Surakarta area. His reasons for staying underground and his activities while in Central Java remain unknown. Former party leaders, when I asked them about the subject, either said they did not know or did not want to talk about it. He might have been trying to organize some kind of resistance, hoping that the province could serve as a secure base for the party. It seems unlikely that he would have stayed there just to save his own skin, without thinking of what was best for the party. But his hiding there was inconsistent with the party's official policy, which was to deny responsibility for the Movement and remain passive so that President Sukarno could investigate the event and work out a "political resolution." In accordance with that policy, he should have been in Jakarta making public statements that explained the party's position. By acting like a fugitive, he gave the impression that the party had indeed been involved in the Movement and was still plotting some kind of action.

Perhaps Aidit expected Suharto and Nasution to quickly overthrow Sukarno, in which case Sukarno could move to Central Java and join forces with the PKI. Or perhaps Aidit hoped the pro-PKI troops in Central Java could regroup and take the provincial capital, Semarang, and then he could bargain with Sukarno from a position of strength. Whatever Aidit intended to do, nothing came of it. The fragile, covert network of pro-PKI troops was already in disarray after October 1 and could not be revived for another action. The PKI back in Jakarta was rudderless in the absence of Aidit. Other Politburo members in Jakarta, such as Njoto and Lukman, were flummoxed in October and November. The party as a whole was paralyzed while its leader was underground in Central Java.[54]

The Politburo member from Surakarta, Rewang, was in Jakarta at the time. He admitted that the party leaders did not know what to do after October 1. They did not issue calls to resist the army's onslaught: "There wasn't any instruction to take action or launch a movement. Nothing like that. So when we were hit we were completely passive. People were arrested and nobody resisted. Nobody ran away. It was only after a lot of arrests that people began hiding."[55]

The RPKAD Invasion and the Mass Arrests

When the RPKAD troops arrived on October 22, Surakarta was like an open city before an invading army. The communists who had dominated the town were disorganized and defenseless. PKI leaders had not instructed villagers to build barricades in the roads, and the troops moved all over the area, from Boyolali to Klaten, without facing serious obstacles.[56]

The number of paracommandos entering Surakarta was not large. Two companies meant about 150 troops. Their importance did not lie in their firepower. Their main task was to force the army troops and the police already in and around Surakarta to start attacking the PKI. Sarwo Edhie transmitted the orders from Jakarta to the top military officers in the area: the PKI must be annihilated, and anyone not cooperating would be treated as a PKI supporter. It was necessary for such orders to be conveyed personally, since Sukarno was ordering the military to remain calm at that time and not attack the PKI. Direct pressure needed to be placed on military officers wary about defying Sukarno's orders. They had to be convinced that Suharto's orders overruled those of the president and that there would be consequences for their future careers in the military if they did not comply. To display the newfound unity of purpose among the armed forces of Surakarta, Sarwo Edhie led a massive cavalcade of armored vehicles, trucks, and jeeps through the streets of Surakarta during the afternoon of October 22.

Since Surakarta and its surrounding regencies formed the center of the PKI's strength, they were given special attention. Suharto's army hyperbolically imagined the triangle formed by Surakarta, Boyolali, and Klaten to be an "area of death."[57] Sarwo Edhie set up his headquarters at the RPKAD base just to the west of Surakarta and directed a new army command called the Surakarta Joint Security Staff. His authority was confirmed in a letter from the Kodam commander for Central Java on October 27, assigning him the task of "controlling [*menguasai*] the area of the former Surakarta Residency, with a radius of action encompassing Boyolali to the west, Sragen to the east, and Wonogiri to the south."[58]

Sarwo Edhie, wielding emergency powers, initiated a purge of the civil administration of the Surakarta area. The army took over the administration. The mayor of Surakarta, Utomo Ramelan, was arrested on October 23 and replaced by an army officer, Lieutenant Colonel Soemanto. The *bupatis* for Karanganyar and Boyolali were replaced with military officers on October 24.[59] Even the lowest-level officials, the *lurah*, were systematically purged.[60]

To help the army and police round up PKI supporters, Sarwo Edhie summoned the leaders of the various non-PKI youth and paramilitary organizations in the Surakarta area. These groups were affiliated either with the Muslim organizations Muhammadiyah and NU or with the political parties, such as the PNI. In effect, the army deputized thousands of civilians, giving them authority to arrest and even kill PKI members. The army officers conveyed to them the propaganda line, that the PKI was secretly organizing to carry out mass murder, that it was a time of kill or be killed, and assured them of impunity for any violence they committed against PKI supporters.

The brief training sessions and guns were of less significance than the simple act of licensing them to kill. Bronto noted that many of the non-PKI militias in the Surakarta area had already received training from the army over the previous years. The short training sessions in late 1965 were superfluous.

Moreover, the number of guns provided was not large. These militias did not need many military skills and weapons to rampage through the streets and capture or kill unarmed civilians.

Sarwo Edhie recounted to a journalist some months later while in his office in Jakarta: "In Solo, we gathered together the youth, the nationalist groups, the religious [Muslim] organizations. We gave them two or three days' training, then sent them out to kill the Communists."[61] The journalist to whom Sarwo Edhie spoke was John Hughes, a correspondent for American newspapers. Hughes uncritically reported the colonel's version of events. Supposedly, the PKI ordered a "general offensive" in the villages and cities of the Surakarta area in mid-October and began attacking "police stations and army compounds." The communists systematically slaughtered noncommunists. In the city of Surakarta itself, "anti-Communists were killed by the hundreds, houses were burned, and there were many calls for help." The paracommandos arrived on October 22 and magically put a stop to this offensive in one day: "On October 23, the Gestapu forces surrendered."[62] Hughes's reporting was deeply misleading. There was no PKI offensive. Police and army posts were not attacked. Noncommunists were not slaughtered in large numbers in Surakarta. There were no organized PKI armed forces that could formally "surrender" on October 23. As the paracommandos and their allied militias rampaged through the city, they provoked skirmishes in which people on all sides were killed. But the PKI did not organize mass murder in the Surakarta area.[63] Hughes had an inkling that his story was not accurate. As much as he tried to follow Sarwo Edhie's account and tell a story of a battle between two armed forces, he knew that the army had simply slaughtered civilians. He commented after listening to Sarwo Edhie: "unspoken between us lay the knowledge that the real purpose of his assignment in Central Java had been the extermination, by whatever means might be necessary, of the core of the Communist Party there."[64] In a campaign of extermination, there are no battles. Hughes's story of a PKI "general offensive" and a "surrender" obfuscated this other story about extermination.

Soon after the paracommandos arrived, mobs looted the stores owned by Sino-Indonesians. That appears to have been part of the agreement with the local militias.[65] In authorizing the militias to attack PKI supporters, the army authorized them to raise their own funds by stealing from the Sino-Indonesians.

Bronto recalled that some of the batik merchants of the Laweyan neighborhood of Surakarta, whose ancestors had started Sarekat Islam back in the 1910s, gave money to the paracommandos. The Indonesian army was not flush with funds at the time and was open to receiving donations from private citizens. These wealthy donors were able to guide some of the army personnel

The ruins of stores owned by Sino-Indonesians after a riot, Surakarta, late October 1965. Journalist Don North estimated that thirty shops and two hundred homes were burned down in the riot. Photo by Don North.

and determine the targets to be attacked. The power of these civilians to influence the army does not mean that they were in charge. They were able to influence the army only because the army had already decided to carry out the full-scale repression of the PKI.

Interviews with the victims in the Surakarta area reveal that the general pattern appears to have been for police, army soldiers, civilian militias, or some combination thereof to descend upon houses where PKI supporters lived and then force-march them or truck them to the nearest police station or army headquarters. The detainees were then transferred to the city's prison or Balai Kota (City Hall), a large compound in the center of town that was turned into a detention camp. A building in the back of the City Hall compound remained a detention site for years, but by the end of December 1965, most of the detainees at the City Hall had been transferred to Sasono Mulyo, a building owned by the Kasusunan royal family that had been used for ceremonial occasions. The US ambassador reported, after a week-long tour of the area around Yogyakarta and Surakarta in October 1966, that the number of political prisoners "in one prison on the grounds of the palace in Solo," meaning Sasono Mulyo, was 400, down from "an original 1,200." He did not mention how the number of prisoners had gone down, whether through releases or executions.⁶⁶

Once held in these locations, the detainees were interrogated and classified according to the Interrogation Team's threefold classification system (A, B, or C). The military police headquarters, close to the City Hall, was the main place for interrogations.⁶⁷ A typical experience was Haryono's.⁶⁸ He was a teenager from a poor family who had played in the drum band of the PKI's youth group, the Pemuda Rakjat. A neighbor of his in the Laweyan neighborhood, a PNI supporter, reported him to the police, who grabbed him at his home in December and threw him into the jail at the police station in Laweyan. He was briefly interrogated and then transferred to Sasono Mulyo. After further interrogations, he was deemed a person of little importance and was released in May 1966. His neighbors refused to accept his presence and called the police again. He was rearrested and held in the City Hall detention camp until 1969, when he was exiled to Buru Island.

Ibu Marniti was held at the same locations.⁶⁹ She was arrested with dozens of other people as part of a police dragnet one evening in a neighborhood. They were trucked to a police station, where they spent one night, and then shifted to City Hall. During the interrogations, she had to explain her life history. She had joined a series of PKI-affiliated organizations—IPPI in high school, Pemuda Rakjat once she had graduated from high school, and Gerwani once she married. Her husband was the head of Surakarta's chapter of Pemuda Rakjat. With a resumé like that, she was deemed a diehard party loyalist and was kept in detention indefinitely without charge in Plantungan, a prison camp for women political prisoners near Semarang. The Plantungan prisoners were released in 1979 at roughly the same time as the men in the prison camp on Buru Island.

Ibu Sunarti was a thirty-one-year-old schoolteacher in Solo who was active in Gerwani.⁷⁰ She was married to Soejatno, who was a schoolteacher as well. He was a veteran of the armed struggle against the Dutch and, after the district elections of 1957, became a member of Surakarta's local administration representing the PKI. He was arrested soon after the RPKAD arrived and was held in the military police headquarters. She was grabbed by an anticommunist militia about a week later and deposited in a nearby police station in the Banjarsari neighborhood. The police sent her to the City Hall detention camp. She was taken out one night, probably in December, to be interrogated by the military police. She was tortured as the interrogators insisted she tell them about events that never happened, such as her military training and her preparations for the September 30th Movement. After the torture session, she was returned to City Hall. It was in detention that Ibu Sunarti learned that her husband had disappeared.

All the survivors have stories about people who disappeared. Some of the captives at City Hall, Sasono Mulyo, the Kodim, the prison, and other detention sites around Surakarta were taken out and executed. Ibu Sunarti, Ibu Marniti, and other women held at the City Hall detention camp recounted the disappearance of four high-profile women. The four included Ibu Kustinah Sunaryo, a PKI representative to the provincial parliament, and Ibu Haroen Rasjid, a leader of Gerwani in Surakarta and the wife of an associate of Haji Misbach and a veteran of Boven Digoel, Haroen Rasjid. A detainee who shared a cell with Ibu Haroen Rasjid recalled:

> I was arrested on December 5 and taken to the City Hall on the ninth. . . . Ibu Haroen Rasjid was already there. So about one week later, she was taken out and then brought back and she said good-bye to her friends. The four women were taken out again and until now they haven't been found. . . . She knew she was going to be killed but she kept smiling, "Don't be afraid! Don't be afraid! Keep up the struggle."[71]

Most of the detainees who disappeared were men. Many women were left widowed. Ibu Wiwik, who was twenty-five years old at the time, watched from their home in the Jagalan neighborhood as her husband was taken prisoner in November 1965. Both of them had been leading fulfilling lives as members of Lekra. In their free hours, when he was not working in a cigarette factory, they played in a gamelan orchestra. He played the gongs while she danced. She regularly brought food and clothes to him while he was held in the central prison in downtown Surakarta. Then, one day in December, the guards told her he was no longer there.

> I sent them like usual but they were returned. The clothes and the food were returned. They said he had been moved, but where he had been moved to I wasn't allowed to know. "Don't bother looking for him. Look for someone else." That's what they said, the guards. "He's been moved far away." Until now there still hasn't been any word about him.

Ibu Paini had a similar experience.[72] Her husband had been the *lurah* of a neighborhood just to the west of Surakarta, in the *kecamatan* of Gatak. She had been the head of the local Gerwani chapter. Their residential compound had been the center of cultural life in the neighborhood. Lekra members practiced gamelan there and listened to the radio together. She and her husband owned one of the few radios in their neighborhood. They also owned several bicycles that functioned as collective property, with their friends and neighbors freely borrowing them. As the army and militias were rounding up people in late October and early November, she persuaded him that he should turn himself into the police at the *kecamatan* rather than wait for a mob to appear at their house. It seemed the safer option. "Just turn yourself in, I said, instead of being hunted down and then beaten up." Some of the police at the *kecamatan* were their friends, and they could protect him. But the police soon transferred him to the prison at Sukoharjo. She brought clothes and food to him there, and she sold a water buffalo to obtain the money needed to take care of him in prison. Meanwhile, the local young toughs of the PNI invaded her house and stole the radio, bicycles, and everything else of value. When she walked in the street, they cursed her and threatened to burn down the house with her in it.

Ibu Paini bravely aided her husband in prison for about three months, ferrying food and supplies to him, and then was told by the guards one day that he was no longer there. She traveled to other prisons around Central Java looking for him. Eventually she resigned herself to the probability that he had been executed at the Bacem Bridge.

Conclusion

Colonel Sarwo Edhie, the RPKAD commander and temporary martial-law dictator for the Surakarta area, concluded in late December that the repression of the PKI had been largely accomplished and that his troops could return to Jakarta. Instead of having his men board military transport airplanes for the trip back, he had them ride on trucks in a large cavalcade. Instead of sending the trucks by the most direct route, he had the cavalcade zigzag its way through Central Java to directly spread the message that the PKI had been "crushed." The march of triumph started from the RPKAD base on the western outskirts of Surakarta on December 25. Its first stop was the city of Surakarta itself, requiring a detour to the east. The RPKAD repeated its "show of force" parade that it had held when it entered the city on October 22.

As the troops passed through the small towns in Central Java, they staged similar "show of force" parades, driving all around the streets of the towns, instead of just passing through. The troops demonstrated that the army was the new master of Central Java and that the PKI was powerless. They arrived back in Jakarta on December 31 as if they were an imperial army returning to the capital from a foreign conquest. At the head of the so-called long march was Major Santoso, nicknamed Commander Napoleon for his short stature.[73]

The anticommunist student groups in Jakarta that had been demonstrating in the streets and ransacking PKI buildings and homes since early October hailed Sarwo Edhie as a great hero. He had slain the dragon in its Central Javanese lair. The students did not clearly understand that he had killed the dragon as it lay still and refused to fight. Their image of him was as a courageous warrior whose manly exploits had saved the nation from an evil villain. Leaders of the student coalition Kesatuan Aksi Mahasiswa Indonesia (KAMI, Indonesian Student Action Front), such as Fahmi Idris, went to RPKAD headquarters to ask Sarwo Edhie to speak at a large rally to be held at the medical school of the University of Indonesia campus in Salemba on January 10. The rally was held to protest the devaluation of the currency and to mark the start of a weeklong seminar on the economy. One of the KAMI leaders, Cosmas Batubara, recalls that they invited him "because of his success in destroying the PKI in Central Java." The students were "very impressed" with him. Sarwo Edhie agreed to speak at the rally, much to their delight. The students felt "they had received a new power" with his support since "KAMI always felt it was necessary to get *back-up* from the army."[74]

The students who participated in the 1966 demonstrations cultivated an image of themselves at the time as the moral voice of the nation, pure and idealistic, unsullied by any vested interests. They hardly cared to know at the time of the army's torture, summary executions, and disappearances of those labeled PKI. Many of them did not care to know in later years. Idris and Batubara, after condemning the tyrannical rule of Sukarno and the antidemocratic nature of PKI, happily supported the Suharto dictatorship for decades and accumulated large fortunes. The former KAMI leaders sustained a social memory of the 1966 demonstrations as a glorious time. History textbooks invariably mention their role in demanding the banning of PKI, the lowering of prices, and the appointment of new cabinet ministers. To honor their supposedly heroic struggle, Idris and Batubara funded the construction in the early 1990s of a large statue of the numbers 66 and placed it in the central business district, right in front of the five-star Regent Hotel owned by Idris.

One of the few KAMI leaders who had regrets later was the precocious and principled Soe Hok Gie. He learned of the atrocities once the demonstrations in Jakarta were over and he had a chance to travel to other parts of Java. In a private letter to a friend in late 1967, he wrote:

> What mainly disturbs my thoughts are not economic issues but problems of human values in the Indonesian society of the future. It was two years ago when the tragedy of mass murder in East Java and Central Java occurred.... The event will be forgotten but its "echoes" will gradually

enter the hearts of the children and youths who grow up in this intolerant environment. And "history" will teach them that if there are conflicts of values then the grave must be the result of their resolution.[75]

It is unfortunate that Soe Hok Gie died in 1969 in a mountain-climbing accident, one day shy of his twenty-seventh birthday, and could not continue to criticize his friends as they celebrated Suharto's apparent success with "economic issues."

A medical student at the University of Indonesia who joined some of the KAMI rallies, Firman Lubis, was just as shocked as Soe Hok Gie on learning of what had transpired in Central Java. Lubis traveled to Surakarta in late March 1966 as part of a group of volunteers from KAMI to help the victims of the flood that covered the city on March 16. While there, he heard "horrific stories about the massacres of PKI people." He wrote in his memoir:

> I shuddered while listening to the stories about the methods used to murder the people accused as communists. They were dreadful and hard to understand rationally. . . . Even though I did not like communist ideas, these arbitrary actions outside the law that were approved by the military authorities at that time made me disgusted, especially since many of the victims were not even communists. . . . The event produced an antipathy within me toward the military authorities and the civilians who were involved in the mass murder. . . . Probably the natural doctrine of war— "kill or be killed"—influenced them. But still, their actions cannot be justified. The PKI that they fought was not a military power with troops. It was just a legal political party consisting of civilians. The situation can't be compared to a time of war.[76]

In sober and unadorned prose, Lubis expressed humanitarian sentiments that have been rarely heard in Indonesia's public discourse about the events of 1965–66. Such sentiments are usually drowned in a flood of hysterical denunciations of the absolute evilness of the PKI. By holding onto simple ethical principles, Lubis was able to make a radical break with those around him, such as his former KAMI associates, who have routinely denied or justified the atrocities.

The massacres in the Surakarta area did more than destroy the PKI as a political party. They destroyed a culture that had been built there over two generations from the 1910s to the 1960s, a culture based on the egalitarian principles articulated by Mas Marco, who coined the phrase "*sama rata, sama rasa*," which can be roughly translated as "equal standing, shared feelings." The railways, plantations, and factories were sites where the workers organized themselves and influenced the character of the nationalist movement. The PKI in the Surakarta area grew out of the mass mobilizations of workers and peasants during the colonial period and the armed struggle in the second half of the 1940s. Those who had been powerless under colonial rule claimed the rights of citizenship in the new nation-state and ended the special privileges of the royal houses of Surakarta. Following Haji Misbach's example, some Islamic scholars in the area joined the PKI and promoted Islam as a religion of social justice and equality, requiring selfless service to the poor and oppressed.

Suharto's army buried this decades-long experience of egalitarian politics and rehabilitated the colonial-era culture of the hereditary aristocracy of Surakarta. Suharto's wife, Siti Hartinah, was a proud scion of that aristocracy. Suharto, a common villager of uncertain parentage, identified so much with her royal ancestry that he had himself and his wife buried near Surakarta in a marble mausoleum next to the graves of the old sultans of the Mangkunegaran dynasty. As Suharto now lies in regal repose, the corpses of the plebeians his troops executed at the Bacem Bridge lie dishonored in scattered and unknown locations, at the bottom of the riverbed or somewhere under the Java Sea.

5

Vanishing Points

Disappearances in Bali

Gusti Nyoman Gede knew that he was to be killed. The militiamen in his village, the Tameng, could not keep their orders secret, and the news spread by word of mouth, reaching even the men to be targeted. He did not think it was possible to flee. Even if he could somehow escape the village without being noticed, there was nowhere on the island for him to hide and no way off the island. He decided to face his upcoming execution as a matter of fate. He was fifty-two years old. In his family's compound early in the morning, he composed a final message to the musicians and dancers with whom he had played for years performing Legong, a dance accompanied by gamelan music. He inscribed the message on a dried palm leaf, a *lontar*, using a metal writing instrument with a sharpened tip. He must have been calm at the time: the intricate Balinese letters he engraved into the hardened fibers of the *lontar* are precisely formed.

Nyoman wished to tell his friends in the gamelan and dance group that they had nothing to regret. Their shared ideal of fighting for "millions of poor people" was a noble ideal that they should never disavow: "I am not dying as a coward. I am dying for our struggle to build a state that is just and prosperous in all of Indonesia." He understood the death warrant against him to be an act of political repression: "My death is related to our Legong group." He requested they take care of the troupe's gongs and drums and make offerings for him during Bali's religious holidays. Believing that the repression would be only a temporary setback and that some of his friends would resume their struggle, he asked them to one day build a monument to him and other victims in the middle of the village's main intersection.

The *lontar* written by I Gusti Nyoman Gede, with the date of the text's composition in the lower right corner: 16-12-65. Photo by John Roosa.

His fellow musicians and dancers who survived did not learn about his final message until five years later. His son found the *lontar* hidden in the roof of one of his family's ancestral shrines. His son had been working in a bank in Jakarta in 1965 and had been spared the terror of the death squads. Returning to live in the village in 1970, he began asking relatives and friends about what had happened to his father. His stepmother told him about the hidden *lontar*. Even once Nyoman's friends learned about his dying wishes, they could do nothing to fulfill them. Four other members of the troupe had disappeared as well, and the survivors did not attempt to rebuild the group with new members. They did not even meet for social occasions for fear of arousing the suspicions of the village's murderers. They were never able to build the monument he requested.

Although the history of Nyoman's troupe has vanished, one trace of his artistic genius has been on public display for decades. A painting of his hangs in the collection of the main art museum in the center of Ubud, the Puri Lukisan (Palace of Painting), which opened its doors in 1956. It has been seen by countless numbers of tourists. Nyoman was not just a musician; he was also a painter. He was a multitalented artist influenced by the cultural efflorescence around Ubud that started in the 1930s. The painting depicts the thick foliage of a Balinese forest, with many different kinds of trees and plants. The leaves, with their edges outlined in white, seem to shine. The text posted on the museum wall next to Nyoman's painting supplies the title, "The Monkey Is Playing the Drum to Wake Up the King"; the year it was painted (1934); and Nyoman's birth and death years, 1913–65. The text does not mention how

Nyoman came to die in 1965. The museum's beautiful catalog, which contains a reproduction of the painting, also does not mention the circumstances of his death.[1]

Nyoman's painting follows the convention of Balinese painting at that time: it is depthless. All the elements of the picture—the foliage, an old woman making offerings, and a monkey in a tree—are in the same plane. Balinese artists around the Ubud area began to depart from that convention and to represent depth in the early 1930s, precisely when Nyoman was painting this masterpiece. With patronage from some members of the local nobility and advice from two European artists resident in Ubud, Walter Spies and Rudolph Bonnet, Balinese artists in the area created a new style of painting that came to be called "the Ubud school." They reworked Balinese artistic traditions to appeal to the international tourists who started to arrive on the island by steamships and airplanes in the 1920s. The new paintings had vanishing points and leading lines, foregrounds and backgrounds, illuminated parts and shadows.

When I visited Nyoman's son, Mangku Kebyar, in 2012, he pulled out one of his father's drawings that was left unfinished at the time of his death. He pointed out the exquisite, expertly drawn detail on the foliage and noted that its style, unlike the 1934 painting in the museum, reflected the influence of "the Ubud school." Mountains are in the distance, a temple's tower in the mid-distance, and figures standing in a rice field in the foreground. Palm fronds bend gracefully in the wind. I imagined how beautiful the painting would have been had it been completed and how many more paintings Nyoman could have completed had he lived longer.

Mangku Kebyar described to me how his father's Legong troupe played at the events held by the PKI and its various mass organizations. The PKI in Bali was a small party in the 1950s, earning only 7 percent of the vote in the 1955 elections. It had no long-standing roots in Bali, unlike in Central Java. But it grew quickly in the early 1960s. Former supporters of the party recall ceremonies being held just about every week to inaugurate the opening of a new chapter of a PKI-affiliated organization somewhere or other on the island. Many villagers flocked to the party for help in taking advantage of the national laws on sharecropping and land ownership passed in 1960. Nyoman, as an artist, played a role in this mobilization of poor people challenging the hegemonic power of the Indonesian National Party (PNI) in Bali.[2]

His connection with the PKI may have begun when his troupe toured Eastern Europe in the mid-1950s under the auspices of Indonesia's Directorate of Culture.[3] Mangku Kebyar specifically remembers that his father's troupe played in Czechoslovakia. With the money Nyoman's troupe earned from the tour, they purchased land in the village. They managed the land as a collective and used the earnings from it to finance their artistic work. Nyoman decided to spend his last minutes on earth writing a message to the other members of the troupe because they meant so much to him. They were a tightly knit group.

Mangku Kebyar pieced together the story about how his father was killed from conversations with relatives and friends in the village over many years. A group of local Tameng, the militia of the PNI, captured him in the community hall, the *bale banjar*, and marched him to a nearby village. It was a large-scale, noonday dragnet of the whole Bedulu area, with Tameng from every village, supervised by army soldiers, grabbing suspected communists. The Tamengs' assignment was easy enough: the names of all the suspects were already on a list because they had been reporting daily to the police for about a month. Some were grabbed when they came to the police station for their daily check-in. Nyoman was placed in the back of truck with about thirty other captives and taken to the police station in the nearby town of Gianyar. The following day he was trucked with others to Masceti Beach, about ten kilometers to the southeast. Large numbers of Tameng were involved in the roundup, but only a core group accompanied the truck to the beach to serve as executioners and gravediggers. As night fell, with a few stray witnesses present from the village of Saba, the detainees were executed on a patch of land adjacent to the beach and buried in an unmarked mass grave.

Nyoman engraved a crucial piece of information on the *lontar* at the very end of the text, in the bottom corner of the *lontar*—the date: December 16, 1965.

The vanishing of Nyoman in Ubud fits into a pattern. The large-scale killing in Bali began only in mid-December, soon after the army high command in Jakarta sent RPKAD troops there. In the two months after the October 1 crisis, there were no massacres on the island. The situation was tense but not especially violent. PKI supporters, fearing they would be attacked, took refuge in police stations, army buildings, and neighbors' houses. Some remained in their homes and, starting in early November, reported daily to the police or army. The governor, Anak Agung Bagus Sutedja, and the army commander, Brigadier General Sjafiudin, endeavored to prevent the slaughter of PKI supporters. They did not authorize the police, army, or civilians on Bali to kill. They were doing what Major General Adjie was doing in West Java—trying to prove to the army high command that the PKI was under control and that there was no need for a murderous campaign of repression.

The case of Bali highlights the issue of genocide prevention. In addition to the basic triadic paradigm of perpetrator, victim, and bystander, a fourth category should be added: resister. In any case of genocide, there are always people who endeavor to prevent the killing from happening in the first place or to halt it as soon as possible after it has begun. Resisters include people who are expected to be perpetrators, such as state officials who refuse to be complicit in murder and who wield their authority to stop the perpetrators from committing violence. Any analysis of genocide has to consider how the resisters become disempowered and sidelined.[4] From village heads to governors of provinces, there was a wide range of people who tried to stop the killers in Indonesia, and sometimes they succeeded. Much of the literature on genocide prevention focuses on the methods by which outside powers can intervene.[5] Equal attention must also be paid to the internal forces that attempt to prevent genocide from happening and continue to work, even as the killing has begun, to limit or end it.

Sutedja and Sjafiudin's policy was not allowed to succeed. Rival politicians and army officers in Bali discredited it in the first week of December, claiming that mass violence in the regency of Jembrana, on the western corner of the island, on November 30 was evidence that the PKI was not under control. The generals of the army high command in Jakarta intervened and sent batches of RPKAD troops on December 7–9 for the purpose of organizing an island-wide campaign of violence against the PKI.

The role of the RPKAD troops was twofold: (1) to disempower the state officials who wished to protect the lives of PKI supporters, and (2) to empower the militias, the Tameng especially, that could help the army carry out the killings. The RPKAD commander sent to Bali, though only a major, arrived with orders from his superiors in Jakarta. All the police and army officers in Bali understood that they could not obstruct his campaign without being labeled "PKI" and punished. If they wanted to keep their jobs and perhaps even their lives, they needed to comply with the new orders.

The RPKAD troops arrived on an island where the PKI was not a large and powerful organization, as it was in Central Java. The bulk of the Balinese elite was a landed elite that was passionately anticommunist because of the struggles with the PKI over land ownership and sharecropping. The PNI politicians, representing this landed elite, wanted the PKI to be violently repressed. They were successful in lobbying the army high command in Jakarta to end Sutedja and Sjafiudin's policy. Still, it should be recognized that the army high command in Jakarta could have chosen to maintain the existing policy. If they had, the PNI and its Tameng militia might have committed violence on their own, but the number of fatalities would have been far lower. As it was, the RPKAD organized the PNI supporters so that they could systematically kill every person with a connection to the PKI. Given that the campaign of mass murder had official sanction, even PNI supporters who did not approve of it felt that they had to either participate or remain passive.

The killing of unarmed, defenseless civilians on a small island containing about two million people was relatively quick work for the army and the PNI. Those already in custody were taken out of their places of detention in batches, trucked at night to quiet locations, cold-bloodedly executed, and then buried in unmarked mass graves. Those who had been reporting daily to a police or army post were rounded up from their neighborhoods and murdered in the same way. Beaches, cremation grounds, and forests were the preferred sites for the mass graves. As the young Indonesian intellectual Soe Hok Gie remarked after speaking with some Balinese people about one year after the violence, the killing was a unilateral slaughter: "A war? There was absolutely no sign of it. In a war, however unequal the sides may be that are facing each other, they will definitely attempt, in however small a way, to defeat the other side or at least defend themselves."[6]

It is indicative of the abysmally poor quality of the literature on the 1965–66 violence that the massacres in Bali, like those in Aceh, have been understood as the epitome of spontaneous violence. This gross misinterpretation largely derives from the reporting of American journalists. Many writers, even those who study Indonesia, have treated the book *Indonesian Upheaval* (1967), by the Pulitzer Prize–winning correspondent John Hughes, as a reliable primary source on the events in Bali.[7] Using only the military and civilian perpetrators as his sources, he portrayed the violence as a welling up of a deep-seated hatred for the communists among otherwise peaceful Balinese. The communists had supposedly made themselves so hated that ordinary Balinese jumped at the chance to slaughter them: "Whole villages, including children, took part in an island-wide witch-hunt for Communists, who were slashed and clubbed and chopped to death by communal consent."[8]

Horace Sutton from the *Saturday Review* continued the same tropes of communal violence. He reported that the Balinese civilians had carried out the slaughter after working themselves into a "religious fervor" and attaining a "suspended state of trance." They were barely conscious of what they were doing. They were righteous perpetrators, spiritually cleansing their island, and could not be considered criminally responsible for murder. The only people to blame for the violence were the PKI members themselves who had been disrespectful toward Balinese traditions.[9] The role of the army in Bali, according to both Hughes and Sutton, was to stop the killing by the frenzied masses.

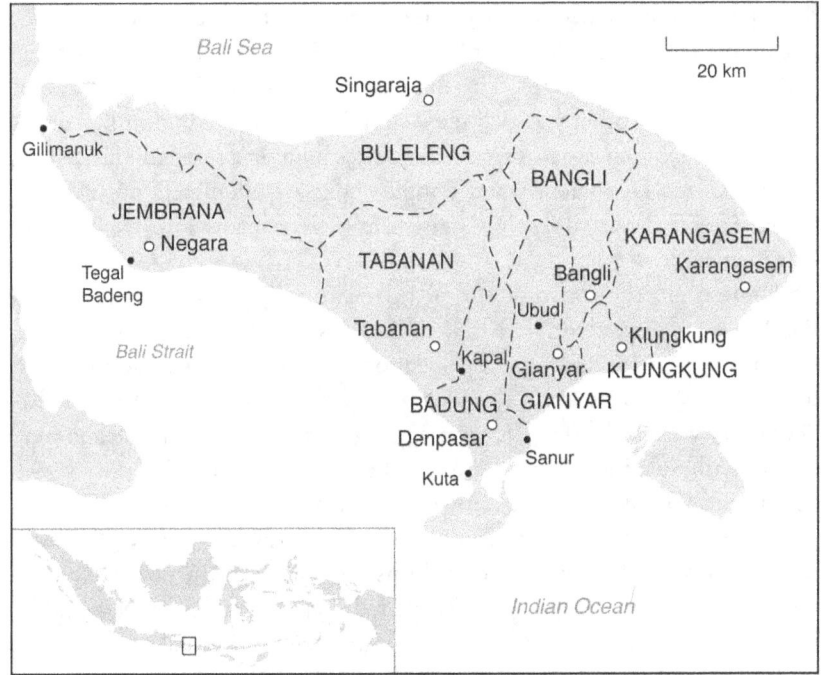

Bali in 1965

They presented the army as a rational agent, ending the excesses committed by the momentarily insane civilians and responding proportionately to the dangers posed by the PKI's revolt. Such reporting did not reflect a serious investigation into the course of events in Bali.

The army's decision to organize the slaughter in Bali was like a vanishing point in a painting: it accounts for the coherence of the entire picture but does not itself appear in the picture. It can be pinpointed only once one notices the patterns in the picture and extrapolates the leading lines. In the case of the killings in Bali, all the lines converge on a spot in the picture that has been covered up by the contorted visage of a fanatical civilian.

Preventing Mass Murder

During Guided Democracy, Bali appeared to be a safe haven for President Sukarno. Most of the educated elite of Bali had grouped themselves behind the PNI in the early 1950s. The party was closely associated with

Sukarno and represented mainstream nationalism. It was all-inclusive; it was not a party meant for adherents of just one religion (as the Muslim, Catholic, and Christian parties were). The Balinese looked upon Sukarno as one of their own—his mother was Balinese—and Sukarno looked upon Bali as his second home. In the late 1950s, he had a palace built on a forested hillside near Tampaksiring, an ancient water temple about six kilometers northeast of Ubud. He often hosted foreign dignitaries there, such as Tito, Nehru, and Khrushchev.

Underneath the romanticism of the relationship between Sukarno and Bali lay much discontent. The PNI in Bali was unhappy during the Guided Democracy years. It had won 51 percent of the vote in the 1955 elections and held the majority of seats in the provincial parliament. The PNI leaders believed they were entitled to choose the first governor for Bali in 1958 and were furious with Sukarno when he appointed someone from outside the party—Sutedja, a scion of the royal family of Negara and a veteran of the independence struggle. Their anger was compounded the following year when Sukarno, as part of his Guided Democracy reforms, reconstituted the national parliament and the provincial parliaments. He reduced the number of seats held by political parties and introduced representatives of "functional groups." The PNI in Bali went from holding sixteen of the twenty-five seats in the provincial parliament to holding just seven. The Sukarno of Guided Democracy was not the Sukarno that the PNI leaders in Bali had idolized earlier.

The PNI's frustration with Sukarno only grew in the early 1960s as the PKI in Bali gained more supporters and Governor Sutedja refused to use the coercive powers of the state to suppress the communists. The property owners in the villages, who tended to identify with the PNI, were being challenged by tenants, sharecroppers, and menial laborers. Those opposed to the PNI in their villages found in the PKI a larger network of people who could help them in their local struggles for land and grain. Sutedja, as a Sukarno loyalist, followed the president's policy of allying with the PKI to achieve common anti-imperialist goals, even if that meant antagonizing the Balinese elite. The PKI had won only 7 percent of the vote in Bali in the 1955 elections but was becoming a serious rival to the PNI in the early 1960s.

For his part, Sukarno saw the PNI in Bali as an organization of a conservative, narrow-minded elite that thought more of securing its property than engaging in his "progressive revolutionary" agenda and thinking about the international politics of the Cold War. He consistently undermined this group of Balinese who loudly proclaimed their commitment to him. Sukarno preferred Sutedja not simply because he was, as a politician unattached to a large party, more pliable; he was also more cosmopolitan—an all-important virtue for Sukarno. He fully understood the significance of Sukarno's anti-imperialist campaigns, unlike most PNI leaders, whose frame of reference barely extended beyond Bali.[10] Sukarno appreciated Sutedja's loyalty so much that he appointed him in 1964 to be the Regional Military Authority for the campaign against Malaysia—a position that was normally handed to a military officer.[11] With that position came emergency powers.

As governor, Sutedja handed the big government contracts and the directorships of state-run companies to non-PNI businessmen. A lot of revenue and employment was channeled away from the PNI. The situation was intolerable for the PNI members: they thought of themselves as the lords of the land, yet they were denied state power and the spoils of office. They were being squeezed by a combination of state action from above and popular mobilization by the PKI from below. Because of Sukarno's strictures against "*Komunistofobi*," they could not openly express their hatred of the PKI. The conflict between Sutedja and the PNI reached a crisis point in March 1965 when Sutedja placed a PNI leader, Wedastera Suyasa, under house arrest.

The political watchers at the US embassy in Jakarta kept an eye on the conflict in Bali. They saw both Sutedja and Sjafiudin as Sukarno loyalists. The US Embassy's political affairs consular, Edward Masters, notified the State Department in March 1965 that Sutedja was "a leftist governor." Later, he reported that Sjafiudin was pro-PKI: he was "either a Communist, pro-Communist or an opportunist bent on pleasing Sukarno no matter what the damage is to the non-Communists." Masters based this evaluation solely on the fact that Sjafiudin made pro-Sukarno statements at a May 1965 meeting of all of the army's Kodam commanders. He was the only general "to go out of his way to compliment Sukarno's address to the conference" and to "employ in any marked extent the 'newspeak' of the Sukarno regime."[12]

In the wake of the October 1 crisis, Sutedja and Sjafiudin strictly followed Sukarno's orders to prevent mass murder. After meeting the president in Jakarta on October 29, they returned to Bali and issued a statement insisting that they did not want to exceed Sukarno's orders: "we do not want to go beyond what is in the statements about the September 30th Movement issued by the Great Leader of the Revolution Bung Karno." They said that they "did not want to take actions that would pre-empt Bung Karno's *political solution*."[13] That meant that they did not want to encourage or permit violent actions against PKI members when Sukarno was demanding peaceful conditions. Sukarno did not state that the PKI was the mastermind of the September 30th Movement, and he refused to ban the PKI, even as the army went ahead with its operations to "crush" the PKI. Sutedja and Sjafiudin did not want the kind of violence that was happening in Central and East Java to happen in Bali.

Sutedja and Sjafiudin's policy was initially viable because there had been no action by the September 30th Movement in Bali. Nothing happened on October 1. No one was kidnapped or killed. No pronouncements were made. According to the newspaper reporting at the time and the Suharto regime's official history of the Movement, the troops in Bali did not take any action and PKI members did not demonstrate in the streets. A detailed investigation by Akihisa Matsuno reveals that some troops in Bali had been in contact with the Movement and had been planning on taking some kind of action. But the Movement collapsed in Jakarta before they did anything. Matsuno confirms that there was no manifestation of the Movement in Bali.[14]

Once the Indonesian army started to move against the PKI in early October 1965, the PNI in Bali saw its chance to get rid of Sutedja, Sjafiudin, and the PKI. The PNI leaders in Bali condemned the governor and the Kodam commander for their refusal to support harsher measures against PKI members. While the two men were in Jakarta in late October, the PNI held a large rally in the main square in Denpasar. The head of the PNI in Bali, I Gusti Putu Merta, delivered the main address to a crowd of thousands. He lamented that the anti-PKI campaign in Bali was far behind the campaign in Java and denounced Sutedja for allowing Bali to become "its own state separate from the central state."[15]

In early November, Sutedja and Sjafiudin made some concessions to the anti-PKI campaign. They created an "Inspection Team" on November 1 that would determine who had been involved in the September 30th Movement in Bali. On November 3, they took away the licenses of two newspapers, *Fadjar* and *Bali Dwipa*, that had been supportive of the PKI.[16] On November 5, they issued an order "freezing" the PKI and its affiliated organizations. This "freezing" was not a banning of the organizations; it was a temporary suspension of their activities. The order also required the members of the organizations to report daily to the police or army.[17] The political party of Sukarno loyalists, Partindo, was also the target of this repression. Sutedja and Sjafiudin intended these measures to demonstrate to the anticommunists that there was no need for violence: PKI members were under control, and those who had been involved in the September 30th Movement conspiracy were being rooted out. Under duress, many members of the PKI and Partindo announced the disbandment of their local chapters in late October and November.[18]

Sjafiudin explained his policy at a mass rally on November 10, on the occasion of an annual national holiday commemorating veterans. He noted that Bali had not had any mass violence because the army had been successful in taking preventive measures and ensuring that everyone could see that the PKI did not present any danger: "Outside of Bali there have been physical clashes, murders, kidnappings, and burnings. Bali has been considered weak and people have ridiculed it. These people, not stopping at ridicule and slander, want to imitate what is going on elsewhere." Bali remained "orderly and peaceful" because there was "no movement that was posing a threat."[19] The PKI had been frozen. On November 24, Sjafiudin went further and established an Interrogation Team (Teperda). He also turned the PKI's office in Denpasar into a detention camp for the suspects to be interrogated.[20]

The policy of freezing the PKI, however, did nothing to placate the PNI, which saw its chance to finally take control of the government in Bali. The PNI ramped up a campaign against Sutedja in November. Its newspaper, *Suara Indonesia*, ran condemnations of Sutedja on an almost daily basis, with news of some organization or another—the National Front, a group of district officials, university students, the provincial parliament for Bali—refusing to recognize him as governor.[21] The PNI, in a coalition with four other small parties, demanded on November 10 that Sukarno remove Sutedja and ban the PKI, Partindo, and their affiliated organizations.[22] To discredit Sutedja, the PNI even claimed, on the basis of circumstantial and fabricated evidence, that he had been directly involved in the September 30th Movement.[23] The PNI held frequent rallies in the capital city, Denpasar, and in smaller towns.

A key target for the PNI was the Bali Beach Hotel in Sanur, which was still under construction. The project managers were busy recruiting and training employees. As Bali's first large, multistory hotel, it was one of the most valuable projects on the island. The executive director of the project was Ida Bagus Kompiang, who had founded Segara Village Hotel and who had played a key role, along with his wife, in developing Bali's tourist industry in the 1950s.[24] The PNI alleged he was a member of Partindo. Whether or not he was a member is immaterial now; the salient fact was that he was not part of the PNI. The number of applicants for jobs at the hotel had been far in excess of the available positions, and the PNI alleged that Kompiang had influenced the selection process so that people affiliated with the PKI and Partindo were given most of the jobs. The PNI held rallies demanding that PKI supporters be fired. Merta told the crowds that the hotel was "owned by the public not by Partindo or one individual." He absurdly claimed that the hotel's training center in Sanur, where future waiters learned how to set silverware and pour beer, was a "nest of the September 30 Movement."[25]

The Arrival of the Paracommandos

If Sutedja and Sjafiudin's policy had continued, Bali would have gone down in history as a province like West Java, where the Kodam commander, Ibrahim Adjie, had prevented his troops from permitting or committing mass murder. As it turned out, the policy lasted only two months, and Bali became a province where the killings were extraordinarily extensive, where the deaths per capita were perhaps the highest in the country. The difference was that no powerful political force within West Java was mobilizing to oppose Adjie and make the province ungovernable. In Bali, the PNI, representing the landed elite, was determined to force Sutedja and Sjafiudin out and eliminate the PKI. To achieve those goals, it invited Suharto's army to intervene.

The situation was confusing for everyone in Bali in late 1965: the PKI in Bali was passive, but army propaganda coming from outside Bali kept making it appear that the PKI was still armed and dangerous. Every day *Suara Indonesia* reprinted the army's psywar stories from elsewhere in the country about the PKI stockpiling weapons, digging mass graves, and plotting to kill all noncommunists. The reports made it seem as though the PKI's responsibility for the September 30th Movement was an established fact and that everyone involved with the PKI had been secretly involved in it. The headlines were alarmist: "Captured!," "Help the Military Crush the Remnants of the Counter-Revolution," "Monitor the Activities of the PKI," "PKI Gangs Are Kidnapping, Looting and Burning." Even if PKI supporters in Bali were inactive, they were inevitably perceived in the atmosphere of the time as ever-present threats. Their ostensible inactivity was assumed to conceal secret planning.

The PNI, organizing militias and crowds, was waiting for a chance to break its stalemate with Sutedja and Sjafiudin. Anticommunist officials within the Kodam and the government were also eager for a change of policy. Their chance came with an incident in the Jembrana Regency, on the western side of the island. They used that incident as proof that the PKI was taking advantage of the government's lax policy and organizing an armed resistance. The incident occurred in the village of Tegalbadeng, which is about two kilometers southwest of Jembrana's urban center, Negara. On November 30, the army and a local militia raided what they thought was a nighttime PKI meeting in the village, and in response the people there defended themselves. A policeman in the village shot and killed a soldier and two militiamen. It appears the people gathering in Tegalbadeng were seeking protection, as all other PKI supporters in the area were doing. But the rumor circulated that the PKI had organized a mass meeting and had started to go on the offensive.[26]

In response to the three deaths, the army troops of the Kodim and the Tameng militia in Jembrana went on a rampage in early December, massacring people throughout the regency. One eyewitness, a PNI supporter, recalled that the slogan in the streets expressed the going rate on the comparative value of lives: "One soldier's life must be paid for with 1,000 PKI lives."[27]

The killers may have reached that exchange rate. In the town of Negara alone, about three hundred PKI supporters who had been held for weeks by the police and army in a large store called Toko Wong in the commercial district were taken out in batches and massacred near a desolate beach about three kilometers to the west. They had had nothing to do with the events in Tegalbadeng and had not been plotting an uprising: they had not attempted to escape from the Toko Wong and had sheltered there, expecting to be protected by the police and army. The Tegalbadeng incident on November 30 became the pretext for the mass murder in Bali in much the same way that the September 30th Movement became the pretext for mass murder in Indonesia as a whole. Indeed, it became known in Bali as G-30-N (Gerakan Tigapuluh November), the November 30th Movement, in imitation of the acronym G-30-S (Gerakan Tigapuluh September).[28]

Since Jembrana was Sutedja's home area—it was where his ancestors had been the kings before independence—the chaos there signaled Sutedja's inability to control events in all of Bali. A mob raided his family's compound on December 2, looting valuables and burning down some of the structures.[29] Sutedja's younger brother, A. A. Dhenia, who was a supporter of the PKI, was killed while under police protection, and his corpse was taken out and sadistically mutilated in front of a crowd of people on a main street.[30] Leading these attacks were men from several elite pro-PNI families of Jembrana who had long resented the power and prestige of the Sutedja family's royal status and the family's closeness with Sukarno. One such family was that of Wedastera Suyasa, the PNI leader whom Sutedja had placed under house arrest in March.

For Sutedja's enemies in Bali, the Tegalbadeng incident and the subsequent carnage in the area was proof that his policy toward the PKI was not working. They had an interest in exaggerating the scale of the violence and claiming that Jembrana was the scene of a PKI revolt.[31] The events there became the leading topic of discussion within the government and among the military officials. The army high command in Jakarta interpreted the violence to mean that the anticommunist civilians were impatient for a more violent suppression of the PKI and that they would, if left to themselves, victimize many innocent people.

The generals in Jakarta decided to intervene. Four brigadier generals working on Suharto's staff arrived in Bali on December 7: Soemitro, H. S. Dharsono, Hartono, and Suharto.[32] The latter, Brigadier General Suharto (not to be confused with his superior of the same name who was a major general) told the journalists: "What motivated our visit to Bali was the need to follow up reports that we received about the situation in Bali and we thought it important to see the situation for ourselves."[33] From what transpired after their visit, it is clear that these generals decided that PKI members would be slaughtered in Bali. They overturned Sutedja and Sjafiudin's policy. Instead of preventing mass murder, the army troops would facilitate it. The plan was to let the civilians loose while still restraining them so that they killed only full-fledged members of the PKI.

With the brigadier generals came platoons of RPKAD troops. The first batch, which arrived by plane on December 7, was accompanied by a platoon of troops from the East Java military command and armored personnel carriers. More RPKAD troops arrived on either December 9 or 10.[34] Sjafiudin was kept in his post as Kodam commander even as his policy was being reversed. He welcomed the initial batch of the paracommandos at a ceremony in Denpasar on December 8, explaining to journalists that the troops had come "for the purpose of wiping out the counterrevolutionary September 30th Movement."[35] The number of RPKAD troops was very small when compared to the number of troops already stationed on Bali. Their main purpose was not to carry out the mass murder themselves but to force the local Kodam troops and police forces to cooperate with the new policy of mass murder. That had been their role in Central Java.

It was not difficult for the RPKAD to bypass Sjafiudin. He was the commander of the Kodam that covered Bali and many of the islands of eastern Indonesia. Directly under him was the commander of the Korem that covered only Bali. That Korem commander from 1965 to 1967 was Lieutenant Colonel Soekarmen. He was in charge of the eight Kodims that covered the eight regencies of Bali. The RPKAD needed to work only with Soekarmen to carry out the "crushing" of the PKI in Bali. Soekarmen must have done his job well because Suharto rewarded him by appointing him governor of Bali in 1967, a position he held for the next ten years. Sjafiudin, meanwhile, saw his career reach a dead end once he was removed as Kodam commander on June 21, 1966.

Even if there had been a PKI offensive in Bali, there was no military necessity for additional troops or equipment to be brought in; the Kodam in Denpasar had more than enough of both to deal with a group of unarmed civilians. Sjafiudin pointed that out at the sendoff ceremony for the RPKAD troops before their return to Java in early January. In the reception hall of the Bali Hotel in Denpasar, he said, "Actually the counterrevolutionary adventurist September 30th Movement in Bali could have been overcome just with the power of ordinary infantry troops." He explained that the RPKAD had arrived to "lead and direct the enthusiasm of the people" so that there would not be "unnecessary victimization."[36]

Sutedja was forced out of office with the arrival of the RPKAD. Sukarno, meeting Bali's top state officials at the presidential palace in Jakarta on

A group of the PNI's Tameng militia, Bali, ca. late 1965. The Tameng wore black clothes and badges with a five-cornered star, the logo of the party's student organization, Gerakan Mahasiswa Nasional Indonesia (GMNI). Photo from National Library of Indonesia.

December 8, decided that he could no longer serve as the governor. He could see that Sutedja was powerless and could not even reside in Bali because of fears for his safety. Sukarno still did not want to fully capitulate to the PNI: instead of firing Sutedja, he "suspended" him and appointed a temporary acting governor. Sutedja's replacement was the obvious choice: the PNI leader for Bali, I Gusti Putu Merta.[37]

With Sjafiudin bypassed and Sutedja out of the governor's office, the RPKAD troops sent to Bali had a free hand to work with the army personnel of the Territorial Command and the PNI, especially its militia, the Tameng, to organize the mass murder of PKI members. The army, with a dubious interpretation of the Jembrana events, justified the bloodshed in the name of preventing more numerous, less selective murders.

Setting the Rules for Mass Murder

The commander of the RPKAD troops in Bali, Major Djasmin, placed a high priority on the mobilization of the militias. Within two days of his arrival, he put together a coalition of militias from five anticommunist political parties: PNI, NU, Ikatan Pendukung Kemerdekaan Indonesia (IPKI, League of Supporters of Indonesian Independence), the Catholic Party, and the Christian Party. The coalition was announced on December 9 with an ungainly name: Coordinating Body for Unifying the Actions to Crush the Counterrevolutionary September 30th Movement. Former Tameng members remember the organization being known by the abbreviation KOKAP.[38] Within this coalition, the PNI's militia, the Tameng, had the greatest number of followers and was the dominant force.

Major Djasmin wanted to ensure that the upcoming slaughter exclusively targeted PKI members. He did not want militiamen to kill people because of personal grudges or steal property for personal enrichment. In inciting the Tameng and then letting them loose to break the law, he still wanted them to follow certain rules. Their madness had to be methodical. The day after he set up the militia coalition, an army officer in Bali, a member of the Mental Operation Team, released a statement that put the rules for the "crushing" in writing:

> In the crushing of the September 30th Movement:
> (1) the target must be appropriate;
> (2) the method of implementation must be appropriate;
> (3) arson is strictly forbidden;
> (4) foodstuffs and motor vehicles must be secured;
> (5) actions must be carried out in a coordinated and guided manner;
> (6) always be alert and vigilant against efforts at subversion, incitement, and slander.[39]

Rule number 4 required the militiamen to report valuables stolen from PKI supporters to the army so that the army could ensure a proper distribution. The army was especially strict about vehicles since they were expensive, strategic assets; all cars and trucks that had been "secured" had to be reported to the army.[40]

Major Djasmin explained these rules at a briefing for the leaders of Bali's political parties and mass organizations on the morning of December 11 in the chamber of Bali's provincial-level parliament. His main point was that "the actions of the military and the popular masses have to be in harmony during the crushing of the September 30th Movement down to its roots."[41] He was worried about anarchic actions by civilians that would lead to excessive violence and looting outside the army's control.

The PNI kept a handwritten record of one of the meetings with the army. Representatives of the five political parties met with officers of the army and police at the Kodim in Denpasar on December 10 to discuss "the crushing."

They agreed that the targets had to be "definite and appropriate" (*djelas dan tepat*). The targets would be "PKI leaders from the CR to the CDB," that is, everyone from the village-level chapters to the provincial-level committee. Additional targets would be "cadres, organizers, and those responsible behind the scenes [*kader-kader, penggerak, dan dalangnya*]."[42] That definition of the targets was quite loose. It made anyone associated with the party vulnerable to being killed. A point emphasized at the meeting was that all of their actions had to be coordinated with the army.

The attendees at the December 10 meeting at the Denpasar Kodim also agreed that the process of the "crushing" should not be done in a spectacular fashion. Their rules on that score were:

(a) Don't be demonstrative.
(b) It should not be seen by children, women, and people who don't need to know.[43]

One of the PNI representatives to the Kodim meeting was Dewa Made Wedagama, who became well known for assuring the Balinese that God approved of the killing of PKI supporters.[44]

Once the killings were under way, Major Djasmin felt compelled to clarify the meaning of his order to destroy the PKI "down to its roots." Speaking to an audience at the main university in Bali, Udayana University, on December 18, he stated: "Don't let it come to burning down rice storehouses and annihilating little girls and even grandmothers." At later public gatherings, he insisted that buildings owned by PKI supporters should not be torched but instead confiscated so that "we can use them."[45] Again, he urged all the militiamen to follow orders from their local Kodim commander.[46]

The Mental Operations officer who had issued the six rules for the "crushing" of the PKI on December 10, Major Matnoer, issued his own clarification eleven days later. His statement was titled "On the Understanding of Annihilating the September 30th Movement 'Down to Its Roots.'" He frankly called for the killing of everyone with any association with the PKI, even those with an incidental connection. Matnoer's statement of December 21 explained that the "crushing" was not analogous to "cutting the grass until it is level with the ground." It was not enough just to eliminate the appearance of the PKI when it was possible that it could grow back again: "we have to completely destroy their Physical Existence and their Ideology."[47] Not just PKI leaders would have to be killed but also ordinary members and their enablers.

The head prosecutor in Bali, Purwanto Sastroatmodjo, also contributed to this discussion about the correct policy that could guide the campaign of mass murder. He issued a statement meant to clarify the term "appropriate target" (*sasaran jang tepat*). He listed three types of targets: (1) those who consciously joined the September 30th Movement; (2) ordinary PKI members; (3) incidental, halfhearted supporters of the PKI. He suggested that the first group should be "completely finished off" (*mutlak habis*) and the second group "finished off" (*dihabiskan*). He did not explain the difference between being "completely finished off" and just "finished off." For those placed in the third group, he suggested indoctrination sessions. If they refused to repent and renounce the party, "they too must be finished off" (*mereka juga harus dihabiskan*).[48] In other words, anyone with a connection to the PKI should be executed without trial. Such was the judgment of a leading expert on the law.

The RPKAD arrived in Bali with the aim of leading a campaign of mass murder that carefully selected its victims. The rules they promulgated, however, encouraged an indiscriminate slaughter, sparing only "little girls and grandmothers." The pressure the RPKAD placed on army officers in the Kodam and the leaders of the political parties was transmitted down to all the lower levels. The message that ordinary Balinese received was that everyone connected to the PKI had to be killed and that anyone protecting the PKI from being killed would be suspected of being pro-PKI.

Those Not Finished Off

The thoroughness of the killing in Bali after the arrival of the RPKAD is truly astonishing. When I first came to Bali to interview former political prisoners in 2000, I was surprised to discover that so few of them were alive. On the island of Java, I was able to interview former PKI provincial committee members and the heads of the mass organizations. While the killing in Central and East Java had been extensive, it had not resulted in the death of every political prisoner. Even some high-level PKI leaders survived. In Bali, all the PKI leaders—Ktut Kandel, Anom Dada, Ida Bagus Dhupem, Badam Wirka, among others—had been executed, as had nearly all of the rank-and-file members. The prisons had been emptied out in December 1965. Thousands of low-level supporters like the painter and gamelan musician I Gusti Nyoman Gede, who had not been detained but had been reporting daily to the local army command, were rounded up in their villages and executed.

The army's campaign could be so effective because the island had already been sealed off beforehand. The PKI supporters had no place to go. The army set up checkpoints at the ports. Anyone leaving the island had to have a travel permit (*surat jalan*) issued by the police.[49] In Java, people wanted by the death squads were sometimes able to flee to different cities and survive by hiding out in poorly policed neighborhoods. In Bali, they were trapped, surrounded by sea.

Despite the wish of the army and the PNI that the executions be committed discreetly, hidden from the view of women and children, some parts of their campaign in December were entirely open. Informal, unrecorded discussions with a variety of elderly Balinese over the years have indicated that one form of killing was for a PNI leader with an army escort to arrive in a village in the middle of the day and order the residents to assemble the PKI supporters and immediately execute them in the village's cremation ground. Everyone in the village, women and children included, saw what was happening. The residents were summoned by the banging of the *kul-kul*, a kind of resonating wooden gong that was usually used to summon villagers for collective funerary ceremonies. Ordinary villagers would feel compelled to carry out the order lest they be suspected of being PKI supporters themselves. Under such conditions, it is impossible to speak of "communal consent," as the journalist John Hughes did. The consent was forced. For instance, one elderly man I met by chance at a village ceremony mentioned that he had taken part in this kind of killing in his village though he thought it was sinful and entirely unnecessary.

Just about every person in custody in Bali was taken out and executed. The former political prisoners I met had for exceptional reasons been passed over and allowed to remain alive. One former political prisoner I met, Bhadra, had been in the Denpasar prison in December 1965; he watched as batches of his fellow political prisoners were taken out every night by the truckful and never heard from again.[50] Before his arrest, he had been a mechanic for the army, repairing its cars and trucks in a large garage. He was thirty-eight years old and had a lot of experience. He had been working as a mechanic and driver since he was a teenager accompanying his father, who worked in a workshop in the early 1940s during the Japanese occupation. He and the other workers at the army's garage were members of a union affiliated with SOBSI, the trade union confederation led by the PKI. He described his arrest at the garage around mid-October 1965.

> I was called to the office, and a lot of my friends, especially the union leaders, were called there too. Even though I wasn't the head of the union, I was just an ordinary assistant for it, we were all summoned. Some military personnel were also summoned. Then we were taken to the military police. We weren't told anything. They just wrote down our names and gave us a tin plate for food and a reed mat and took us straight to the prison, and then I was holed up there for fourteen years.

The prison to which he was taken was the main prison on the island. It was located in the Pekambingan neighborhood of Denpasar. The Dutch colonial rulers built it in 1916, only a decade after their conquest of southern Bali.[51] The army packed the prison full of PKI supporters in late 1965, including even the prison guards who had been active in the union for prison guards. Bhadra witnessed many of his fellow prisoners being hauled out of prison. The military police officers running the prison yelled out the names of the prisoners and gathered them at the front gate. The guards never told them where they would be taken.

> It was difficult to know in the prison. Some were taken out to be interrogated. Others were taken out to be executed. Some were moved to a different prison. Their strategy was to prevent us from knowing whether they were to be killed or interrogated or moved.

From inside their cells, they could not see or hear well enough to know where the men were to be taken. They just saw the men leave and never come back. Sometimes they heard from newly arrived prisoners about the massacres on the outside. Bhadra described the attitude of the prisoners as one of total resignation: "Those of us on the inside were hopeless [*pasrah*], it was all up to God. We couldn't do anything. There was no way to defend ourselves."

He does not know or does not want to tell me why he was passed over. He thought it might be because of his daily prayers. When his family members discovered around mid-1966 that he was still alive, they were shocked.

> The story in the village was that I was dead, that I had been shot, shot in Bangli. Other families had given up, but my wife and kids wanted to pay their last respects to me and wanted to be clear, if I had been shot they wanted to know where, and so they kept asking around for me and finally they heard that I was still alive in the prison.

I was told by another former prisoner that Bhadra had been spared because an army officer protected him. He was an experienced mechanic who was needed to work on the army's vehicles. That is a distinct possibility. Bhadra described how he was put to work as a mechanic and driver for the military police once the emergency conditions were over.

> Once the situation improved and was calmer, I was asked by the CPM to work outside. I was put to work in their garage. I was picked up in the morning and brought to the workplace, the CPM garage, and I repaired the cars there and, in the afternoon, I was taken back to the prison. After

some time, I went there by myself, I rode a bike. In the morning, I biked to the garage and came back to the prison in the afternoon. Later on, as I became trusted, a driver's license was made for me and I was told to become a driver. So I was a driver, going all over the city.

He was never paid for all the years of work he did. Even after his release in 1979, the military police required him to continue working there for free for another six months. His life had been saved, but in exchange he was enslaved for twelve years.

Another former political prisoner who was not killed was I Wayan Santa. I met him at the house in which he grew up, in a densely packed neighborhood near Renon in Denpasar.[52] In 1965 it had been a small village surrounded by rice fields. His father was a sharecropper who gave half of the harvest to the landlord, and his mother ran a small shop near their house. He came from a poor family and had many siblings, so the course of his schooling was never smooth; he was still a high school student at age twenty. The family had trouble coming up with enough money to buy him shoes when his school required that all students wear them.

In high school, Wayan joined IPPI, the PKI organization for his age group. It was, he believed, a perfectly normal, patriotic organization that counted among its members the governor's own son. He sang in IPPI's choir, which often practiced at the governor's residence since it had a large room that could accommodate them. He attended IPPI's monthly study group that discussed the key documents of Guided Democracy, such as Sukarno's Political Manifesto. The PNI had an organization for high school students as well, and some of his close friends belonged to it. He nearly joined it himself. He happily stood in the crowds of students mobilized by the government to wave flags along the roadsides to greet visiting foreign heads of state being driven with Sukarno up to the state palace at Tampaksiring.

In October 1965, the atmosphere in Denpasar was tense and fearful, with many rumors circulating. But Wayan still moved around freely. He joined the village's nightly patrols, walking around with PNI supporters to guard the village. He continued going to IPPI meetings. For the annual commemoration of the Oath of Youth, on October 28, IPPI members marched from their office on Jalan Kedondong a few blocks south to the city's central green space, the Puputan Badung Field, and were surprised that the organizers refused to allow them to enter the field. He started to notice the repression of the PKI only at that time. He was obliged to report regularly to a police station in the Pekambingan neighborhood beginning in November. After the order about "freezing" PKI organizations, IPPI announced that it was suspending all its activities. Attackers targeted the houses of PKI supporters. Someone tried to burn down the shed holding Wayan's family's stock of rice.

Wayan described how he was taken into custody in mid-December.

> Wayan: The head of the *banjar* [community association] came to my house with some soldiers. They identified themselves, but I forget their names now. What I clearly remember was that they were wearing black uniforms and red berets. I was asked to go to the *bale banjar* [the community association's building], and so I went with them.
> John: Was it nighttime?
> Wayan: At night, around ten o'clock I think. Ten at night. At the *banjar* I met some other men from my village. We were gathered at the *banjar*. Then we were told to get into a truck. From my own *banjar* there were three men. From the adjacent *banjar* there were two, and from the *banjar* to the left were about seven. Altogether we were twelve men from this village.

The truck stopped at other neighborhoods and picked up more men as it made its way to the Pekambingan prison. One was an official of the National Front. Another was the governor's driver.

> I remember that the person at the front office of the prison was from the military police, a fellow named Hadi Samiaji. I still remember his name! We were brought in, and information about us was written down. Our names, the names of the organization we belonged to. Mine was IPPI. Others were listed as Pemuda Rakjat, SOBSI, and so on.

Wayan recounted how the guards called out the names of some prisoners at night: "They were called and told to get their things ready. After that, they went out and never came back." Since prisoners were routinely called to be taken out to be interrogated or transferred to some other location, they were not certain that they would be executed, especially when they were called to bring their belongings, usually nothing more than their tin plate, sleeping mat, and change of clothes. Some assumed that they were heading home. The prisoners still inside realized that those taken out had not been sent home when their relatives came to the prison over the following days to deliver food: "The family didn't know where he was. The prison guards told them that the fellow wasn't inside. Then his family would have to search for information and try to figure out where he had disappeared to."

The prisoners began hearing stories about massacres: "I heard stories about how those who were called were immediately handed over to villages as 'quotas' [*jatah*], that was the term used then." Wayan first heard about the massacres from a fellow prisoner, Pak Bagus, who was on good terms with the soldiers who were on duty at the prison. The soldiers had told Pak Bagus that the prisoners taken out at night were being executed. The prisoners saw the pattern: every night around 11:00 p.m. about twenty prisoners were taken out. The nightly extractions stopped around mid-January 1966. Wayan was surprised when two cellmates of his were taken out in March 1966. He thought the executions were starting up again but was relieved when no further prisoners were taken out at night.

Wayan did not understand the selection process that determined which prisoners would live and die. He noticed that the soldiers avoided killing children:

> One case that was kinda funny was that there was one prisoner from a village, a small fellow. He was from the Pemuda Rakjat. His name was called. When he got to the front gate, since he was young and had a small body, they thought he was just a little kid. He was sent back [to his cell] and he survived—even up to now, he's still alive.

Wayan assumes that he too was not taken out because he too was deemed to be a minor. He was still a high school student. He was released from the prison in 1967, having been categorized as a "C" prisoner.

Among those taken out and executed during those weeks from mid-December to mid-January were his neighbors and relatives. Of the group of twelve men from his village trucked to the prison with him, nine disappeared. He kept a mental record of the death toll for his village and remembered seven of the nine names. One of them was his cousin who had been a member of the SOBSI union federation.

> Wayan: From this village, the ones that entered the prison and whose names were called out were Swena, Kaler, Muajo, Bagong, Dapur, Retan, Cetat—those were from my village, who had been arrested with me. Once inside their names were called out.
> John: And they never came back?
> Wayan: They never came back.

Upon returning to the village, he learned that another villager, named Mohon, had disappeared but he was not among the twelve taken to the prison: "He was taken out from the Kodim and then just disappeared. He had not been taken to the prison, but he was among the victims in this village." Wayan also learned that the village had been the site for the execution of three men from outside the village.

From Wayan and the other former political prisoners who survived, I learned that the military personnel being held in the prison were not taken out and executed. Even those accused of having been involved in the September 30th Movement were spared.[53] The military did not massacre its own men. Wayan recalled that at the time he was released, in 1967, "there were only a small number of civilians left but there were a lot of military personnel since they had not been taken out." About four hundred political prisoners, including three lieutenant colonels, were still being held in the Denpasar prison at least until 1968.[54]

Those Finished Off

Since there were so few former PKI members to interview in Bali, I decided to focus on interviewing the widows of the men who had disappeared. Their stories were similar: their husbands were taken into custody in December 1965 and then were taken out one night and executed. Here are the stories from two widows in Denpasar about the disappearance of their husbands.

Ni Made Intaran

Ni Made Intaran was married to I Wayan Serata, who was a member of the PKI's leadership council for Bali, the CDB. They were both health professionals in Denpasar. He worked in the government's public health department as an expert on the eradication of malaria while she worked as a nurse in a hospital, specializing in obstetrics. When I met her in 2000, she was working as a midwife from a clinic in her home.[55]

A fixed point in her memory is the birth of her fourth child, a daughter, on December 2, 1965. She began her story with that date and sequenced the events by their relationship to it. The atmosphere of Denpasar was already tense and foreboding. Her husband was holed up inside the house, and she had to rely on neighbors for help in delivering her baby.

> At that time, what date was it?, well, the thing is, I gave birth on December 2, and the situation was getting really dangerous . . . and I was feeling sick to my stomach, I was about to give birth. I told that to the policeman, the fellow next door, Pak Bambang. He said, it's better if you don't go to the

hospital, in this dangerous situation; it's safer if you just stay at home and don't go out. I gave birth in his house; they were close to us, Pak Bambang and his wife. I gave birth there. A midwife was called in, a midwife who was a friend of mine. Then after delivering there, I moved back into my home.

She was uncomfortable in speaking about that time. She spoke haltingly and then rapidly and then haltingly again. Her stories were disjointed as she tried to put the events in order. She had rarely narrated aloud her experience of the violence.

About five days after her daughter was born, a Tameng gang showed up at the house.

> I heard a lot people making noise outside. They were carrying swords and wearing black clothes. I called my husband, "Hey what's going on outside?" I really didn't understand it at all. How come so many people had come? With swords and black clothes. What was happening? I didn't get it. So, I was confused, and thought, OK, well, whatever this is, I'm going sit in front of the house. It was early morning; my friends were already walking along the road to work.

She recognized some of the gang members.

> Those people walking back and forth in front of the house, those Tameng, yeah, there were some who I knew. They wanted to get inside the house, but they didn't, maybe because they saw me. I was on good terms with them, those families of the Tameng. Whenever I was called, yeah, I was willing to help out with a birth or whatever, so maybe those guys felt ashamed in front of me. This one guy kept acting like he was going to rush inside and kept staring at me.

One fearless midwife sat before the front door to her house facing down a mob and held them at bay by her sheer maternal presence. In the midst of this standoff, her neighbor, the policeman, came out of his house, walked through the crowd, and approached her. The crowd called for him to grab Serata and bring him outside. It was a great relief for her when Pak Bambang turned to the crowd and told them to disperse.

> "Go on, get out of here, later I'll take care of this myself." After persuading them to leave, he came to me and said, "Look, your husband, a lot of

people are looking for him, asking that he come out. I stopped them. But it's better if I protect him at the police station."

Pak Bambang escorted her husband in a police jeep to the station in the neighborhood later that day. He was shifted to a makeshift detention camp at a building on Diponegoro Street, not far from their house. Over the following days, she brought food to him: "He kept requesting that I bring the kids so, yeah, I brought them along too." Other relatives also brought food to him. As the campaign against the PKI turned murderous, she realized that a CDB member had little chance of survival. She was not surprised when her husband's youngest brother came to the house one morning in mid-December to tell her that Serata had vanished from police custody. The news left her numb: "That was it, that was all, I couldn't say anything, I was speechless."[56]

Another man arrived at her house not much later that day carrying Serata's wedding ring, his watch, and a final message.

> He came and told me, "Last night your husband was taken away, here are some things, his ring, his watch, he asked me to pass them on to you," that's what he said. He asked that you raise the children well. I couldn't say anything in response.

She is not sure where Serata was killed. She heard from some people who he had been killed in Panjer, a neighborhood in Denpasar. Some friends of hers believed that he had been killed in the Kapal massacre (see chapter 6), where most of the other PKI leaders were killed. She never received official notice from the police or army as to the fate of her husband.

Ni Made Intaran was left on her own to raise four children, all under age five. She was never detained by the police or army. She did not have to face harassment from the state. Her problem was that the society began to treat her as a social leper. Old friends were fearful of associating with her lest they become known as PKI as well. She felt like "an old mangy street dog." She worked as a nurse until 1974, by which time she was able to buy some land and start her own practice as a midwife. The stigma gradually wore off, and, as a health professional, she became a pillar of the community. Among her patients were those who had been Tameng militiamen.

> I've seen them quite often around town. They even call for me to help them, "Help me, Ibu, please rush to my house, my wife is about to give birth." I go. Such people, they call me and, you know, they don't seem ashamed to call for me, old Ibu Intaran. Before they were ready to kill me.

Well, my attitude is humanitarian. I can't refuse them. Even the big figures of the old neighborhood, like the wife of Pak K., came looking for me. Yeah, I went and helped her. He used to be a leader of the Tameng. I helped them, as usual. These people, they don't feel any shame in asking for my help. Before they were Tameng, really vicious then, but it's no problem for me.

She does not know what the former militia members think now about what they did then; they have not spoken to her about why they killed, just as she has not expressed her pain to them. Living quietly in Denpasar, never speaking about her husband's disappearance, she has kept her thoughts upon the starting point of the circle of life and seen in the face of every baby, even those born of murderers, a hope for a different future.

Ibu Pasek

In 1965, Ibu Pasek was a member of Gerwani who lived in the Pekambingan neighborhood, not far from the prison. Her husband of thirteen years was a merchant who regularly made trips to Surabaya by ship to buy cloth. He was not a formal member of any organization, but he supported his wife's social activities and allowed his house to be turned into a kind of community center. Ibu Pasek started up a crèche there for preschool children and an adult literacy class. Many prison guards lived in the neighborhood, and they occasionally held their union meetings in her house. I spoke with Ibu Pasek and her daughter, Putri, in 2000, in a newly built house on the same property on which they were living in 1965.[57]

Putri remembers that her father was taken away one night in early December. The next night someone threw a lit bottle of kerosene through a window of their house while she, her mother, and her five siblings were sleeping. The flames quickly consumed their house along with several neighboring houses. The family fled to the father's parents' house, located in the same neighborhood, for shelter. While homeless, Putri and her siblings searched the detention centers in the city for their father. They finally found him in a makeshift detention camp near the hospital. Since the central prison in their neighborhood was already overflowing with detainees, the police and military had pressed other government buildings into service.

Every day, she and her older sister carried food to him. Ibu Pasek explained to me that she sent her daughters to deliver food since all her adult friends were scared of approaching the detention centers. The police and army were indiscriminately rounding up people. If they saw that another adult had a connection with a detainee, they might throw him or her into prison too. The children were occasionally allowed to see their father, but they weren't allowed to speak with him for very long. During one of these brief meetings, Putri's father asked her to bring him eucalyptus oil that he could rub on his chest to ward off a cold and a fresh set of nicely ironed clothes. He handed over his gold wedding ring and his watch and asked her to have her mother sell them to pay for the things he needed.

After Ibu Pasek heard stories from neighbors and friends about detainees being killed, she sent her husband a secret note inside a bar of soap urging him to escape and not to trust the assurances from the police that he was safe and would be released once the chaotic violence in the streets had ended.

> When Putri's older sister delivered food to him, she whispered to him, "Dad, Dad, there's a bar of soap, it's for bathing, but there's a letter inside." He read it. Then when he was giving back the container in which she had brought the food, he said, "Everyone here is going to be sent back home, why am I told to escape?" "That's what Mom said," she answered. I had already heard about lots of people who were sent home who did not actually return home. They were killed, it was like that. Rather than him being locked up and then later—what's going to happen, right?—better that he just get out of there. That's the way I saw it. But my husband didn't want to escape. Those inside didn't know the situation outside. I was outside, I heard about this case, that case. But he didn't want to flee.

When Putri came back to visit him with the oil and the clothes he had requested, she discovered that he was missing. The police told her he was no longer there, that he had been "moved." Putri described her feeling at that time.

> Where is he? I demanded to know. Where is my father? I was still a little kid, running all over. The house was already burnt down. I was so confused, running around like a chicken with its head cut off looking for him. When I think about it now, I just want to cry.

Her family looked all over the city for him, inquiring at the prison, the police stations, the army offices. They never found him. Putri said:

> I didn't know where he had been taken, whether he died or what. We prayed to God, may he still be alive. We were hoping that he would just come home.

The dates still stick in Ibu Pasek's mind. He was taken from their home on December 7, the day before it was burned down, and he disappeared on January 4, 1966. At the time of his disappearance, she herself was sitting in a detention camp as a political prisoner. Her daughters, as they had been doing for her husband, delivered food to her. They were the ones to tell her that he had been "moved."

> After they told me that he had been "moved," well, those were terms people used then, you know, "moved" and "safeguarded" [*diamankan*], yeah, safeguarded indeed—in a grave. I knew what it meant.

Although she was confident in her interpretation of the euphemisms, she never convinced herself she was correct. She retained the hope that he was still alive and might show up any day. Putri spoke about her mother:

> Sometimes my mother, if someone came to the house begging, my mother would say "Give him something, hurry, give him something." Who knew? Maybe the beggar was him. Every time a person came to the door, ah, it must be him, that's what we thought. I so hoped that he would show up.

Ibu Pasek was first detained in December 1965 in the local Kodim and released after nine months. Her name remained on the military's list of potential troublemakers. She was one of their usual suspects to be brought in anytime there was a public disturbance. She was detained for three months in 1968, during another large wave of arrests, then again in 1974, when riots broke out in Jakarta. Without an arrest warrant, without charges, she was held that last time for three years, from 1974 to 1977.

As a single mother living under the ever-present threat of detention and socially stigmatized by the label "Gerwani," she had to struggle to feed and clothe her six children. She returned to sewing as a hired hand and sent her children out to sell things in the street. She bought her children's clothes on installments, paying one rupiah a day.

> I used to work until 1 a.m., 2 a.m. in the morning. I would work for people who had sewing machines. I never took an afternoon nap, I never slept during the day. Never. I never slept before 10 p.m. It was always 2 a.m., 1 a.m. Then I could earn enough to buy rice.

In those late nights, huddled over a sewing machine, worried about her children and their uncertain future, she suppressed all feelings of nostalgia for the life she had before. When she looks back over her life now, she cannot even describe a pleasant memory. The difficulties after 1965 have colored everything so that the entire thread of her life appears black, as one long, tangled saga of work and pain: "That's how it's been my life; there was no happiness, just sadness; inside is only sadness."

> I can't get rid of these scars, these wounds. If someone says, "Yeah, just try to forget about it," I can't. I can't forget about it at all. No matter what other people say, I can't forget it at all. On the outside I smile, you know, but my heart inside just can't, it just can't.

On saying this, she breaks down in tears, and her daughter Putri joins her. Inside their house flow two generations of tears.

Conclusion

The decision-making process behind the mass murder in Bali is fairly clear. Who made the decision and when they made it are known in rough outline. Four brigadier generals on the army's General Staff, men working directly under Suharto as his assistants, came to Bali in early December and decided to introduce RPKAD troops to organize the mass murder. The commander of the contingent of RPKAD troops sent to Bali was Major Djasmin. The officers most responsible for implementing the plan were the Korem commander, Lieutenant Colonel Soekarmen, and the eight Kodim commanders. These officers supervised the PNI's Tameng militiamen as they destroyed the PKI "down to its roots," to use the term they used at the time. The RPKAD commander, Colonel Sarwo Edhie, was responsible for Djasmin's actions, and he visited Bali in late December to check on his subordinate's work.[58]

The myth that the RPKAD troops were dispatched to Bali to put a stop to the PNI's killings appears to have begun with John Hughes, who wrote, after his interviews with Sarwo Edhie in 1966, that the "worst was over" before the RPKAD's arrival.[59] Many years later, Major Djasmin, who had risen up the ranks to become a brigadier general, continued the myth, telling an American writer, Ken Conboy, that the killings were committed entirely by the PNI and that he and his men were horrified by their violence. Conboy accepted Djasmin's version of events, writing, "As the RPKAD companies stood by, Balinese society continued its bloody convulsions."[60] It is clear just from the newspaper reports about the methods for "crushing" the PKI in December 1965 that the claim of RPKAD passivity is entirely incorrect.

The massacres in Bali took a variety of forms. Some of the detainees were removed from the detention centers by people they knew and were taken back to their own neighborhoods or villages to be executed. Other detainees were removed by army personnel and trucked to villages where they were executed by strangers. Those grabbed from their homes were either executed the same day in the own villages or were placed in trucks to be executed elsewhere, days later. Some massacres were committed in a largely clandestine manner, at night, in remote locations with few witnesses. Others were committed in front of crowds of villagers in the middle of the day. In some cases, the executioners were civilians. In other cases, they were army personnel or a combination of civilians and army personnel.

The leaders of the PNI took full advantage of the crisis to eliminate their rivals, occupy the posts of the provincial government, and seize the spoils of office. The Bali Beach Hotel employees who were killed were replaced by PNI members. The directors and commissioners were changed. Attendees at a meeting of the PNI in December 1965 decided who the new commissioners would be.[61] The director of the state-run Bali Beach Hotel project and head of the Tourism Board, Ida Bagus Kompiang, was dismissed from his posts and came close to being killed. He flew to Jakarta before the violence in December. Knowing his life was still in danger even outside Bali, he laid low in a small town in Java for several years and then returned to Bali in the late 1960s to run his own hotel on Sanur Beach.[62]

The governor, Sutedja, and his wife stayed in a government house in the Senayan area of Jakarta once he was removed from office in mid-December. They were safe as their relatives, friends, and political associates were being massacred in Bali. When a car arrived at their house with four men in army uniforms on the morning of July 29, 1966, they did not sense danger. The men asked Sutedja to accompany them to the Kodam to meet their superior officer, a captain. He left without protesting, "before he had drunk his morning coffee," as Ibu Sutedja recalls. She became worried when he had not returned by the afternoon. She spent the next days visiting military bases and government offices, inquiring about her husband and finding no one who could tell her where he was.[63] The former governor disappeared in Jakarta, just like so many ordinary men and women in Bali. His assassins were never caught. I heard from Balinese who were in a position to know that Sutedja's assassination was ordered by PNI leaders back in Bali who paid a group of army personnel to carry it out.

This chapter began with the murder of I Gusti Nyoman Gede, a painter and musician in the Ubud area. In his final message on the palm leaf, he asked the surviving members of his Legong troupe to build a monument in the village to him. They were unable to do that. His son, in partial fulfillment of his father's wishes, has placed statues of musicians in front of his residential

Statues in honor of I Gusti Nyoman Gede and his Legong group, Bedulu, Bali. Photo by John Roosa.

compound. The statues, on an island that has promoted its music and dance for the global tourist trade, look unremarkable. A passerby on the street would think that it was just a typical, perhaps even clichéd Balinese scene. For the son, however, these statues represent his father and the murdered musicians of the Legong troupe and are meant as a coded form of memorialization, an invisible form of resistance to the oblivion into which the victims of the massacres of Bali have vanished.

6

Invisible Worlds

The Kapal Massacre in Bali

Entering the cremation ground of the village of Kapal, one passes a towering banyan tree that looks as if it has stood for centuries, somberly marking the passage into a magical world where imperceptible souls separate from burning corpses. Souls are believed to be attracted to these strange trees that grow ever outward, with roots descending to the ground to start new trunks, just as the living are attracted to their sprawling, luxurious shade. After a cremation, the soul lingers near the tree until the villagers take the ashes to the sea for the final funerary ceremony. Once freed of all ties to the contaminations of corporal existence, the souls are able to transmigrate into other, higher states of being. Most cremation grounds in Bali are graced by banyan trees. For the living, they ease the transition to the world of the dead, and for the dead, they ease the transition to the great beyond.

Balinese funerary ceremonies are extraordinarily elaborate and have been the wonder of droves of tourists from all over the world for decades. The loved ones of the deceased go to great lengths to ensure that the soul has a safe passage to the afterlife, and they proceed cautiously since the eternal fate of the soul is in their mortal, fallible hands. The Balinese are famous for the richness of their invisible world, inhabited by gods, spirits, and demons. The island feels enchanted. Every family's compound has a cluster of shrines to which the ancestral spirits, propitiated with daily offerings of flowers, regularly return to bless their descendants. Every person belongs to a *banjar*, a neighborhood association whose key function is to coordinate the mutual assistance at the time of the labor-intensive funerary ceremonies. After a death, the Balinese

The cremation grounds of Kapal village, 2012. Photo by John Roosa.

almost invariably consult a spiritual medium, a *balian*, to communicate with the deceased and ensure that he or she is making the transition to the afterlife without a problem.

If one walks past the banyan tree, further into this cremation ground in Kapal, down the dirt path, past the black burnt-out circle in the middle of a small clearing, past a cluster of palm trees, past the area where villagers assemble for the cremations, one will find a mound carpeted with long grass, indifferently tended and littered with plastic wrappings left by the attendees of previous ceremonies. The mound seems unremarkable; it is part of the background that one overlooks. People walk by it and sometimes over it. What is extraordinary there is invisible. Underneath is a mass grave containing the skeletons of thirty-five Balinese men who were massacred in mid-December 1965. Most unnaturally, their bodies were never cremated. They were shot and buried, and their relatives were never officially informed of their deaths.

I am certain the skeletons are there belowground even though no physical evidence is visible aboveground. Nothing marks the spot—not a stick, stone, or tree. It is just a mound, one among many in this field, that could have formed for any number of reasons. My knowledge of the unseen does not derive from Bali's specialists of the invisible world, the spiritual mediums, the *balian*, who communicate with the souls of the departed. I have not interviewed the dead.[1] I have instead resorted to the ancient art of historians. I have spoken with the living: with four villagers who helped prepare the execution ground and bury the victims, two eyewitnesses from Denpasar, the widows and other relatives of two of the victims, one man jailed with some of the victims just prior to the massacre, and one man in Denpasar with extensive secondhand knowledge. I have compared their stories and tried to figure out how the massacre was carried out.

The Kapal massacre is not a documented historical event. One will not find descriptions of it in the history books, even though the victims included high-profile public figures, such as Ktut Kandel, the head of the PKI's Provincial Committee in Bali, and I Gde Puger, a wealthy businessman, cultural impresario, and honored veteran of the national struggle for independence. Their execution was an open secret at the time; many Balinese, including some of the families of the victims, heard stories about the Kapal massacre. Among the many massacres on this island, this one was the best known since it claimed the top leaders of the organization that was being "crushed to its roots," as the army's slogan put it. The story of what happened in Kapal traveled by word of mouth until it acquired the status of a legend.[2] But it did not enter the written records, at least not those publicly available. For instance, the one daily newspaper still being published in Bali in December 1965, *Suara Indonesia*, did not report on it or any other massacre on the island.

Working entirely from oral interviews, I am proposing to turn this non-event into an event, one that can enter the historical record as a fact and be treated as being as real as the other mass deaths that marked the epochs of Bali's twentieth-century history: the mass suicides (*puputan*) of two royal families when facing the Dutch conquests in 1906 and 1908 and the massacre of nationalist troops, including the commander Ngurah Rai, by Dutch troops on November 20, 1946. That massacre, though not a mass suicide, is also called a *puputan* because of the willingness of Rai's troops to fight to the death. These previous cases of mass death were documented, and all sides to the conflicts acknowledged that they happened.[3] It is impossible not to notice the memorials to them in Bali. The international airport is named after Ngurah Rai. The massacres of 1965–66, however, have been shrouded in mystery, and no single massacre in Bali has been studied in any detail. The perpetrators have been free to keep silent or, when pressed, to advance the absurd claim that the mass killing in Bali was actually a form of mass suicide, along the lines of the 1906 and 1908 *puputan*. Some journalists have accepted this claim and have written stories about how the victims were not really victims at all but people who wanted to be killed, who realized their iniquity and went willingly to their deaths.[4]

That there should be such ignorance about the 1965–66 massacres is surprising since Bali has been intensively studied by legions of foreign researchers. The literature on Bali is voluminous. Anthropologists, historians, and other researchers have spent a lot of time speaking with the Balinese and observing their actions. Wishing to avoid ethnocentric approaches, they have valorized some form or another of the "emic" approach that calls for understanding a culture in the terms that it understands itself. The Balinese, as one writer in this vein has explained, divide the world into the visible (*sekala*) and invisible (*niskala*) realms.[5] Researchers have been particularly attentive to the invisible realm and have held extensive discussions with the Balinese about, for instance, their gods, spirits, demons, temples, shrines, offerings, artwork, musical performances, and dances. The Balinese, for a variety of reasons, have tended to keep quiet about the massacres. Bali's post-1965 transformation from a site of mass graves to a site of mass tourism has been predicated on the premise that the Balinese are a peaceful, artistic, prepolitical people who prioritize aesthetic beauty and social harmony above all else.

To understand the massacres, one must adopt an approach that transcends the dichotomy of "the visible" and "the invisible." The relevant category could be called "the unseen seen," meaning that which is seen but is then treated as something unseen. The Balinese since 1965 have lived in full awareness of the mass graves lying all around the island, and many of them have become adept at pretending that those graves are not there. Understanding Balinese culture requires an attentiveness not just to the invisible world that the Balinese see but also to what they pretend not to see.

The Gravediggers of Kapal

From the main road that bisects the village, all one sees of Kapal are the stores lining both sides of the road, many selling shrines that families place in the corner of their compounds to honor their ancestors. Travelers passing through the village after the 1999 elections found it difficult to avoid noticing a large wooden double-door on which was painted the head of a wild bull in bright red and jet black. I was led to this doorway by the son of the man who had been the village head in the 1950s and 1960s. He told me that the patriarch of the extended family who lived there, I Made Poniti, had been a leader of the PNI in the village in the 1960s. Poniti was still active in electoral politics, as was evident from the fact that he had turned his front door into a billboard for a party that grew out of the PNI, the PDI-P, whose logo is a wild bull's head.

Poniti was seventy-two when I first met him in 2000. Healthy and confident, with a firm handshake, he was proud to tell me of his career highlights, even the time when he arranged the execution site in the village cremation grounds in December 1965. At that time, he worked as a schoolteacher and in his off hours volunteered as the leader of Kapal's chapter of the PNI militia, the Tameng Marheinis.[6] He explained that an army officer approached him about using Kapal as the execution site, or, in the euphemistic language of the time, a site for "securing" (*pengamanan*) a group of detainees to be brought there from Denpasar.

> The army came to me and explained that those who had already been interrogated would be finished off. They would be secured. And the best place for securing them would be Kapal. I was appointed as the one to receive them. I asked whether this was official. We were worried; if our village went ahead and carried out this order, we didn't want our village to be taken advantage of [*dijadikan objek*]. I said something like that. If it was official, give us a written order, spelling out how it was to be implemented. . . . We insisted on getting a written order.[7]

Poniti claimed that the army officer who approached him for this task was Colonel I Gusti Putu Raka from the Kodam headquarters in Denpasar: "He was the one who ordered it." The colonel was the head of the Kodam's Judicial Inspectorate in late 1965. On November 1 the governor of Bali appointed him as the head of a special Inspection Team to investigate the September 30th Movement in Bali.[8] Poniti remembered the name of the colonel's agency as "Team for Crushing [the September 30th Movement]" (Tim Penumpasan). In this case, his mistaken memory is more accurate than the real name in capturing the essential significance of the team's work, which involved more "crushing" than "inspecting." Poniti recalled that the colonel had been in frequent contact with him during October and November 1965, asking him how the PKI suspects were being dealt with in his district: "He often requested news from me—'How is the situation now in Kapal?'"

I asked Poniti why the army chose his village to be the place for the massacre. He did not know or did not want to tell me. I suspect part of the reason was its location. Kapal was along a paved road about fifteen kilometers away from Denpasar. The massacre could not be committed in or near the city without large numbers of people gaining firsthand knowledge of it, but it could not be held in a faraway place that would require the army's convoy of vehicles to undertake a lengthy drive.

Once Poniti and his PNI colleagues in Kapal had the written order from the army, they went to work preparing the execution site. It was as if they were staging a performance, thinking about the lighting, the backdrops, the position of the spectators. He gestured with his hands as he described the staging.

> We inspected the site in the early afternoon. Here was an embankment, here was the cremation ground, and here was some flat ground. This became the *background* [in English] for the crushing. Here we hung some kerosene lamps. After that, we would put the two tanks here. And then here would go the firing squad, lined up. And the PKI leaders would be lined up along here.

They chose to line up the detainees in front of an existing earthern embankment about four feet high so that the bullets from the firing squad would be absorbed into the earth and would not endanger the villagers. The place for the mass grave was about thirty feet to the west of that spot, toward the edge of the land reserved for the cremation ground.

Poniti ordered the men in the neighborhood, the *banjar*, adjacent to the cremation ground to dig the mass grave. These were men of a lower caste who were accustomed to being ordered around by the members of the dominant caste in the village, many of whom lived along the main road, at some distance from the polluting presence of the cremation ground.

> The people who prepared the place were those in the *banjar* nearby, just for digging the pit. The pit was dug in the afternoon and then by evening it was ready. "What's this for?" [they asked]. "I don't know, just dig it" [I said].

That night the army arrived with the detainees.

> Then the tanks came, about 11:30 p.m. The tanks came. They [the captives] got out and then sat in a row. The total number in the twenties, not less than that. I don't remember exactly. . . . They were all tied up. When it came time to kill them, their blindfolds were taken off, one after the other, they all had their heads bowed.

By tanks (*panser*), Poniti was referring to armored personnel carriers that were like tanks on truck tires instead of treads. They were probably British-made Saracens, which were in common use by the Indonesian army then.[9]

He had reserved an area where the spectators, the high officials from Denpasar, could stand. He claimed that the head of the PNI in Bali, I Gusti Putu Merta, and the commander of the Kodam, Brigadier General Sjafiudin, watched the massacre: "I accompanied them, as did the village head." He claimed that he ordered his men to keep all the locals out of the field and posted guards to ensure they did not enter. Very few villagers saw the executions, he said. "They only heard the sound of the gunfire."

Poniti became dramatic when recounting the shooting, raising and lowering his voice, gesturing with his hands, voicing the sound of the army officers and the gunfire.

> "Firing squad, get ready!" The guns were inspected. "Shoot!" Tarrrrr. All I could see was the flashes. It was all fire. Everything in sight was covered with flashes. "Stop!" Just as he said stop, they all collapsed on the ground. Whether they were already dead before falling, I don't know. "Inspect them!" A few soldiers went over to see if all of them were dead. If one was still moving around a little, he was shot again. After that I was told: "Our job is done here. Secure this place and clean it up." They left, and we were the ones who cleaned up the blood and all the rest.

I asked Poniti if he remembered seeing I Gde Puger, the most recognizable of the victims since he was, for a Balinese, unusually tall and fair-skinned. Poniti said that Puger was given special treatment since he was considered the ringleader of the PKI in Bali. He was killed last. Instead of being shot like the rest, he was killed by a sword.

> Puger was a famous figure who worked with the PKI in Bali. He alone was tortured; it was after all the others were shot. He was brought down [from the armored vehicle] alone. [Someone said,] "Puger! Look at your followers [*anak buah*]."

Poniti would not say who called for volunteers from among the Tameng of Kapal for the task of killing Puger with a sword. Poniti thought one of his followers, a man who lived near the village temple, would be the best one for the task. He urged him to volunteer but explained to him that he was not ordering him to do it: "If you're brave enough go ahead; if not, don't force yourself." The man came forward: "I want to do it, sir!" A second villager volunteered. One held Puger while the other amputated his arms at the shoulder. As the two became covered in blood, some of the spectators, and even one of the soldiers, fainted. "It didn't last long, one could say about five minutes, and then he wasn't breathing anymore." Puger was also given special attention in the burial. His corpse was placed at the very bottom, and all the other corpses were laid on top of his.

When I spoke with Poniti again, years later, I reviewed his story with him, double-checking some of the details. He recounted the same information except when it came to the mutilation of Puger. On that part, he identified different individuals stepping forward as volunteers. To identify perpetrators from within the village itself was a sensitive matter. He had no problem recounting the massacre by the army soldiers. His conscience was clear since he did not kill anyone; he prepared the place where they were to be executed and helped bury the bodies. Both the perpetrators and the victims came from outside the village. He could candidly admit his role. Indeed, he emphasized his leadership over the entire operation, omitting mention of other PNI leaders in the village who must also have been involved.[10] But when it came to the complicity of his own Tameng members in the murder of the one of the detainees, his story became murky.

I asked Poniti whether he still had the written order from the army. He regretted he did not: "Before I had all my notes and papers, I wrote some notes myself, but I was ordered by my superiors to get rid of everything and make sure there wasn't any trace left."

Poniti once paused during our last conversation and looked off in the distance. It seemed as if he was viewing scenes from that time in his mind's eye. After a while, he shook off the reverie and looked at me again, saying that he knew that he had done nothing wrong, "Look at me. If I had done something wrong, I never would have been able to live to this age."[11]

In Kapal, I also visited the house of a former member of Poniti's Tameng group. I will call him Putu.[12] He was a bit nervous in speaking about the massacre since he was worried about contradicting Poniti's account or revealing something that was not supposed to be revealed. He told me that he was only an underling who was following orders and that I should just talk with Poniti. He avoided going into the details of the event but confirmed that the RPKAD soldiers had brought prisoners to the village for execution in the cremation ground. He referred to a Soviet-made Gaz truck coming to Kapal as well, apart from the armored personnel carriers.

Putu mentioned that as the prisoners were brought out of the vehicles, blindfolded, with their hands tied behind their backs, the soldiers double-checked the names on their list and discovered that one of the prisoners was a Javanese army officer who was not meant to be executed with the PKI leaders of Bali. He was spared at the last minute. Putu confirmed that Puger was the last one to be killed and that he was mutilated but declined to name the people who did it. He just said that "the masses" did it. I find it hard to believe one of his stories. He claimed that one of the prisoners was shot three times and rose up each time shouting, "Long live the PKI." No other eyewitness mentioned such a dramatic and physically unlikely event.

Putu was more forthcoming about politics in the village before October 1965. His family owned some land and was part of the dominant caste. His ambition at that time was to move out of farming and become a policeman. By a combination of bad luck and bad performance, he was never selected, and it still rankled him decades later. He wanted access to state power because his family was facing protests from the sharecroppers working their land. Putu complained to me about how the PKI organized the sharecroppers in the early 1960s and how his family found it difficult to obtain the customary share of the harvest from them. He recalled confrontations in the fields between the sharecroppers and the landowners.

Putu looks back at the slaughter of PKI supporters in Bali with contentment. He felt more secure afterward. He is proud that he eventually gained government employment as a driver entrusted with chauffeuring the top army commanders in Denpasar. It was not as manly a career as being a policeman, but it did allow him to spend his days close to powerful men. As someone for whom manliness has been a highly prized virtue, he feels pathetic in the decrepitude of old age, no longer able to even earn some pocket money by dressing up in a uniform for a day and parading around as part of a Satuan Tugas (Task Force), a purely symbolic paramilitary hired by political parties as a show of force.

I spoke to another former member of the Tameng in Kapal. Stooped and bow-legged, bearing the marks of a lifetime of hard labor in the rice fields, Pan Wayan (a pseudonym) still lived in the neighborhood next to the cremation ground.[13] He had been a member of the PNI militia before October 1965 and was among the many villagers who, under Poniti's orders, dug the mass grave. He does not know how old he is. He guesses he is in his late seventies. He does not know Indonesian very well. The son of the former village head brought me to his house and helped translate the Balinese words he used. When we asked him about the massacre, his immediate response, in Indonesian, was, "Oh, the 35 one." It turned out that he meant that thirty-five people had been killed. He remembered the number clearly, without hesitation, without prompting. It is only on the basis of his recollection that I am claiming that there were thirty-five victims. All the other witnesses made rough guesses between twenty and fifty. He was the only one to provide a precise number, and he was in a position to know: he had helped dig the mass grave and place the corpses there. He claimed there were two mass graves dug side by side: one held seventeen, the other eighteen.

We walked over to the cremation ground, and he pointed out the place where he remembered the graves to be. I asked how the corpses had been dragged from the execution site by the embankment over to the mass grave, and he insisted they had not been dragged (*diseret*) but had been respectfully carried (*diangkat*). The site of the mass grave is a mound because the villagers kept piling dirt on top for months to compensate for the sinkage of the loose dirt that had been used to fill the hole. They had wound up overcompensating.

Pan Wayan remembered that the RPKAD soldiers stayed behind until all the bodies were buried, and then an officer instructed them to keep quiet about what they had just witnessed: "If anyone comes around here asking about it, just tell them 'I don't know.'"

It turned out that Pan Wayan had said "the 35 one" (*yang 35*) because there was another massacre there in the cremation grounds a few days after the first. Poniti also confirmed that there was a second one. The army brought about five people and carried out the execution quickly, without prior preparation or elaborate staging. Poniti believed the victims were men brought from the Jembrana Regency in western Bali. After this second massacre, there were no further executions in Kapal.

I asked Pan Wayan if his community has been bothered by the ghosts of those thirty-five who had died an unnatural, violent death. He said no, they had not. Several days after the massacre, they brought offerings to the mass graves and begged the spirits not to disturb them, saying that they had only done what the army had ordered them to do. The spirits must have listened. They kept quiet, unlike the ghost of a foreign tourist who accidentally drowned in a nearby stream sometime in the 1980s and was continuing to haunt Pan Wayan and his neighbors, even though they had nothing to do with his death.

Poniti, wishing to depict himself as a noble-minded hero, sparing his fellow villagers from seeing such a ghastly sight that fateful night, claimed that the residents of Kapal did not witness the massacre: "All the gates for entering and leaving the area were closed. I was the one who ordered them closed." Actually, the whole village turned out to see what was going on. It was no secret in Kapal. It could not have been. There was much commotion in the village during the day as dozens of people were digging the mass graves and walking back and forth on the village streets between the cremation ground and their homes.

Agung, an eighteen-year-old at the time, recalled standing among a large crowd of villagers watching the goings-on.[14] He lived in the same family compound as the village head, a relative of his, while attending high school in Denpasar. The village of Kapal, situated on a paved road, was convenient for his daily commute on a bicycle. Agung played a small role in the preparations for the massacre. In the evening, as it was getting dark, he carried about six kerosene lanterns from the village head's house to the cremation ground. The village head, as one of the more prosperous members of the village, owned more of these lanterns than the average villager. There were no street lamps then, and the cremation ground was pitch black at night. The lanterns were hung in the trees and placed on the ground to light up the area where the prisoners were to be executed. Agung recalls that reflectors were slid behind the glowing mantles so that the light could be concentrated on the area where the detainees stood.

According to Agung, the cremation ground was surrounded by a low hedge. There were no gates to open or close, as Poniti claimed, but there was a row of bushes behind which the villagers were grouped. They could still peer through, above, and around the bushes. It was not a solid wall of foliage. Some climbed trees to get a better look. Agung said the soldiers instructed the villagers to face away from the cremation ground and stand guard in case the area was attacked by PKI supporters. Agung understood that the idea of a potential attack was an excuse to encourage them to look away. Like most of the villagers, he kept watching the area illuminated by the kerosene lanterns he had carried.

Agung knew the sergeant who commanded the eight soldiers in the firing squad. His name was Abdul Syukur. He gave the commands to fire and stop firing. He had often come to Kapal to provide military training to villagers during the months prior to October 1965 as part of Sukarno's campaign to recruit volunteers for the Confrontation against Malaysia. Syukur was a Javanese Muslim who was born and raised in Bali. He was stationed at the Kodam in Bali and was not part of the RPKAD.

Agung, standing with a close friend, watched from the southern edge of the cremation ground behind the RPKAD soldiers as they lined up with their machine guns. His body trembled once the shooting began. He had never seen anything like it. Sparks and bursts of flames came from the guns, illuminating the soldiers' faces, and then, in an instant, a long row of standing bodies slumped lifeless to the ground. The loud staccato of gunfire rang in his ears. His heart was racing. He was so nervous and terror stricken that he urinated in his pants.

Abdul Syukur and the RPKAD soldiers walked forward once they stopped firing to inspect the bodies and see if any of the men were still alive. One man—Agung remembers him being referred to as Dupem—was still alive. The soldiers thought he must have received some magical power of invulnerability (*kekebalan*). They shot him at point-blank range.

Unlike Pan Wayan, the poor farmer ordered to dig the graves, Agung does not remember the precise number of victims. He thinks Pan Wayan is wrong about there being two graves. He is certain there was only one. Perhaps Pan Wayan's memory is wrong about the number of victims as well. I will continue

I Gde Puger and Ida Ayu Rai Parmini, Denpasar, Bali, ca. 1960. Photo from the Indonesian Institute of Social History.

to use his figure of thirty-five while emphasizing that it is based only on one man's memory and happens to be in the middle of the range of estimates that other witnesses have offered.

Like all the other witnesses to the massacre, Agung mentioned that Puger was killed only after the firing squad had finished killing all the others. He was singled out for a particularly brutal execution by a sword and was placed in the mass grave first, below all the other corpses. But Agung provided details the other witnesses did not. He said the person who called for volunteers to wield the sword and kill Puger was not a soldier; rather, he was a Tameng leader from Denpasar. That man strode over to Poniti's group of local Tameng from Kapal and demanded that volunteers step forward. At first, none did, and he called them cowards and "sissies" (*banci*) for not being eager to kill the man who was supposedly the most powerful communist of Bali. Agung named the two men who ultimately did step forward and briefly described them. They were different from the two described by Poniti. Whoever they were, they were two men of Kapal who had not expected to become killers that night and who did not personally know Puger. One held onto Puger as the other cut off his arms and then stabbed him in the chest. None of the people I spoke with in Kapal could explain why Puger was killed in this way.

When I met Agung in 2013, it was still difficult for him to talk about the atrocity he had witnessed. He had never told his own children about it. He bravely summoned up the fortitude to describe the executions in a clear and matter-of-fact way and temporarily suppress the disgust he felt. When the soldiers ordered the men of Kapal to clean up the execution site, he moved forward with the rest, though still only a high school student, and helped place the bodies into the mass graves. He wound up carrying Puger's severed right arm. He remembers the ring on one of the fingers. It was a horrific, nauseating experience. He described how, to this day, he could still hear Puger's screams in his head: "If I recall that event I break out into a cold sweat. I'm traumatized [*saya trauma*]."

Witness-Perpetrators from Denpasar

Poniti mentioned the presence of government officials from Denpasar. It was not just the villagers of Kapal who witnessed this theater of atrocity. The army had invited a select number of key figures of the anti-PKI campaign to come to Kapal. The army had drawn up a guest list, contacted the guests, and informed them of the time and place of the event. It was a pre-planned army operation. The men to be executed were picked up from their places of detention and brought in armored personnel carriers to Kapal at the scheduled time. I do not know all the names on that guest list. I know of only two: I Wayan Dhana, the *bupati* (the regency-level civilian administrator), and Pugeg, a Tameng leader of Denpasar.[15] In 1965, both were leaders of the PNI. I spoke with them independently in Denpasar.

In late 1965, I Wayan Dhana was the *bupati* in charge of the regency of Badung, which covers both the capital city, Denpasar, and the small, undistinguished village of Kapal. During his tenure as *bupati*, from 1965 to 1975, he facilitated the mass tourism industry; the tourist hotspots of Kuta, Nusa Dua, and Sanur all lie in Badung. I met him at his home in Denpasar in 2001. It sat across the street from a busy shopping mall. While pointing out the window, he said that all of the nearby land had been covered with rice fields back in 1965. He was proud of having put it most of it under pavement, even the roaring, multilane road in front of his house. I interviewed Dhana in his study, surrounded by racks of law books, government reports, and piles of papers—the legacy of many years of desk work. Dhana became the *bupati* at age thirty-three, just four months prior to the October crisis.[16]

Between October 1, when the September 30th Movement erupted, and December 7, when the RPKAD troops arrived, Dhana recalls being scared of the PKI. He organized a group of youths from the PNI to serve as his bodyguards. He thought the PKI was organizing a revolt and that he was in danger. He and his followers started attacking people they suspected of being PKI supporters.

> I didn't feel safe. At night, a lot of people I didn't recognize, a lot of unknown guys, would pass in front of my house wearing black clothes. I felt threatened. I gathered together a lot of youths to guard the house, to safeguard this area. After a while these youths started to think, "Instead of being attacked, it would be better if we attacked."[17]

Dhana claimed that his group beat up people in various unspecified ways or stabbed them but that they never shot anyone. His gang felt confident to take more drastic action only after the RPKAD troops arrived in December. Dhana recalled their arrival as a clear turning point.

> It only became really vicious after the RPKAD came. We felt we had *backup* from the army. And RPKAD really knew how to use weapons, how to shoot on target, you know. That was really admired. Once they were supported by the RPKAD, the youths felt a lot braver.

The army invited him to Kapal to see the RPKAD put their marksmanship to work using machine guns to mow down standing, unarmed captives. When I asked about the event, his answers became terser, and I had to ask more questions to prompt him.

> Question: Do you know about the Kapal massacre?
> Answer: I was invited to watch it. I couldn't do anything to stop it. I was invited by the Muspida—at that time it was called the Pancatunggal. I was asked to witness it.
> Q: The army invited you?
> A: The army.
> Q: The local army or . . . ?
> A: Yes, the Kodam. I was invited to witness it.
> Q: Did a lot of people witness it?
> A: A lot.
> Q: A lot of local Kapal people?
> A: A lot. The residents there knew about it. I was there, but it was dark; I couldn't see everything, but I came using my official car, because I was asked by the security forces.
> Q: Do you remember who was killed there?
> A: No, I don't remember. There were too many of them. Over fifty.
> Q: Over fifty?
> A: Yes, over fifty. They were the prominent figures [*tokoh-tokoh*].
> Q: I heard Puger was one of them.
> A: Oh yes, among them was Puger. He was among them. I don't really know the process of how they were brought there. I don't know.
> Q: But it was the RPKAD that did the killing?
> A: Yes, the RPKAD. They used armored vehicles [*panser*].
> Q: To kill?
> A: Yes, they used an armored vehicle with a 12.7 gun, "taat, taat, taat."[18] Even I was actually asked to [shoot], but I didn't want to. I had weapons. As a *bupati* I had weapons—a pistol and a sten gun. I brought them.

Dhana insisted that the killings in Bali were the responsibility of the army—both the Kodam, which consisted of soldiers permanently based in Bali, and the RPKAD troops flown in from Java—and that he, as a *bupati*, was in charge only of economic development. He claims he did not kill, even when given the chance: "At Kapal I was actually asked to [shoot], but I didn't want to." His vocabulary became rich as he emphasized the proper division of labor: it was not his "duty" (*tugas*), "field" (*bidang*), or "profession" (*pekerjaan*). He carried guns but did not know how to shoot them properly. He was a bureaucrat, a man of the pen. Army officers invited him to witness more massacres at Sibang, Kuta, and other villages, but he declined, having seen enough bloodshed in Kapal. In speaking with me, he positioned himself as best he could as a witness to the mass murder in his regency, not a perpetrator, even if he had headed up a Tameng gang.

Dhana's gang was just one among many Tameng groups within the PNI. The main Tameng gang in Denpasar, according to Dhana and others, was led by a man named I Made Pugeg. He was living in his ancestral compound in the center of Denpasar, on Jalan Arjuna, when I interviewed him in 2000.[19] One could tell by the intricately carved walls and gates facing the street that he was wealthy. He had done well for himself as a businessman and politician during the Suharto years. Before 1965, he ran a business importing textiles from Surabaya and used some of his income to finance the PNI. He was the treasurer of the party. At age seventy-six, he was still fit and spoke with the confidence of a respected, successful man. He was one of the few surviving veterans of the armed struggle against the Dutch and was the head of the veterans' association in Bali, a position that had been held before 1965 by Puger.

Pugeg, like Dhana, recalled the arrival of the RPKAD as a turning point in the campaign against the PKI. He talked about the Kapal massacre as the first major massacre in southern Bali.

> The PKI really began to be destroyed when hit by the RPKAD. The number of PKI people killed was far more than the number of RPKAD troops. For instance, Puger, he was grabbed. He had surrendered himself first to the police, and then he was grabbed. Some more PKI people were taken from the jails by RPKAD and then shot in Kapal. RPKAD did the shooting. One mass grave, a lot of them were placed in it, how many I forget.

Pugeg knew all about the RPKAD actions in Bali because he was, according to his own account, the key contact person between the RPKAD and the Tameng. The RPKAD commander, Major Djasmin, drove to Pugeg's house soon after he flew in from Jakarta.

> The officer who led the RPKAD troops in Bali was Major Djasmin. He came straight to my house. Not to the Kodam [*laughing*]. He was lodged over at the RPKAD's place, but with his commander of the operations section—Captain Urip was his name—came here to my house.[20] The person who escorted them here was a doctor. He was a doctor in the RPKAD. A Balinese man. He happened to be a relative of mine. Probably he was the one who told them, "If you've got business like this then you should see him." That's what he told me. They came, the three of them:

the commander Djasmin, Major Djasmin; the operations section officer, Captain Urip; and that doctor, Ketut Purwana. They came.... It happened to be in the afternoon, near lunch time; we had lunch together.

What was Major Djasmin's "business" (*urusan*) with Pugeg? One of the RPKAD's tasks in Bali was to work with the Tameng so that together they could overwhelm the forces in the government and the military that were resisting a murderous crackdown on the PKI. Both Dhana and Pugeg claimed that the top army officer in Bali, the Kodam commander, Brigadier General Sjafiudin, and the governor of the island, Sutedja, were overly sympathetic to the communists. Before the RPKAD arrived, these two men, working with other officials in the army, police, and civilian administration, were able to limit the violence and prevent mass murders. They did not give the Tameng gangs legal immunity to kill. Many of the people accused of being PKI supporters turned themselves over to the police and army for protection from Tameng attacks in October and November.

The top state officials, once sandwiched between the paracommandos coming into Bali in December and the local Tameng mobilizing from below, were rendered powerless. The officials who did not agree with mass murder could not resist the new policy of mass slaughter. Pugeg explained: "But eventually those who didn't agree became passive. When the RPKAD started coming, they got scared. Silent. If they disagreed, they didn't do it openly." The officials could no longer guarantee the protection of those who sought refuge in police stations, prisons, and army buildings. With the RPKAD's arrival, the thousands sheltering from the Tameng attacks were taken out and executed.

Pugeg described his meeting with Major Djasmin, who had come with instructions from the top RPKAD commander in Jakarta, Colonel Sarwo Edhie.

> He told me here, "Pak Pugeg, here it is; I've been entrusted by Pak Sarwo Edhie to work through Pak Pugeg here, to see how our operations should proceed." That's what he said. At that time, it had already become really tense. We had already burned down some houses of the PKI. Also, there were some people involved in the party who had been murdered. The PKI had already been weakened, and some had been killed. The idea was that if they resisted, they should be killed. So he had this letter from Sarwo Edhie, to discuss the issue of the operations in Bali. Well, we discussed it.

Pugeg spoke in euphemistic and ambiguous terms about the plan for killing off large numbers of PKI supporters. There were "operations" and "affairs." After the Kapal massacre, there were a series of massacres: "and so began constant operations." But he disowned any responsibility: "I didn't want to get too deeply involved." Like Dhana, he shifted responsibility for the massacres to Major Djasmin.

Djasmin, upon arriving in Bali, set up a network of largely PNI contacts throughout the island so that his troops could use them for identifying and killing PKI supporters. The network, called KOKAP, reached down to every village: "He was the one who drew that up." Djasmin must have also relied on information from anticommunist officers in the Kodam who had been working with the PNI gangs over the previous months.

Pugeg spoke with pride and pleasure about his bravery in the two months before the RPKAD arrived. A group of about fifty youths stayed day and night in his compound, fearful of sleeping in their own homes. "I was powerful here, so these youths decided to stay with me." He was the wealthy patron of a mini-army of young men, supplying them with food, coffee, and cigarettes. In October and November, they would venture out to attack PKI neighborhoods around the city and even villages outside the city, as far as Mengwi and Gianyar. He recalled a village where the PNI youth called for backup to attack the PKI supporters there. No other PNI groups would come to help them "because they were scared of being stopped on the roads by the government as they headed there." Pugeg was proud that his group was brave enough to go help them. With some of his youths, he drove there in his jeep, carrying the two guns he owned.

> The PKI there turned out not to have any guns, just some swords and spears. . . . We helped the PNI there and destroyed the place. We burned down the whole community center [*bale banjar*]. I went there and I led the attack. The military police [CPM] came later. I was in my jeep and was stopped by the CPM. The *bale banjar* was already destroyed, burned down. I was stopped by the CPM. I was going to be arrested. I said, "I don't know anything about this. I was just driving past in my car."

He laughed about avoiding arrest by pretending to be an innocent bystander. For him, those were times of daring deeds. When speaking about the mass killings after the RPKAD arrived, he became circumspect and repeatedly emphasized his noninvolvement and lack of knowledge. Once the "operations" were under way, he was supposedly just a low-level subordinate, even if he had an important role to play as a kind of consultant in identifying those who should be killed.

Another contact in Bali for the RPKAD was Pak Reti, who had been a leader of the Balinese chapter of the Partai Sosialis Indonesia (PSI,

Socialist Party of Indonesia). Reti was about the same age as Pugeg and lived just a few blocks away from him in downtown Denpasar.[21] Much like his idol, the PSI leader Sjahrir, Reti considered himself a cosmopolitan and modern intellectual. He spoke condescendingly of the PKI leaders as charlatans, mobilizing poor people with grandiose dreams and false promises. Reti was a principled anticommunist who could speak knowledgeably about political theories and current events. He had studied socialism in the 1950s with Daino, a famous PSI organizer from the city of Yogyakarta, who regularly came to Bali to build up the party there. Reti was critical of the PNI in Bali as well, perceiving it as having been led in the 1950s and 1960s by narrow-minded men more interested in piggybacking on Sukarno's popularity to gain power inside Bali than in engaging in national-level politics.

Several RPKAD officers, after arriving in Bali in early December 1965, often visited him to ask him about the political affiliations of various public figures. His wife provided them home-cooked meals as they discussed the operations against the PKI. One of the officers showed him the list of men who were to be killed at Kapal and asked him to confirm whether the men were really PKI leaders. Every member of the PKI's provincial leadership for Bali, the Comite Daerah Besar (CDB), was on the list, such as Ktut Kandel, Anom Dada, and Ida Bagus Dupem. With a heavy heart, he confirmed that they were PKI leaders: "Goodness, they were all my friends. . . . There wasn't a CDB member who wasn't my friend." He had attended primary school in Denpasar in the 1930s with some of them and had fought against the Dutch during the Revolution (1945–49) with all of them. He praised Ktut Kandel: "He was very congenial, very charismatic, a real populist who could speak with everyone." As much as he disliked their political practice, he couldn't bring himself to see them executed: "I was asked to witness the Kapal massacre, but I didn't want to."

Reti later heard from RPKAD soldiers what had happened in Kapal. He was shocked by the treatment Puger had received. "It was disgusting to hear the story. Whatever he had done, there was still a memory of him as a friend, as a classmate, as a fellow fighter in the nationalist movement. He was killed with a sword and mutilated."

In an earlier interview with another researcher in 1996, he repeated the same story. Reti claimed that when he was shown the list of men to be killed at Kapal, he was also informed that Puger was to be mutilated. It was already part of the plan: "I was invited to watch the spectacle of him being chopped up. I didn't have the heart for it and I said to him, honestly, these are all my friends. I didn't have the heart to watch something like it. If he was to be shot I could stand to watch it."[22]

The Victims and Their Families

While the names of most of the victims of the Kapal massacre remain unknown, the identity of one of the victims is definite: I Gde Puger.[23] There are two points on which all the witnesses agree: I Gde Puger was killed last, and he was killed by amputating his arms with a sword. It was a horrific form of execution that made a deep impression on everyone who saw it. The story about it quickly spread all over Bali by word of mouth, since Puger had been one of the island's most prominent public figures. From my informal discussions with elderly people in Bali over the years, I believe that many adults at that time heard some version or another of the story.

Horace Sutton, an American journalist, heard a garbled version of the story from an employee of the Bali Beach Hotel in late 1966.

> There was the tale of Gde Buger, who was an exporter and a contractor in league with the former Communist governor. When Buger was caught they marched him to the cemetery. He was a fat man and seemed to epitomize one who had grown rich at the expense of the people. They shot nine of his companions in front of his eyes and taunted him with their deaths. Then they slashed Buger with a *pedang*, a curved and ominous sword, and the blood ran from the flesh where the fat had bulged. He fell at last and then they shot him in the head and dumped his body in a common grave, piling his dead cohorts on top of him.[24]

It is remarkable how many inaccuracies are packed into this short passage.[25] Despite these inaccuracies, several elements of Sutton's version are in accordance with all other stories about the killing: Puger was killed after others had been shot, he was mutilated with a sword, and he was the first to be placed in the mass grave. Robinson heard stories about Puger's death when conducting his doctoral research in Bali in the 1990s. He was much more circumspect than Sutton in handling these stories: "One of those targeted was the former *pemuda* [youth] leader G. P. [Gde Puger], Sutedja's close associate. According to reports that are difficult to confirm, G. P. was tortured and dismembered by his captors before being killed."[26]

To find out more about Puger, beyond the manner of his death, I spoke with his widow, Ida Ayu Rai Parmini, known informally as Dayu Rai, who lived in Puger's ancestral compound in downtown Denpasar.[27] Over the years since that interview with her in 2000, I have met most of the couple's children and several other relatives and have collected written documentation about Puger's life. I have found him a fascinating and tragic figure. As a respected veteran of the nationalist struggle, wealthy businessman, parliamentarian, and patron of artists, he had a hand in just about everything going on in Bali up to 1965. He was a close friend of the governor and the Kodam commander. The leader of the nascent tourist industry, Ida Bagus Kompiang, was his brother-in-law. No one in Bali then could have imagined someone so prominent and well respected suddenly being treated as an evil and dangerous traitor, someone worthy of being killed in such a brutal manner.

Because his activities were numerous and varied, it is difficult to write a barebones account of his career. Born in 1925, he grew up in Denpasar and attended the Taman Siswa school, which produced many of the young nationalists. He joined the struggle against the Dutch and spent a couple of years in prison. Immediately after independence, he devoted himself to business and became a wealthy man in the 1950s as he built up a diversified company, Majapahit, that exported cattle, sold construction supplies, transported cargo, and ran an automobile repair shop, among other things. The company employed many of his fellow veterans. Puger was a close friend of Governor Sutedja and frequently met President Sukarno, who often visited Bali. At one of the soirées in 1958, Sukarno asked Puger's then-pregnant wife to name her child after him. She did. She named him Jaya Karna.

Sukarno liked Puger so much he appointed him in 1960 to his parliament in Jakarta to represent, on a national level, the nonparty "functional group" for businessmen. Both he and his wife were in the Balinese chapter of the National Front, an organization that Sukarno had set up to unify all elements of the state and civil society. He was a commissioner of the Bali Beach Hotel, which was under construction in 1964–65. Puger patronized Balinese artists and, as a master of the logistics of transport and methods of accounting, sometimes served as the coordinator of state-sponsored tours of artists to other countries. When the writers of the Asia-Africa Association held a conference in Bali in 1963, Puger and his wife served as the hosts, making the arrangements for the international guests. Many of them stayed at the Segara Beach Hotel, run by Ida Bagus Kompiang.

In the literature on Bali, Puger is routinely referred to as a "PKI leader." Such labeling distorts his relationship to the party. He had no formal position in the party and never identified himself as a member or even leader of the PKI. He was a wealthy businessman who took his orders from Sukarno, not the PKI. In the 1950s, as he was building his business and dealing with the affairs of the veterans, he had no connection to the PKI. His connection began only when he became an official of Sukarno's Guided Democracy in 1960. Sukarno wanted to build up a counterweight to the PNI, the hegemonic political party on the island, which did not fully understand or support his anti-imperialist policies, even as it cultivated a personality cult around him.

Puger helped finance the Balinese chapter of the PKI in the interest of supporting Sukarno's one-man regime, not because he was a PKI loyalist. One way he supported the PKI was by paying for the publication of its newspaper *Fadjar*.[28] He also patronized another political party, Partindo, which was Sukarno's own national-level project to create a more leftist alternative to the PNI.[29] Puger highlighted international issues in the hope of rallying the Balinese behind Sukarno's grand foreign policy agenda, such as the Confrontation against Malaysia. Puger was a leader of the Balinese chapter of the Soviet-sponsored World Peace Council (WPC), whose head office in Jakarta consisted of many prominent noncommunists.[30] The overriding concern of both Puger and Governor Sutedja was to ensure that the Balinese supported Sukarno's Guided Democracy.

These peculiarities of the political dynamics of Bali were entirely lost on the journalist John Hughes, who briefly visited the island in 1966 and obtained all of his information about the victims from the perpetrators. He described Sutedja as an "openly pro-Communist governor" at whose elbow always stood "his old friend and crony, Gde Puger, leader of the island's Communist Party." Hughes uncritically relayed the slanderous stories the murderers told to justify their crimes: "Puger had acquired funds in plenty, which many Balinese believe came from Peking. Whatever Sutedja wanted—advice, money, girls—Puger was ready to supply." Unfounded rumors became material for his journalism: "The amount of cash found, or said to have been found, in his home after his death has now become legend."[31]

The basic tension in Balinese politics goes unmentioned in Hughes's account: the PNI leaders in Bali headed up the largest party on the island and felt entitled to the governor's office. They felt aggrieved that Sukarno's appointee, Sutedja, did not represent their interests. They wanted to use the police to crack down on the PKI and wanted to control the state businesses so that they could gain more money and employ their supporters. It was infuriating for them to see Sutedja standing in their way and protecting the PKI as it challenged the PNI's hegemony in the early 1960s.[32] In the aftermath of the October 1, 1965, crisis, the PNI leaders saw their chance to overthrow Sutedja.

Puger's widow, Dayu Rai, recalled that Denpasar was tense after October 1 but that she and her husband continued many of their daily activities as before. There were no actions in Bali, whether by troops or civilians, in support of the September 30th Movement. Puger remained in the open, hosting the delegates to the International Conference against Foreign Military Bases for several days of rest in Bali before the business of their conference began in Jakarta on October 16.[33] Puger continued to live with his family through October and

November even as the Tameng terror prompted many others to seek refuge. He and his family were living in a house on what was then the southern edge of urban habitation in Denpasar, on the newly paved Yos Sudarso Street. They had moved out of his ancestral compound in downtown Denpasar several years earlier in search of more space for their children. The house was near the Kodam offices and the home of the Kodam commander, Sjafiudin. He was probably receiving protection from Sjafiudin, whose wife was a good friend of Dayu Rai's.

Puger and Dayu Rai were increasingly anxious over October and November. They had been expelled from the National Front and banned from speaking on the state radio station, Radio Republik Indonesia (RRI, Radio of the Republic of Indonesia), in Bali. The paper Puger had helped finance, *Fadjar*, was banned. The organization that Dayu Rai had supported, Gerwani, was being demonized in the press. The PNI militiamen, the Tameng, such as those backed by Dhana and Pugeg, were roaming the streets.[34]

Sometime in early December a mob attacked their house. It was midday. The eldest child, Jaya Wardhana, remembers seeing the mob in the streets in the neighborhood of Sanglah after he got out of school at 11:30 a.m.[35] He recognized some PNI supporters, such as a shopkeeper who had a store near his school. He rode his bike home and told his family about it. Puger and Dayu Rai were not at home, and his paternal grandfather assured the ten children there was no reason to worry. But about an hour later the mob appeared in front of their house. The family ran out a small alley in the back and took shelter in a neighbor's house as the mob entered the house and looted its contents. The mob did not chase them and attempt to kill them. The mob was interested only in looting and destroying property, such as the family's small Morris car, which was torched.

At nightfall, under the cover of darkness, the ten children trekked north to Puger's ancestral compound in downtown Denpasar, breaking up into groups of two and three and staying off the main streets to avoid being noticed. Their house on Yos Sudarso Street was taken over by the army, and they never stepped foot in it again. The charred remains of their Morris car sat in front of the house for weeks, reminding passersby of the violence that had taken place there.[36]

It was around the time of the mob attack that both Puger and Dayu Rai sought police protection. Puger rode his Vespa to the police headquarters, and the police placed him and dozens of other detainees, including most of the other leaders of Bali's PKI, in a newly built government housing complex in Sanglah.[37] Dayu Rai turned herself over to the Mobile Brigade Police, where a relative of hers worked. They assumed that once the chaos on the streets ended, they would be able to leave police protection. The children were left in the care of the grandparents.

Puger's nephew, Raka Suasta, who had been living with the family since infancy as an adopted son, delivered food to Puger in the Sanglah housing complex, which was guarded by the police. Raka, in his early twenties, was a painter who had studied at an art school in Yogyakarta. He remembers that Puger disappeared from the place of detention sometime in mid-December. He arrived to deliver food and the guards told him that Puger was no longer there: "I don't remember the date. The way I remember it is this: I had stopped delivering food for about two weeks when I myself was arrested on December 28."[38]

Dayu Rai was not taken out of detention and killed like her husband. She survived, though confined as a political prisoner off and on for the next fourteen years. She assumed that the perpetrators tended to spare mothers to avoid creating thousands of orphans, who would then be a burden on the state.

The chaotic atmosphere at the time engendered many rumors. When one of Sukarno's ministers, Oei Tjoe Tat, came to Bali in late December as part of the Fact-Finding Commission, he snuck out of Bali Hotel in downtown Denpasar to make his own inquiries. At night, he left the hotel by the kitchen door in back and walked to the house of a police officer whose name had been given to him by Sukarno's private secretary. The officer told him about "the sadistic killing of nearly the whole family of a member of parliament (named Puger?)."[39] Oei placed a question mark after the name because he had not heard of Puger beforehand. The story of the Kapal massacre had become garbled as it spread by word of mouth. Puger's wife and children had not been killed.

Dayu Rai heard about the massacre in Kapal from some policemen while still in custody.

> I just heard about it. It was said that some people watched. Lots of officials brought all their cars. I heard some of the policemen who were watching cried and said, "Oh, the poor man. Even someone as dignified as him gets killed. He was a good man."

Dayu Rai and her children do not remember the precise date Puger disappeared from police custody. One man who remembers the date is I Wayan Jendra, who was being held in the same detention center in Sanglah as Puger. I met Jendra by chance. I was speaking with his wife, who had been a political prisoner in Bali, and he piped up when I mentioned the Kapal massacre.

Jendra had been an ordinary policeman with little connection to the PKI, but he had been detained nonetheless. From inside the Sanglah compound, he saw Puger and several PKI leaders, including Anom Dada, being taken away one night. Before I had the chance to ask him for an approximate date of that event, he stated, without equivocation or hesitation, that it was on December 16. When I asked him how he could remember the date with such certainty, he explained, "Puger was a very important man in Bali. I made a note of it."[40]

The PKI in Kapal

The Kapal massacre did not claim the lives of any of the PKI supporters who lived in Kapal. All of the victims had been brought there from elsewhere. Kapal merely served as the site of their execution, and the villagers served as gravediggers rather than executioners (except for the two recruited on the spot to kill Puger). But there were PKI supporters living in Kapal. What became of them?

The same people I interviewed in Kapal as witnesses to the massacre in the cremation ground also recounted a story about three villagers being murdered in a gruesome way on the main street. They told the same basic story. The village head, who was a PNI supporter, had agreed to protect some of the PKI supporters by allowing them to live in his residential compound in November 1965. I met one of the individuals who took shelter with him. She was his neighbor. She was teenager at the time and a member of a choir that sometimes performed at the opening ceremonies for new PKI offices in southern Bali. She was perhaps the most innocuous of PKI supporters, yet she felt her life was in danger as well. Other PKI supporters in Kapal fled to other places, such as Denpasar, and willingly placed themselves under police and army protection. Still others were arrested and placed in custody. One of them was Bhadra, the auto mechanic mentioned in chapter 5 who was held in the prison in Denpasar.

Kapal's village head, who resisted the genocide, could no longer protect those sheltering in his residential compound once the RPKAD arrived and initiated the massacres. Kapal was like a miniature version of Bali as a whole, with the village head playing the role of Sutedja in preventing violence in October and November. Poniti claims that he and the other PNI leaders in Kapal were being mocked and even threatened by PNI supporters from the surrounding villages for allowing that group of PKI supporters to remain alive. At some time in the days before the massacre at the cremation ground, a PNI crowd assembled in front of the village head's compound and insisted that the

PKI supporters inside be sent out. The village head relented. Three of them were killed on the road right in front of the compound. The PNI in Kapal had proved their anticommunist credentials. The army must have chosen Kapal as the site for an important massacre because the village PNI had already driven out or killed all of the PKI supporters.

The village head was not happy with all of the killing. Several villagers told me about an incident that occurred sometime in late December. An army truck arrived in the village and dropped off about a dozen tied-up prisoners. It was common practice: many villages received an "allotment" (*jatah*) of prisoners to execute and felt they could not resist orders from army personnel. But the village head of Kapal refused to arrange the execution of this *jatah*. He told the soldiers that the village had seen enough bloodshed and had already contributed more than its share to the anti-PKI campaign. The soldiers relented and took the prisoners down the road to the next village to find executioners and gravediggers.

The Lives of Documents

An event that I will call the Kapal massacre can be understood to be a fact. The uncertainties, inconsistencies, and gaps in the various stories presented here do not diminish the reality of the event. About thirty-five men, on or about December 16, 1965, were killed in the cremation grounds of the village of Kapal and buried there in one or two mass graves. All except one man were executed by the firing squad of RPKAD soldiers wielding machine guns. The one exception was I Gde Puger, who was killed by two men from Kapal on orders from someone who had come with the army from Denpasar. At least some, if not most, of the victims had been taken from police custody in Denpasar and brought to Kapal in armored personnel carriers. The victims included the leaders of the PKI in Bali. The massacre was organized by officers of the Kodam and RPKAD and witnessed by a group of government officials from Denpasar.

The families of the victims of this massacre never received official notification of the execution of their loved ones. They heard about the massacre from people who witnessed it or from people who had heard about it second or thirdhand. Puger's adopted son, Raka Suasta, heard about it while he was a political prisoner in 1966; his source was a policeman who had been assigned to guard the Kapal cremation grounds that night. Puger's family, certain that Puger had indeed been killed, held funerary rites for him in 1978. His widow, Dayu Rai, was allowed out of prison for several days to attend the ceremonies.

The office of the Legal Department of Kodam IX, Denpasar, Bali, 2012. Photo by John Roosa.

(In cases where the body of the deceased has disappeared, as with drownings at sea, the Balinese cremate an effigy made of reeds and soil.) The members of Puger's family, like all other families of the victims, have not demanded an exhumation of the bodies and have resigned themselves to trusting in the power of the law of karma to punish the perpetrators.

Puger's children, however, found one way to resist by using the law of the land. They launched a court case in 2004 to demand the return of the property that the Kodam had confiscated from Puger. Ironically enough, Puger's house on Yos Sudarso Street had become the office for the Kodam's Legal Department. The illicit transfer of ownership of that piece of property to the army's legal specialists says much about the status of law in Indonesia. The lawyers defending the army in court against the Puger family's suit were occupying the very land that was in contention. Another plot of Puger's land had been transferred by the army to the main university in Bali, Udayana University, which used it for its Economics Department. Two prominent institutions in Bali's capital, one for law, one for economics, were housed on stolen land.

The army's lawyers, determined to avoid the humiliation of their own eviction, fought the case for six years all the way up to the Supreme Court. The only justification they had for the confiscation of the property was the claim that Puger had been a communist. But they could not prove that claim in court. The army had executed Puger before he had ever been charged with a crime, much less proved to have been a PKI member. Puger's political affiliation also turned out to be irrelevant: the two pieces of property had been owned by Puger's father (d. 1998), who had never joined the PKI. The army lost the case at every level of the judicial system.[41] The university followed the Supreme Court's order of 2011 and vacated the property, but the Kodam refused to do likewise. The Kodam's Legal Department has persisted in its illegal occupation of the Puger family's house. There has been no police force willing to enforce the court's order on army personnel.

When Puger's house was attacked by a mob in early December 1965, the family's legal documents, like all their other belongings, were stolen. The family was able to prove ownership of their properties in court only because some of those documents had been fortuitously returned to them. Dayu Rai recalled that a woman in the mob who had grabbed the rattan case containing the documents later felt guilty about her action. Perhaps she had also decided that since the documents were worthless to her, she might as well return them. Whatever the case, it was an act of kindness. She came to Dayu Rai, then living in Puger's ancestral compound in downtown Denpasar, and apologized while returning the rattan case to her.

Other documents in Puger's house found their way into the hands of the Kodam, which then turned over the documents to the Komando Operasi Tertinggi (KOTI) in Jakarta. Officers at KOTI took it upon themselves to collect information about the PKI and its connections with international communism. The army deposited with KOTI many of the documents it confiscated from the homes and offices of PKI supporters. Once Suharto disbanded KOTI in 1967, its files were kept at the State Secretariat, which transferred them to the Arsip Nasional Republik Indonesia (ANRI, National Archives of the Republic of Indonesia) in 1980. ANRI opened up the KOTI files in 2013. It was in that year, when reviewing the list of those files, that I noticed an entry for Puger's papers. The illicitly obtained personal papers of a man who was disappeared by the army had been made public property. Any researcher in ANRI now can consult the results of the army's theft of Puger's papers, such as his personal business correspondence and family photos.[42]

One of the documents that the army found important enough to archive is a postcard to Puger from his eldest daughter. She was a talented Balinese dancer on her way to perform at the World Festival of Youth and Students in Finland in 1962. While on a stopover in Tashkent, she dashed off a postcard with a picture of the city's grand opera house. The entirety of her handwritten message is: "Wishing you a happy Galungan/Kuningan [Balinese festivals]. I hope father is healthy and in good spirits." The formerly secret archive in

Jakarta kept by military intelligence about the communist movement pretends to hold documents that reveal clandestine plotting and criminal actions. It holds instead the innocuous personal correspondence of a teenage Balinese dancer.

The Mystery of Another Burial

One of the oddities of the Kapal massacre is the mutilation of Puger. Why was he not shot like the rest? In an army operation to massacre the top communists of Bali, why should Puger have been singled out when he was not part of the PKI leadership? Even if the perpetrators believed that his patronage had been a crucial factor behind the growth of the PKI, why should they have considered Puger to have been somehow more responsible for the party's actions than the party leader himself, Ktut Kandel?

One clue that can help explain this oddity lies in Puger's relationship with Pugeg, the Tameng leader of Denpasar, who worked closely with the RPKAD commander, Major Djasmin. Pugeg was present at the massacre. It turns out that Puger and Pugeg grew up together. They were neighbors. Puger's ancestral compound is on the same street at Pugeg's, about two hundred meters to the south. Puger's widow, Dayu Rai, recalled that in the late 1940s, during the life-or-death struggle against the Dutch, they were such close friends that the two men took a vow to protect each other's families. They spent days and nights together: "they slept using the same pillow [*tidur sebantal*]." After independence, both men, respected veterans, went into business. The office of Puger's company, Majapahit, was just two doors down from the office of Pugeg's company on Gadjahmada Street, right in the middle of Denpasar's commercial district. Their friendship turned into a rivalry, and Puger was clearly the winner in this rivalry. By the early 1960s, he was much closer to Governor Sutedja and President Sukarno, and his business was much more prosperous. Pugeg, hitching his fortunes to the PNI, was marginalized.[43] I suspect that Pugeg was the one who informed the RPKAD officers that Puger was the key ringleader of the PKI who deserved special punishment. Pugeg mentioned that the RPKAD commander, Major Djasmin, came to his house immediately upon landing in Bali and consulted with him about how to attack the PKI.

Before I interviewed Pugeg in 2000, I had been told by some Balinese friends that he had become a controversial figure because he had announced that he wanted to be buried, not cremated. When I asked him about this issue, he did not give a clear reason for his unorthodox position. I thought perhaps he had been motivated by theological reasons. I asked whether it was an attempt to return to the original Vedic-era form of Hinduism in which the deceased were often buried. He replied that he had not heard about Vedic burials but was delighted to learn of them. I had unintentionally provided him a justification for a position that he had adopted for other reasons that he declined to explain to me. I suspect—this is only a suspicion—that he was committed to being buried so that he could reassure himself that the many people he was responsible for burying in mass graves in 1965–66, such as his former close friend Puger, were not suffering in the afterlife. He wanted to prove that the burial of a body is not a crime against the cosmic order. Pugeg passed away in 2008 and, instead of being cremated in the *banjar* where he lived, he was buried far away in a private plot of land that he had purchased in the southernmost part of Bali.

7

Dead Labor

Disappearances in Sumatra

The union hall was packed. People had come from all over Jakarta and the surrounding areas, even Sumatra, to attend a Cultural Night organized by the country's largest trade union confederation, SOBSI. Men and women, young and old, filled the capacious auditorium of the railway workers' union hall. They stood in the doorways and hallways and spilled out into the yards on the sides. It was a swelteringly hot evening, but the atmosphere was festive. The unionists had just participated in the grand May 1 celebrations about two weeks earlier and were still enthusiastic for more events affirming their communal solidarity.

The highlight of the evening's entertainment was a drama titled "The Brave Ones," about plantation workers struggling against the "capitalist bureaucrats" who were mismanaging the plantation. Artists of the left-wing cultural organization Lekra had collaborated with the workers of the Plantation Workers Union (Sarbupri) to write and perform the drama. One plantation worker in the audience commented afterward that he thought the drama was so true to his experiences that he could play a role in it without having to learn any acting skills. The journalist covering the event for the PKI's newspaper told him encouragingly, "Lekra is always ready to help activists from social organizations who want to improve their skills."[1] Other workers in the audience commented that the stage props were so effective that they made it seem as if the action was really at a plantation.

A contingent of SOBSI's choir performed as well. For the May 1 ceremony at Senayan Stadium, the full choir of three hundred workers had performed, but for this smaller event only forty of them were present. Their

Drawing of the Railway Workers' Union Hall near Manggarai Station, Jakarta. Image from *Sunday Courier* (Jakarta), March 8, 1953.

voices resounded within the union hall and thrilled the audience. The traditional arts were also represented on the evening's bill. A female singer of West Java, a *pesinden*, performed, as did a dance troupe, a *reog*, from East Java. For workers whose weekdays were full of sweated labor, the free entertainment and the relaxed socializing with so many other people were welcome pleasures. It was a magical night when social identities were in flux, when workers felt like artists and artists felt like workers.

The union hall that was so alive that night in May 1963, pulsing with the creative energies of working people, had been designed precisely for such events. The Railway Workers Union (SBKA) had constructed it in 1953, soon after the attainment of national independence, so that it could accommodate large crowds.[2] The union did not just want an office space for its staff. It wanted a large hall that could be used for music and dance performances and rented out at below-market rates to other organizations, especially other unions, for their meetings. The Indonesian trade unions of the time, in their literature and their meetings, repeatedly emphasized the goal of expanding educational and cultural opportunities for workers.[3]

Railway workers from all over the country chipped in small amounts of money to help build it, and some volunteered their labor to erect the high brick walls and lay the baked-clay tiles on the roof. Having been forbidden to organize and forced to accept the unilateral dictates of management during the years of Dutch and Japanese colonialism, the workers were hopeful of becoming full members of the new democratic society of independent Indonesia, on an equal standing with their better-paid and better-educated managers. They were proud of having constructed what they called a "monumental" building on land rented at a low rate from the state's railway company. Having lived through many years of war and deprivation, the workers felt as if they were finally gaining greater control over their lives.

The SBKA union hall was just two hundred meters down the street from the entrance to Manggarai Station, one of Jakarta's busiest stations. The union chose this area for its headquarters because it was home to the largest concentration of railway workers in the capital city. Just south of the station, on the far side of the tracks, tucked away from the view of train passengers, was a massive workshop, spread over many hectares of tall sheds. When the elegant, gleaming white station was opened, in 1918, so too was this workshop containing the heavy, modern equipment needed to assemble and disassemble broken-down carriages and repair locomotive engines. Hundreds of workers were employed there by the Dutch colonial state's company, Nederlandsch-Indische Spoorweg Maatschappij, from highly paid engineers to the low-paid lumpers. One still finds in the neighborhoods around the workshop many of the stately and spacious houses that were built for the white-collar employees. The less sturdy housing for the waged workers has not survived the ravages of time.

By the time independence was attained in 1949, the older members of SBKA had a wealth of experience in the politics of union organizing. They knew about the first big railway workers union, Vereeniging van Spoor en Tramweg-Personeel (VSTP, Union of Rail and Tramway Personnel), and its leaders, Sneevliet and Semaoen, and the PKI revolt in 1926–27. They had experienced the crackdown on radical unions in the aftermath of the revolt and the terrible years of the economic depression in the 1930s when many workers were fired. They had suffered under the brutal discipline of the Japanese managers and had seen fellow workers forcibly taken away to work as unpaid laborers (*romusha*) on rail lines in Burma and Malaya.

Once the Japanese surrendered in August 1945, the railway workers felt liberated. They quickly seized control of railway stations across the country. SBKA was established in early 1946 at a time when railway workers were the de facto managers of the rail network and were negotiating with the nationalist leaders over how it was to be managed in the future. The union often came into conflict with the nationalist leaders Sukarno and Hatta. At the time of the

The PKI's thirty-fifth anniversary celebration, held in the Railway Workers' Union Hall in May 1955. Photo from Oey Hay Djoen Collection, Indonesian Institute of Social History.

workers' strike in Delanggu in 1948 (see chapter 4), the SBKA, meeting for its Third Congress in nearby Surakarta, decided to send nine tons of rice to the striking plantation and factory workers. It was a direct snubbing of the nationalist leadership and a remarkable act of solidarity from a union that had little surplus rice to spare.[4]

With decades of political experience, the SBKA leaders were not just thinking about higher wages and better working conditions. It was a union that, as its bulletin stated, wished to do more than just bargain for more "sugar and coffee" for its members.[5] The members had sacrificed for the national struggle and wanted to play a role in running the country. All the political and cultural activities at the union hall represented victories for them, victories over the forces that wished to reduce them to mere drones, working all day at subsistence pay, without the ability to pursue any higher callings in life.

The SBKA was the vanguard of the union movement in all of Indonesia and a key component of SOBSI. By the 1950s, it was a large and well-organized union that was close to the Communist Party. Many of the recruits to the PKI in the early 1950s were urban workers. Indeed, during those early years, when the party was rebuilding after the murderous repression of 1948, the party was a kind of appendage of the trade unions. Aidit and his fellow youths who had taken over the Politburo were then quite poor and relied on financial support from the unions.[6] When the PKI celebrated its thirty-fifth anniversary, in May 1955, four months before the momentous general elections, it did so in the SBKA union hall, with hundreds of people in attendance. By contrast, for its forty-fifth anniversary, the party used Senayan Stadium, the largest venue in the country, with more than one hundred thousand people in attendance.

Suharto's army banned the SBKA in late 1965 and arrested nearly all the railway workers at Manggarai Station who belonged to the union, accusing them of being "directly or indirectly involved" in the September 30th Movement, even though they had done nothing to support the Movement. Military officers took over the management of the railways and then found themselves unable for many months to have the trains running because they had dismissed and imprisoned so many workers. The SBKA union hall and a workshop shed became temporary prisons. The army confined hundreds of railway workers there. Once the workers had been sent to prisons and other detention camps in the city, the SBKA building was confiscated by the state. The union was completely destroyed and the union hall—a building that represented the union's collective identity and power—was stolen from the workers.[7]

The SBKA union hall still stands near Manggarai Station. According to several local residents, the police used it for some years as a dormitory and then rented it out to the private cargo company that currently occupies it. What used to be the function hall where artistic performances, international exhibits, and PKI conferences were held is now used as a warehouse for cargo. It is filled with stacks of wooden crates and cardboard boxes. Looking around the grounds, I see no indication that it was once a union hall, though the Art Deco touches to the front and back sections of the building prompt one to suspect that it must have served a different purpose in earlier years. It has to be the most stylish warehouse in the city. At its front entrance, a steady stream of motorcycle drivers picks up packages and then drives off to deliver them. Other workers load boxes onto trucks. None of the workers I ask knows anything about the history of the building.

The 1965–66 mass violence in Indonesia appears at first glance to be a matter of politics. It was a purge of a political party, the removal of a political tendency from the body politic, a political genocide. The targets of the mass arrests and killings were people affiliated with the Communist Party. The victims came from a great variety of occupations; they were farmers, middle-class professionals, artists, small-business owners, soldiers, students, teachers, bureaucrats, and housewives. What they had in common was some kind of connection to the PKI and its mass organizations. The army that carried out the genocide was supported by the United States, which was then waging a global crusade against communism. One can understand much about the repression by using the ordinary categories of political analysis: the state, military, political parties, militias, contestation between groups within the civil society, US global power, and the Cold War.

These categories of political analysis, however, do not grasp the economics of the genocide. The army's attack on the PKI was also an attack on the working class. The literature on the mass killings has often glossed over this point. Hilmar Farid was one of the first historians to prioritize the experience of the working class in the 1965–66 violence. He wrote of a "blindspot" in political analyses that fail to connect state violence "to economic struggles over property and wealth." He complained that the human rights discourse that had dominated the writing about the violence had not attended to the question of class.

> Violations remain understood at the level of state politics, and not in the context of the dynamics of the existing capitalist order. The killing of trade union activists and workers in the plantations of North Sumatra, for example, signifies more than just a violation of human rights. It signifies a defeat for the workers and a reduction of the remaining workers' will and capacity to resist the plantation owners. Conventional human rights research does not include within its scope the profound effects that such an event can have on the hopes, expectations, self-organization, and cultural life of a community of workers.[8]

Farid's brief essay opened up a wide-ranging debate about how the 1965–66 violence should be understood within a narrative of capitalism and class struggle.[9] This chapter does not address the intricacies of that debate, which have often turned on the question of "primitive accumulation"—Marx's term in the first volume of *Capital* for the violent origins of capitalism in land enclosures, slavery, and colonialism. It is meant only to provide some insight into how the labor movement was destroyed by the army in 1965–66. It focuses on the oil workers in two provinces of Sumatra—Riau and South Sumatra. The oil industry of Indonesia at that time was concentrated in those two provinces. The main oil workers union, Persatuan Buruh Minyak (Perbum), was affiliated with the PKI's trade union confederation, SOBSI. I have chosen to focus on this particular group of workers within SOBSI because they worked at an especially strategic site of struggle; oil was one of the country's most valuable exports. Also, these two provinces have been neglected in the literature on the 1965–66 violence. By comparing these two provinces, we can gain some insight into the pattern of the mass killings. In Riau, there were very few killings. In South Sumatra, many thousands of people were killed. What explains the difference?

To place the mass killings within the narrative of class struggle requires a focus on the experience of workers both before and after 1965. As we have seen in the case of the SBKA, union workers lived with knowledge about their past and with a plan for their future. During the years from 1950 to 1965, they saw history moving in their direction for once. They had been involved in the struggles to end both the Dutch and the Japanese colonial states—states that did not recognize workers' rights. National independence brought about substantial changes: the workers had more control over their workplaces and enjoyed greater respect in the society. They could dream that their children would attend universities. The destruction of the union movement cut them off from both their sense of the past and their plans for the future.

The label "genocide" encourages us to think about the particular social groups that are listed in the 1948 Convention: ethnicities, religions, races, and nations. The label "political genocide" brings political groups, such as political parties, into the picture. We are not used to thinking about organized labor as a social group that can experience genocide. But something like a genocide did occur for union members in Indonesia: they were killed in large numbers, and their collective existence as union workers was entirely suppressed. Under the Suharto regime, all unions had to belong to one federation, and the regime exercised total control over that federation. Suharto followed a corporatist model of the state in which no organization could exist outside the state. All Indonesians were meant to be members of one big family, with Suharto as the stern (but smiling) patriarch.[10] The terminology of the regime is revealing: it banned the word *buruh* (worker) because of its association with the history of trade unionism and insisted on using the words *karyawan* and *pekerja* (employee) instead.[11]

The incarceration and killing of workers during the army's generalized repression of the PKI deserves special attention. The army was partly motivated to attack the PKI because of the party's hold on the labor movement—and that movement was very powerful in 1965, especially in the sectors that earned the most foreign exchange. Unions were demanding the nationalization of foreign-owned companies, such as the oil companies. The army generals, as they contemplated taking state power in the several years before the final showdown with the PKI, which by chance came in October 1965, believed that the destruction of the unions would be a precondition for a restoration of economic growth. To bring foreign investment back and reassure domestic investors, they knew they would have to arrange a vast reassertion of managerial control over the workplaces.[12] Major General Mokoginta, the army commander for all of Sumatra, standing above the island's four Kodam commanders, was in constant touch with the US consulate in Medan in 1964–65 to discuss strategies to counter Sarbupri's actions affecting US businesses there, such as Goodyear's rubber plantation.[13] The army was intimately involved in workplace struggles prior to 1965 because it owned and managed many companies and enforced labor discipline on behalf of foreign-owned companies.

From the Russian Revolution in 1917 to the collapse of the USSR in 1991, nearly all, if not all, of the murderous anticommunist campaigns in the world were simultaneously campaigns against organized labor. The converse is also true: nearly all the murderous campaigns against organized labor were justified as campaigns against communism, whether the unions had a connection to a communist party or not. Marxist historians have been particularly concerned to document the mass violence against unions and communist parties. It is a kind of violence that is understandable within the dynamics of capitalism. A list of the massacres that unionized workers and communists suffered worldwide during the decades of communism includes the massacres of coal miners at Blair Mountain in West Virginia in 1921, communists in Shanghai in 1927, plantation workers in Colombia in 1928, peasants in El Salvador in 1932, a great variety of laborers and leftists by the Franco regime in post-1936 Spain, Greek communists in 1944–45, Kuomintang's opponents in Taiwan in 1947, imprisoned communists in Korea in 1950, and many more besides. These individual massacres were often part of a broader campaign of terror against working-class organizations.

If scholars of genocide, following Lemkin, have tended not to write about the violence of class conflict, Marxists have tended not to write about genocide, or at least not to write about it in insightful ways. The historian Enzo Traverso has shown that Marxists have been inept at grasping the specificity of the Holocaust.[14] Two separate literatures on mass violence have emerged with little contact between them. One literature prioritizes the categories of ethnicity, race, nation, and religion; the other prioritizes class. It is possible to read the literature on genocide without ever finding a connection with capitalism, and it is possible to read Marxist histories without finding a substantive analysis of genocide.[15] The story of the complete destruction of organized labor and the mass murder of workers in Indonesia in 1965–66 lies at the intersection of the two.

It is usually assumed that workers, as people to be employed rather than eliminated, cannot be the targets of a genocide. Capitalists cannot seek to kill off all the workers when they need workers to produce the commodities they sell. But the Indonesian case suggests that when the workers are organized into a powerful union and linked to a broad-based social movement gaining hegemony over the civil society, a state may resort to large-scale massacres that approach an eliminationist logic.

Oil Workers in South Sumatra

The main city in the province of South Sumatra, Palembang, lies on the Musi River. It was constructed centuries ago by sultanates earning money from maritime trade. Ships entered the river from the Java Sea and headed about eighty kilometers upstream, where they found an amphibious city built on stilts, canals, and floating decks. When oil was discovered there in the 1890s, the landscape of the city was quickly transformed. Shell built a refinery in the early 1900s on the south bank of the river just east of the city proper in a hamlet called Plaju. Stanvac, coming to explore for oil in the Palembang area at the same time, discovered a massive oil field in its concession in 1922 and opened its own refinery four years later right next to Shell's in a hamlet called Sungai Gerong. With all the new wells being drilled in the area, Palembang was a boom town in the 1920s and 1930s, becoming the home for an unprecedented influx of managers, workers, and merchants arriving from Europe and other parts of the Netherlands East Indies. Many of the workers came from Java. The two refineries became the largest in Southeast Asia and were connected by networks of pipelines with the oil fields lying largely to the southwest. The two refineries together produced a total of about ninety thousand gallons a day, much more than the other oil-producing areas of the Netherlands East Indies.[16]

Acquiring the oil of Palembang was the single most important motivation for Japan's full-scale invasion of Southeast Asia in December 1941. Once the United States and the Netherlands East Indies imposed an embargo on oil exports to Japan in August, the Japanese government decided that it had to directly seize the oil through what it called a "southern operation." As an expert on the subject puts it, "The principal aim of the southern operation lay in getting hold of the Dutch East Indian oil resources."[17] All the military operations, from the attack on the US Navy at Pearl Harbor to the attacks on British positions in Singapore, Malaya, and Burma, were necessary consequences of the decision to occupy the oil fields and refineries of the East Indies.

An aerial view of the oil refineries in Palembang, Sumatra, ca. 1930. The Shell refinery is in the center of the photo, and the Stanvac refinery is on the left. Photo from Leiden University Libraries Digital Collection.

The refineries in Palembang and the nearby oil fields of South Sumatra produced most of the oil in the East Indies.

The Dutch, in their hasty retreat from the invading Japanese troops, inexpertly torched the Shell and Stanvac oil refineries in Palembang. The fires did not completely destroy the facilities, and the Japanese had them running again soon enough, pumping out millions of barrels of oil during the war years. Most of the fuel for the Japanese Air Force was produced at the Plaju refinery. The Allies went to great lengths to bomb Palembang and put the refineries out of commission. The US Air Force set new distance records for the Boeing B-29 Superfortress plane by flying fifty-four of them nonstop from Sri Lanka in August 1944 to bomb the refineries and drop mines in the Musi River.[18]

Once Japan surrendered in August 1945, the Indonesian workers themselves occupied the refineries and ran them in coordination with the local leaders of the Republic. The Japanese officials formally handed the refineries over to the Republic in early October at a gathering in Plaju attended by about one thousand workers. The officials of the Republic and the workers retained control of the oil refineries as more and more British troops (largely Sikhs and Gurkhas) entered Palembang from late October 1945 to March 1946 to arrange the repatriation of the Japanese and the prisoners of war.[19] The British troops left in November 1946, but not before facilitating the entrance of Dutch troops intent upon recolonizing the Indies. The British turned the fortress in the city over to Dutch military officers, not to the officials of the Republic.[20]

The local Republican leaders did not put up much resistance to the arrival of the Dutch troops. They expected that the Dutch would respect Indonesian sovereignty over the oil industry as negotiations proceeded to determine the colony's fate. The Republic, with the support of the workers' unions, had been running the industry for more than a year and had assembled a semiregular army of thousands of soldiers. The Dutch, however, had no interest in accommodating Republican control over the most valuable resource in the Indies. The Dutch reoccupation of its former colony had the same basic motivation as the Japanese occupation five years earlier: to seize the oil. Within two months of arriving, the better-organized and better-equipped Dutch troops had gone on the offensive and forced the ragtag Republican troops out of the city. In the process, they committed war crimes: Dutch planes bombed the city and navy ships shelled it from the river in early January 1947, reducing much of the city to ashes and killing between 1,000 and 3,500 civilians.[21]

During the three years of the Dutch occupation of Palembang, the executives and managers of Shell and Stanvac returned and reclaimed the oil fields and refineries. The two companies kept control of their facilities once the Dutch finally gave up on the recolonization attempt and left in December 1949. The new republic was bankrupt and disorganized; it was unprepared to either purchase or expropriate the companies' properties. As Sukarno explained in a speech to the Stanvac refinery workers in September 1950: "You will certainly ask me why it is that foreign industries are still permitted to operate in our country." His answer was simple: "We need foreign capital."[22] State officials begrudged Shell and Stanvac their oil businesses and offered only perfunctory assistance. The army occasionally confiscated pieces of their land. With the memory of the atrocities committed by the Dutch troops still fresh in their minds, Indonesians found the presence of well-paid Dutch personnel at Shell and Stanvac difficult to tolerate.

The oil workers union, Perbum, launched a strike at the Sungai Gerong refinery in January 1950, only a month after the Dutch troops had departed, and made it clear that it was the union with which the oil companies would have to negotiate. Stanvac entered into a formal process of collective bargaining with Perbum the following year. Perbum represented about eight thousand Stanvac workers at the time.[23] The union caused "continuous labor unrest, punctuated by work stoppages," in 1953 but tended to seek government mediation after that, bringing grievances before a Central Mediation Board, which then issued binding decisions that sometimes favored the union. For instance, the Board, in 1954, ruled that Indonesian workers had to be granted the same forty-five-day-long vacation that the foreign workers were granted every six years.[24]

The oil facilities of Palembang again became a source of armed conflict in the late 1950s—this time between different groups of Indonesians. The army's Troop and Area Command covering the southern half of Sumatra was headed up by Lieutenant Colonel Barlian, who decided in January 1957 to support a revolt against the central government. He allied himself with the commander of the Troop and Area Command covering the northern half of Sumatra, Colonel Maludin Simbolon. These two colonels, taking over the civilian administrations of their areas, assumed that with the country's largest foreign-exchange earners—the oil and rubber industries—in their hands, they would be able to force Jakarta to grant Sumatra greater autonomy. Barlian, headquartered in Palembang, threatened to blow up the oil refineries if central government troops attacked. His deputy requisitioned trucks and radios from Stanvac and planned on using the Sungai Gerong refinery as the rebels' headquarters.[25]

For all the bluster, Barlian could not fully commit himself to the revolt. He was constrained by the oil workers in Palembang, who were opposed to it.[26] They were capable of shutting down the refineries and sabotaging the colonels' plans. Negotiations with Jakarta dragged on for months until Simbolon and other officers decided, with encouragement from the US, to declare a parallel government, the Pemerintahan Revolusioner Republik Indonesia (PRRI), in February 1958. No longer demanding greater autonomy for the outer islands, the officers committed themselves to the establishment of a separate state. At that point, Jakarta sent troops to Sumatra to crush the rebellion and bring the oil fields back under central government control. Barlian backed out of the PRRI rebellion and refused to order his troops to fight. Many other rebel troops remained passive, though scattered bands continued a low-level guerrilla war for several years.

With the defeat of the PRRI, which had been supported by the Masjumi party, and the banning of Masjumi in 1960, the PKI's position in South Sumatra improved, even though its supporters remained a small minority in the province up to 1965. Masjumi had been the dominant party in the province, and it had promoted strident anticommunist campaigns in the name of protecting Islam. In South Sumatra, Masjumi won 42 percent of the vote in the 1955 election for the national parliament and saw its share decline slightly to 38 percent in the 1957 election for the provincial council. The PKI's share of the vote increased over those two elections, from 12 percent to 16 percent. Because the votes were distributed among a large number of political parties, the

PKI, with only 16 percent, was the second largest party in the province. Most of its votes came from the Javanese farmers and oil workers in the province who were familiar with the party in Java.[27]

Bhaskoro's Story

To understand the history of South Sumatra in the 1950s and 1960s on a more personal level, we can turn to the life history of Bhaskoro, a Javanese migrant who joined the army in Palembang. He was interviewed by a colleague of mine in 2000.[28] Relishing the role of the storyteller, he spoke in great detail about his life in the army in South Sumatra, even though he occasionally broke down in tears when recounting the suffering he had witnessed and endured.

He grew up in a village in the Sragen Regency in the Surakarta Residency during the chaotic 1940s, when just about everyone in rural Central Java was impoverished. With his mother, father, and many other relatives, he came to Sumatra in 1956 looking for land and work. Too impatient to wait for the government's transmigration office to process their application, they came on their own, without any guarantees of land ownership. After arriving at the ferry terminal in Lampung, the port city on the southern tip of Sumatra, they immediately started strategizing on how they would survive. Bhaskoro joined the army after a couple years of dead-end odd jobs in Lampung.

Bhaskoro moved to Palembang, the capital of South Sumatra, in 1958 just after the central government troops had evicted the PRRI troops. He spent nine months in basic training and then joined the South Sumatra Kodam as a private. His battalion's first assignment was to move into a remote part of the province to guard Stanvac's oil wells. Roving bands of PRRI rebels were threatening to sabotage the wells. Bhaskoro and his fellow grunts endured many deprivations and bouts of illness over six months of trekking through the jungles and engaging in firefights with the rebels.

He was relieved to be stationed in the relatively peaceful and comfortable city of Lampung in the early 1960s. His official duties were not burdensome, and he had spare time for money-making activities to supplement his meager salary. He scalped tickets at the theater owned by the Kodam and tickets for the ferry to Java. He married and started raising a family. To advance within the army, he attended a training course for the military police. He passed the course and was accepted into the military police in Palembang as a corporal in 1963.

His parents, meanwhile, had to fend for themselves since his salary was not enough to cover their expenses. As farmers, they were determined to have

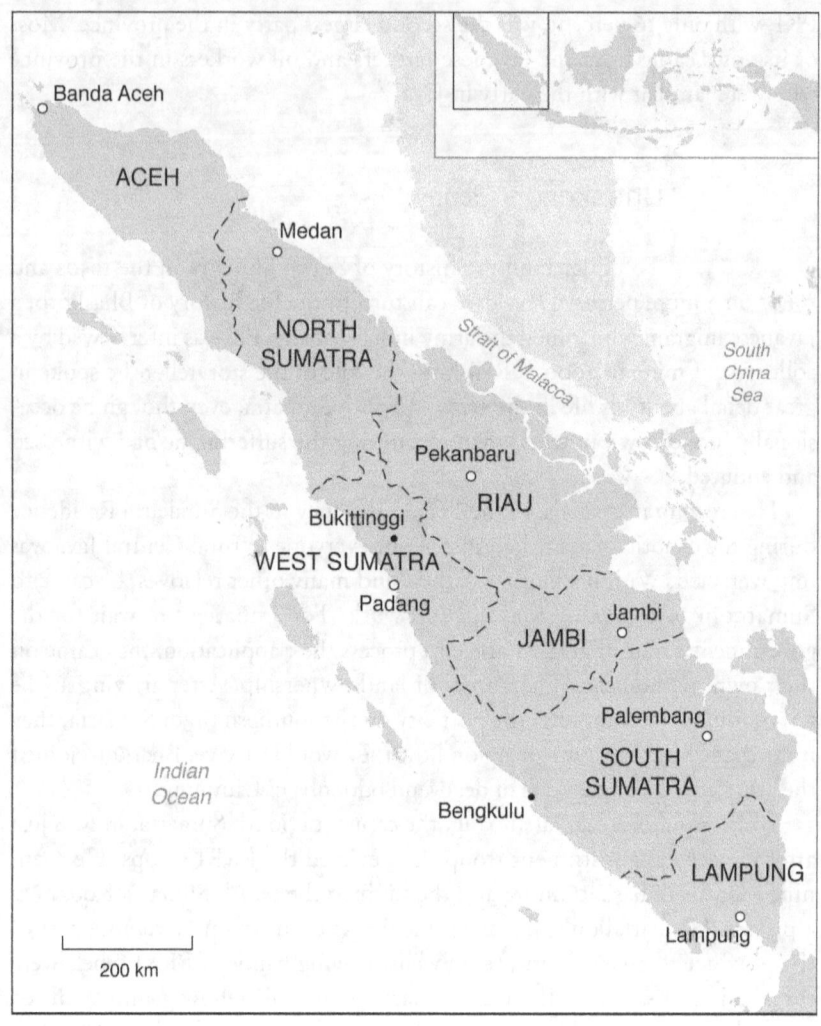

Sumatra in 1965

their own land. Barisan Tani Indonesia (BTI), the peasant union affiliated with the PKI, organized the confiscation of a large tract of state-owned land near the city of Lampung, distributed the land to poor people who wanted to farm it, and fended off the state officials who wished to evict them. Bhaskoro's parents received a piece of the land and joined the BTI. Many of those who received the land were, like them, Javanese migrants. The region of Lampung contained large numbers of Javanese. As a relatively unpopulated area, it became a frontier for Javanese settlement.

Bhaskoro, while his parents were struggling for land, was working for the military police in Palembang and was largely preoccupied with investigating military personnel accused of engaging in corruption or fighting with other military personnel: "There were thefts that involved soldiers, thieves who were protected by the police, policemen who were shot by soldiers. Those cases became routine for me. There was a soldier who opened up a brothel, things like that."

The nature of his work changed after the September 30th Movement occurred. He was assigned the task of arresting PKI supporters in Palembang. He became the adjutant of the head of the intelligence section of the military police, Captain Benny Pasuma, from Manado. They started arresting people sometime around October 6–7. Bhaskoro did not have any principled objection to these mass arrests. He was not a PKI supporter. His superior officers had told him that there had been a revolt in Jakarta and that the PKI had been responsible for it. They had to arrest everyone connected with the PKI to prevent a revolt from erupting in South Sumatra. The matter seemed simple enough to him.

Their first target was the office of the PKI's Provincial Committee. Finding no one there, they ransacked it looking for documents. The next night they raided and ransacked the Baperki building, called the Great Wall; the printing house next to it, named Krakatau; and a pharmacy run by the treasurer of Baperki's Provincial Committee.[29] They did not find many people to arrest in these raids.

Their next target was the oil workers union, Perbum, at Shell. They drove over to the Plaju refinery in the afternoon, put soldiers at all the gates, and then waited for the workers to exit at the end of the workday.

> I was ordered to close all the exit gates. There were three gates. We had a document that listed the employees who were leftists. Now I was always with Benny Pasuma, the captain. It was then that I started to feel really proud, because there were about 40 names on that document, and if I'm not mistaken, we got about 17—or was it 27?—no, it was 17 I think.... A lot of workers came out, and we asked them, "Who are you?"
>
> "My name is Pono."
>
> "OK, sir, please, um, don't go home just yet." We would ask them to stay.
>
> "Sir," he would ask. "What's up?"
>
> And then another fellow came out, the engineer Sofian Rusli, and we asked, "Sir, is this your name here?" And he said, "Yes, sir."
>
> "Please come over to this room first."
>
> "What do you want with me?"

My goodness, that engineer Rusli was really something, really first class. He even had an Italian wife, Italian!

Having taken the Shell workers into custody, Bhaskoro's team trucked them over to an empty building owned by the Forestry Department that was next to the military police headquarters. The detainees were told they would be held for questioning. The whole process was, at first, entirely polite. The families were notified and allowed to bring toothbrushes, a change of clothes, and food. Bhaskoro even took some of them to their homes to retrieve things: "They were all smart people, they owned radios, and all sorts of other stuff."

The next day, the military police repeated the same procedure at Stanvac's Sungai Gerong refinery and netted some more prisoners. The day after that, they descended upon a tire factory and the large fertilizer factory in the city, Pabrik Pupuk Sriwijaya (PUSRI), and grabbed more union workers. PUSRI was located on the north bank of the Musi River, directly across from the refineries on the south bank. There they discovered that their list of leftist employees contained an error: they had detained a chemical engineer, a Balinese man, who, it turned out, had no connection to the PKI-affiliated union. They let him go. When his family picked him up in his brand-new Chevrolet Impala, he invited a group of them to accompany him home and have dinner at his house, as a show of gratitude for being released. Bhaskoro, from a family of poor peasants, was awestruck by the luxury of his car and his home.

A US embassy official visited Palembang in late October, and Ambassador Green summarized his report on November 1 for the benefit of the State Department back in Washington: "Reportedly 600 Communists already jailed and arrests continuing. Top SOBSI officials at both the Shell and Stanvac refineries and at PUSRI Fertilizer Plant among those picked up." All the leaders of the oil workers union, Perbum, had been detained within one month of the outbreak of the Movement. The embassy had the precise numbers: "24 Perbum members picked up by Army at the Pladju refinery and 35 at the Prabumulih oil fields." The personnel managers at the refineries estimated that about fifty to seventy-five Perbum members remained to be arrested. Army officers arrived one morning at the home of a Dutch executive working for Shell and explained that they wished to arrest his cook, a suspected supporter of the PKI. The executive asked that the arrest be delayed until the cook had finished preparing lunch. He told them, "I've a big party planned." Ambassador Green recounted the incident as if it were humorous: "Arrest made after lunch."[30] A cook entrusted with preparing food for an executive's family suddenly found his life turned upside down.

Over the following weeks, the military police arrested more and more people. The middle-class detainees, like the engineers, were kept at the Forestry Department building next door while the rest were placed in Blocks B and C of the prison, which stood opposite the military police headquarters on Merdeka Street. Hundreds of detainees were crowded into these places. Soon, all the other regencies of South Sumatra and the neighboring province of Jambi (also under Kodam IV) sent their PKI detainees to Palembang for interrogation. There were so many detainees in the city that the army decided to move a portion of them to an unused warehouse on Kemaro Island, lying in the middle of the Musi River.

Bhaskoro remembers how the first detainees were killed. It was sometime in early 1966. The army's Interrogation Team had chosen four men to be executed for reasons he did not understand. A warehouse in the back of the military police compound was used as the place to beat the four men with metal rods. Their dead or unconscious bodies were then stuffed into sacks, the kind used for fertilizer and cement, "so that the blood wouldn't leak out." The sacks, weighted down with metal objects taken from the city's main scrap metal dealer, were thrown into the back of a van that the army had requisitioned from the PUSRI fertilizer factory. Bhaskoro sat in the van with several other soldiers as they headed to Ampera Bridge, the bridge over the Musi River that had just been opened (coincidentally) on September 30, 1965, to connect the north and south halves of the city. En route, they were shocked to hear a cry for help from one of the sacks but decided to ignore it.

The van stopped in the middle of the bridge. Bhaskoro kept a lookout near the vehicle while other soldiers stood at each end to block traffic. It was after midnight. Two soldiers threw the sacks into the water below, and the boatmen, plying their old wooden crafts, paddled madly to move away. Bhaskoro returned to headquarters, trembling and unable to eat. He did not realize that was only the start.

As he spoke during the interview in 2000, Bhaskoro occasionally stopped, took a deep breath, and reminded himself that he needed to tell these stories. He tried not to lose his composure: "I need to explain something—all this, what I'm talking about now, it's not meant to open up secrets for the sake of provoking revenge. I'm talking about this for the sake of justice and humanitarianism. What was done by those people was really heart-breaking." Knowing there was no justification for killing people who were already in custody, he felt compelled to speak. But knowing that other military personnel would not like him speaking about the atrocities, he also felt compelled to reassure them that he did not wish them harm.

According to Bhaskoro, the months of February to April 1966 were the peak months of killing. On many nights, batches of forty prisoners were called out of the prison, escorted across the street to the military police headquarters, beaten to death, and stuffed into sacks. With so many people to kill, the soldiers arranged the killing in the manner of an assembly line. They turned the warehouse in the compound of their headquarters into a slaughterhouse. The prisoners were brought in, one at a time, whacked on the back of the head with a metal rod until lifeless, and then stuffed into burlap sacks. The sacks (made in the Delanggu factory in Java) were then tied with wire at the top. Blunt force to the head was the preferred method of killing since gunfire created too much noise. The headquarters was downtown, close to many other buildings, and people would hear the shots and become curious about what was happening. The soldiers could not continue to use the Ampera Bridge in the middle of the city. Throwing that many corpses into the river would attract too much attention. They started to truck the corpses to uninhabited spaces outside of the city and bury them in mass graves. To complete the whole process under the cover of darkness, the killing squads began around 8:00 p.m.

> The quota [*jatah*] for each night was about forty people, because with forty, you had time to execute them, get them into the truck, and take them to the mass grave. That was the quota because everything had to be finished by 3:00 a.m.

Bhaskoro was invited to be one of the killers inside the slaughterhouse, but he declined, appealing to superstition. He said his wife was pregnant and that killing at such a time could bring bad luck upon the baby. His wife lived in Lampung, and so his fellow soldiers would not easily discover the fact that she was not pregnant. The brutality of the beating was more than he could bear.

> It was the Interrogation Team that determined who had to be executed. We just picked them up [from the prison]. But I didn't enter the warehouse, using that excuse, that my wife was pregnant. It was only an excuse. I just couldn't take it. I can't stand the sight of blood. I know it sounds strange, a soldier who can't bear to see blood, but, well, that's the way it was. If I had been ordered to shoot them maybe I would have been able to.

One night, as the prisoners were being executed, he recognized some of the union activists he had rounded up months earlier.

> Among the places we used for the mass graves was Kampung Kenten [about twenty kilometers outside the city]. I helped transport them to that place two times, and one of the times I knew a lot of the guys from their

time in detention. Hey, there was a guy from Sungai Gerong, others from Plaju and PUSRI, the ones that I had captured earlier. The one whose name I remember is Pono, he was a chemist, if I'm not mistaken. He was part of the company's staff, a Javanese guy. Then there was Sofian Rusli, who wore his sunglasses day and night, and they were really striking. Today, they would probably cost hundreds of dollars.

The fancy sunglasses were memorable objects for Bhaskoro: "probably only Sukarno had glasses like that then." The soldiers took his glasses from him and blindfolded him before leading him into the slaughterhouse for execution. One of Bhaskoro's friends received the glasses as his share of the loot taken from prisoners.

As the adjutant for the military police officer in charge of the anti-PKI campaign in Palembang, Bhaskoro understood exactly *how* the prisoners were executed. But he did not understand *why* the prisoners were executed. The order must have come from the Kodam commander, Brigadier General Makmun Murod. Bhaskoro did not know what motivated Murod. He assumed the order to kill the prisoners was a result of the army's lack of money to keep feeding them. The army had taken into custody far more people than it could afford to feed. By March and April 1966, "the budget wasn't enough, and then the places of detention were overcrowded, and the army troops were getting tired."

Bhaskoro was a perpetrator—a low-level one, but still a perpetrator. He later became, surprisingly enough, a victim. He was arrested in 1970 and held as a political prisoner. At the time of the arrest, his career prospects seemed bright. He had been promoted to sergeant in 1967 for his work in Palembang and then put in charge of a newly opened military police post in a district in Lampung.

His troubles began in Lampung. He came into conflict with a superior officer who resorted to the underhanded tactic of reporting him as an underground agent of the PKI. The fact that his parents in Lampung had been members of the PKI-affiliated peasants' union, BTI, was used against him. His parents had been classified as C prisoners and released in the late 1960s, but they were required to remain within the city limits and seek permission from a government official if they wished to travel outside Lampung. Bhaskoro, guilty by association, was held for nine years without trial.

It was precisely because he had become a victim that he was willing to speak at length about the army's crimes of 1965–66 in a recorded interview. He admitted that if he had not been imprisoned he would probably be unwilling to talk about the disappearances: "At that time I had no idea that later I would become a victim. I was still committed to guarding state secrets." He regretted that he did not compile a set of documents that could confirm all of his stories: "If I had known that I would become like this I would have kept a lot of documents."

Many of the elements of Bhaskoro's story of the killings in Palembang are confirmed by other victims and witnesses.[31] Ibu Murtini, a senior Gerwani activist in Lampung, was held in Palembang in early 1966.[32] She had been captured in a village on January 1, after several months of disguising herself as a peasant. The military police, viewing her as a PKI "kingpin," escorted her and a member of the PKI's Provincial Committee to Palembang for questioning. While being held for the month of February in the military police headquarters, she saw the warehouse that was used as the place of execution. She remembers seeing Sofian Rusli, the engineer with the expensive sunglasses. He had studied chemical engineering in the Soviet Union, and PKI supporters in South Sumatra admired him for his intelligence and prestigious position.

Ibu Murtini is one of the few survivors of the detention camp on Kemaro Island. She was confined there from March 1966 until late 1967. Some of the prisoners, she reports, were taken away and executed. Most died of starvation and the diseases brought on by malnutrition. She recalls that the military police stopped providing food to the camp in early June 1966 and allowed the prisoners to slowly starve to death. The guards cleared out the dead bodies daily, placing them in sacks, weighting them with scrap metal, and then throwing them in the river. She survived by eating scraps of food, such as banana peels, obtained from vegetable sellers plying the river in small boats.

One of the witnesses to the mass death in Palembang was Taufik Keimas, who later became a powerful politician in the country. He married Sukarno's daughter, Megawati, in 1973 and helped her lead the Partai Demokrasi Indonesia-Perjuangan (PDI-P, Indonesian Democratic Party of Struggle), a political party that grew out of the PNI in the 1990s. When she ruled as president of Indonesia (2001–4), he wielded much power behind the throne. But in 1965, he was an ordinary twenty-three-year-old activist in Palembang affiliated with the PNI's youth wing. He spent six months helping the army arrest PKI supporters after the September 30th Movement but found himself sharing the same prison with them when he protested the anti-Sukarno campaign backed by the Kodam. He was arrested by the military police along with twenty other PNI activists in March 1966. He then saw firsthand how the PKI prisoners were being treated.

Imprisoned for more than a year, Keimas witnessed the gradual removal of all of the PKI prisoners. He estimated that about ten thousand political prisoners were held in South Sumatra and that fewer than one hundred of them survived: "Every night, about one hundred were executed."[33] In one respect, he thought the Indonesian state at that time was worse than Nazi Germany, which at least kept some written records of their killings: "Any one alleged to be associated with the PKI was tortured and then finished off just like that, without any documentation or court trial."[34]

The PNI prisoners like Keimas were treated much better than the PKI prisoners. None were taken out at night and disappeared. Still, they suffered malnutrition from the meager rations—"four spoonfuls of rice a day." One of Keimas's fellow student activists died because of the poor prison conditions.[35] Keimas survived, and his faithfulness to Sukarno served him well, making him a suitable match for Megawati. Despite his prominence, his statements in 2008 about the executions and starvation deaths in Palembang did not attract attention.

The brutalities in Palembang became widely known among political prisoners being held elsewhere in Indonesia at that time. The PKI leader Sudisman, in his last statement before he was to be executed in late 1968, mentioned Kemaro Island in a list of detention camps in Indonesia where prisoners had died of starvation. He must have received information about the deaths from party activists before he was thrown in prison in Jakarta in December 1966 or from his fellow political prisoners thereafter. It turned out to be accurate information.

> In Kemarau Island in South Sumatra about 10,000 comrades died because they had only been given 50 kernels of corn and one small mug of water a day; they were PKI supporters from Jambi, Bengkulu, Lampung, and South Sumatra. They died without having been processed and an interrogation report typed up; they had only their age, name, and address noted down. They died because the calories of their rations were only a little more than those of the rations for prisoners during Japanese military rule. But they were, in terms of both quantity and nutritional quality, far below the rations during the Dutch imperial occupation, before and after World War Two.[36]

Today, Kemaro Island is a tourist attraction in Palembang. The local government built a Buddhist pagoda on the island in 2006 to honor a legend about the drowning deaths of four individuals: a Muslim princess who belonged to the precolonial Palembang sultanate, her husband, their faithful servant, and a Chinese merchant. The story about these four deaths in the Musi River is drawn from an old folktale, not from real-life events. The folktale is recounted on a plaque next to the pagoda as "The Legend of Kemaro Island."

This patently obvious invention of tradition, encouraging tourists to imagine a local heritage of interethnic, interreligious, and interclass harmony, hides the horror of the recent violence. There is nothing on the island to commemorate the real deaths of hundreds, if not thousands, of Indonesians at the hands of other Indonesians within meters of the pagoda. The skeletons of the victims lie in the riverbed all around the island, but tourists are asked to think about a mythical story of four bodies lying underwater. The barracks and the barbed-wire fence of the prison camp no longer exist, and most sections of the camp's concrete perimeter wall are covered by thick vegetation.

The army's destruction of the oil workers union in Sumatra allowed the army to dominate the oil industry after 1965. The key man in the Suharto regime in charge of the oil industry was Ibnu Sutowo, a doctor turned army officer who had gained his initial knowledge of the industry while in Palembang from the mid-1940s to the mid-1950s. His commissioned memoir, written by the same author-for-hire who wrote Suharto's memoir, barely acknowledges the existence of oil workers and is written as if the oil came out of the ground of its own accord, ready for him to sell. Sutowo mentions the oil workers only once in the five-hundred-page memoir, and that brief mention is in relation to 1965: "Arrests of people happened. The dismissal of some employees affiliated to the PKI had to be done."[37] It would be difficult to compose a more euphemistic description of the events.

Ibnu Sutowo was a physician. He understood the physical effects of starvation. He had seen those effects with his own eyes in Palembang when he was posted there in late 1945 to help restore the Dutch, British, and Australian prisoners of war to good health so that they could be repatriated. The Japanese had held the POWs in a prison camp near the Sungai Gerong oil refinery and had provided very little food to them. As he recounted in his memoir, "The prisoners were in a really sad state. Their body weight was on average less than 50 kilograms."[38] Some 350 POWs died of starvation in that camp during the war years.[39] Ibnu Sutowo must have known but could not admit what Sudisman had pointed out: the Indonesian army in 1965–66 outperformed the Japanese army in killing off and starving prisoners in Palembang.

Oil Workers in Riau

Yoseph Taher grew up around the oil wells in the province of Riau in the 1950s.[40] His father worked for Caltex, an American company that resulted from the merger of the Texas Company (later Texaco) and Standard Oil of California (later Chevron) and that had only just started drilling for oil in that area in the early 1950s. Although Caltex was a newcomer to the Indonesian oil business, it quickly outproduced the older companies, Shell Oil and Stanvac, because, by chance, it had discovered the largest oil field in Southeast Asia—the Minas Field just north of the provincial capital, Pekanbaru. Taher and his family lived in Pekanbaru when Caltex was rapidly growing and recruiting more workers.

Taher's parents had come to work in Sumatra as indentured laborers, or "contract coolies" as they were called, from Central Java in the 1920s. His mother and father met on a rubber plantation where his father had worked his way up to be a foreman by virtue of his ability to read and write. Taher, born in 1938, spent his first years in a coal-mining town, Sawahlunto, in West Sumatra, where his father had found work, again as a foreman.[41] When the Japanese invaded in 1942, the family fled into the forest and succeeded in eking out a subsistence from hunting and gathering for some months before they were discovered and forced into unpaid labor. The Japanese put Taher's father to work with hundreds of other men on the construction of a rail line leading from the small, remote town of Singingi to Pekanbaru. Among his fellow starving *romusha* was a Dutch man who had been his boss at the rubber plantation years earlier.

The defeat of Japan meant liberation for Taher's family. The call of *merdeka* (independence) in August 1945 meant more than national liberation for them. It meant an end to decades of coolie labor. They moved to Pekanbaru, and Taher's father joined the ill-organized Indonesian army as a sergeant. He fought against the Dutch troops who reoccupied Riau in 1946. Upon the withdrawal of the Dutch troops in 1949, Taher's father quit the military and sought a steady job that did not involve combat. He became a worker in the maintenance department at Caltex, painting the buildings. His job at Caltex was different from all of his previous jobs: for the first time in his life, he was protected by a union. Independent Indonesia had new labor laws that recognized the right of workers to form unions. Taher's father volunteered for the union and served as the treasurer of the local branch. As a veteran of the struggle for independence, he was a respected member of the society.

For Taher, the oil workers union in Pekanbaru was just one organization within a whole constellation of like-minded organizations. As a high school student in the 1950s, he had joined the PKI's youth group, Pemuda Rakjat, because it was related to his father's union. A large number of his friends and neighbors belonged to the PKI or one of its affiliated organizations. Within one family, it was common for individuals to belong to the different PKI-affiliated organizations according to their age, gender, occupation, or personal inclinations: university students joined Consentrasi Gerakan Mahasiswa Indonesia

(CGMI, Indonesian Student Movement Center), housewives joined Gerwani, those with artistic talents joined Lekra, and so on. His girlfriend's uncle was a union member, and her aunt was a Gerwani leader and a member of the provincial parliament. Her grandfather had led the PKI's armed revolt in West Sumatra in 1926–27 and had been exiled to Boven Digul.[42]

To some extent, the left movement in Riau and other provinces in Sumatra represented an importation of the political culture of Java. The coolies who had come to Sumatra during Dutch colonial rule, like Taher's parents, were from poor Javanese communities that had been influenced by the PKI. Taher's father had been raised in Semarang by an uncle who was a railway worker. When the uncle was imprisoned by the Dutch colonial state at the time of the 1926–27 PKI revolt, Taher's father was orphaned and had to find work on his own. In that desperate situation, he was willing to submit himself to the indignities and deprivations of coolie labor in Sumatra. Many Javanese workers recognized the PKI as a party that represented their interests, and they carried that loyalty to the party when they moved to find work in Sumatra. Not all of its supporters on the island were Javanese. The family of Taher's girlfriend, for instance, were of the Minang ethnic group from West Sumatra. But most of the non-Javanese ethnic groups in Riau supported other parties. The PKI won only 6 percent of the vote in the province of Central Sumatra in the 1955 elections.

For Taher, being a PKI supporter in Riau was not something radical and subversive. It was quite conventional. Communists formed a large minority in the provincial capital where the union members lived. They did not constitute a small, inward-looking cult. His ambitions were similar to those of his non-communist peers: a university education, a good job, and a family. In the early 1960s, Taher and his girlfriend hoped to attend university together at the Patrice Lumumba University in Moscow.

Taher wound up staying in Pekanbaru and abandoning his plan for a university education after he obtained a job at Caltex in 1962. He recalls that competition for the jobs there was fierce. The pay was high, and the benefits were extraordinary. Caltex had its own hospital with ultramodern equipment. The company once paid for his whole family to fly in a plane to and from Java for a vacation. It may seem odd that PKI supporters were happy to be working for an American multinational company, but Taher believed that the good wages and working conditions at Caltex were products of the union's struggles. If Caltex was willing to negotiate agreements with Perbum, then working for it was perfectly acceptable. Many Caltex managers prioritized on-the-job performance and did not make an issue of the political leanings of the unionists. An American manager was so pleased with the work of Taher's communist father that he arranged for him to do the same work as a private contractor after he reached the mandatory retirement age of fifty-five.

Nevertheless, at the national level, the relationship between Caltex and the Indonesian government was always tense. Many officials, not just PKI leaders, did not like the idea of foreign companies profiting from the country's natural wealth. The government did not award any new concessions to foreign oil companies in the 1950s, hoping to build up domestic companies to replace them. The American government's support for the PRRI Revolt in 1957–58 in Sumatra made business much more difficult for American companies such as Caltex. They were widely suspected of being extensions of the CIA, bent on sabotaging Indonesia while using their businesses as covers.

The nationalization of Dutch enterprises in 1958—a consequence of Indonesia's campaign to gain sovereignty over West Papua, which was still under Dutch control—established a precedent. The PKI saw that nationalization as a great victory against imperialism and consistently pressured the government to nationalize all other foreign enterprises. The trade union federation SOBSI wrote up a manual on nationalization and held training sessions for its members on how they should fight for it.[43] The government resisted nationalizing the oil companies, seeing them as too important to the economy. It treated the Anglo-Dutch multinational Shell as a British company rather than a Dutch company so that it did not have to nationalize it in 1958.

Relations deteriorated even further once Sukarno's Confrontation against Malaysia began in 1963. This time British companies were nationalized because of Britain's support for Malaysia, and a mob burned down the British embassy in Jakarta. Sukarno issued his Deklarasi Ekonomi (Dekon, Economic Declaration), which was partly written by PKI leaders. Shell was still allowed to operate, but its executives had lost the determination to stay and planned on selling the company to the government. In this hostile political climate, other foreign companies believed that their turn would come soon. American companies were especially vulnerable because the US was supporting Britain and Malaysia.

The crisis for the US companies, Caltex and Stanvac, came in March 1965 after the US sold weapons to Malaysia. In Palembang, a coalition of the oil workers unions affiliated with the PKI, PNI, and NU declared on March 18 that Stanvac's Sungai Gerong refinery was the property of the Indonesian state. Their declaration was for symbolic purposes. Instead of occupying the facility, they called upon state officials to carry out the nationalization of Stanvac.[44] In Riau, a similar action was taken, though the PKI leader in Jakarta overseeing the provincial committee complained that the unionists of Perbum at Caltex hesitated for days in deference to the PNI-affiliated union, which was not in favor of demanding immediate nationalization.⁴⁵ In Jakarta, at the same time, the PKI led demonstrations at the head offices of Stanvac and Caltex.⁴⁶

The Indonesian government responded immediately to the workers' actions. The Third Deputy Prime Minister, Chaerul Saleh, summoned representatives of the oil companies, such as Caltex, Shell, and Stanvac, to his office in Jakarta on March 20, where they were informed that the government was taking temporary "control" of the companies. It was a vague formulation that seemed largely meant to placate the workers and allow oil production to resume. Saleh did not nationalize the oil companies at that time, but he indicated that the government was working toward that end.⁴⁷ The oil companies continued operations as before, with the sword of Damocles over their heads, up to the October crisis.

The September 30th Movement was a nonevent in Riau. Nothing happened there in connection with the Movement. Taher recalls the great confusion among PKI supporters in Pekanbaru in October. They had taken no actions in support of the Movement and knew nothing about it, but they were quickly accused of being traitors and killers.⁴⁸ The anticommunist groups in the city demonstrated in the streets in October and called for the banning of the PKI. Taher and his family moved to the house of his wife's relatives in the hope that they might be safer staying together. Tense weeks passed. Taher kept going to work as usual and hoped the crisis would pass. Instead, the situation worsened. The military police raided their house on November 17 and took away his wife's aunt, Ibu Jainsah, who was the local Gerwani leader and a member of the provincial parliament.

The next day at work, his supervisor handed him a list of several names of his coworkers and ordered Taher to round them up and truck them over to a nearby school, where the military police wanted to question them. He did as he was told. Once that task had been completed and the workday was over, his supervisor drove him over to the same school and, much to his surprise, handed him over to the military police as well. The detainees were nervous but not especially fearful. "We all thought, 'Ah, it will just be one or two days.'"⁴⁹ They had not been part of the Movement and had done nothing criminal, so they assumed that they would be released once the military discovered that.

Taher and the other detainees from Caltex were trucked from the school to the military prison in Pekanbaru that night. There, they met other detainees who had come from all over the city and the surrounding districts. Altogether, there were about five hundred of them. Many of them he knew: "They were all members and leaders of Perbum, BTI, Pemuda Rakyat, IPPI, CGMI, SBPP, SBKB, Lekra, SOBSI, and the PKI itself. About twenty-five women were there, Gerwani members, including my wife's aunt Ibu Jainsah, and some others whom I knew, who were kept in one room reserved for women."⁵⁰ The detainees were kept there week after week, housed in barracks, with no further information provided as to what would happen to them. In January 1966, Taher and the other Perbum members received letters from Caltex telling them that they had been "dishonorably discharged" from their jobs. He heard around the same time that Caltex had purged nearly all Perbum members from its workforce. It was a mass firing: about 75 percent of the employees were Perbum members.

The approximately five hundred detainees in the military prison in Pekanbaru were interrogated one by one during 1966. Torture was standard operating procedure during the interrogations. The detainees were assigned a classification of either A, B, or C. Taher, like most of them, was classified as B. He was considered too much of a danger to be released back in the society (as the C prisoners were) but not significant enough to be put on trial (as the A prisoners were). The B prisoners were in legal limbo and faced indefinite detention. Nearly all the B prisoners in Java, some eleven thousand of them, were shipped to Buru Island in 1969–70, but most of those in Sumatra were kept in prisons in Sumatra, where they suffered from hunger and disease. The forced labor of the Dutch and Japanese periods was reintroduced, and the political prisoners were put to work as unpaid laborers on construction projects around Pekanbaru, such as the project to build the city's grand mosque, the An-Nur Mosque.

The key army officer in Riau at the time was Brigadier General Kaharuddin Nasution. He had led the operation to attack the PRRI troops in Riau in 1958 and had stayed on after the operation to control the province for the central government. He had established the new Korem that covered all of Riau. The Korem was directly under Kodam III, which was headquartered in the city of Padang, in the neighboring province of West Sumatra. Even after he became governor of Riau in 1960, he wielded a great deal of influence over the Korem commanders. He remained an active-duty officer, and he outranked them. Moreover, Nasution, not the Korem commander, was the regional authority in charge of the campaign for the Confrontation against Malaysia (the Pepelrada).

Kaharuddin Nasution ordered the mass arrests and incarcerations of the PKI supporters in October but not their executions. As long as he was in charge, the political prisoners in Pekanbaru were not disappeared from their places of detention. He did what a fellow Sukarnoist officer, Ibrahim Adjie, did in West Java: repress the PKI without mass murder. The Kodam III commander in Padang, Brigadier General Panuju, was following the same policy. There were not many massacres in the other Korem under Panuju's control, the one covering West Sumatra, and those that did occur there seem to have taken place after Panuju was dismissed, in February 1966. The new commander encouraged the militant anticommunist civilians—such as those who had supported the PRRI before—to attack the PKI.[51]

The executions of prisoners that occurred in Pekanbaru were in September 1966, when Nasution was away in Jakarta to attend a meeting of provincial leaders.[52] His temporary replacement, Colonel Subrantas Siswanto, either organized the executions himself or acquiesced to the demands of others. It is possible that civilian anticommunists, especially those who had supported PRRI and wanted revenge on the PKI, demanded the executions and Colonel Subrantas capitulated to their demands, hoping to curry favor with them. Starting in May 1966, the new anti-PKI student groups in Riau, the chapters of Kesatuan Aksi Mahasiswa Indonesia (KAMI) and Kesatuan Aksi Pemuda Pelajar Indonesia (KAPPI, Indonesian Youth and Student Action Front), condemned Nasution for being too soft on the PKI, though the party had been already thoroughly repressed, and insisted that he be dismissed.[53] The civilian elite of the province, including many of the businessmen, largely consisted of Masjumi supporters, and they saw a chance during the anti-PKI campaign of staging a comeback after being banned during Sukarno's Guided Democracy. Nasution, the governor, was an obstacle for them since he had been enforcing the ban on Masjumi and had even arrested some of the party leaders.

During Nasution's absence in September, forty-nine detainees were taken out of the military prison and were never heard from again. Taher kept a count at the time. Among the victims was his wife's uncle: "He embraced me and whispered into my ear in the Minangkabau language: 'I know where I'm being taken. Take care of your younger sisters and brothers. OK!' With tears falling from my eyes, I nodded, even though I didn't know what was going to happen to myself. . . . He, Muhktar Bagindo Marajo, was taken out by the authorities and disappeared in who knows what forest!"[54] His uncle and the others were taken out at night, loaded onto trucks, and then massacred in remote locations where there were few witnesses.

The executions would have probably continued had Nasution not returned to Riau. Another prisoner, a close friend of Taher's, was told by a guard that the military had created a kill list that ranked the prisoners in order of priority. Nasution wound up stopping them after they had reached the forty-ninth prisoner on the list. Taher himself can remember the names of twenty-one of the disappeared. Fellow prisoners who survived can remember the names of twenty more. There are still eight victims whose names they do not know. Ten of the forty-one individuals whose names they can remember were Perbum members at Caltex, and one of those was the head of SOBSI in Riau, a man named Zainuddin. Taher and his fellow prisoners heard through prison guards and their networks of friends in Pekanbaru about four different locations for the mass graves on the outskirts of the city.[55]

Prisoners elsewhere in the province were likewise vulnerable, even if the general policy was not to kill all of them, as was the policy in South Sumatra. Nasution, like the Kodam commander headquartered in West Sumatra, Panuju, could not control all of the troops and anticommunist civilians. Taher and other surviving victims compiled information on massacres outside the provincial capital, Pekanbaru, and estimated the number of dead to be about three hundred. The prisoners were taken out in boats or trucks and disappeared. The three members of the provincial committee for Riau, including its head, Abdullah Alihamy, were not summarily executed. All three were put on trial. Alihamy was executed after being sentenced to death, while the other two were sentenced to life in prison.[56]

The anticommunists of Riau, encouraged by like-minded officers within the army, denounced Nasution in 1966 for being too soft on the PKI and lobbied Jakarta for his removal as governor. The Suharto regime concurred and removed him in October 1966. The next governor, an army officer originally from Riau and with ties to the civilian elite of the area, did not resume the execution of prisoners, though the officer who had been responsible for executions in September 1966, Colonel Subrantas Siswanto, remained in good standing in Riau. He served under the new governor and then became governor himself in 1978.

Taher and the other political prisoners being held indefinitely without charge in Pekanbaru were freed in 1978–79. It was a time when the Suharto regime was releasing political prisoners throughout the country (excepting those already put on trial and convicted). Taher found his newfound freedom intolerable: he was under constant surveillance by the state and treated as a pariah by the society. He left the country soon after his release and became a migrant worker in Malaysia and Singapore. History had come full circle: his father had been a migrant worker from Java who settled in Sumatra and, after many sacrifices, had helped build unions that guaranteed stable, well-paying jobs from 1950 to 1965. Workers in Riau became full citizens with rights, creating communities where the children attended school and adults engaged in cultural activities. The army's repression of the unions in 1965 ended one generation's struggle and returned Indonesian workers to the conditions of colonial-era coolies and *romusha*.

The denial of workers' rights in the oil sector was ongoing. In 1985 the Suharto regime forced Caltex to fire 600 of its workers and forced other oil companies to fire 1,400 of their workers. The regime alleged that all of those workers were still secretly working for Perbum, the union that it had banned twenty years earlier. The oil companies themselves were upset by this unnecessary disruption in their operations. An industry bulletin noted that "labor problems on Indonesian oilfields have been minimal, and company sources were at a loss to explain why government security agency Kopkamtib ordered the purge."[57] The official who ordered the arbitrary purge was the labor minister, Sudomo, whose previous position was Kopkamtib commander.

During the Suharto years, workers were strictly policed. Kopkamtib, the army's special agency set up in late 1965 to organize the repression of the PKI, remained in existence, complete with unchecked emergency powers. Instead of being concerned about external threats to Indonesia, it was focused on citizens deemed by the regime to be internal enemies, such as striking workers. Kopkamtib put itself in charge of industrial labor relations and worked through the army's Territorial Command to expand its interventions after a rash of wildcat strikes in the early 1980s. With a name change to Bakorstanas in 1988, it continued the same function: using the emergency powers of the army within Indonesian society to wage war on striking workers.[58] One of the first acts of the post-Suharto reformers in 1999 was to disband Bakorstanas.

Conclusion

If one visited the oil-rich provinces of South Sumatra and Riau in December 1965, one would have found thousands of people being held in prisons and detention camps. The oil workers union, Perbum; the PKI; and the broad range of organizations affiliated with the PKI had been targeted for a thoroughgoing campaign of political repression. One would not have found, however, that many people had been killed. The anticommunist civilians, who far outnumbered the PKI supporters, had not immediately set about slaughtering them after October 1. In both provinces, the army's Territorial Command had organized the arrest and detention of vast numbers of people without much bloodshed. The army had not set civilian militias loose to massacre the PKI supporters. If one had returned one year later, one would have found that nearly all the prisoners in South Sumatra had been killed but that most of prisoners in Riau were still alive. Why should the fate of the prisoners been different?

The Kodam based in Palembang, covering South Sumatra and the neighboring provinces of Lampung and Jambi, organized a massive operation to capture PKI supporters and then transport them to Palembang for processing. By early 1966, the Kodam and its military police detachment assigned to interrogate the prisoners were overwhelmed. Army officers either could not obtain enough money to feed the prisoners or did not want to spend any more money on them. The army officers decided that they could not continue to hold the prisoners but that they could not be returned to their communities.

The decision taken around February 1966 was to reduce the prison population by executing batches of prisoners every night. Their bodies were trucked to uninhabited locations outside the city to be buried in unmarked mass graves. Later, around June 1966, food rations were stopped and the remaining prisoners were allowed to starve to death. All of these deaths were disappearances: the families of the prisoners were not informed of their deaths much less the location of their corpses.

The timing of the killings within the area covered by Kodam IV suggests that the army did not begin the repression of the PKI with the intention of killing the people it arrested. The executions and starvation deaths occurred after it was already clear to the officers of Kodam IV that the lives of the PKI prisoners had no value. The army high command in Jakarta had by early 1966 ordered killings in Central Java, East Java, and Bali and had at least approved of mass killings in other provinces, such as Aceh. The killings in Palembang could have easily been avoided if the army had been willing to commit the resources to either keep the prisoners alive while in prison or arrange their release.

One might suppose that the fact that Riau had far few killings was the result of a simple demographic difference: Riau (the mainland part, excluding the Riau Islands) had a little over one million people in 1965 whereas the area covered by Kodam IV had about five million. Riau also had fewer Javanese people, while the area under Kodam IV included Lampung Province, where there were many Javanese migrants who were more likely than native Sumatrans to support the PKI. The Korem covering Riau imprisoned fewer people than the Kodam in Palembang. But a purely demographic explanation for the difference in the death toll does not take into account the fact that the Korem in Riau could have decided to kill the prisoners there, regardless of the relative lack of pressure on its resources, and some officers within the Korem were willing to order executions of the prisoners. One has to consider the politics of the army officers within the Territorial Command and the civil administration.

The governor of Riau, Brigadier General Kaharuddin Nasution, who largely controlled the Korem for the province, had been a stalwart of Sukarno's Guided Democracy and was not ready to countenance massacring people with whom he had been working for years. The Kodam covering Riau and the neighboring province, West Sumatra, was commanded by an officer with similar ideological leanings, Brigadier General Panuju. He tried to limit the killings in West Sumatra and was removed from his post in February 1966 as the anti-Sukarnoists in the army high command (such as the commander for all of Sumatra, Major General Mokoginta) consolidated their grip over the army. The replacement for Panuju as Kodam commander, Colonel Poniman, took his orders from Mokoginta and imposed the same harsh policies on Riau and West Sumatra:

he vigorously purged the army and the government of Sukarno supporters (considered to be too weak in repressing the PKI) and whipped up crowds of students and youths to denounce and intimidate Sukarnoists and communists. The massacres in West Sumatra began at that point.[59] Kaharuddin Nasution, having spent six years building the provincial administration of Riau after the military operation against the PRRI, had a firm grip on power and could not be easily undermined or dismissed by Poniman. He held onto power long enough to prevent the large-scale massacres that some anticommunist officers and politicians were demanding. He faced much opposition over the course of 1966 until he too was finally forced out of office in October 1966.

In both Riau and South Sumatra, the PKI was a small political party overshadowed by anticommunist parties. After October 1, 1965, the anticommunist civilians did not immediately rise up and slaughter the PKI supporters, even though their numbers suggest that they could have. The army and the civil governments of these areas in late 1965 were behaving much like their counterparts in Bali: they were not in favor of a policy of repressing the PKI through mass murder, and they were able to keep the civilian anticommunists in check. The repression proceeded through mass arrests and detentions. Riau, under Nasution, was able to sustain that policy, though some massacres did take place there, while Kodam IV in Palembang, under Brigadier General Makmun Murod, ended the policy in early 1966 and murdered nearly all of its prisoners. He was rewarded for his service. Murod remained as Kodam commander until June 1967 and then rose through the ranks to become chief of staff of the army for four years in the 1970s.[60]

The mass arrests and massacres in Riau and Palembang were part of a more general campaign against the oil workers union and the PKI. All of the gains that the union movement had made over the first twenty years of national independence, from 1945 to 1965, were suddenly and irrevocably wiped out.[61] The activists of a movement committed to working-class power were systematically hunted down and killed off. Some of them starved to death on Kemaro Island in the middle of the Musi River, situated directly north of the oil refineries. As they died behind barbed wire, they could see the refineries standing on the opposite bank, with the steam billowing up from the cooling towers and the bright lights shimmering across the water at night. The Suharto regime reduced the value of their lives to nothing and welcomed foreign investors back to operate the refineries. Ibnu Sutowo and many other state officials became immensely wealthy, building fortress-like mansions in Jakarta, while the workers and the Indonesian public were excluded from sharing that wealth. The oil tankers that motored up and down the Musi River passed over the skeletons of union activists lying in the riverbed below.

Conclusions

Building on the findings in the preceding chapters, we can venture some conclusions that go part of the way toward answering the questions raised in the introduction about the spatial and temporal patterns of the 1965–66 massacres and the relationship between army personnel and civilian perpetrators. Material from the case studies of particular provinces (chapters 4–7) can be put together at this point to create a picture of the nationwide patterns. These case studies can also be combined with material from previously published case studies of other regions to fill out the picture.

Much of the literature on the killings has worked with a dichotomy between "the army" and "the civilians." One of the arguments here is that "the army" needs to be more precisely defined. The roles of the different levels of the army's hierarchal structure and the internal dynamics of the army's Territorial Command need to be examined. The army was not a monolithic entity at the time, and the tensions within it affected decisions on how the PKI was to be repressed. Another argument is that "the civilians" need to be understood in the context of the political history of the specific provinces in which they operated. Given the great variation in the pre-1965 politics of different provinces, the composition and power of the civilian anticommunist forces varied significantly. It is difficult to generalize for the whole country about the role of the anticommunist militias beyond the basic observation that they played a subsidiary role.

To understand why massacres occurred in some provinces and not others and why they occurred when they did, one needs to consider three different levels of armed power: (1) the army high command in Jakarta, (2) the Kodam commanders, and (3) the civilian anticommunist militias. The three had separate roles and motivations and should be examined separately. But they should

Art installation, *Penggalian Kembali* (Re-excavation), by Semsar Siahaan, exhibited at the Jakarta Biennale of 1993–94, Taman Ismail Marzuki cultural center. Siahaan dug up the ground at a disused pavilion and then sculpted humanlike figures at the bottom of the pit to create a realistic scene of a mass grave. Late in 1994 he was beaten by police at a demonstration against censorship and was left with a permanent limp. Traumatized by the riots and the disappearances of activists in 1998, he moved to Victoria, Canada. He passed away from a heart attack at age fifty-two soon after his return to Indonesia in 2005. Photo by John Roosa.

also be seen in relation to one another. The triangular relationship between these levels in every province determined the severity and timing of the massacres. The army high command created national-level conditions favoring mass murder (as described in chapters 2 and 3), but it did not intervene in every province to ensure that mass murders were carried out. The army high command sometimes did intervene by replacing a Kodam commander who was repressing the PKI through mass arrests rather than mass murder. The Kodam commander stood in the middle between the high command above him and the civilian militias below him. The militias chose to work with or resist the Kodam commander and could appeal to the army high command to urge them to pressure the Kodam commander. Each province had its own particular configuration of this triangular relationship. Let us consider each level in more detail.

The Army High Command in Jakarta

By the term "army high command," I am referring to Suharto, the generals on his staff, and his closest assistants, Ali Moertopo and Yoga Sugama. The fact that there was so much variation in the severity and timing of the massacres in the provinces suggests that the high command did not issue a single order to the troops in the nationwide Territorial Command to kill PKI supporters. It did not insist that army commanders in every province arrange for large numbers of PKI supporters to be killed. They did not issue an explicit call to the public to murder all PKI supporters. They did take actions, however, that encouraged commanders and civilians to kill. These actions can be described as *incitement, precedent-setting,* and *personnel selection.*

The high command was in charge of the takeover of the media and the generation of a steady stream of propaganda that incited people to "crush" and "annihilate" the PKI. As chapter 2 demonstrated, the army's propaganda had definite, predetermined protocols about what should be said and not said. The chief propagandists, Sugandhi and Ibnu Subroto, created a delusional reality where PKI supporters were dangerous traitors bent on mass murder. If anyone did choose to kill a PKI supporter, then that killing would automatically appear to be a reasonable act. The high command's incitement amounted to granting a general license to kill rather than an order to kill.

The high command was directly responsible for the killings in Central Java that began in late October 1965. Suharto and his generals in Jakarta sent RPKAD troops to that province and gave them supreme authority, with the power to arrest and kill civilians and army personnel in the Territorial Command. Central Java was one of the first provinces where mass killing took place. It set a precedent for other army commanders around Indonesia to follow. Harold Crouch observed this effect for the neighboring province of East Java: "the army-supervised killings" in Central Java "removed the inhibitions of troop commanders in East Java."[1] The massacres were not reported in the newspapers, but what was clear to the reading public and to army personnel was that RPKAD had approached PKI supporters in Central Java as if they were combatants who should be killed.

Both the incitement to kill and the precedent of the killings in Central Java created an atmosphere of war in the entire country. It was obvious that the army high command believed that the crisis was not to be treated as a criminal matter that should be handled by the police and the authorities of the civil administration. The PKI supporters were presented as dangerous internal enemies who could be killed with impunity. These two actions of the army high command—incitement and precedent-setting—did not by themselves cause the mass killings in the other provinces outside Central Java. The Kodam commanders needed to authorize a policy of mass killing for it to happen.

The army high command in Jakarta involved itself in choosing Kodam commanders according to whether or not they were willing to support a campaign of mass murder. Its selection of army personnel made it culpable for mass murder in a number of provinces. It did not remove every Kodam commander who followed a repression-without-massacre policy. It removed at least two of them—Daryatmo of Kodam II and Panuju of Kodam III—and thus became culpable for the massacres in North Sumatra and West Sumatra that occurred under the new commanders. It did not remove the Kodam XVI commander, Sjafiudin, but it did overrule him by sending central government troops to Bali in December 1965. It thus became directly responsible for the mass murder in Bali.

The army high command kept in power Kodam commanders who had committed mass murder. For instance, Djuarsa remained the commander of Kodam I until 1967. He was then rewarded for his service by being appointed the commander of Kodam IV, covering the oil-rich province of South Sumatra. Murod, the previous commander of Kodam IV, had been responsible for thousands of deaths in 1966. Once he was replaced by Djuarsa, he too was promoted. The army high command's policies of personnel management indicate that it worked against the repression-without-massacre approach and favored the repression-with-massacre approach.

The Kodam Commanders

After October 1, 1965, there were two different leaders in Jakarta: President Sukarno and Major General Suharto. Some of the Kodam commanders had supported Sukarno's Guided Democracy and had acquired a personal loyalty to Sukarno. Those army generals, such as Ibrahim Adjie in the Kodam covering West Java and Sjafiudin in the Kodam covering Bali and eastern Indonesia, after October 1 followed Sukarno's orders, which were to avoid bloodshed and limit the repression of the PKI to mass arrests. The Kodam commander for the provinces of West Sumatra and Riau, Panuju, headed up a large contingent of Javanese troops there and was loyal to the president. He tried to prevent the killings by the anticommunists in those provinces. Panuju was assisted by the governor of Riau, Kaharuddin Nasution, who largely controlled the Korem covering that province. Nasution followed the same policy.

These Kodam commanders following a repression-without-massacre policy were constantly undermined by lower-level officers and civilian elites. The fate of the policy depended on how strong those challenges were and how well the commanders were able to fend them off.

The Kodam commanders can be ranked on a spectrum of success in maintaining the policy. On one extreme of the spectrum, Adjie in West Java was able to maintain a firm grip over both the officers in the Kodam and the civilian elites. Very few massacres occurred there, and Adjie remained the commander of Kodam VI until July 1966. Panuju faced more substantial challenges in West Sumatra and Riau. He was forced out as the commander of Kodam III in February 1966. At that point, the killing proceeded without obstruction in the West Sumatran half of the Kodam's territory. Meanwhile, in Riau, the other half, Governor Nasution stayed in power until October 1966 and prevented massacres there. Panuju, with his mixed success in maintaining the policy, can be placed in the middle of the spectrum.

On the other end of the spectrum, where the policy completely collapsed, was Bali. The civilian elites on the island of Bali, grouped behind the PNI, were very powerful and wanted to use the October crisis to regain control of the provincial government and suppress the PKI. They undermined Sjafiudin's policy by creating crisis conditions and inviting the army high command in Jakarta to intervene. The high command agreed to intervene in early December and sent RPKAD troops to organize a systematic slaughter of PKI supporters. The civilian elites of Bali could not have achieved such a systematic slaughter on their own. Sjafiudin and the governor, Sutedja, had prevented them from killing for two months. But the arrival of the RPKAD troops with orders from the high command led to a reversal of their policy; the Korem and its eight Kodims covering Bali, instead of trying to rein in the PNI members, ordered them to clear the island of PKI supporters. The Kodam commander's Sukarnoist policy was ended by a combination of civilian actions from below and the army high command's actions from above.

In the case of southern Sumatra, the Kodam commander, Murod, initially followed the repression-without-mass-murder policy, but once he and the other officers of Kodam IV found themselves responsible for many thousands of detainees in Palembang in early 1966, they began killing the detainees. As described in chapter 7, some were taken out by the truckload every night and buried outside the city, while others were left to starve to death in a concentration camp in the middle of the Musi River.

In both Aceh and North Sumatra, the Kodams started murdering PKI supporters from the earliest moments of the repression in October. The Kodam commander in Aceh, Ishak Djuarsa, was part of a militantly anticommunist group of army officers led by Colonel Suwarto, the key thinker at the army's think tank in Bandung.[2] Djuarsa immediately mobilized his troops to murder PKI supporters in October, making Aceh the first province where mass killings took place.[3] Djuarsa received approval for this policy from Mokoginta, the army commander who stood above the four Kodam commanders in Sumatra and was also a committed anticommunist with no interest in heeding Sukarno's orders.[4]

Mokoginta ensured that PKI supporters were violently attacked in Kodam II, covering the province of North Sumatra, just south of Djuarsa's Kodam I. Mokoginta's headquarters was in the provincial capital, Medan, and he became directly involved in organizing the repression of the PKI in that province. The PKI-affiliated plantation workers' union was powerful in the province's plantation belt and was the main target of the repression. Mokoginta arranged with the army high command in Jakarta for a new Kodam II commander to be appointed in late October 1965; the new commander was Brigadier General Sobiran, who was "violently anticommunist," according to the US Consulate in Medan.[5] One remaining obstacle to the campaign was the governor of North Sumatra, Brigadier General Ulung Sitepu, who was a Sukarno loyalist and had some influence over the troops in the Kodam. Mokoginta and Sobirin organized rallies to denounce him as a communist and then had him removed from office on November 16 and thrown in prison. Directing the work of civilian militias, the Kodam organized the killing of tens of thousands of PKI supporters in North Sumatra.[6]

The Kodam for East Java followed a policy similar to the one followed by the Kodams for Aceh and for North Sumatra; murdering PKI supporters was the policy from the start. There was, however, one difference: the start of the policy was slightly delayed. The Kodam commander in October and November 1965 was Basuki Rahmat, who initially did not support the policy. He was known for being a Sukarno loyalist.[7] Some of the Korem and Kodim commanders under him worked with NU militias in the province to begin violent attacks on the PKI supporters in mid-October. The typical tactic was to hold a large gathering (*apel akbar*) in the central square of a city (the *alun-alun*) and then lead the crowd through the streets to physically attack the offices of the PKI and its affiliated organizations. Young toughs in the demonstration would assault and kill any PKI supporters they encountered. These were what can be called "public killings." Rahmat did not approve of such attacks and prevented them in the capital city where he was headquartered, Surabaya. An intelligence report on East Java in late November complained that Rahmat's resistance prevented more extensive attacks on the PKI. The report claimed that

Rahmat, at a briefing where his subordinates were urging him to take a firmer line against the PKI, said, "I have my own instructions."[8] Presumably, those were Sukarno's instructions.

Rahmat, upon seeing the RPKAD campaign of mass murder in Central Java, realized by early November that Sukarno's orders were null and void. Rahmat accommodated himself to Suharto's approach and did not impede the wild campaign of mass murder in East Java in November, though complaints about his lack of enthusiasm for it were voiced.[9] The army high command removed Basuki Rahmat on November 26, 1965, and brought him to Jakarta.[10] The new Kodam commander, Sunarijadi, continued the same policy of mass murder but tried to ensure that the NU militia followed the army's lead and did not kill PKI supporters on its own.[11]

Because of the terror in the streets of East Java that began in October, many PKI supporters allowed themselves to be taken into custody. They did not find safety in the detention camps. The army culled the prison population in late 1965 and early 1966 and turned over truckloads of tied-up prisoners to NU executioners to kill in the villages. Subchan, a prominent NU leader well known for his anticommunism, explained the army's policy in East Java to an Australian researcher in 1970: "they took quotas from the camps and handed them over to us."[12] The death toll in East Java was perhaps the largest of any province. It may have been as high as 150,000.[13]

Civilian Anticommunist Militias

The role of the civilian militias greatly varied from province to province. The variation was caused by two factors: (1) the preexisting relative strengths of the PKI and the anticommunist parties, and (2) the decision of the Kodam covering the province on how to employ civilian militias in the campaign of repression.

In Central Java, the PKI was a popular party that had supporters in the provincial government, in the military, and in the mass organizations of peasants, workers, artists, students, and women. In some parts of the province, such as Surakarta, it was the dominant party. It had fairly good relations with some sections of the second-largest party in the province, the PNI, and had supporters within the police and army troops of Kodam VII. The militant anticommunists did not immediately attack the PKI supporters after October 1 because they expected a strong counterattack. They needed backing from outside the province before they could move against the PKI. It was only after the RPKAD troops came and subordinated or removed the pro-PKI troops that the militias felt confident enough to rampage through the streets and attack the homes and offices of the PKI supporters. Even then, they tended not to kill the PKI supporters in the streets. Rather, they tended to terrorize them and force them into detention camps. The executions were carried out later, as select batches of prisoners were taken out at night and executed.

In those provinces where the PKI did not have a powerful presence, the actions of the anticommunist militias depended on how well organized and committed those militias were and whether they had the backing of the army. In Bali, the PKI was not as powerful as the PNI, and the PNI was militantly anti-PKI. The PNI in Bali quickly transformed its groups for students and youths into a militia, the Tameng, in October and began attacking the homes of PKI supporters, driving many of them to seek shelter with the police or army or neighbors. The Tameng militia was very powerful, but it did not kill PKI supporters in the streets. It did not have the backing of the Kodam commander and the governor; the militiamen did not have a license to kill. That changed in early December, when the PNI, drawing upon its powerful network of Balinese elites, was able to lobby the army high command to send RPKAD troops and overrule the Kodam commander and the governor.

In the southern and central provinces of Sumatra, under Kodams III and IV, the PKI's supporters constituted a small minority of the population. The anticommunists, though far more numerous, were not well organized. Most had been affiliated with the PRRI rebels back in 1958 and had suffered because of the military repression of that rebellion. The army troops in these two Kodams were wary about reempowering the anticommunists for the purpose of repressing the PKI in late 1965. Most of the work involved in the repression was done by army personnel themselves, with select groups of civilians recruited as assistants. Still, the anticommunists were able to organize themselves in certain parts of West Sumatra and Riau (under Kodam III) to carry out violent acts on their own. The appointment of a new Kodam III commander in February 1966, arranged by Mokoginta, resulted in a greater role for the anticommunist militias.

Civilian militias had the greatest solidity and autonomy in the provinces of North Sumatra (under Kodam II) and East Java (under Kodam VIII). But even there, from the start of the violence they worked closely with army officers at various levels of the Territorial Command. Some were not sui generis civilian organizations. In North Sumatra, the Pemuda Pancasila militia, made famous by Joshua Oppenheimer's films, had been the youth group of an army-sponsored political party founded in 1954.[14] It contained many young toughs from the gangs that the plantation companies used to intimidate union organizers and break up strikes. Some of those plantation companies were managed by army officers. Mokoginta worked closely with Pemuda Pancasila so they could begin attacking PKI supporters in October.[15]

Like the militias in North Sumatra, the leaders of the NU militia in East Java were constantly coordinating their actions with the officers of the Territorial Command. The NU published a book on the role of its militia, Banser, to establish the point that "the crushing actions that involved Banser were always under the chain of command, the orders, of the army."[16] Even the writers who have emphasized the autonomy of the NU have acknowledged that the army was deeply involved in all aspects of the actions carried out by NU members. Army officers provided the license to kill, the trucks for transporting NU members and the captives, and armed escorts for the killing squads. The NU may have initiated some of the mob attacks on PKI supporters in October, but its adherents were relegated to the role of mere executioners over the course of November and December as the army turned over nightly "allotments" (*jatah*) of tied-up prisoners to them. The journalist Stanley Karnow reported that the prisons of East Java were emptier than those of Central Java because "fewer captives were allowed to live." The captives with their thumbs tied together behind their backs "were unloaded from army trucks into villages" as army commanders ordered "black-shirted Ansor youth" to execute and bury them.[17]

An important role of the militias was to determine the individuals to be arrested and kept in detention.[18] Militiamen either provided information to the army about the identity of the PKI supporters so that the army could arrange their arrest or arrested those persons themselves and turned them over to the army for detention. Many civilians, even large crowds, could be involved in the process of capturing PKI supporters in their homes and neighborhoods. Within detention sites, however, a smaller core group of committed militiamen helped the army interrogate the detainees and determine which ones should be executed. In many provinces, the army personnel relied on the militiamen for personalized information about the identity of the detainees. The decision on whether to execute detainees rested with the army, but if the army permitted executions, the militiamen had some power to select the victims.

The threefold division of the perpetrators outlined here is meant to help move the analysis of the massacres beyond the dichotomy between the military and civilians.[19] The analysis can become more refined if one considers the layers of the Territorial Command below the Kodam. The commanders of the Korems and Kodims had some room for maneuver and could either impede or accelerate a policy of mass murder. Likewise, the role of governors and police chiefs needs to be more carefully examined. Each province had its own particular combination of forces, and there were variations in the intensity of the mass murder in the various regencies of each province.

Apart from a more refined analysis of the different kinds of perpetrators, much progress can be made by closely analyzing the precise chronology of the killing. Historians writing case studies of individual provinces have revealed that there were two phases to the killing in the provinces that they studied.[20] We are now in a position to affirm that this was a nationwide pattern. The first phase involved mass detention, resulting in large populations of detainees. The second phase involved the execution of the detainees.

In some provinces, such as Aceh and East Java, the first phase was accompanied by murders in the streets. In other provinces, such as Bali and South Sumatra, it was carried out with very few public killings. In all places, it entailed terrorizing the PKI supporters. The actions included street demonstrations, threats, mob attacks, house burnings, and physical assaults. The result was that PKI supporters either allowed themselves to be taken into custody without resisting or voluntarily placed themselves in the custody of the police or military. Staying in detention seemed to be a preferable alternative to remaining at home. Some PKI supporters fled to other areas and disguised themselves.

The second phase does not seem to have been planned from the start in all cases. When the army began keeping people in detention, its officers had not always determined what the ultimate fate of the detainees would be. The decision to execute and disappear prisoners was taken in different provinces at different times. Much more information is required to establish when such decisions were taken and by whom. At some point, one army officer made the same decision that Henry V made at the Battle of Agincourt in 1415: to violate "the law of arms" and order "every soldier to cut his prisoner's throat" (as Shakespeare put it in his play *Henry V*).

The lag between the time of arrest and the time of execution could be many months. On the island of Lombok, for instance, hundreds of prisoners were killed from August 1966 to early 1967, according to a former perpetrator there. Prisoners spent up to a year in custody before being executed. The euphemism used at the time was "clearing out the warehouse and selling the inventory" (*mencuci gudang dan mengobrol isinya keluar*): almost every night ten to fifteen detainees were taken out of a detention camp, a former ice factory, and executed until none were left in the camp.[21]

In some cases, the time of detention was only a matter of hours. Army officers rounded up large numbers of people in their neighborhoods and villages and then arranged for them to be executed immediately. In these cases, like the case in Bali mentioned at the start of chapter 5, officers had already decided that the people taken into custody would be killed. The victims were detainees even if their detention was not part of the first phase and was only one brief step in the process of their execution.

If the repression of the PKI had been limited to the first phase, the number of deaths would have been far fewer. The killings in the first phase often occurred during mob attacks on urban neighborhoods or villages. Such attacks came with some forewarning, and the people to be targeted often had time to flee and hide. Even during the attacks themselves, the individuals targeted could still manage to escape wounded but alive. It was the killing of defenseless prisoners that was horrifyingly efficient: many people could be killed in a short amount of time, and very few were able to escape.

Once one recognizes that the killings were of two different types, one can avoid generalizations drawn from only one type. The killings of the first phase would lead one to overestimate the agency of the civilian militias, whereas the killings of the second phase would lead one to overestimate the agency of the army. The distinction between the two phases can also allow one to understand the confused picture in the social memory of the killings. It has been easy for the public to imagine that civilian militias were the main perpetrators because the killings in the first phase were public knowledge. The killings were done in front of other people, and the corpses were left in the streets. There were dramatic and traumatic scenes of bloodshed. The killings in the second phase were done more discreetly, so that most people did not have direct knowledge of them. One young bystander in the city of Kediri in East Java, Pipit Rochijat, saw mutilated corpses in the street, the results of the first phase, but saw only indirect signs of the killings of the second phase. The army trucked detainees up a mountain: "Who knows what the army did with them there—what was clear was that the trucks went off fully loaded and came back empty."[22] Even though the slaughterhouse-style killing of truckloads of prisoners claimed more lives than the rampages in the streets, the rampages made a much greater impact on the minds of the bystanders.

By distinguishing between the two phases, one can also understand why the PKI supporters were vulnerable to the campaign of mass murder and why they did so little to resist. During the first phase, the PKI supporters sometimes did resist the mob attacks. Such violence was a continuation of the kind of brawls that youth organizations had been involved in before October 1965. If only mobs and militiamen were attacking, the PKI supporters were willing to fight back. In neighborhoods and districts where the PKI supporters were numerous, the militias either did not attack or quickly backed away from the attacks they attempted. But the PKI supporters tended not to resist being taken into custody by state officials. They often had friends, relatives, and neighbors among the state officials and presumed that they would be afforded some level of protection. They were trapped, however, once the army decided to start executing them. As prisoners, they were not in a position to resist.

The execution of prisoners cannot be justified on any grounds. Nothing in Indonesian law permitted state officials to murder prisoners. Even the law code for martial law (Undang-Undang Keadaan Bahaya of 1957) did not permit extrajudicial executions. Basic principles of human rights had already been articulated before 1965, for example in the United Nations Universal Declaration of Human Rights of 1948, which included the right to "a fair and public hearing by an independent and impartial tribunal" for anyone charged with a crime. Those who wish to claim (contrary to all of the existing evidence) that it was a time of war when the PKI was engaged in an armed uprising will have to admit that the Geneva Conventions of 1949 (which Indonesia signed in 1958) would then apply. While the Geneva Conventions were mainly designed for international armed conflicts, they contained a clause regarding internal armed conflict. Article 3 common to all four Geneva Conventions concerns "armed conflict not of an international character." It states: "Persons taking no active part in the hostilities, including members of armed forces who have laid down their arms and those placed *'hors de combat'* by sickness, wounds, detention, or any other cause, shall in all circumstances be treated humanely." Article 3 explicitly forbids "cruel treatment and torture" and "the carrying out of executions without previous judgment pronounced by a regularly constituted court."

This chapter has outlined a methodology that can be used for studying the massacres of 1965–66 in Indonesia in regions other than the ones that served as the case studies in the preceding chapters. It has suggested using a tripartite categorization for the perpetrators and examining the role of each group and the relationships among the three groups in specific spatial contexts. This chapter has also suggested distinguishing between two phases in the killing—an initial phase that resulted in large numbers of detainees and a subsequent phase in which the detainees were summarily executed. The most important finding is that the mass killings of the second phase were usually mass disappearances. Relatives were not informed of the executions, and the bodies of the victims were either hidden in unmarked mass graves or thrown into rivers.

When one employs a methodology with such spatial and temporal determinants, one discovers the importance of the resistance to the massacres. Historians have tended to focus on people who could be categorized as perpetrators, victims, or bystanders. Resisters have been neglected. From Kodam commanders down to village heads and ordinary citizens, some Indonesians tried to prevent the massacres. Their stories need to be told as well. Such a methodology also helps one discover the economic interests of the perpetrators. The existing literature has taken it for granted that the perpetrators were animated by political and religious grievances. That is how the perpetrators themselves in later years explained their behavior. But when one more carefully examines the various groups of perpetrators within local contexts, one finds that they had economic motivations as well, such as destroying labor unions and seizing control of state resources.

Afterlives

It was an unprecedented break from the fifty-year reign of official silence. It was the first public discussion organized by the Indonesian government about the violence of 1965–66.[1] On April 18, 2016, in a grand, high-ceilinged ballroom of a five-star hotel in downtown Jakarta, the highest officials of the country opened an unscripted, two-day discussion among a variety of people, including perpetrators and victims. Former political prisoners and former PKI supporters were given the right to speak about their experiences and aspirations. The coordinating minister for politics and security sat in the center at the front of the room, flanked by the minister of the interior, the head of the police, the attorney general, and the minister of law and human rights. These men were the appointees of President Joko Widodo, commonly known as Jokowi, who had been elected two years earlier. The event was a fulfillment of one of his campaign promises: to address past human rights violations. The two hundred attendees, sitting along the edges of the room behind tables arranged in a single large square, recognized that they were witnessing a historic moment. Journalists and cameramen were everywhere. The organizers had arranged for the proceedings to be livestreamed over the internet so that Indonesians all over the country and the world could watch it.[2]

The key architect of the symposium was Lieutenant General Agus Wijoyo, who was the head of the National Resilience Institute (Lemhanas), an institute that runs educational training sessions for state officials. In his opening address, he explained that the intention of the "national symposium" (*simposium nasional*) was to place different perspectives on the events of 1965–66 in dialogue with one another. Laying out the ground rules for the dialogue, he asked that all of the participants be prepared to listen to one another and be willing to acknowledge that no one has a monopoly on truth. The symposium

A session of the national symposium titled "Dissecting the 1965 Tragedy: A Historical Approach," in Jakarta, April 18, 2016. Photo from Tempo / Aditia Noviansyah.

was not meant, he said, to establish the truth of what had happened; it was to embrace the diversity of views and serve as the first step toward reconciliation. He noted that the attempt to create a truth commission had failed and that court trials were impossible for such a complicated event so long ago. Reconciliation, he affirmed, was still a possibility because it did not rely on a truth arrived at through a process of verification; it could be achieved through a rough consensus on particular points. He urged the participants to think beyond the question "*who* was wrong?" to the question of "*what* was wrong?"—what was wrong with the Indonesian nation as a whole such that large-scale violence could occur?

Wijoyo's speech, with its embrace of multiple perspectives on historical truth and its call for analyzing impersonal, structural problems, was an appropriate opening for a discussion involving people who had been on opposite sides of a violent conflict. The very fact that the speech was delivered by Wijoyo, an army general who was the son of one of the seven officers killed by the September 30th Movement, carried a powerful message. If the son of Major General Sutoyo Siswomiharjo, a sacred icon of the Suharto regime, one of the "Seven Heroes of the Revolution" whose statue stands atop the monument at Lubang Buaya, could endorse the idea of reconciliation with former PKI supporters, then the idea had to be taken seriously. The Suharto regime's propaganda, such as the widely watched 1984 film about the September 30th Movement, had demonized the PKI by emphasizing the suffering of the families of the seven slain officers. With reconciliation receiving Wijoyo's stamp of approval, die-hard anticommunists could not dismiss it as a clever PKI ploy designed to legitimate the party and bring it back to life.[3]

Wijoyo's speech reflected the thinking of a larger group of people. For many years he had been meeting the sons and daughters of prominent public figures involved in past armed conflicts, such as the revolts of Darul Islam and PRRI. Many of the children of the "Seven Heroes of the Revolution," such as Yani's daughter, Amelia, were members, as was Aidit's son, Ilham, who had been living a low-profile life as an architect. Their group, founded in 2003, was called Forum Silaturahmi Anak Bangsa (FSAB, Friendship Forum of the Nation's Children). The idea was to demonstrate to the public that past conflicts were indeed in the past, that the children of earlier generations of political leaders were now living in peace with one another.[4] The key intellectual in the group was Wijoyo's own sister, Nani Nurrachman Sutojo, a professor of psychology in Jakarta. In her writings, she had been concerned about the category of "the victim" (*korban*). She positioned herself as a victim but one willing to recognize that many people had been victimized by the anti-PKI campaign. Wijoyo's speech at the symposium echoed her ideas about how all Indonesians could be considered victims of one or another of the many conflicts in the nation's history.[5]

After Wijoyo's speech, the coordinating minister for politics and security, General Luhut Panjaitan, delivered his speech. He explained the basic motivation for the symposium. It was to prove to the world that Indonesia was a "great nation" (*bangsa besar*) that could resolve its own problems and "make peace with its past" (*berdamai dengan masa lalunya*). He became emotional, angrily repeating the point that Indonesians should not be appealing to foreign countries and citizens to become involved in condemning Indonesia for past human rights violations or demanding that Indonesia take a particular course of action in addressing those violations. "I am not prepared," he shouted into the microphone, "for us to be controlled by another state." This "national symposium" was meant to affirm a patriotic spirit.

The cause for his emotional outburst was left unnamed, but the audience knew what it was. A group of human rights NGOs and victims' organizations had held what it called an International People's Tribunal (IPT) in The Hague in November 2015. It was an entirely unofficial, self-financed affair, involving much volunteer labor. It was held in a church and did not involve any governments or international agencies. Victims testified about the atrocities of 1965–66, historians reported on their findings, and seven individuals playing the role of judges delivered a final report.[6] Even though this tribunal had only symbolic importance, it still generated much consternation back in Jakarta, especially at Panjaitan's office. The *national* symposium was meant to be a refutation of that *international* tribunal. Panjaitan made it clear that he believed that no atrocities had occurred in 1965–66 and that the state had no reason to apologize: "You need to realize, the government is not so stupid as to offer apologies here and there." And he repeated the phrase for emphasis: "We aren't that stupid."

Panjaitan's speech did not follow Wijoyo's high-minded plan for setting aside disputations of facts. He homed in on a factual question: How many people were killed? He dismissed the numbers that he had heard from the victims' organizations and IPT, which were in the hundreds of thousands, and insisted the actual number had to be much lower. To establish the point, he arranged for an army officer who had taken part in the RPKAD's operations in Central Java in 1965–66 to speak after him. That officer, Lieutenant General Sintong Panjaitan, told the audience that those killed in 1965–66 included many people killed by the PKI and that the total number of dead did not even reach the 78,500 reported by the Fact Finding Commission in January 1966. He claimed that when he was in charge of the area around Pati as a twenty-five-year-old platoon commander in late 1965, his troops killed only one person, and that was a prisoner who was trying to run away.[7]

For a forum meant to be open to multiple perspectives, it was an unpromising beginning. All speakers in the first session were uncompromising in upholding the perpetrators' version of history: it was a time of kill or be killed, the PKI committed atrocities, very few PKI supporters were killed, and so on. The victims did eventually have a chance to speak about their experiences, though most of the high state officials, Wijoyo excepted, had left after the opening speeches and were not present to hear them. One elderly woman, Ibu Sumini, who had come to Jakarta to attend the symposium all the way from Pati, directly refuted Sintong Panjaitan's claim that only one person was killed there. "There are seven mass graves around Pati!" she said, her voice trembling. Only eighteen years old in 1965, she was kept in prison for years without charge and was still, in her old age, stigmatized as an immoral PKI woman. One could hear a lifetime of desperation in her voice as she ended with a plaintive question: "What was my crime?"[8]

The symposium was a rare moment when the state's version of history was challenged at a forum organized by the state. A young human rights activist from Palu, Sulawesi, Nurlaela Lamasitudju, countered General Luhut Panjaitan's opinion that an apology from the state was a "stupid" idea. Because of the work of activists like her in Palu, the mayor had apologized to the victims in 2012 on behalf of the city government. The mayor, Rusdy Mastura, had witnessed the abuse of prisoners firsthand in 1965 when he, as a teenager, was recruited by the army to help guard them. His simple acknowledgment that they were victims, that they had been wronged, she explained, fulfilled an all-important aspiration of the former political prisoners: to be recognized as good Indonesians.[9]

Lamasitudju also challenged Wijoyo's relativistic approach to the truth. In an eloquent and moving statement, she asserted a simple truth: much could be known about the events of 1965–66 if Wijoyo's own institution, the army, opened up its records. Her organization had managed to obtain some of the records of the local Kodim that showed that 7,179 individuals had been detained as political prisoners in Palu. She and other researchers, apart from consulting army records, had conducted hundreds of oral interviews and had arrived at a well-documented account of a variety of human rights violations in Palu, such as the substandard conditions of detention, forced labor, and execution of prisoners.[10]

Despite its limitations, the symposium was well received by the victims and the human rights activists such as Lamasitudju. It was a sign that reformers within President Jokowi's administration, Wijoyo most notably, were willing to move beyond the customary demonization of the people who had supported the PKI. By recognizing all Indonesians as victims, the symposium had recognized the former political prisoners and the families of the disappeared as victims, not as evil perpetrators with no right to speak.

Even the denial by the two Panjaitans (Luhut and Sintong) of the reality of the massacres had a positive outcome. Luhut Panjaitan challenged the victims and activists to produce evidence of the mass graves. He wanted to prove that the long-standing claim that there were hundreds of thousands of victims was false: "Go ahead and show us the proof, dig up the mass graves if indeed there were hundreds of thousands of people [killed]. Don't just say it."[11] He was certain that very few mass graves existed. After meeting the president the following week, he told reporters that Jokowi had approved of his plan: "The president has just instructed me to search, to see if there are any mass graves."[12] Planning on demonstrating that the evidence was nonexistent or inconclusive, he aimed to improve Indonesia's international reputation: "It's so that our nation isn't said to have had a Holocaust."[13]

The response to the symposium from the old guard within the army and various Islamic organizations was hysterical. Agus Wijoyo had initiated the symposium to prove that Indonesia was a "great nation" that could approach fifty-year-old events with a mature and dispassionate attitude. The virulence of the right-wing reaction proved that the past was not past. The president's own defense minister, General Ryamizard Ryacudu, denounced the symposium, as did the military commander, General Gatot Nurmantyo. Both spoke, along with Sintong Panjaitan, at a rival symposium held on June 1–2 and meant, as its title put it, to save the country from "the threat of a reawakening of the PKI." A procession of speakers at that event pointed to the efforts by the victims to organize meetings and publish books as evidence of a vast international conspiracy to revive the PKI so that it could resume its pre-1965 killing spree. The speakers insisted that the PKI supporters were perpetrators, not victims, and that they should apologize to the Indonesian nation for their actions. Ryacudu insisted that the mass graves must remain untouched: "If the graves are dug up then what happens if everyone is angry? Everyone is going to be fighting."[14]

The right-wing organizations went on a media offensive after mid-April, filling the TV talk shows, Twitter, and print news with reassertions of the vulgar Suharto-era anti-PKI propaganda. Much of the information they spread was obviously absurd and designed only to gain attention and sow confusion. The retired major general Kivlan Zein claimed that the PKI had been secretly organizing and had already gained 15 million members throughout the country. He even invented a name for the leader of this ghostlike network that had magically escaped detection by the police and the army's Territorial Command: Wahyu Setiaji.[15] Perhaps most of his allies in the anti-PKI campaign understood that he was just making up stories, but they hardly cared. They were playing the role of agents provocateurs. The more outrageous the lies, the better. Some of the campaigners even claimed that Agus Wijoyo and Jokowi were communist agents.[16]

The hysteria about a "PKI revival" had its intended effect. It made Jokowi back off from the plans for facilitating further discussions and pursuing reconciliation with the victims. Dealing with the history of 1965–66, he decided, was going to stir up controversy that would damage the stability of his presidency. He removed Luhut Panjaitan as coordinating minister for politics and security in July 2016, shifting him to the less sensitive position of coordinating minister of maritime affairs. That put an abrupt end to the plan to document and exhume mass graves. Panjaitan's replacement was General Wiranto, who was the epitome of a Suharto loyalist. He had been Suharto's personal adjutant for four years and the military commander at the very moment Suharto's regime faced its final crisis, in 1998. Wiranto was expected to continue the old approach to the mass murder of 1965–66.

Wiranto did not defy expectations. On the occasion of the annual ceremony commemorating the September 30th Movement at the Lubang Buaya monument in 2016, he delivered a brief statement that was meant to put an end to the raging controversy set off by the national symposium back in April.

It was titled "Resolution of the Alleged Serious Past Human Rights Violations Related to the September 30 Movement/PKI Event." The title was strange. It was proposing a resolution (*penyelesaian*) to a problem whose existence it did not acknowledge. It proposed to resolve allegations of violations, not the violations themselves. The text of the statement was just as strange. Wiranto's resolution of the "alleged violations" was to proclaim that there had been no violations. And there were no violations because there had been no law to violate. What follows is the statement's main section, translated in a way that is faithful to the odd word choices, spellings, and grammar of the original.

> From a judicial approach, an in-depth study has been done about the aforementioned event [the September 30th Movement/PKI]. From a criminal law study, the aforementioned event falls into the category of "*the principle clear and present danger* [in English]," the state can be said to have been in a state of real danger, so that actions related to *national security* [in English] form actions of rescue. From the aforementioned event, the adage was also in force "*abnormoal recht voor abnormoale tijden* [in misspelled Dutch]," emergency actions for emergency conditions (abnormal) that can be legally justified and cannot be evaluated according to the character of present-day law.[17]

Wiranto's alleged "resolution"—the claim that the September 30th Movement had created a state of exception—is clearly incorrect. President Sukarno did not declare a state of emergency after the Movement occurred. Indonesia had a law for a state of emergency, Undang-Undang Keadaan Bahaya, and that law was in force from 1957 to 1963. Sukarno did not reinstate that law after October 1965. He repeatedly explained that the Movement was a relatively minor affair. It was Suharto who usurped the role of the sovereign in late 1965 and created a de facto state of exception, against the president's wishes. Even in the areas where the army itself proclaimed that the law of "*keadaan bahaya*" was in force, as in Central Java, that law did not permit massacres of unarmed civilians and prisoners.

Wiranto, with his statement at Lubang Buaya in 2016, protected Suharto's legacy, just as he had protected Suharto's life and vast fortune amid the street protests and riots of 1998–99. There was no acknowledgment of massacres and disappearances, no mention of reconciliation with the victims, and no call for further investigations. The basic message of his statement was that the official version of history, with all its salacious slanders and outrageous lies about the PKI, on full display at Lubang Buaya, was to remain unchanged, even as he called for people to avoid "blaming each other" and "provoking hatred." The state would sustain its hate speech against the PKI and would not sponsor any further open discussions of the 1965–66 events. It would continue to consider the victims evil traitors to the nation with no right to demand an apology, compensation, or official inquiry.

The implacable resistance to a reexamination of the 1965–66 history can be explained at least partly by the stories and arguments presented in the preceding chapters. The killings represented a unilateral slaughter of unarmed civilians; they were unjustifiable, inexcusable atrocities. Perpetrators have known that any open discussion of the violence of that time that involved survivors and witnesses would inevitably reveal the atrocious nature of the violence. Despite their bravado about the "crushing of the PKI," they have been fairly scrupulous in not delving in the details of that "crushing." That is why the massacres, such as the ones discussed in this book, have been difficult to investigate. Given the clandestine or semiclandestine manner in which many of the massacres were carried out, the perpetrators understood at the time that these were events that were not supposed to be proudly narrated to others in the manner of heroic war stories. Perpetrators have understood that their narrative of valiant battles of self-defense against a dangerous and evil foe would crumble to pieces if the precise circumstances of the battles came to light. They have been like the character in one of Sartre's plays who responds to an army colonel beginning to describe a battle that his troops had just won: "No, no! No details! Especially no details. A victory described in detail is indistinguishable from a defeat."[18] If the victory over the PKI is described in detail, it is indistinguishable from an atrocity.

In the documentary film *The Act of Killing*, Adi Zulkadry, a man who served as an executioner of prisoners in Medan, cautions his friends against making a film about their exploits: "If this film is a success, it will make us look crueler than the PKI. We have to be aware of this." Zulkadry thinks more deeply than his friends about how the public will view them and is worried about ruining the perception of the anticommunists as heroes. "The evaluation of this history will be overturned, not just by 180 degrees, but by 360 degrees." His geometrical metaphor was confused, but his message was clear: showing how they tortured and executed prisoners was going to make them look like the villains of the story.

The danger of holding any kind of open discussion about the 1965–66 violence also stems from the implications for property ownership. The perpetrators confiscated many buildings and plots of land at that time. Militiamen, government officials, and military personnel grabbed property for themselves and for the state. It was a massive bout of looting. If the victims are given the chance to speak and they are not delegitimated from the start, then they will inevitably speak about the property that was stolen from their families and social organizations. Wijoyo and his colleagues in the Friendship Forum had hoped they could open up Pandora's box while keeping the malevolent spirits trapped inside. It turned out to be an impossible maneuver. Behind many great fortunes in Indonesia lies the great crime of 1965–66.

The resistance to films, books, and public discussions about the massacres does not derive solely from the perpetrators' wish to hide evidence of their crimes. The delusional reality described in chapters 2 and 3 became the official story of a regime that lasted thirty-two years. The propaganda that enabled the killings in 1965–66 became the unquestioned truth for a generation of officials. Millions of Indonesians, from elementary school teachers to cabinet ministers, spread stories about how the PKI supporters were cruel, sadistic, and immoral and deserved whatever violent punishments were meted out to them. With a large institutional investment sunk into that storyline during the Suharto years, officials have been averse to changing it. Even those born after 1965, who have no direct knowledge of the events, have acquired a passionate commitment to upholding its validity. Textbooks, monuments, museums, annual ceremonies, and countless speeches have made the statement "*PKI kejam*" (the PKI was cruel) seem to be an obvious and incontrovertible truth. Surveys indicate that communists are still the most hated group in Indonesia.[19]

The part of the state most committed to sustaining the old myths is the army's Territorial Command, described in chapter 1. It still exists, even though the reasons for its creation in the late 1950s no longer obtain. There are no armed rebellions (except for the one in Papua), and there is no communist movement. The active-duty soldiers placed within the civil society are superfluous and could easily be removed without affecting the security of the citizenry. The police forces are sufficient to handle the kinds of threats that do exist. After Suharto's fall, in 1998, the new reform-minded governments drew up plans to reduce the Territorial Command, but the military leaders "put up fierce opposition" and "took every opportunity to consolidate, and even expand, their network of local commands."[20] To justify the retention of the Territorial Command, the army has continually appealed to what it calls the "latent danger of the PKI." Since there are no communists left, it must create them out of thin air. Inquisitive university students holding discussions, naïve youths wearing hammer-and-sickle T-shirts, and geriatric former political prisoners meeting in their homes have been the typical internal enemies to be combatted by active-duty army soldiers.[21]

The presence of about 150,000 troops within the civil society gives the army commanders a powerful voice within national politics. When Jokowi took office, in 2014, he contemplated reducing the Territorial Command, as many politicians, academics, and even some military officers had been recommending for years. The reformers have been committed to creating a more professional army (one that focuses on external threats) and improving the functioning of the civil administration (so that unaccountable army personnel are not interfering in its work).[22] The officer who had been the most prominent advocate of the reform of the Territorial Command was the same one who had organized the national symposium: Lieutenant General Agus Wijoyo.[23] The two issues, reform of the Territorial Command and reconciliation with the former supporters of the PKI, have been interrelated. If the state acknowledges that there is no longer a "latent threat of the PKI," then the Territorial Command loses a substantial part of its raison d'être. Jokowi understood that the two were connected. Amid the anticommunist hysteria after the symposium, he spoke at a gathering of thousands of army personnel at army headquarters and announced that he would neither reform the Territorial Command nor issue an apology to the victims of 1965–66.[24]

The president canceled his tentative steps toward reform in June 2016 because he believed that he could not afford to alienate the hard-liners in the army when he was facing a serious threat from other quarters: the Islamic right wing. Jakarta's gubernatorial election was coming up in early 2017, and the right-wing Islamic organizations were mobilizing against the candidate he was backing, who was both Chinese and Christian. Jokowi, declining to fight on two fronts, embraced the old guard of the army. In the face of an unprecedented mass mobilization of Islamicists in the second half of 2016 (which brought about a half-million of them to Jakarta in December to protest a trumped-up case of blasphemy), Jokowi lost all interest in addressing past human rights violations. Thereafter, he made special efforts to speak at gatherings of the Territorial Command troops, where he praised their work and announced massive increases to their salaries.[25]

One of the attendees at the national symposium in Jakarta in April 2016, where Lieutenant General Agus Wijoyo took the simple but daring step of allowing the victims to speak, was Yunantyo Adi, who had come by train from the city of Semarang. He was a lawyer, journalist, and all-around community activist with a passion for studying local history. I had first heard of him in connection with his work on preserving the building that had served as the headquarters of Sarekat Islam in Semarang in the 1920s. It was the building where the trade unionist and the PKI activist Semaoen had formed the "red" faction of the Sarekat Islam and spoke about a synthesis of Islam and communism. It was a large open hall used by many nationalist organizations, including the unions for the workers of the railways, docks, and sugar mills of the city. It was at the center of the nationalist movement in Semarang up to 1945. Ownership of the building changed hands over the decades until it came to be owned by a foundation that proposed to tear it down and construct a five-story office building in 2012. Adi and his colleagues lobbied government officials and publicized the history of the building in the local media. They succeeded in preventing its demolition by having it recognized as a heritage building. Unlike many other activists staging sensationalist actions to grab headlines, he engaged in patient, low-profile work that produced concrete results.

Adi had come to the symposium fresh from another achievement: he had led a successful effort to erect a plaque at the site of a mass grave near Semarang. He and his colleagues concerned with local history and human rights had spoken with many older residents and had learned of a number of mass graves ringing the city. The one about which they were able to obtain the most reliable and detailed information was near the village of Plumbon, about ten kilometers west of the city center. Multiple eyewitnesses could describe it and pinpoint the location. It was a spot in the middle of a teak forest.

The massacre in the Plumbon teak forest was carried out in the same way that so many other massacres were carried out elsewhere in the country, from Aceh in the west to Flores in the east. Detainees were trucked to a remote location at night, shot to death as they stood blindfolded and tied up, and then buried in a mass grave. One of the witnesses, Sukar, was a teenager at the time, eager to accompany an older friend who headed up the local chapter of the PNI's youth group for what promised to be a dramatic event. The youth group, helping the army decide where to massacre the detainees being held in the small town of Kendal, suggested an uninhabited part of Plumbon. On the appointed night, Sukar and his friend waited in the forest, along a dirt road, for a truck to arrive carrying the human cargo. It arrived after midnight, escorted by three uniformed army men in a jeep. The detainees were unloaded from the truck and marched down to a spot where pits had been dug in the ground. In the quiet of the night, Sukar watched as they were positioned on the edges of two pits, shot, and buried. He felt nauseous and regretted that he had volunteered to come.[26]

Adi and his colleagues first learned about the mass grave because of its already existing fame in the Kendal area as a place to request spiritual help to win lotteries. The villagers had marked the two graves with piles of stones immediately after the massacre. Stories about the event traveled by word of mouth, and a legend sprung up around one of the victims, a female shadow puppet performer (*dalang*) named Moetiah from the town of Kendal. She was the only woman among this "allotment" (*jatah*) of detainees and was famous enough to be recognized by some of the witnesses. It was extraordinarily rare for a woman to be a puppet master. Around the 1990s, people from outside the village began arriving to consult her spirit for help in choosing lottery numbers. Her talent as a *dalang* was believed to endow her spirit with mystical abilities, and, because she died an unnatural death, her spirit was believed to still linger around this world, disgruntled but willing to help fortune-seeking mortals. Those visiting the mass grave brought gifts to propitiate her, such as lipstick, facial powder, and perfume.[27]

Adi and his fellow researchers collected as much information as they could about the massacre. The precise number of victims remained uncertain: some witnesses said twelve, others said twenty-one or twenty-four. The precise date also remained undetermined; it was sometime in late 1965 or early 1966. One elderly man in a nearby village told them the names of eight victims that he had learned about in the 1970s when speaking to local army soldiers.[28] The researchers hoped that the remains could be exhumed, studied by forensic experts, and given a dignified reburial. Finding that plan too complicated and expensive, they turned to a simpler way of showing their respects to the dead. They held a religious ceremony at which representatives of Islam, Catholicism, and Kejawen (an indigenous tradition of Java) said prayers and placed a marble plaque at the site to serve as a collective gravestone.

To erect that plaque, Adi and his colleagues spent months patiently explaining their idea to a great variety of state officials. They had to obtain permission from every level of the bureaucracy: the *lurah*, the *camat*, the Semarang city government, the army, the police, and the Forestry Department (on whose land the grave is located). They also had to approach two anticommunist organizations to ensure that they would not be physically attacked. They explained that this was a purely humanitarian gesture for fellow Indonesians who had not received proper funerary rites. Their success in being able to obtain all the approvals came as a surprise to many human rights activists. The fear and hysteria surrounding all events related to 1965 had subsided enough in Semarang in 2015 to allow this initiative to proceed. Because it was such a rare achievement, many journalists from the national and international media attended the ceremony in the middle of Plumbon's forest and have visited it since.[29]

That the marking of a mass grave with the names of the dead and the holding of a religious ceremony for their souls should be so unusual testifies as much to the unusual Antigone-like persistence of human rights activists like Adi as it does to the stifling, decades-long political climate that has prevented investigations into the massacres and exhumations of mass graves. As much as one would like to construe the Plumbon plaque as a victory for human rights, as an act of defiance against the secrecy that surrounds the disappearances of 1965–66, one has to acknowledge that the perpetrators have been remarkably successful in keeping the history of those disappearances secret.

It would be comforting to end this book about the massacres with the story about the Plumbon plaque. It is a story about secrets being revealed. It offers some hope that ultimately many more secrets will be revealed. Such an

Sukar standing next to a plaque marking the mass grave near the village of Plumbon, Semarang, Central Java. He was one of the villagers who helped dig the mass grave in late 1965 or early 1966 and was a key source of information for researchers about it. Photo from Ulet Ifansasti / Getty Images.

ending, however, would hide the bitter truth: most of the relatives of the victims of the 1965–66 massacres have passed away by now without being able to recover the remains of their loved ones and provide proper funerary rituals. Even in the Plumbon case, Adi and his colleagues could not locate the relatives of the victims. Army officers hid many corpses at that time, and now the current generation of army officers points to the absence of the corpses as proof that the massacres never happened. The secrets have remained buried. Some victims were thrown in rivers and will never be found. The locations of countless mass graves remain unknown, just as countless stories of the relatives of the victims remain untold. For every individual disappeared, there were many relatives and friends left with lifetimes of uncertainty. At the gates of prisons and detention camps throughout the country, spouses, children, and siblings were overcome with grief and confusion upon being told that their loved ones were no longer inside. There was never a narrative closure for them to enjoy. They never reached a point at which they could say that they had closed the book on the history of the massacres of 1965–66.

Notes

Introduction

1. The organization of former political prisoners, YPKP, published its findings on the Wonosobo exhumation in its newsletter: Femi Adi, "Tentang Kuburan Massal di Hutan Situkup," *Soeara Kita*, no. 11 (January 2001): 15–16, and no. 12 (February 2001): 15–16. A summary of YPKP's raw data can be found in Deny Tjakra-Adisurya, "Die Exhumierung des Massengrabes in Wonosobo," *Indonesien-Information*, no. 1 (2001), http://www.watchindonesia.org/II_April_2001/Exhumierung.htm. Katherine McGregor has written more about the exhumation and the subsequent attempt to rebury the skeletons: "Mass Graves and Memories of the 1965 Indonesian Killings," in *The Contours of Mass Violence in Indonesia, 1965–68*, ed. Douglas Kammen and Katherine McGregor (Singapore: National University of Singapore Press, 2012), 234–62.

2. On the purge at Gadjah Mada University, see Abdul Wahid, "Counterrevolution in a Revolutionary Campus: How Did the '1965 Event' Affect an Indonesian Public University," in *The Indonesian Genocide of 1965: Causes, Dynamics, and Legacies*, ed. Katherine McGregor, Jess Melvin, and Annie Pohlman (London: Palgrave Macmillan, 2018), 157–69.

3. Stanley Harsha, "An American Library in 1965 Indonesia: From Enlightenment to Torture," *Strategic Review*, March 4, 2019, http://sr.sgpp.ac.id/post/an-american-library-in-1965-indonesia-from-enlightenment-to-torture.

4. *Shadow Play*, directed by the Australian filmmakers Chris Hilton and Sylvie Le Clezio, was broadcast on the PBS network in the US in June 2002.

5. At the same time, the Ford Foundation was helping develop the economics department at the University of Indonesia (UI) in Jakarta. The University of California, Berkeley, was responsible for the training of UI economists. They became famous as "the Berkeley mafia" after 1965. Suharto appointed them to work as his top economic policymakers. The parallel Ford Foundation–funded program at Gadjah Mada University run by the University of Wisconsin faded into obscurity. John Bresnan,

the in-country director of the Ford Foundation in 1961–65, has written about his experiences: *At Home Abroad: A Memoir of the Ford Foundation in Indonesia 1953–1973* (Singapore: Equinox Publishing, 2006).

6. L. Reed Tripp (1913–1994) was a professor of economics at the University of Wisconsin–Madison from 1950 to 1964 and the director of its Industrial Relations Center. He moved to Lehigh University and later donated the gamelan instruments to Bucknell University.

7. Jon Tripp, personal email communication, October 25, 2017.

8. Komando Operasi Tertinggi, *Laporan tentang Hasil Fact Finding Commission*, Jakarta, January 10, 1966. Photocopies of the original report circulated privately for years. Its first appearance in print appears to have been as an appendix to Oei Tjoe Tat's memoir: Oei Tjoe Tat, *Memoar Oei Tjoe Tat: Pembantu Presiden Sukarno*, ed. Pramoedya Ananta Toer and Stanley Adi Prasetyo (Jakarta: Hasta Mitra, 1995), 348–66. Oei was an FFC commissioner, a minister in Sukarno's cabinet, and the head of a political party that Sukarno favored, Partindo. As a Sukarno loyalist, he was one of fifteen ministers imprisoned in March 1966 when Suharto took control of Sukarno's cabinet.

9. Oei Tjoe Tat, *Memoar Oei Tjoe Tat*, 355.

10. Telegram from US Embassy in Jakarta to Secretary of State, "Joint Sitep no. 70," December 29, 1965. National Security Archive, Indonesia and East Timor Documentation Project, File 16, p. 16.

11. Oei Tjoe Tat, *Memoar Oei Tjoe Tat*, 186.

12. "Sukarno Reports Killing of 87,000," *New York Times*, January 16, 1966, p. 12.

13. Nugroho Notosusanto and Ismail Saleh, *The Coup Attempt of the "September 30 Movement" in Indonesia* (Jakarta: Pembimbing Masa, 1968), 77.

14. M. D. Poesponegoro and Nugroho Notosusanto, *Sejarah Nasional Indonesia*, 6th ed., vol. 6 (Jakarta: Balai Pustaka, 1990), 403–4. Notosusanto played a key role in shaping the historical profession in Indonesia, with effects that persist to the present day. On his career, see Katherine McGregor, *History in Uniform: Military Ideology and the Construction of Indonesia's Past* (Singapore: National University of Singapore Press, 2007).

15. John Hughes, *The End of Sukarno: A Coup That Misfired, a Purge That Ran Wild* (1967; repr., Singapore: Archipelago Press, 2002), 167.

16. Agus Sunyoto et al., *Banser Berjihad: Menumpas PKI* (Tulungagung: Pesulukan Thoriqoh Agung, 1996). The book contains some of the first published descriptions by civilian perpetrators of the massacres.

17. Greg Fealy and Katherine McGregor note that the phrase was "the most commonly encountered comment in interviews with NU members involved in the killings." "East Java and the Role of Nahdlatul Ulama in the 1965–66 Anti-communist Violence," in Kammen and McGregor, *The Contours of Mass Violence in Indonesia*, 123.

18. Sunyoto et al., *Banser Berjihad*, 154–55.

19. Sunyoto et al., *Banser Berjihad*, 156–60.

20. Nugroho Notosusanto, *The National Struggle and the Armed Forces in Indonesia* (Jakarta: Centre for Armed Forces History, 1975).

21. The talk show was held in the Medan studio of the state-owned channel TVRI. It was not broadcast throughout TVRI's nationwide network. It was broadcast only locally by the Medan station.

22. Slavoj Žižek, "On *The Act of Killing* and the Modern Trend of 'Privatising Public Space,'" *New Statesman*, July 12, 2013, https://www.newstatesman.com/culture/2013/07/slavoj-zizek-act-killing-and-modern-trend-privatising-public-space. He repeated the argument in his book *Event* (London: Penguin, 2014), 168–69. One may note that Žižek makes many factual errors, such as the claim that the victims were "mostly ethnic Chinese" and that the death toll was "2.5 million."

23. John Roosa, "Interview with Joshua Oppenheimer," *Rethinking History: The Journal of Theory and Practice* 18, no. 3 (2014): 419.

24. Joshua Oppenheimer and Michael Uwemedimo, "Show of Force: A Cinema-Séance of Power and Violence in Sumatra's Plantation Belt," *Critical Quarterly* 51, no. 1 (2009): 94.

25. The transcript of the show appears in Gantyo Koespradono, *Kick Andy: Kumpulan Kisah Inspiratif* (Yogyakarta: Benteng, 2008), 240–47. Both words, "Kick" and "Andy," are names in Sulawesi; they should not be read as English words.

26. This same photographer, Moelyono, was interviewed by an American anthropologist. She notes that he was embedded with the army in late 1965 and was told "what, when, and how to photograph." The army forbade him to photograph acts of killing. He was allowed to photograph corpses as long as their faces were not visible. Karen Strassler, *Refracted Visions: Popular Photography and National Modernity in Java* (Durham, NC: Duke University Press, 2010), 239.

27. Robert Cribb, ed., *The Indonesian Killings 1965–1966: Studies from Java and Bali* (Monash: Monash University Centre of Southeast Asian Studies, 1990), 3.

28. Kenneth Orr drew upon studies that Indonesian graduate students of his had conducted in two subdistricts of Central Java. The students collected information about the 1965–66 violence in the course of a study focused on educational facilities. "Schooling and Village Politics in Central Java in a Time of Turbulence," in Cribb, *The Indonesian Killings 1965–1966*, 177–94.

29. Robert Cribb, "Genocide in Indonesia, 1965–1966," *Journal of Genocide Research* 3, no. 2 (2001): 235.

30. Taufik Abdullah, Sukri Abdurrachman, and Restu Gunawan, eds., *Malam Bencana 1965 Dalam Belitan Krisis Nasional, bagian 2: Konflik Lokal* (Jakarta: Yayasan Pustaka Obor, 2012). This project was greatly influenced by an earlier book that contained one chapter on the massacres in two areas of East Java: Hermawan Sulistyo, *Palu Arit di Ladang Tebu: Sejarah Pembantaian Massal yang Terlupakan* (Jakarta: KPG, 2000). I have criticized the methods of these "local conflicts" studies: "Who Knows? Oral History Methods in the Studies of the Massacres of 1965–66 in Indonesia," *Oral History Forum d'histoire orale* 33 (2013): 1–28.

31. Geertz's brief account of the mass killings, largely based on discussions with perpetrators and bystanders in a small town in East Java, uncritically relays their version of the story: *After the Fact: Two Countries, Four Decades, One Anthropologist* (Cambridge, MA: Harvard University Press, 1996), 6–10. His memoir reveals the limitations of an interpretive approach that does not concern itself with the validation of truth claims. For more on those limitations, see Ben White, "Clifford Geertz: Singular Genius of Interpretive Anthropology," *Development and Change* 38, no. 6 (2007): 1187–1208.

32. Christian Gerlach, *Extremely Violent Societies* (Cambridge: Cambridge University Press, 2010), 17–91.

33. Jess Melvin, *The Army and the Indonesian Genocide: Mechanics of Mass Murder* (London: Routledge, 2018).

34. Gerlach, *Extremely Violent Societies*, 35.

35. Melvin, *The Army and the Indonesian Genocide*, 194.

36. Melvin, *The Army and the Indonesian Genocide*, 228.

37. Geoffrey Robinson, *The Killing Season: A History of the Indonesian Massacres, 1965–66* (Princeton, NJ: Princeton University Press, 2018), 7, 17, 19, 22.

38. Robinson, *The Killing Season*, 293. Robinson here builds on earlier arguments by other historians on the differences between the army high command in Jakarta and the regional commanders: Douglas Kammen and Faizah Zakaria, "Detention in Mass Violence: Policy and Practice in Indonesia, 1965–1968," *Critical Asian Studies* 44, no. 3 (2012): 441–66; John Roosa, "The State of Knowledge about an Open Secret: Indonesia's Mass Disappearances of 1965–66," *Journal of Asian Studies* 75, no. 2 (2016): 281–97.

39. Robinson, *The Killing Season*, 152.

40. Jacques Semelin, *Purify and Destroy: The Political Uses of Massacre and Genocide* (New York: Columbia University Press, 2009), 9–51.

41. One precedent occurred in 1958. The army officers behind the Pemerintahan Revolusioner Republik Indonesia (PRRI, Revolutionary Government of the Republic of Indonesia) revolt in Sumatra in 1957–58 killed many of their prisoners, who were mainly PKI supporters, as they were being attacked by the central government troops. The leader of the PKI's West Sumatra chapter reported three massacres of prisoners in that province: 137 prisoners killed in Situjuh on May 23, 1958; 179 in Suliki on May 27, 1958; and 54 in Atar on August 5, 1958. Nursuhud, "Pidato," *Bintang Merah, Nomor Special Jilid II, Dokumen-Dokumen Kongres Nasional Ke-VI, 7–14 September 1959* (Jakarta: Yayasan Pembaruan, 1960).

42. This paradigm is defined in Patrick Ball, *Who Did What to Whom? Planning and Implementing a Large Scale Human Rights Data Project* (Washington, DC: American Association for the Advancement of Science, 1996).

43. On East Java, see Vannessa Hearman, *Unmarked Graves: Death and Survival in the Anti-Communist Violence in East Java* (Singapore: NUS Press, 2019), 68–111. On North Sumatra, see Yen-Ling Tsai and Douglas Kammen, "Anti-communist Violence and the Ethnic Chinese in Medan, North Sumatra," in Kammen and McGregor, *The*

Contours of Mass Violence in Indonesia, 1965–68; Oppenheimer and Uwemedimo, "Show of Force."

44. For a listing and a description of these interviews, see "Tentang Arsip Suara," http://sejarahsosial.org/arsipsuara/.

45. History writing contains more than narrative and analysis, and even these two terms can be defined in a variety of ways. The dichotomy is meant only as an opening move toward differentiating the component parts of history writing. The chapters in this book also aim to establish the veracity of the stories being told, interpret the meaning of the past events for the present, reflect on the kind of narratives being told, and situate the author within the story.

46. Robert Cribb, "Political Genocides in Postcolonial Asia," in *The Oxford Handbook of Genocide Studies*, ed. Donald Bloxham and A. Dirk Moses (New York: Oxford University Press, 2010), 449; Cribb, "Genocide in Indonesia, 1965–1966."

47. Melvin, *The Army and the Indonesian Genocide*, 45–49.

48. Cribb, "Political Genocides in Postcolonial Asia."

49. Beth van Schaack, "The Crime of Political Genocide: Repairing the Genocide Convention's Blind Spot," *Yale Law Journal* 106, no. 7 (May 1997): 2259–91; David Nersessian, *Genocide and Political Groups* (New York: Oxford University Press, 2010).

50. Barbara Harff and Ted Gurr, "Toward Empirical Theory of Genocides and Politicides: Identification and Measurement of Cases Since 1945," *International Studies Quarterly* 32, no. 3 (1988): 360.

51. Barbara Harff, "No Lessons Learned from the Holocaust? Assessing Risks of Genocide and Political Mass Murder since 1955," *American Political Science Review* 97, no. 1 (February 2003): 57. In a more recent essay, Harff has defined politicide the same way as genocide: "Genocides and politicides are the promotion, execution, and/or implied consent of sustained policies by governing elites or their agents—or in the case of civil war, either of the contending authorities—that are intended to destroy, in whole or part, a communal, political, or politicized ethnic group." Barbara Harff, "Genocide and Political Mass Murder: Definitions, Theories, Analyses," in *States and Peoples in Conflict: Transformations of Conflict Studies*, ed. Michael Stohl, Mark Lichbach, and Peter Nils Grabosky (New York: Routledge, 2017), 216.

52. Frank Chalk and Kurt Jonassohn, *The History and Sociology of Genocide: Analyses and Case Studies* (New Haven, CT: Yale University Press, 1990), 12–27.

53. Alexander Hinton, "Critical Genocide Studies," *Genocide Studies and Prevention* 7, no. 1 (Spring 2012): 10.

54. A. Dirk Moses, "Genocide vs. Security: A False Opposition," *Journal of Genocide Research* 15, no. 4 (2013): 492–93. This argument also appears in his article "Paranoia and Partisanship: Genocide Studies, Holocaust Historiography and the 'Apocalyptic Conjuncture,'" *Historical Journal* 54, no. 2 (June 2011): 573–577.

55. Roger Clark, "History of Efforts to Codify Crimes against Humanity: From the Charter of Nuremberg to the Statute of Rome," in *Forging a Convention for Crimes against Humanity*, ed. Leila Nadya Sadat (Cambridge: Cambridge University Press,

2011). Philippe Sands, *East West Street: On the Origins of "Genocide" and "Crimes against Humanity"* (New York: Vintage, 2016).

56. Scott Straus, *Fundamentals of Genocide and Mass Atrocity Prevention* (Washington, DC: United States Holocaust Memorial Museum, 2016), 30–41.

57. Stéphane Courtois et al., *The Black Book of Communism: Crimes, Terror, Repression*, trans. J. Murphy and M. Kramer (Cambridge, MA: Harvard University Press, 1999). The original French-language edition was published in 1997.

58. Franz Magnis-Suseno, "Membersihkan Dosa Kolektif G30S," *Kompas*, September 29, 2015.

59. A good expression of his views is found in Abdurrahman Wahid, "Keadilan dan Rekonsiliasi," *Kompas*, February 14, 2004.

60. Katherine McGregor, "A Bridge and a Barrier: Islam, Reconciliation, and the 1965 Killings in Indonesia," in *Reconciling Indonesia: Grassroots Agency for Peace*, ed. Birgit Bräuchler (London: Routledge, 2009).

61. Ralph McGehee, "The C.I.A. and the White Paper on El Salvador," *The Nation*, April 11, 1981, 424.

62. Peter Winn, "The Furies of the Andes: Violence and Terror in the Chilean Revolution and Counterrevolution," in *A Century of Revolution: Insurgent and Counterinsurgent Violence during Latin America's Long Cold War*, ed. Greg Grandin and Gilbert Joseph (Durham, NC: Duke University Press, 2010), 271.

Chapter 1. Unarmed Fortresses

1. The name of the Staff College was SESKOAD (Sekolah Staf dan Komando Angkatan Darat). Its deputy commander, Colonel Suwarto, was its most important strategist. As a committed anticommunist, he turned the institution into "the political think-tank of the army headquarters." Ulf Sundhaussen, *The Road to Power: Indonesian Military Politics, 1945–1967* (New York: Oxford University Press, 1982), 139.

2. D. N. Aidit, *PKI dan Angkatan Darat (SESKOAD)* (Jakarta: Jajasan Pembaruan, 1963), 25.

3. Aidit, *PKI dan Angkatan Darat*, 5.

4. D. N. Aidit, *Angkatan Bersenjata dan Penyesuaian Kekuasaan Negara dengan Tugas-Tugas Revolusi; PKI dan Angkatan Darat—SESKOAD II* (Jakarta: Pembaruan, 1964), 9.

5. Antonio Gramsci, *Selections from the Prison Notebooks*, ed. and trans. Quintin Hoare and Geoffrey Nowell Smith (New York: International Publishers, 1971), 243.

6. Gramsci, *Selections from the Prison Notebooks*, 233.

7. The Gramscian character of the PKI has occasionally been noted by scholars of Indonesian politics. Edward Aspinall has mentioned in passing that "the PKI was essentially engaged in a classical Gramscian 'war of position.'" "Indonesia: Transformation of Civil Society through Democratic Breakthrough," in *Civil Society and Political Change in Asia: Expanding and Contracting Democratic Space*, ed. Muthiah Alagappa (Palo Alto: Stanford University Press, 2004), 66. Hilmar Farid Setiadi has

analyzed the writer Pramoedya Ananta Toer, who was part of the PKI-affiliated cultural organization Lekra, in Gramscian terms: "Rewriting the Nation: Prameodya and the Politics of Decolonization" (PhD diss., National University of Singapore, 2014).

8. Robert Cribb, "The Indonesian Marxist Tradition," in *Marxism in Asia*, ed. Colin Mackerras and Nick Knight (London: Croom Helm, 1985), 252.

9. On the strategy of Aidit's group in the late 1940s and early 1950s, see Siswoyo, *Siswoyo dalam Pusaran Arus Sejarah Kiri: Memoar Anggota Sekretariat CC PKI* (Bandung: Ultimus, 2015), 102–26.

10. Cribb, "The Indonesian Marxist Tradition," 252–53.

11. Busjarie Latif, *Manuskrip Sejarah 45 Tahun PKI, 1920–1965* (Bandung: Ultimus, 2014), 380–81. The author, Latif, was a member of the PKI's thirty-five-member Department of History. He completed this manuscript in early 1965 as a first draft of a comprehensive and detailed party history that was to be revised by other members of the department. Because of the assault on the party in late 1965, there was never a chance for the party to revise it. The manuscript remained unpublished and largely unknown until 2014. For more on the background of this important document: Rukardi Ahmadi, "Ketika Partai Perlu Belajar Sejarah," *Historia*, September 13, 2017, https://historia.id/modern/articles/ketika-partai-perlu-belajar-sejarah-P7xdQ.

12. Latif, *Manuskrip Sejarah*, 384.

13. Latif, *Manuskrip Sejarah*, 379–83.

14. Latif, *Manuskrip Sejarah*, 372–409; John Roosa, "Indonesian Communism: The Perils of the Parliamentary Path," in *The Cambridge History of Communism*, vol. 2, ed. Norman Naimark, Silvio Pons, and Sophie Quinn-Judge (Cambridge: Cambridge University Press, 2017).

15. The leading exegete of Gramsci's ideas, Perry Anderson, has not mentioned the PKI in relation to them. His two recently published books on Gramsci are exercises in European intellectual history: *The H-Word: The Peripeteia of Hegemony* (London: Verso, 2017); *The Antinomies of Antonio Gramsci* (London: Verso, 2017). The lacuna may be because his older brother, the late Benedict Anderson, a well-informed expert on Indonesian politics, believed that the PKI was "wholly barren of Gramscian strategic thinking." He did not elaborate on this comment; it was made in passing. It represents a condescending attitude toward the PKI's strategizing and an overestimation of the sophistication of Gramsci's thinking. Benedict Anderson, review of Keith Foulcher, *Social Commitment in Literature and the Arts, Pacific Affairs* 61, no. 1 (Spring 1988): 197.

16. For example, Laclau and Mouffe, prominent Gramsci-inspired political theorists, have prescribed strategies that are silent on the military violence that has so often doomed left-wing movements. One may consult, among their many publications: Chantal Mouffe, ed., *Gramsci and Marxist Theory* (London: Routledge & Kegan Paul, 1979); Ernesto Laclau and Chantal Mouffe, *Hegemony and Socialist Strategy: Towards a Radical Democratic Politics* (London: Verso, 1985); Ernesto Laclau, *The Rhetorical Foundations of Society* (London: Verso, 2014). Consider the neglect of military matters in Peter Thomas, *The Gramscian Moment: Philosophy, Hegemony, and Marxism* (Leiden: Brill, 2009). One may also note that the Subaltern Studies group of historians

in India, while initially inspired by Gramsci's ideas—evident from the use of the term "subaltern"—largely avoided dealing with the history of the Communist Party of India and its armed struggles. The one member of the group who was concerned about that issue, Sumit Sarkar, left the group. Sumit Sarkar, "Orientalism Revisited: Saidian Frameworks in the Writing of Modern Indian History," *Oxford Literary Review* 16, no. 1–2 (1994): 205–24.

17. Military strategy is emphasized in Daniel Egan's incisive book *The Dialectic of Position and Maneuver: Understanding Gramsci's Military Metaphor* (Leiden: Brill, 2016). Egan suggests that war of position and war of maneuver should be seen not as stages but as interrelated and simultaneous elements of political strategizing. Struggles for hegemony inevitably entail moments of coercion, and military struggles inevitably entail efforts to gain consent.

18. V. I. Lenin, "Terms of Admission into the Comintern" (1920), in *Collected Works*, vol. 31 (Moscow: Progress Publishers, 1965), 206–11.

19. As quoted in David McKnight, "Work in the Army: Introduction," *Revolutionary History* 8, no. 2 (Summer 2002), https://www.marxists.org/history/etol/revhist/backiss/vol8/no2/comintern.html. A Comintern committee that included Ho Chi Minh issued a book in German in 1928 on the art of armed insurrection. The chapter titled "Communist Activity to Subvert the Armed Forces of the Ruling Classes" explained the necessity for communists to organize military personnel: A. Neuberg, *Armed Insurrection*, trans. Quintin Hoare (London: New Left Books, 1970), 151–70.

20. Leon Trotsky, *The History of the Russian Revolution*, vol. 3, trans. Max Eastman (New York: Simon and Schuster, 1932), 181–82.

21. Musso, "Jalan Baru Untuk Republik Indonesia," 1948, https://www.marxists.org/indonesia/indones/1948-JalanBaru.htm.

22. On the significance of Sukarno's visit to China in 1956, see Hong Liu, *China and the Shaping of Indonesia, 1949–1965* (Singapore: NUS Press, 2011), 205–33.

23. The start of Guided Democracy is often mistakenly dated to 1957, when Sukarno floated his "concept" (*konsepsi*) of it in February and proclaimed martial law in March. But he did not put an end to parliamentary democracy until July 1959.

24. The PKI explained its support for Guided Democracy in two key documents: D. N. Aidit, "Kembali ke UUD 1945 untuk Perubahan dalam Politik dan Penghidupan!," *Bintang Merah* (July–August 1959): 291–320; and Sakirman's article, published in two parts: "Apa Arti Sokongan PKI kepada UUD 1945 dan Demokrasi Terpimpin," *Bintang Merah* (May–June 1960): 194–219; (July–August 1960): 320–40.

25. Drew O. McDaniel, *Broadcasting in the Malay World: Radio, Television, and Video in Brunei, Indonesia, Malaysia, and Singapore* (Norwood, NJ: Ablex Publishing, 1994), 215.

26. McDaniel, *Broadcasting in the Malay World*, 218. If we assume the average household size at that time was five, then there was one radio for every twenty households.

27. Soekarno, *Genta Suara Revolusi Indonesia* (Jakarta: Departemen Penerangan, 1963), 9. See also S. H. M. Maiddin, "Microphone Republic: Propaganda and Indoctrination in Guided Democracy Indonesia" (PhD diss., University of Sydney, 2016).

28. Latif, *Manuskrip Sejarah 45 Tahun PKI*, 386.

29. Daniel Lev, *The Transition to Guided Democracy: Indonesian Politics 1957–1959* (Ithaca, NY: Cornell Southeast Asian Studies Publications, 1966), 59.

30. "An Indonesian Reds Hate: Abdul Haris Nasution," *New York Times*, July 11, 1959. The US State Department compiled a favorable profile of him in 1958: "Memorandum from the Director of the Office of Southeast Asian Affairs (Mein) to the Assistant Secretary of State for Far Eastern Affairs (Robertson)," April 14, 1958, in Department of State, *Indonesia*, vol. 17 of *Foreign Relations of the United States, 1958–1960* (Washington, DC: US Government Printing Office, 1994), 101–6.

31. A. H. Nasution, *Tjatatan-Tjatatan Sekitar Politik Militer Indonesia* (Jakarta: Pembimbing, 1955), 188.

32. On the formation of the TT structure in 1950–51, see Sundhaussen, *The Road to Power*, 58–60.

33. Dushan Kveder, "'Territorial War': The New Concept of Resistance," *Foreign Affairs* 32, no. 1 (October 1953): 91–108.

34. Nasution's ideas on guerrilla warfare are discussed in Robert Cribb, "Military Strategy in the Indonesian Revolution: Nasution's Concept of 'Total People's War' in Theory and Practice," *War & Society* 19, no. 2 (2001): 143–54.

35. Guy Pauker, *The Indonesian Doctrine of Territorial Warfare and Territorial Management* (Santa Monica, CA: RAND, 1963), vi.

36. Quoted in Sundhaussen, *The Road to Power*, 175.

37. Despite its historical importance, the formation of the Territorial Command has not been studied in detail, and only the basic facts about it are described in the standard works on Indonesian military history. Sundhaussen, *The Road to Power*, 125, 175–76; Robert Lowry, *The Armed Forces of Indonesia* (St. Leonards, New South Wales: Allen and Unwin, 1996), 91–94. Harold Crouch did not mention it in his chapter on Guided Democracy in *The Army and Politics in Indonesia*, rev. ed. (Ithaca, NY: Cornell University Press, 1988.), 43–68. Daniel Lev focused on martial law, not the Territorial Command, in *The Transition to Guided Democracy*, 59–74.

38. Ayesha Jalal, *The State of Martial Rule: The Origins of Pakistan's Political Economy of Defence* (Cambridge: Cambridge University Press, 1990); Robert Taylor, *The State in Myanmar* (Singapore: NUS Press, 2009).

39. Sukarno, "The Revolution Goes On" (1965), in *Indonesian Political Thinking, 1945–1965*, ed. Herbert Feith and Lance Castles (Ithaca, NY: Cornell University Press, 1970), 119.

40. Pauker, *The Indonesian Doctrine of Territorial Warfare*, 145.

41. Pauker, *The Indonesian Doctrine of Territorial Warfare*, 2.

42. Cosmas Batubara, *Cosmas Batubara: Sebuah Otobiografi Politik* (Jakarta: Kompas, 2008), 58–61, 72–73.

43. On Pauker's career, see William Bradley Horton, "Guy Pauker and US-Indonesia Relationships of the 1950s–1970s," *Journal of Asia Pacific Studies* 29 (October 2017): 85–104.

44. Sundhaussen and Pauker overstated the PKI's opposition to the Territorial

Command and misinterpreted Aidit's statements. While the party did not want the army to wield martial-law powers or establish civilian fronts (the BKS), it did not criticize the Territorial Command as such. Aidit criticized only the "reactionary" and "anti-people" tendencies of unnamed army officers. Given that Aidit believed that the army and "the people" were fundamentally unified, the particular institutional structure of the army was immaterial for him. Sundhaussen, *The Road to Power*, 175; Pauker, *The Indonesian Doctrine of Territorial Warfare*, 45–46. Rex Mortimer's description of the PKI's views on the army are more accurate: *Indonesian Communism under Sukarno: Ideology and Politics, 1959–1965* (Ithaca, NY: Cornell University Press, 1974), 102–17.

45. Latif, *Manuskrip Sejarah 45*, 438–39.

46. For instance, one will not find reference to MKTBP in the three key books about the PKI's history: Donald Hindley, *The Communist Party of Indonesia, 1951–1963* (Berkeley: University of California Press, 1964); Justus van der Kroef, *The Communist Party of Indonesia* (Vancouver: University of British Columbia Press, 1965); and Mortimer, *Indonesian Communism under Sukarno*.

47. D. N. Aidit, *Kibarkan Tinggi Pandji Revolusi!* (Jakarta: Jajasan Pembaruan, 1964), 34.

48. The Suharto regime's many propagandistic writings about PKI history misrepresent MKTBP as a doctrine of warfare, as though the definition Aidit gave of it in relation to the war of independence was also applicable to the postindependence period.

49. "Djadilah Komunis jang Baik dan Lebih Baik Lagi," *Harian Rakjat*, June 11–12, 1964.

50. Mortimer, *Indonesian Communism under Sukarno*, 337. Mortimer quoted this passage without mentioning MKTBP.

51. At a 1962 party congress, Anwar Sanusi, a PKI leader, described how the National Front worked and encouraged party members to join it: "'Front Nasional' yang Diketuai Presiden Sukarno Mulai Bergerak Serempak Ke Luar dan Ke Dalam," *Bintang Merah, Nomor Spesial, Kongres Nasional Ke-VII PKI* (Jakarta: Pembaruan, 1963).

52. Rosihan Anwar, *Sukarno, Tentara, PKI: Segitiga Kekuasaan Sebelum Prahara Politik* (Jakarta: Obor, 2006), 287–88.

53. The Masjumi leader, Natsir, admitted that the PKI played a crucial role in the suppression of the PRRI rebellion that he had helped to lead in Sumatra. PRRI forces were initially able to fend off the troops brought in from Java in 1958, but the balance of military power "drastically altered when the Javanese troops developed a technique for using members of the local PKI's Pemuda Rakjat as scouts to trace down the guerrillas in the jungle." Quoted in Audrey Kahin, *Islam, Nationalism, and Democracy: A Political Biography of Mohammad Natsir* (Singapore: NUS Press, 2012), 132.

54. Latif, *Manuskrip Sejarah 45*, 443–45. Aidit spoke to the Air Force in 1963 and again in 1964. D. N. Aidit, *PKI dan AURI* (Jakarta: Jajasan Pembaruan, 1963); *Revolusi, Angkatan Bersenjata & Partai Komunis (PKI dan AURI II)* (Jakarta: Jajasan Pembaruan, 1964). He spoke at various police institutions four times in 1962–63. D. N.

Aidit, *PKI dan Polisi* (Jakarta: Jajasan Pembaruan, 1963). Aidit spoke to the Naval Academy on July 16, 1963: D. N. Aidit, *PKI dan ALRI* (Jakarta: Jajasan Pembaruan, 1963).

55. D. N. Aidit, *The Indonesian Revolution and the Immediate Tasks of the Communist Party of Indonesia* (Peking: Foreign Language Press, 1964), 70.

56. On the Special Bureau, see John Roosa, *Pretext for Mass Murder: The September 30th Movement and Suharto's Coup d'État in Indonesia* (Madison: University of Wisconsin Press, 2006), 139–75. Many elements of my account of the PKI's work within the military have been confirmed by the former PKI leader Siswoyo: *Siswoyo dalam Pusaran Arus*, 193–94.

57. Oei Hay Djoen, oral interview, Jakarta, January 24, 2002. Oei knew this on the basis of his conversations with the Politburo member Njoto, who was a close friend of his. Njoto was one of the founders of the PKI-affiliated cultural organization Lekra. Oei's house in Jakarta served as Lekra's main office. Oei stated that the Dutch scholar W. F. Wertheim asked Njoto about the possibility of the army attacking the PKI in the way that the Kuomintang attacked the Communist Party of China in 1927. Njoto dismissed the possibility.

58. "Prospects for and Strategic Implications of a Communist Takeover in Indonesia," Special Intelligence Estimate, SNIE 55-65, Washington, September 1, 1965, in Department of State, *Foreign Relations of the United States*, 26:289–92.

59. David Hill, *The Press in New Order Indonesia* (Jakarta: Equinox Publishing, 2007), 30.

60. The PKI compiled its many denunciations of BPS from its newspaper *Harian Rakjat* and published them in a pamphlet: *"BPS": Aksi Reaksi* (Jakarta: Rakjat, 1965).

61. The NU's cultural organization, with army encouragement, intended to publish a newspaper, *Abad Muslimin*, in mid-1965 to help counter the PKI. Technical problems delayed the start of the newspaper until October 4, 1965. Roger Paget, "Djakarta Newspapers, 1965–1967: Preliminary Comments," *Indonesia* 4 (October 1967): 212.

62. On the formation of *Kompas*, see the biography of its first editor: Helen Ishwara, *P. K. Ojong, Satu Dari Dua Pendiri Kompas-Gramedia: Hidup Sederhana Berpikir Mulia* (Jakarta: Kompas, 2001), 213–52.

63. For a record of such bannings, see Rhoma Dwi Aria Yuliantri and Muhidin Dahlan, *Lekra Tak Membakar Buku: Suara Senyap Lembar Kebudayaan "Harian Rakjat" 1950–1965* (Yogyakarta: Merakesumba, 2008), 98–101.

64. The book was reprinted once the Suharto regime ended: Pramoedya Ananta Toer, *Haokiau di Indonesia* (Jakarta: Garba Budaya, 1998).

65. David Hill has noted that many newspapers relied on the patronage of military officers who could, for instance, agree to buy a large number of copies for distribution to the troops. Even Mochtar Lubis, a journalist famous for his commitment to a free press, received "irregular but significant financial injections through the intervention of key military intelligence officers" for his paper *Indonesia Raya* in the 1950s. Hill, *The Press in New Order Indonesia*, 32n14.

66. Anwar, *Sukarno, Tentara, PKI*, 150.

67. Sukarno greatly relied on Djawoto. When he started building a much tighter alliance with China in early 1964, he sent Djawoto to Beijing to serve as the ambassador. It turned out to be yet another blow to Adam Malik's Murba party: Djawoto arrived in Beijing in February 1964 to replace Sukarni, a senior stalwart of Murba who returned to Jakarta without an official position. Djawoto wound up stranded as a refugee in China after October 1965.

68. Joesoef Isak, oral interview, Jakarta, December 20, 2003.

69. Ali Moertopo, *Himpunan Pidato Menteri Penerangan RI 1978–1982: Peningkatan Penerangan yang Berwibawa* (Jakarta: Departemen Penerangan, 1983), 201.

70. Quoted in Roosa, *Pretext for Mass Murder*, 235.

71. Sintong Panjaitan, then a lieutenant in the RPKAD, led the operation to take over RRI. Hendro Subroto, *Sintong Panjaitan: Perjalanan Seorang Prajurit Para Komando* (Jakarta: Kompas, 2009), 114–17.

72. Within the state bureaucracy, RRI was under the authority of the Minister of Information, Major General Achmadi, who was a Sukarno loyalist. On October 11, Achmadi appointed a new director and vice director of RRI and "a supervisor/advisor from the military." "RRI ganti pimpinan," *Berita Yudha*, October 12, 1965.

73. I thank Tsabit Azinar Ahmad for giving me a clear photocopy of the Sunday, October 3, issue.

74. *Kompas*, October 6, 1965, p. 1; "Surat2 kabar jang boleh terbit" and "Mulai 6 Okt. 65 surat2 kabar pendukung 'Gerakan 30 Sept.' dilarang terbit," *Berita Yudha*, October 7, 1965.

75. "Undangan KA Puspen AD," *Berita Yudha*, October 7, 1965.

76. The US Embassy learned from an aide of Nasution that Sukarno had wanted to dismiss Sugandhi for being too outspoken against the PKI but, for some unknown reason, decided not to dismiss him. "Telegram from the Embassy in Indonesia to the Department of State," October 18, 1965, in Department of State, *Foreign Relations of the United States*, 26:328.

77. "Fakta Bicara," *Berita Yudha*, October 7, 1965.

78. "Gerakan Kontra Revolusioner 'G30S' Biasa," *Berita Yudha*, October 9, 1965; "Suroto Pem. Red. Antara plintat-plintut: Anggapan terror 'Gestapu' sebagai 'peristiwa biasa,'" *Angkatan Bersenjata*, October 9, 1965.

79. "Panggilan buat Wartawan2/Karyawan2 LKBN Antara," *Berita Yudha*, October 11, 1965; "LKBN 'Antara' dibawah penguasaan Peperda Djaya," *Berita Yudha*, October 12, 1965; "26 Pedjabat/Wartawan Antara 'diambil' Peperda," *Berita Yudha*, October 16, 1965; "Dokumen," *Berita Yudha*, October 20, 1965. The US Embassy noted in a cable of October 17 that the "Army still seems dissatisfied with activities of Indonesia's sole news agency, Antara, and continues to interrogate and harass its staff." "Telegram from the Embassy in Indonesia to the Department of State," October 17, 1965, in Department of State, *Foreign Relations of the United States*, 26:326.

80. "SBPA dukung gerakan 30 September," *Berita Yudha*, October 9, 1965.

81. Hill, *The Press in New Order Indonesia*, 35; David Hill, *Journalism and Politics*

in Indonesia: A Critical Biography of Mochtar Lubis (1922–2004) as Editor and Author (London: Routledge, 2010), 93.

82. Ibu Rusiyati's daughter has posted online an excerpt from an oral interview with her: Ratih Miryanti, "Kesaksian Wartawan Antara Atas Tragedi 1965," September 23, 2006, http://langitkata.blogspot.co.id/2011/05/ratih-miryanti-kesaksian-wartawan .html. She was imprisoned and held without charge for thirteen years. Her name appeared on the list of dismissed Antara editors and journalists published by the army newspapers: "35 orang wartawan Antara diberhentikan," *Angkatan Bersenjata*, October 28, 1965; "SBPA debekukan! 35 wartawan dan anggota redaksi Antara ditjopoti," *Berita Yudha*, October 28, 1965.

83. Oei Hiem Hwie, a journalist for *Trompet Masyarakat*, has written about his experiences with the paper and his detention as a political prisoner for thirteen years: *Memoar Oei Hiem Hwie* (Surabaya: Wastu Lanas Grafika, 2015).

84. H. Suparman, a journalist for the paper, received the order. He was arrested on October 20 at his house by two lieutenants from the military police and detained as a political prisoner without charge for more than twelve years. See his memoir, *Dari Pulau Buru Sampai ke Mekah: Sebuah Catatan Tragedi 1965* (Bandung: Nuansa, 2006), 45, 51, 252. The paper's office was destroyed by a crowd of people a few days after the banning. "Warta Bandung diserbu rakjat," *Berita Yudha*, October 14, 1965; "Warta Bandung dilarang terbit," *Berita Yudha*, October 15, 1965.

85. Hill, *The Press in New Order Indonesia*, 34. "Sedjumlah surat-kabar2 daerah dilarang terbit," *Berita Yudha*, October 11, 1965.

86. "Ditjopot sementara! Anggota2 PWI jang surat kabar/madjalahnja mendukung gerombolan kontra revolusi 'G30S,'" *Berita Yudha*, October 14, 1965.

87. "Rakjat sudah habis kesabarannja: rumah Lukman, Njoto dan Karim DP dapat giliran" and "Rumah Karim DP diobrak-abrik," *Berita Yudha*, October 13, 1965.

88. "Pertemuan rahasia diantara gembong2 PWI mendjelang kup 1 Oktober oleh gerombolan kontra revolusi," *Berita Yudha*, October 14, 1965; "Pengurus PWI tjabang Djakarta petjat 37 orang anggotanja," *Angkatan Bersenjata*, October 26, 1965.

89. *Berita Yudha* claimed that the PWI secretary general, Satyagraha Hoerip, celebrated the September 30th Movement's action on October 1 and was "directly involved" in it. But two days later the paper issued a retraction. "Baginja tidak ada djalan lolos," *Berita Yudha*, October 12, 1965; "Pengumuman," *Berita Yudha*, October 14, 1965.

90. "A. Karim DP Dipetjat: Bersihkan 'Antara' dan 'PWI' dari oknum2 gerombolan 'G30S,'" *Berita Yudha*, October 9, 1965; "PWI petjat anggota2nja jang surat kabarnja terlibat dalam G30S,' *Berita Yudha*, October 26, 1965.

91. "Fungsi Wartawan mendjamin kekompakan ABRI & Rakjat," *Angkatan Bersenjata*, December 10, 1965.

92. Soekarno, *Jo Sanak, Jo Kadang, Malah Jen Mati Aku Sing Kélangan* (Djakarta: Jajasan Pembaruan, 1959). Sukarno delivered the speech at the closing ceremony for the Congress on September 16, 1959, in Jakarta.

93. The PKI published the text of Sukarno's speech, complete with parenthetical

notes on the audience's reactions: Soekarno, *Subur, Subur, Suburlah PKI* (Jakarta: Pembaruan, 1965).

94. (Lieutenant Colonel) Bob Lowry, "Colin East Goes to SESKOAD—in a Year of Living Dangerously, 1964," *Australian Defense Force Journal* no. 183 (2010): 52.

95. Latif, *Manuskrip Sejarah*, 380.

96. Sudisman, *Analysis of Responsibility*, trans. Benedict Anderson (Melbourne: The Works Cooperative, 1975), 5.

97. Siswoyo, *Siswoyo dalam Pusaran Arus Sejarah Kiri*, 169–72, 192–95.

Chapter 2. Mental Operations

1. Sukarno announced Suharto's appointment on October 14 but held the ceremony on October 16. For Pranoto's version of events, see his memoir, *Catatan Jenderal Pranoto Reksosamodra: Dari RTM Boedi Oetomo Sampai Nirbaya* (Jakarta: Kompas, 2014), 181–217.

2. Budi Setiyono and Bonnie Triyana, eds., *Revolusi Belum Selesai: Kumpulan Pidato Presiden Sukarno*, vol. 1 (Semarang: MESIASS, 2003), 22. Words in italics are in English in the original.

3. Setiyono and Triyana, *Revolusi Belum Selesai*, 1:22–23.

4. Marshall Green, "Telegram to State Department," October 13, 1965, National Security Archive, Indonesia and East Timor Documentation Project, File 5, p. 4.

5. John Roosa, *Pretext for Mass Murder: The September 30th Movement and Suharto's Coup d'État in Indonesia* (Madison: University of Wisconsin Press, 2006), 194–95.

6. Setiyono and Triyana, *Revolusi Belum Selesai*, 1:43–44.

7. Sukarno in mid-October ordered his Information Minister, Achmadi, to clamp down on newspapers that were printing inflammatory material. "Menpen akan ambil langkah2 selandjutnja," *Angkatan Bersenjata*, October 15, 1965. But Achmadi could not control the army, and the problem persisted. The *New York Times* noted in mid-November that Sukarno "has voiced disapproval of the way some newspapers have been whipping up public sentiment against the Communist party" and "has complained publicly that he has been misquoted by Indonesian reporters." The press was able to defy Sukarno because it was "guided by anti-Communist army officers." Seth King, "Sukarno Is Losing the Fight over Press," *New York Times*, November 19, 1965, 9.

8. Setiyono and Triyana, *Revolusi Belum Selesai*, 1:50–53.

9. An officer from the army's Information Department conveyed two of these protocols to the Australian ambassador in early November 1965, requesting that the Australian Broadcasting Corporation (ABC) (1) emphasize the role of civilians in the anticommunist campaign; and (2) avoid describing the army as pro-Western and right-wing, which would suggest that it was anti-Sukarno. The ambassador, on his own, had already sent instructions to Canberra in early October suggesting that the

ABC play up "reports of PKI involvement and Communist Chinese complicity in the coup" and downplay "reports of divisions within the army." Karim Najjarine and Drew Cottle, "The Department of External Affairs, the ABC and Reporting of the Indonesian Crisis, 1965-66," *Australian Journal of Politics and History* 49, no. 1 (2003): 52–54. In a similar vein, the US ambassador reported that an army spokesman told the embassy that the US media should not create the impression that the army was "going to massacre Communists." Marshall Green, Telegram from US Embassy, Jakarta, October 7, 1965, National Security Archive, Indonesia and East Timor Documentation Project, File 48, p. 91.

10. US Embassy, Memorandum of Conversation with A. Buyung Nasution, October 15 and 19, 1965. The National Security Archive has posted this document online: https://nsarchive.gwu.edu/briefing-book/indonesia/2017-10-17/indonesia-mass-murder-1965-us-embassy-files. In the early 1970s, Nasution founded the Lembaga Bantuan Hukum (LBH, Legal Aid Society), which grew to function as a kind of civil liberties union. Those who have extolled him as a champion of human rights did not know about his role in helping the army cover up its extrajudicial executions in 1965-66. This document came to light only in 2017, though his anticommunism was already known. Julie Southwood and Patrick Flanagan, *Indonesia: Law, Propaganda and Terror* (London: Zed, 1983), 171–72.

11. Jacques Semelin, *Purify and Destroy: The Political Uses of Massacre and Genocide* (New York: Columbia University Press, 2007), 45.

12. NU leaders, for instance, transmitted the propaganda to their followers. Greg Fealy and Katherine McGregor, "Nahdlatul Ulama and the Killings of 1965-66: Religion, Politics, and Remembrance," *Indonesia* 89 (April 2010): 46–47.

13. The NU drew up a manual in January 1966 for its members who joined the indoctrination teams. The basic message that had to be delivered was that the PKI was against religion; communists were atheists who wanted to destroy religions and create an immoral society. Hamba, *Pedoman Operasi Mental* (Jakarta: Jajasan Perdjalanan Hadji, 1966).

14. Geoffrey Robinson, *The Killing Season: A History of the Indonesian Massacres, 1965-66* (Princeton, NJ: Princeton University Press, 2018), 170. The Bina Mental department of East Java's Kodam still exists; it maintains a military museum in Malang that contains many displays of the Kodam's work in attacking the PKI.

15. Scott Strauss, "What Is the Relationship between Hate Radio and Violence? Rethinking Rwanda's 'Radio Machete,'" *Politics & Society* 35, no. 4 (2007): 631. For an overview of various arguments on the relationship between the media and the violence in Rwanda, see Allan Thompson, ed., *The Media and the Rwandan Genocide* (London: Pluto Press, 2007).

16. Semelin, *Purify and Destroy*, 22.

17. This evaluation is based on a reading of the CIA's daily translations of some of the RRI's news items. See the Foreign Broadcast Information Service reports on Indonesia for 1965-66, available online through research libraries.

18. Najjarine and Cottle, "The Department of External Affairs"; David Easter, "'Keep the Indonesian Pot Boiling': Western Covert Intervention in Indonesia, October 1965–March 1966," *Cold War History* 5, no. 1 (February 2005): 55–73.

19. The name of the organization was slightly changed at a later point in October to Kesatuan Aksi Pengganyangan Gestapu (KAP-Gestapu, Action Front for the Crushing of the September 30th Movement). That was the name it used for its demonstration on October 26, 1965, in Jakarta. "Rapat Raksasa Pengganjangan 'Gestapu' sekali lagi desak: Bubarkan PKI sesuai dengan tuntutan rakjat," *Angkatan Bersenjata*, October 27, 1965. Some of its leaders have left first-person accounts of its activities: Sulastomo, *Hari-Hari yang Panjang: Transisi Orde Lama ke Orde Baru; Sebuah Memoar* (Jakarta: Kompas, 2008), 138–71; Cosmas Batubara, *Cosmas Batubara: Sebuah Otobiografi Politik* (Jakarta: Kompas, 2007), 82–94. The former members of the anti-Sukarno student groups who worked with the army in Jakarta still portray themselves as heroic revolutionaries engaged in daring street demonstrations. Dewan Pakar DPP, *Peristiwa G30S/PKI: 60 Hari yang Mengguncang Dunia; Mahasiswa Melawan Kiri* (Jakarta: Laskar Ampera Arief Rachman Hakim Angkatan 66, 2016).

20. "Rapat Raksasa Ganjang Kontra Rev.: Bubarkan Ormas2 dan Partai2 jang Dalangi Gerakan 30 September," *Angkatan Bersenjata*, October 5, 1965; "Kemarahan Rakjat Tidak Tertahan: Bubarkan Partai2 dan Ormas2 jg. djadi dalang," *Berita Yudha*, October 5, 1965. The United Action's call for banning the PKI was followed by similar calls over the following days. For instance, the NU demanded the banning of the PKI on October 5: "Bubarkan PKI dan Ormas2 jg. Mendukung dan jg. bantu 'Gerakan 30 September,'" *Angkatan Bersenjata*, October 6, 1965.

21. "Masa Rakjat Tidak Sabar Lagi: Mendesak agar Presiden Segera Membubarkan PKI dan Ormas2nja," *Berita Yudha*, October 9, 1965; "Setengah Djuta Massa Aksi Dari 46 Orpol/Ormas Tuntut Pembubaran PKI," *Angkatan Bersenjata*, October 9, 1965.

22. A. M. Mandan, ed., *Subchan Z.E., Sang Maestro: Politisi Intelektual dari Kalangan NU Modern* (Jakarta: Pustaka Indonesia Satu, 2001); J. B. Soedarmanta, *Mempertahankan Cita-Cita, Menjaga Spirit dan Perjuangan: Refleksi 80 Tahun Harry Tjan Silalahi* (Jakarta: Obor, 2014).

23. "PKI, Gerwani, Pemuda Rakjat Terlibat," *Angkatan Bersenjata*, October 6, 1965.

24. "Anwar Sanusi: Situasi Ibukota Pertiwi dlm keadaan hamil tua," *Angkatan Bersenjata*, October 6, 1965; "Sang bayi sudah mati," *Berita Yudha*, October 6, 1965.

25. "Kemarahan rakjat tidak terkendali: Gedung CC PKI dan CDB PKI Djaya dibakar," *Berita Yudha*, October 9, 1965.

26. "Kemarahan rakjat tidak terkendali: Gedung CC PKI dan CDB PKI Djaya dibakar," *Berita Yudha*, October 9, 1965.

27. "Anggota2 PKI & PR lempari massa-rakjat dengan batu," *Angkatan Bersenjata*, October 9, 1965.

28. John Hughes, *From Paper Boy to Pulitzer: A Newsman's Journey* (Glastonbury, CT: Nebbadoon Press, 2014).

29. "Gedung2 SOBSI & PR djadi sasaran Kemarahan Massa," *Angkatan Bersenjata*, October 11, 1965; "Rakjat Serbu Gedung Pemuda Rakjat dan SOBSI," *Berita Yudha*, October 11, 1965; "Gedung Lekra diobrak-abrik rakjat," *Berita Yudha*, October 13, 1965; "Kantor Gerwani diganjang," *Berita Yudha*, October 13, 1965; "Gedung SBPP di Priok diganjang," *Berita Yudha*, October 16, 1965.

30. "Di rumah gembong PKI Njono diketemukan badju berdarah bekas peluru dan seragam tentara dg. pangkat Letnan I. Di rumah Aidit diketemukan Rp. 1 miljar," *Berita Yudha*, October 11, 1965; "Rumah Karim DP diobrak-abrik," *Berita Yudha*, October 13, 1965; "Rumah Karim DP Hantjur," *Angkatan Bersenjata*, October 14, 1965; "Rakjat sudah habis kesabarannja: Rumah Lukman, Njoto dan Karim DP dapat giliran," *Berita Yudha*, October 13, 1965; "Rumah Pramudya digerebeg," *Berita Yudha*, October 15, 1965; "Rumah Tjugito diserbu rakjat," *Berita Yudha*, October 16, 1965.

31. "Djuga 'Double T' djadi sasaran," *Berita Yudha*, October 15, 1965.

32. "Gedung2 SOBSI & PR djadi sasaran kemarahan massa," *Angkatan Bersenjata*, October 11, 1965.

33. "Kantor CGMI Bandung diambil alih," *Berita Yudha*, October 16, 1965; "Kantor SOBSI Medan djadi abu," *Berita Yudha*, October 16, 1965; "Gedung kantor PKI di Surabaja terbakar dan atapnja ambruk," *Berita Yudha*, October 22, 1965.

34. Siauw Tiong Djin, "Baperki, Ureca dan Siauw Giok Tjhan," in *Ureca Berperan dalam Pembangunan Bangsa*, ed. Siauw Tiong Djin (Jakarta: Perkumpulan Res Publica Indonesia, 2014), 17-19.

35. "14 Perguruan Tinggi/Akademi dan Tjabang2nja ditutup," *Berita Yudha*, October 13, 1965. Thayeb also banned student organizations affiliated with the PKI: "Men. PTIP bekukan CGMI, Perhimi dan Univ. jg. bantu Gestapu," *Angkatan Bersenjata*, October 13, 1965; "Organisasi mahasiswa CGMI dan PERHIMI dibekukan," *Berita Yudha*, October 13, 1965.

36. It is indicative of the intensity of anticommunism in Indonesia that Utami Suryadarma avoided any discussion of the events of 1965–66 in her memoir, *Saya, Soeriadi dan Tanah Air* (Jakarta: Yayasan Bung Karno, 2012).

37. "Gedung Ureca Terbakar dan Rontok," *Berita Yudha*, October 15, 1965.

38. "Oknum2 'Gestapu' jang katjaukan demonstrasi2," *Angkatan Bersenjata*, October 19, 1965.

39. "Republika dibakar sendiri oleh CGMI dan Perhimi," *Berita Yudha*, October 19, 1965; "CGMI bakar sendiri," *Angkatan Bersenjata*, October 19, 1965.

40. Tan Ping Ien, "Pembakaran Ureca," in Siauw Tiong Djin, *Ureca Berperan dalam Pembangunan Bangsa*, 223-33.

41. "Lagi dokumen2 disita dari gembong 'Gestapu,'" *Angkatan Bersenjata*, October 16, 1965; "Butki tambah kuat PKI memang dalangnja 'Gerakan 30 September,'" *Angkatan Bersenjata*, November 2, 1965.

42. "Dokumen PKI buktikan: PKI tunggu kesempatan untuk tumbangkan Pres. Sukarno," *Angkatan Bersenjata*, October 26, 1965.

43. "Pak Idham Chalid masuk black-list 'G30S,'" *Berita Yudha*, October 14, 1965.

44. "Lagi Barang bukti ditemukan massa rakjat: Ada daftar orang2 jg mau dibunuh," *Angkatan Bersenjata*, October 28, 1965; "15.000 orang akan dipenggal di Sumatera Utara kalau coup Gestapu berhasil," *Angkatan Bersenjata*, October 30, 1965; "Ratusan orang di Garut njaris dibunuh Gestapu," *Angkatan Bersenjata*, November 3, 1965; "Masuk daftar hitam: Kalau PKI berkuasa 5 hari sadja ratusan pedjabat dan alim ulama dikab. Garut akan menemui adjalnja," *Angkatan Bersenjata*, December 1, 1965; "Di Pati PKI gagal adakan kup: 25 tokoh masuk blacklist didjagal," *Berita Yudha*, November 19, 1965.

45. "30 ribu lembar uang satu rupiahan disita: Akan digunakan sebagai kode oleh anggota2 Pemuda Rakjat," *Berita Yudha*, October 29, 1965; "Gerakan 4P dan rahasia Pil Merah geromb. G30S: Kentong-geropjok tanda dimulainja serangan umum," *Berita Yudha*, November 14, 1965; "Kode 4669: Seorang kurir jang telan beaja Rp. 25 ribu sehari," *Berita Yudha*, November 30, 1965.

46. "'Dewan Kubur' Gestapu di-ubur2 dihutan djati," *Angkatan Bersenjata*, December 3, 1965.

47. "Pasukan PKI: Orang2 Gerwani jg. tjantik disuruh djual diri," *Berita Yudha*, November 4, 1965; "Pasukan 'Kantjing Hitam' ditugaskan melatjur dan meraju tokoh2 Nasa," *Angkatan Bersenjata*, November 4, 1965.

48. "'Operasi Tegak' sita sendjata & dokumen2 penting Gestapu," *Angkatan Bersenjata*, October 20, 1965; "14 Oknum G-30-S ditahan: 13 putjuk sendjata, beberapa pakaian seragam, dokumen2 penting disita," *Berita Yudha*, October 20, 1965; "200 orang ditangkap, 30 sendjata disita oleh Puterpra Kebajoran Lama," *Angkatan Bersenjata*, October 21, 1965.

49. "Senjata api di gedung CC PKI," *Berita Yudha*, October 13, 1965; "KKO sita sendjata gelap jang masuk Tg.-Priok," *Angkatan Bersenjata*, October 20, 1965.

50. "50.000 Putjuk Senjata menurut rentjana PKI akan di drop di Minhasa," *Angkatan Bersenjata*, November 2, 1965; "Pengakuan pengurus BTI Tjiamis: 15,000 senjata gelap sudah masuk Indonesia," *Angkatan Bersenjata*, November 3, 1965.

51. "Bawah pohon tanda Y terdapat senjata!" *Berita Yudha*, November 22, 1965.

52. "Orang2 PKI Aidit gali lobang kubur?," *Angkatan Bersenjata*, October 8, 1965.

53. "Tjatatan Ringan Harian," *Berita Yudha*, October 11, 1965.

54. "Untuk apa lobang2 itu?," *Angkatan Bersenjata*, October 28, 1965; "Untuk apa lobang itu, ha?" *Berita Yudha*, October 28, 1965.

55. Lembaga Ketahanan Nasional, *Bahan-Bahan Pokok G30S/PKI dan Penghancurannya*, March 1969, 17–18.

56. "Inilah Gestapu," *Angkatan Bersenjata*, October 9, 1965.

57. "Inilah cerita ttg. keganasan 'Gestapu,'" *Angkatan Bersenjata*, October 11, 1965. The text as it appears in the microfilm copy is slightly blurry. Benedict Anderson misread the phrase "permainan tjabul" as "permainan djahat" and translated it as "vile plaything." Anderson, "How Did the Generals Die?," *Indonesia* 43 (April 1987): 111.

58. "30 anggota Gerwani menjiksa Pak Jani jang tak berdaja lagi: Penuturan orang jang ikut mentjulik Pak Yani," *Angkatan Bersenjata*, November 3, 1965. The article is based on an Antara report from Tasikmalaya about a man named Memed, twenty-two

years old, who lived in Jakarta and worked at the film studio "Invico" [*sic*, Infico] in Kebayoran Lama. He was arrested after he returned to his home town on October 18. Supposedly, he had been part of the team that kidnapped Yani.

59. "Lobang Buaja & Gendjer2," *Angkatan Bersenjata*, November 4, 1965.

60. "Pengakuan Nj. Djamilah algojo utama di Lobang Buaja: Kami diberi pisau ketjil dan silet utk menusuk djenderal jang dibunuh," *Angkatan Bersenjata*, November 5, 1965.

61. Setiyono and Triyana, *Revolusi Belum Selesai*, 1:89.

62. Setiyono and Triyana, *Revolusi Belum Selesai*, 1:89.

63. Roger Paget, "Djakarta Newspapers, 1965–1967," *Indonesia* 4 (October 1967): 215.

64. Sukarno could not stop *Api*'s patron, Sukendro, from continuing to scheme against him. Sukendro acted as Suharto's emissary to the US embassy in late October to request medical supplies, communications equipment, rice, and small arms. The US did its best to fulfill the request in November, sending covert aid directly to the army. See the cables in Department of State, *Indonesia, Malaysia-Singapore, Philippines*, vol. 26 of *Foreign Relations of the United States* (Washington, DC: US Government Printing Office, 2001), 345–66.

65. Sukarno exclaimed, *"Lā 'ilāha 'illā-llāh,"* which is part of the Muslim profession of faith: "There is no God but Allah." A literal translation of this phrase does not adequately convey how Sukarno was invoking it in this context.

66. "Sekali lagi Bung Karno Djewer Wartawan," *Berita Yudha*, December 14, 1965. The civilian newspaper *Sinar Harapan* also printed an article on December 13, 1965, about Sukarno's statement.

67. *Berita Yudha*'s one article on the theme appeared on November 7: "Wanita sedang hamil 3 bulan dilatih bunuh orang: Inilah moral Gerwani—sendjata silet untuk memotong bagian tubuh si korban." This article largely repeats an article from *Angkatan Bersenjata* that had been published on November 5: "Pengakuan Nj. Djamilah algojo utama di Lobang Buaja."

68. "Tulislah jg benar," *Angkatan Bersenjata*, December 13, 1965.

69. "'Tarian Bunga Harum' Perangsang kotor untuk berbuat a-susila," *Angkatan Bersenjata*, December 13, 1965. Antara was credited as the source in the byline.

70. Setiyono and Triyana, *Revolusi Belum Selesai*, 1:291–92.

71. "Kalau perlu tembak mati orang2 jg tersangkut Gestapu: Tindak orang-orang jang kanankan Revolusi," *Angkatan Bersenjata*, December 18, 1965.

72. "Untung ketawa lebar waktu pembunuhan kedjam Lobang Buaya: Pengakuan seorang anggota Gestapu," *Angkatan Bersenjata*, October 30, 1965. This article, citing a twenty-five-year-old member of Pemuda Rakjat, claims that Untung "heartily laughed when watching the murders."

73. Saskia Wieringa, *Sexual Politics in Indonesia* (New York: Palgrave Macmillan, 2002), ch. 8.

74. Saskia Wieringa, "Sexual Slander and the 1965/66 Mass Killings in Indonesia: Political and Methodological Considerations," *Journal of Contemporary Asia* 41, no. 4

(2011): 544–65; Saskia Wieringa, "Persisting Silence: Sexual Slander, Mass Murder, and *The Act of Killing*," *Asian Journal of Women's Studies* 20, no. 3 (2014): 50–76.

75. "Lagi Kebiadaban Gerombolan PR: 14 anak tanggung didjagal dan dilempar kelobang kuburan anjing," *Angkatan Bersenjata*, November 6, 1965; "4 majat tak bermata terapung dikali Donan," *Berita Yudha*, November 6, 1965; "Adjaran PKI: Tugino bunuh ajah dan adiknja sendiri, karena dua2nja angg. PNI," *Berita Yudha*, November 22, 1965; "Disita: Palu berdarah, pentjukil mata dan sendjata api," *Berita Yudha*, November 25, 1965; "Biadab: Seluruh keluarga Dan Rem 72 ditjintjang," *Berita Yudha*, October 6, 1965.

76. The army's eyewitness reporter at the exhumation on October 4 claimed that the corpses showed signs of having been badly tortured; "some had even been castrated and some had had their eyes removed." "Menjaksikan Kebiadaban Gerakan 30 Sept di Lubang Buaja," *Berita Yudha*, October 5, 1965; "Penjiksaan biadab oleh orang tak ber-Tuhan: Pahlawan2 Revolusi ditjunkil matanja, dirusak wadjahnja hingga tak dapat dikenal," *Angkatan Bersenjata*, October 7, 1965.

77. Setiyono and Triyana, *Revolusi Belum Selesai*, 1:240–41.

78. "Kebiadaban terror kontra revolusi G30S: Bagi yang tidak perlu dibunuh, oleh mereka disediakan alat pentjukil mata," *Berita Yudha*, October 13, 1965.

79. "Alat pentjungkilan mata djuga ditemukan di Garut," *Angkatan Bersenjata*, October 26, 1965; "Satu peti alat pentjukil mata disita," *Angkatan Bersenjata*, November 4, 1965.

80. "Bung Karno: Orang jg tidak bertuhan adalah bukan manusia," *Berita Yudha*, October 11, 1965; "Tak pertjaja Tuhan, makanan setan," *Berita Yudha*, November 14, 1965; "Manusia tak ber-Tuhan lebih ganas dari hewan," *Angkatan Bersenjata*, December 1, 1965; "Tuhan tak perkenankan orang2 anti Tuhan hidup di negara ber-Tuhan," *Angkatan Bersenjata*, December 8, 1965.

81. "Gestapu tak punja hak hidup di Indonesia," *Angkatan Bersenjata*, December 29, 1965.

82. "PKI dan Ormas2nja sudah tidak punja hak lagi utk hidup terus," *Berita Yudha*, November 19, 1965; "Pangdam VII Diponegoro Brigdjen Surjosumpeno: Gestapu hrs dilenjapkan dari bumi Indonesia," *Angkatan Bersenjata*, November 2, 1965; "Kita mutlak mengikis habis Gestapu-PKI: Tak ada tempat bagi mereka dibumi Indonesia," *Angkatan Bersenjata*, December 7, 1965; "Tiada tempat bagi penchianat2 bangsa," *Angkatan Bersenjata*, December 7, 1965; "Tiada tempat bagi pengchianat Gestapu-PKI dibumi Indonesia," *Angkatan Bersenjata*, December 13, 1965; "Gestapu tak punja hak hidup di Indonesia," *Angkatan Bersenjata*, December 29, 1965.

83. "Pendukung2 dan pembela2 gelap G30S masih ada: Mereka masih berusaha lakukan pertahanan untuk lantjarkan kontra revolusi," *Berita Yudha*, November 25, 1965.

84. "Djawa Tengah dlm keadaan perang: Gestapu tingkatkan teror, bakar, tjulik dan garong," *Angkatan Bersenjata*, October 29, 1965.

85. Benedict Anderson and Ruth McVey, *A Preliminary Analysis of the October 1, 1965 Coup in Indonesia* (Ithaca, NY: Cornell Southeast Asia Program, Cornell University, 1971), 63.

86. Anderson and McVey, *A Preliminary Analysis*, 61–62.

87. "Gestapu adakan penjembelihan besar2an di Solo & Boyolali," *Angkatan Bersenjata*, October 27, 1965; "Pesta maut Gestapu di Djateng dan Djatim," *Angkatan Bersenjata*, October 28, 1965; "50 orang Pemuda Rakjat tertembak mati," *Angkatan Bersenjata*, November 1, 1965; "Situasi di Djawa Tengah: 342 angg. pasukan tempur PKI diganjang hidup2," *Berita Yudha*, November 1, 1965.

88. "Gembong2 PKI Djateng diganjang anggota2nja karena ternjata palsu dan suka menghasut," *Angkatan Bersenjata*, November 4, 1965.

89. "Keganasan Gestapu di Jawa Timur," *Angkatan Bersenjata*, November 2, 1965; "Pembunuhan biadab: Tjalon korban digiring kelompak demi kelompok, teriakan 'Allahu Akbar' untuk mengelabuhi rakjat," *Berita Yudha*, November 2, 1965. The total number of victims may have been fewer. A NU leader for East Java announced before the Antara report came out that fifty-one NU members had been killed in the Cemetuk incident: "51 Pemuda Ansor Banyuwangi gugur," *Angkatan Bersenjata*, October 30, 1965.

90. Mohammad Noer, *Mengenang dan Menyelusuri Lubang Buaya di Dusun Cemetuk* (Banyuwangi: Public Policy Institute, 2011); "Wisata sejarah di Monumen Lubang Buaya Cemetuk Banyuwangi," *Merdeka*, May 7, 2016.

91. Firman Syahyudin, "Peristiwa Cemetuk Tahun 1965" (BA thesis, Skripsi Jurusan Ilmu Sejarah-Fakultas Sastra Universitas Jember, 2009); Priya Purnama, "Konflik Berdarah di Desa Krangasem Kecamatan Gambiran Kabupaten Banyuwangi (18 Oktober 1965)" (BA thesis, Skripsi Jurusan Ilmu Sejarah-Fakultas Sastra Universitas Jember, 2012); Ikaning, "Sejarah PKI di Banyuwangi dan Pembantaian Cemethuk 18 Oktober 1965," 2008, https://ikaning.wordpress.com/2008/01/27/sejarah-pki-di-banyuwangi-dan-pembantaian-cemethuk-18-oktober-1965/.

92. "Angg. Pemuda Rakjat meratjuni sumur penduduk," *Berita Yudha*, November 16, 1965; "Penduduk Djakarta njaris djadi korban ratjun," *Berita Yudha*, November 25, 1965.

93. "Madiun Kenangan jang tidak dapat dilupakan," *Berita Yudha*, October 5, 1965.

94. "1/4 djam di kamar maut Madiun: Peluru menembusi orang2 jang tak bersalah," *Angkatan Bersenjata*, December 5, 1965.

95. The banner across the top of the front page of *Angkatan Bersenjata* on December 8, 1965, was "Basmilah Gestapu-PKI sampai keakar2nja agar djangan timbul Madiun ke III."

96. "Kita sudah kenal sikap PKI sedjak 'Madiun,'" *Berita Yudha*, November 5, 1965. The officer quoted in this article, Colonel Soedijono, was speaking in a building in Jakarta that had been confiscated from the Sino-Indonesian organization Baperki.

97. "1/4 djam di kamar maut Madiun: Peluru menembusi orang2 jang tak bersalah," *Angkatan Bersenjata*, December 5, 1965.

98. "PKI de jure belum direhabilitir sesudah pemberontakan Madiun," *Angkatan Bersenjata*, December 4, 1965.

99. Benedict Anderson, "Indonesian Nationalism: Today and in the Future," *Indonesia* 67 (April 1999): 7.

100. I follow Kahin's interpretation of the Madiun uprising as an action initiated by local PKI partisans: George Kahin, *Nationalism and Revolution in Indonesia* (Ithaca, NY: Cornell University Press, 1952), 290–303. That interpretation has been reinforced by later researchers and confirmed by a former party leader: Siswoyo, *Siswoyo dalam Pusaran Arus Sejarah Kiri: Memoar Anggota Sekretariat CC PKI* (Bandung: Ultimus, 2015), 42–50. The key scholarly sources on the Madiun Affair are David Charles Anderson, "The Military Aspects of the Madiun Affair," *Indonesia* 21 (April 1976): 1–63; Ann Swift, *The Road to Madiun: The Indonesian Communist Uprising of 1948* (Ithaca, NY: Cornell Modern Indonesia Program, 1989). For the PKI's own version of the events, see Busjarie Latif, *Manuskrip Sejarah 45 Tahun PKI, 1920–1965* (Bandung: Ultimus, 2014), 277–303. Harry Poeze, while presenting much valuable empirical information, does not provide enough evidence to support his claim that the PKI leaders played a substantial role in organizing the Madiun uprising. For a short version of his arguments, see "The Cold War in Indonesia, 1948," *Journal of Southeast Asian Studies* 40, no. 3 (October 2009): 497–517. A more extended version is in his book on Madiun, which has been published in the original Dutch and in Indonesian translation. I have consulted the latter: *Madiun 1948: PKI Bergerak* (Jakarta: KITLV, 2011).

101. On the Ngalihan massacre, see Poeze, *Madiun 1948*, 294–303.

102. The photographs are reproduced in Poeze, *Madiun 1948*, 275–287.

103. One of the main newspapers, *Jawa Pos*, ran a series of articles in 1989 recycling the standard stories of PKI barbarism and then published the articles as a book: Maksum, Sunyoto, and Zainuddin, *Lubang-Lubang Pembantaian: Petualangan PKI di Madiun* (Jakarta: Grafiti, 1990). The authors reinforced the image of the PKI as murderers who threw their victims into wells and pits (*lubang-lubang*).

104. Bart Luttikhuis and A. Dirk Moses, eds., *Colonial Counterinsurgency and Mass Violence: The Dutch Empire in Indonesia* (London: Routledge, 2014), chs. 7–9.

105. The anticommunist literature on the Madiun Affair published immediately after the October 1965 crisis includes Akhmad Notosutarjo, *Peristiwa Madiun, Tragedi Nasional* (Jakarta: Endang, Pemuda, Api Islam, 1966); Pinardi, *Peristiwa Coup Berdarah P.K.I. September 1948 di Madiun* (Jakarta: Inkopak-Hazera, 1966); Soerasto Sastrosoewignjo, "You Have Stabbed Us in the Back Again" (1965), in *Indonesian Political Thinking, 1945–1965*, ed. Herb Feith and Lance Castles (Ithaca, NY: Cornell University Press, 1970), 373–76.

106. A Suharto regime stalwart and personal lawyer for Suharto, O. C. Kaligis, admitted in 2007 that the propaganda about the killing of the generals was "hyperbolic" and not based on facts. At the same time, he endorsed the suppression of the PKI and claimed that the atmosphere at the time was indeed "kill or be killed." O. C. Kaligis and Rum Aly, eds., *Simtom Politik 1965: PKI dalam Perspektif Pembalasan dan Pengampunan* (Jakarta: Kata Hasta Pustaka, 2007), xvii, 57. An anticommunist politician told George Kahin in 1967 that the stories about the PKI digging holes beforehand were "pure fabrication." Quoted in Robinson, *The Killing Season*, 355n96.

107. Seymour Topping, "Slaughter of Reds Gives Indonesia a Grim Legacy," *New York Times*, August 24, 1965, 1.

108. Salahuddin Wahid, *Negeri di Balik Kabut Sejarah* (Jakarta: Pustaka Indonesia Satu, 2000), 127–28, 125.

109. On Wahid's apology and the controversy around it, see Budiawan, *Mematahkan Pewarisan Ingatan: Wacana Anti-Komunis dan Politik Rekonsiliasi Pasca-Soeharto* (Jakarta: Elsam, 2004), and the articles in the special issue of *Tashwirul Afkar*, no. 15 (2003).

Chapter 3. Tortured Words

1. The former film studio is located on the eastern side of Jalan Kebayoran Lama, just south of the intersection with Gang Buntu. Its GPS coordinates are -6.230573, 106.780319. The building is misidentified in a book written by journalists about torture centers in Jakarta. The book incorrectly claims that the original building was torn down and replaced by housing. The journalists searched only the side alley, Gang Buntu, which is where the original entrance was located. The building is now entered from the main road. Much of the rest of the information in their account, such as the diagram of the interior space, is also mistaken. Margiyono and Kurniawan Tri Yunanto, *Neraka Rezim Suharto: Misteri Tempat Penyiksaan Orde Baru* (Jakarta: Spasi and VHR Book, 2007), 73–94.

2. Kopkamtib, *Himpunan Surat-Surat Keputusan/Perintah jang Berhubungan dengan Kopkamtib 1965–1969* (Jakarta: Sekretariat Kopkamtib, n.d.), 25–26, 31–35.

3. Kopkamtib, *Himpunan Surat-Surat*, 44–54. Suharto's order regarding interrogation teams, dated October 29, 1965, was translated into English and published in Nugroho Notosusanto and Ismail Saleh, *The Coup Attempt of the "September 30th Movement" in Indonesia* (Jakarta: Pembimbing, 1968), 228–46. Justus van der Kroef described the attempts at classification: "Indonesia's Political Prisoners," *Pacific Affairs* 49, no. 4 (Winter 1976–77): 625–47.

4. Kopkamtib, *Himpunan Surat-Surat*, 69. Various subcategories, from A-1 to C-3, were later created to make the classification process seem even more refined.

5. The interviews with former political prisoners are archived at the Indonesian Institute of Social History in Jakarta.

6. Oei Hiem Hwie, arrested in Malang in late 1965, has stated that the military police there did not torture prisoners; they were under a commander who had forbidden it. But other units in the army in East Java did torture detainees. Oei Hiem Hwie, oral interview, Surabaya, July 13, 2000. Suparman, a former political prisoner from Bandung, has claimed that the army in West Java did not make a practice of torturing the detainees, unlike the army commands in Jakarta and Central Java. H. Suparman, *Tragedi 1965: Dari Pulau Buru Sampai ke Mekah* (Bandung: Nuansa, 2006), 53.

7. For instance, it goes unmentioned in Darius Rejali's eight-hundred-page tome that describes and analyzes many cases of torture from all over the world: *Torture and Democracy* (Princeton, NJ: Princeton University Press, 2007).

8. Amnesty International, *Report on Torture* (London: Amnesty International, 1973), 145.

9. Henri Alleg, *The Question*, trans. John Calder (London: J. Calder, 1958); Jean Améry, *At the Mind's Limits: Contemplations by a Survivor on Auschwitz and Its Realities*, trans. Sidney Rosenfeld and Stella Rosenfeld (Bloomington: Indiana University Press, 1980); Jacobo Timerman, *Prisoner without a Name, Cell without a Number*, trans. Toby Talbot (New York: Knopf, 1981).

10. Lesley Gill, *The School of the Americas: Military Training and Political Violence in the Americas* (Durham, NC: Duke University Press, 2004); Alfred W. McCoy, *A Question of Torture: CIA Interrogation, from the Cold War to the War on Terror* (New York: Metropolitan Books, 2006). Given the close ties between the Pentagon and Suharto's army, I suspect some Indonesian officers learned of US interrogation techniques, but there is no indication from the stories of the victims that US training played a significant role. The Indonesian officers used crude methods of physical torture that they either learned from the Dutch and Japanese colonial police forces or improvised at that time.

11. Ulpian quoted in Lucy Grig, "Torture and Truth in Late Antique Martyrology," *Early Medieval Europe* 2, no. 4 (2002): 325.

12. Aristotle, *The Art of Rhetoric*, trans. J. H. Freese (Cambridge, MA: Harvard University Press, 1926), 163.

13. Quoted in Edward Peters, *Torture* (New York: Basil Blackwell, 1985), 34.

14. John Langbein, *Torture and the Law of Proof: Europe and England in the Ancien Régime* (Chicago: University of Chicago Press, 1997), 9.

15. Irene Silverblatt, *Modern Inquisitions: The Colonial Origins of the Civilized World* (Durham, NC: Duke University Press, 2004), 71.

16. Cesare Beccaria, *On Crimes and Punishments and Other Writings*, ed. R. Bellamy (Cambridge: Cambridge University Press, 1995), 44.

17. Quoted in Rod Morgan, "The Utilitarian Justification of Torture: Denial, Desert, and Disinformation," *Punishment & Society* 2, no. 2 (2000): 187–88; William Twining and P. E. Twining, "Bentham on Torture," *Northern Ireland Legal Quarterly* 24 (1973): 305–56. Foucault, when writing about torture, did not specifically address interrogational torture. He focused on the judicial torture and penal torture of medieval and early modern Europe. Michel Foucault, *Discipline and Punish: The Birth of the Prison* (New York: Vintage, 1979); *Wrong-Doing, Truth-Telling: The Function of Avowal in Justice*, ed. F. Brion and B. E. Harcourt, trans. S. W. Sawyer (Chicago: University of Chicago Press, 2014).

18. For critiques of the "ticking bomb" argument, see David Luban, "Liberalism, Torture, and the Ticking Bomb," in *The Torture Debate in America*, ed. Karen Greenberg (Cambridge: Cambridge University Press, 2006), 35–83; Bob Brecher, *Torture and the Ticking Bomb* (Oxford: Blackwell, 2007).

19. Alan Dershowitz, Richard Posner, and Fritz Allhoff have endorsed torture with this kind of reasoning: Alan Dershowitz, *Why Terrorism Works* (New Haven, CT: Yale University Press, 2002), 131–64; Richard Posner, "Torture, Terrorism, and Interrogation," in *Torture: A Collection*, ed. Sanford Levinson (New York: Oxford University Press, 2004), 291–98; Fritz Allhoff, *Terrorism, Ticking Time-Bombs, and Torture*

(Chicago: University of Chicago Press, 2012). The Canadian liberal theorist Michael Ignatieff supports an absolute and unconditional ban on torture while regretting that it might deprive the state of valuable intelligence. He reaffirms the fallacy that torture is effective for extracting information: "If Torture Works . . .," *Prospect Magazine* (April 2006), https://www.prospectmagazine.co.uk/magazine/iftortureworks.

20. The Bush administration opted to practice torture in the belief that it was a quick and effective method of uncovering plots against the US. Mark Danner, *Torture and Truth: America, Abu Ghraib and the War on Terror* (New York: New York Review of Books, 2004); Kenneth Roth and Minky Worden, eds., *Torture: Does It Make Us Safer? Is It Ever OK?* (New York: New Press, 2005).

21. Elaine Scarry, *The Body in Pain: The Making and Unmaking of the World* (New York: Oxford University Press, 1987), 28.

22. Scarry, *The Body in Pain*, 329n7.

23. Scarry, *The Body in Pain*, 58.

24. Carlo Ginzburg, *Myths, Emblems, Clues* (London: Hutchinson, 1990), 160.

25. The US government has used information derived from torture in its official reports. The *9/11 Commission Report* cites interrogation reports 441 times within its 1,700 footnotes.

26. Michel de Certeau understood this point, writing of torture as a matter of imposing a narrative. *Heterologies: Discourse on the Other*, trans. Brian Massumi (Minneapolis: University of Minnesota Press, 1986), 46.

27. Lindsey Dubois, "Torture and the Construction of an Enemy: The Example of Argentina, 1976–1983," *Dialectical Anthropology* 15 (1990): 324.

28. Dubois, "Torture and the Construction of an Enemy," 325.

29. David Sheinin, *Consent of the Damned: Ordinary Argentinians in the Dirty War* (Gainesville: University of Press of Florida, 2012), 30–63.

30. Mark Osiel, "Constructing Subversion in Argentina's Dirty War," *Representations* 75 (Summer 2001): 134. The same point could be made of the Khmer Rouge leaders whose torture house, known as S-21, confirmed their paranoid fantasies about ubiquitous enemies subverting their rule. David Chandler, *Voices from S-21: Terror and History in Pol Pot's Secret Prison* (Berkeley: University of California Press, 1999).

31. Ahmad (pseudonym), oral interview, Ambarawa, July 28, 2000.

32. Hersri Setiawan, *Kamus Gestok* (Yogyakarta: Galang Press, 2003), 214.

33. Setiawan, *Kamus Gestok*, 7–8.

34. Sukrisno, oral interview, Jakarta, May 29, 2000.

35. Kasmin, oral interviews, Rembang, September 8, 2000, and July 25, 2001.

36. Tubagus Suryaatmadja, "Petualangan Politik Seorang Guru Sekolah Rakyat," unpublished typescript (2004), 14.

37. Tan Swie Ling, oral interviews, Jakarta, June 16, 2000, and March 16, 2001.

38. Supardjo, a brigadier general who joined the September 30th Movement, admitted at his trial to having been forced to sign an interrogation transcript. He politely stated that he had signed the transcript to avoid "trouble from the interrogators again." The prosecutor became furious and repeatedly pointed to Supardjo's signature as

proof that there had been no torture. Mahkamah Militer Luar Biasa, *Berkas Perkara Mustafa Sjarif Supardjo* (Jakarta: Mahmillub, 1967), session of February 23, 1967, 650–55.

39. Benedict Anderson, "Tentang Pembunuhan Massal '65," interview with Ben Abel distributed on the Apakabar e-mail list, September 24, 1996. In this interview, Anderson could not recall the name of the Chinese youth he was describing. But he met Tan in Jakarta a few years later, as Tan fondly recounted to me in an interview in 2001.

40. Sarbinatun, "Anggota Lekra Cabang Sala: Laki-Laki Dimanfaatkan Tenaganya, Perempuan Seluruh-Luruhnya," in *Kidung untuk Korban: Dari Tutur Sepuluh Narasumber Eks-Tapol Sala*, ed. Hersri Setiawan (Surakarta: Pakorba Sala, 2006), 56.

41. Bhaskoro, oral interview, Lampung, February 19, 2001.

42. Aristotle thought "many thick-witted and thick-skinned persons, and those who are stout-hearted heroically hold out under sufferings." Aristotle, *The Art of Rhetoric*, 163. Beccaria put a similar idea in different words: torture leads to the "acquittal of robust ruffians and the conviction of weak innocents." Beccaria, *On Crimes and Punishments*, 39.

43. Asep Suryaman, "Asep Suryaman alias Hamim dan Jalan Hidupnya," unpublished typescript (January 1, 1998), 35.

44. Echoes of those debates in 1966–68 within PKI circles can be found in an essay by a trade union activist of Surabaya who thought the idea of an armed struggle in South Blitar was "absurd and suicidal." Adam Soepardjan, "Gerakan Buruh Indonesia pada Prolog, Nalog, dan Epilog G30S/1965," unpublished typescript (December 17, 2000), 4. Vannessa Hearman has discussed these internal party debates: "South Blitar and the PKI Bases: Refuge, Resistance and Repression," in *The Contours of Mass Violence*, ed. D. Kammen and K. McGregor (Singapore: NUS Press, 2012), 182–207.

45. Andre Liem, "Perjuangan Bersenjata PKI di Blitar Selatan dan Operasi Trisula," in *Tahun yang Tak Pernah Berakhir: Memahami Pengalaman Korban 65: Esai-Esai Sejarah Lisan*, ed. John Roosa, Ayu Ratih, and Hilmar Farid (Jakarta: Elsam, 2004), 163–200.

46. The museum of the East Java Kodam in Malang contains a large collection of artifacts pertaining to that invasion of South Blitar, including the stone that was used to smash the head of Hutapea. Schoolchildren in East Java are routinely given tours of this museum that normalizes summary executions of prisoners.

47. Vannessa Hearman, *Unmarked Graves: Death and Survival in the Anti-Communist Violence in East Java, Indonesia* (Singapore: NUS Press, 2018), 171–94.

48. Jatiman, oral interviews, Surabaya, July 16, 2000, and January 2, 2001.

49. Ruswanto, oral interview, Banywangi, East Java, March 21, 2001.

50. Taran (pseudonym), oral interview, Gianyar, Bali. August 18, 2000.

51. Putu Oka, *Merajut Harkat* (Yogyakarta: Pustaka Pelajar, 1999), 62–106. Budiawan has commented on Putu Oka's description of torture: "Tortured Body, Betrayed Heart: State Violence in an Indonesian Novel by an Ex-Political Prisoner of the '1965 Affair,'" in *Violent Conflicts in Indonesia: Analysis, Representation, Resolution*, ed. Charles Coppel (London: Routledge, 2006).

52. Carmel Budiardjo, *Surviving Indonesia's Gulag: A Western Woman Tells Her Story* (London: Cassell, 1996), 4.

53. Budiardjo, *Surviving Indonesia's Gulag*, 6.

54. Budiardjo, *Surviving Indonesia's Gulag*, 29. She uses the term "Satgas-Pusat" (Central Task Force). The former political prisoners I interviewed usually used the term "Satgas Intel" (Intelligence Task Force).

55. Budiardjo, *Surviving Indonesia's Gulag*, 40.

56. Budiardjo, *Surviving Indonesia's Gulag*, 24, 33–34.

57. Amnesty International, *Report on Torture*, 147.

58. Partono, oral interview, Jakarta, November 13, 2000.

59. Partono is mentioned in a wholly uncritical book about the Central Interrogation Team (Teperpu) as a prosecutor "involved" in the September 30th Movement. Aco Manafe, *Teperpu Mengungkap Pengkhianatan PKI pada Tahun 1965 dan Proses Hukum bagi Para Pelakunya* (Jakarta: Sinar Harapan, 2007), 128.

60. Ashar Munandar, untitled and unpublished manuscript, 166–215. When I visited his house in Senayan in 2003, he gave me a copy of the 234-page galley proofs of this memoir, which the publishing house Hasta Mitra was set to publish. As it turned out, it was never published.

61. Pusat Penerangan Angkatan Darat, *Fakta-fakta Persoalan Sekitar "Gerakan 30 September," Penerbitan Chusus*, no. 2, November 5, 1965.

62. Angkatan Darat, Direktorat Polisi Militer, "Berita Atjara Pemeriksaan Abdul Latief," October 25, 1965.

63. Angkatan Darat, Direktorat Polisi Militer, "Berita Atjara Pemeriksaan Abdul Latief," October 25, 1965, 10–11.

64. Angkatan Darat, Direktorat Polisi Militer, "Berita Atjara Pemeriksaan Abdul Latief," October 25, 1965, 10.

65. Abdul Latief, *Pledoi Kol. A. Latief: Soeharto Terlibat G 30 S* (Jakarta: ISAI, 2000), 43.

66. Abdul Latief, *Pledoi Kol. A. Latief*, 56.

67. Komando Operasi Pemulihan Keamanan dan Ketertiban, Team Pemeriksa Pusat, "Berita Atjara Pemeriksaan Abdul Latief," December 21, 1965, and December 23, 1965.

68. Notosusanto and Saleh, *The Coup Attempt*. The book cites the interrogation reports for Sakirman (pp. 9, 11, 110), Supardjo (pp. 34–35), Moeljono (p. 45), Wirjomartono (pp. 45, 47), Raden Mas Koesdibjo (p. 45), and Bambang Setijadi (p. 45).

69. In December 1965, the army distributed what it purported to be a confession by Njono that the PKI had led the Movement. Most foreign observers believed the confession was a forgery. The army published the transcript of Njono's trial: *"Gerakan 30 September" Dihadapan Mahmillub, Perkara Njono* (Jakarta: Pusat Pendidikan Kehakiman A.D., 1966).

70. Notosusanto and Saleh, *The Coup Attempt*, 116.

71. Notosusanto and Saleh, *The Coup Attempt*, 117.

72. Notosusanto and Saleh, *The Coup Attempt*, 120.

73. Notosusanto and Saleh, *The Coup Attempt*, 117.
74. Notosusanto and Saleh, *The Coup Attempt*, 119.
75. Notosusanto and Saleh, *The Coup Attempt*, 121.
76. Helen-Louise Hunter published the 1968 CIA report under her own name with an academic press in 2007: *Sukarno and the Indonesian Coup: The Untold Story* (Westport, CT: Praeger Security International, 2007). She and the publisher did not see fit to mention in the book that it was nothing more than a republishing of the 1968 report, which had been freely available for decades. An unwary reader would believe that it was a newly composed, original, scholarly work.
77. Dake was responsible for the publication of the Widjanarko interrogation transcript and its translation into English: *The Devious Dalang: Sukarno and the So-Called Untung Putsch* (The Hague: Interdoc, 1974). Dake also published two books based partly on the Widjanarko transcript: *In the Spirit of the Red Banteng: Indonesian Communists between Moscow and Peking 1959–1965* (The Hague: Mouton, 1973); *The Sukarno File, 1965–67: Chronology of a Defeat* (Leiden: Brill, 2006). Fic used the Widjanarko transcript and many more fake sources besides: *Anatomy of the Jakarta Coup: October 1, 1965* (Delhi: Abhinav, 2004). For a more detailed critique of Hunter's CIA report and the books by Dake and Fic, see my review essay "President Sukarno and the September 30th Movement," *Critical Asian Studies* 40, no. 1 (March 2008): 143–59.
78. A projectionist in Bandung happened to have preserved a reel of the 16 mm film. A post-Suharto-era project to preserve the country's film heritage was able to digitally restore it. By virtue of his association with Lekra, Siagian is known as a "left-wing" director. But his films were not clearly "left wing." *Violetta* appeals to basic nationalist ideals. A fatherless teenaged girl, raised by a humorless mother who represses her sexuality, falls in love with a jaunty, chivalrous army corporal.
79. On Siagian's career, see Windu Yusuf, "Bachtiar Siagian dan Misteri Realisme Sosialis Dalam Film Indonesia," *IndoProgress*, November 5, 2013, https://indoprogress.com/2013/11/bachtiar-siagian-dan-misteri-realisme-sosialis-dalam-film-indonesia/; Krishna Sen, "Death of a Film Legacy: Remembering Indonesia's Bachtiar Siagian," *The Conversation*, October 12, 2015, http://theconversation.com/death-of-a-film-legacy-remembering-indonesias-bachtiar-siagian-48444.
80. *Surat untuk Bidadari* (1991), made by Garin Nugroho, was "the only film of the 1990s to gain a degree of international critical acclaim." It won awards at film festivals in Germany, Italy, and Japan. Sen and Hill, *Media and Politics in Indonesia*, 154–55.
81. "TNI Publikasikan BAP Tokoh PKI Agar Sejarah tak Diingkari," *Media Indonesia*, October 1, 2003.
82. Manafe, *Teperpu Mengungkap Pengkhianatan PKI*.
83. On torture in East Timor, see chapter 7.4 of the final report of the Commission for Reception, Truth, and Reconciliation: Comissão de Acolhimento, Verdade, e Reconciliação Timor Leste, *Chega!*, 5 vols. (Jakarta: KPG, 2013). On torture in Aceh, see Human Rights Watch, *Aceh at War: Torture, Ill-Treatment and Unfair Trials* (2004). A recent overview of human rights violations in West Papua includes a long

section on torture: International Coalition for Papua, *Human Rights in West Papua 2017* (Wutterpal, Germany: ICP, 2017), 48–78.

84. Utomo (pseudonym), oral interview, Jakarta, November 13, 2000.

85. Guritno (pseudonym), oral interview, Bandung, April 1, 2001.

Chapter 4. Surprise Attacks

1. Martin Aleida, "Malam Kelabu," *Horison* 5, no. 2 (February 1970): 36–40.

2. Personal communication from Martin Aleida, December 1, 2005.

3. Ayu Ratih et al., "Nyadran di Bengawan Solo," in *Kidung untuk Korban: Dari Tutur Sepuluh Narasumber Eks-Tapol Sala*, ed. Hersri Setiawan (Surakarta: Pakorba Sala, 2006), 1–13.

4. The city of Surakarta is also known as Solo.

5. Edward Luttwak, *Strategy: The Logic of War and Peace* (Cambridge, MA: Harvard University Press, 2001), 4.

6. The two royal houses were the Kasunanan and the Mangkunegaran. Each had its main palace in the city of Surakarta, and each maintained its own bureaucracy to collect taxes from its lands scattered throughout the Residency. The Dutch supervised the two royal houses through an official called a Resident.

7. John Ingleson, *Workers, Unions and Politics: Indonesia in the 1920s and 1930s* (Leiden: Brill, 2014).

8. Michael Williams, "Sneevliet and the Birth of Asian Communism," *New Left Review* 123 (September–October 1980): 81–90. Sneevliet, as a Comintern agent, played an important role in the Communist Party of China's strategizing in the early 1920s: Tony Saich, *The Origins of the First United Front in China: The Role of Sneevliet (Alias Maring)*, 2 vols. (Leiden: Brill, 1991).

9. Semaoen wrote a brief history of the social movements in the Indies up to 1921: "An Early Account of the Independence Movement," trans. Ruth McVey, *Indonesia* 1 (April 1966): 46–75. His novel *Hikajat Kadiroen* was first published by the PKI in Semarang in the early 1920s. The English translation of it contains informative essays by H. M. J. Maier and Paul Tickell: *The Story of Kadirun*, trans. Ian Campbell et al. (Jakarta: Lontar, 2014).

10. On Sarekat Islam in the Surakarta Residency, see Takashi Shiraishi, *An Age in Motion: Popular Radicalism in Java, 1912–1916* (Ithaca, NY: Cornell University Press, 1990); Syamsul Bakri, *Gerakan Komunisme Islam Surakarta 1914–1942* (Yogyakarta: LKiS, 2015). Rianne Subijanto has studied the *Sinar Hindia* newspaper: "Enlightenment and the Revolutionary Press in Colonial Indonesia," *International Journal of Communication* 11 (2017): 1357–77.

11. The PKI in the 1920s is extensively described in Ruth McVey, *The Rise of Indonesian Communism* (Ithaca, NY: Cornell University Press, 1965).

12. Haji Misbach's newspaper articles from 1915 to 1926 have been collected in H. M. Misbach, *Haji Misbach: Sang Propagandis* (Temanggung: Kendi, 2016).

13. Harry Benda and Ruth McVey, eds., *The Communist Uprisings of 1926–1927 in*

Indonesia: Key Documents (Ithaca, NY: Cornell Modern Indonesia Project, 1960); Michael Williams, *Communism, Religion, and Revolt in Banten* (Athens: Ohio University Center for International Studies, 1990); Audrey Kahin, "The 1927 Communist Uprising in Sumatra: A Reappraisal," *Indonesia* 62 (October 1996): 19–36.

14. Takashi Shiraishi, "The Phantom World of Digoel," *Indonesia* 61 (April 1996): 93–118; Harry Poeze, "From Foe to Partner to Foe Again: The Strange Alliance of the Dutch Authorities and Digoel Exiles in Australia, 1943–1945," *Indonesia* 94 (October 2012): 57–84.

15. Dasuki and Rasjid's names appear on the list of prisoners in Koesalah Soebagyo Toer, *Tanah Merah yang Merah: Sebuah Catatan Sejarah* (Bandung: Ultimus, 2010), 40, 62. Rasjid was the imam of the mosque at Boven Digoel.

16. Mas Marco's writings on Boven Digoel have been collected in *Pergaulan Orang Buangan di Boven Digoel*, ed. Koesalah Soebagyo Toer (Jakarta: KPG, 2002). Other writings by and about the prisoners have been collected in Prameodya Ananta Toer, ed., *Cerita Dari Digul* (Jakarta: KPG, 2001). See also Elizabeth Chandra, "From Sensation to Oblivion: Boven Digoel in Sino-Malay Novels," *Bijdragen tot de Taal-, Land- en Volkenkunde* 169, nos. 2–3 (2013): 244–78.

17. George Larson, *Prelude to Revolution: Palaces and Politics in Surakarta, 1912–1942* (Dordrecht: Foris Publications, 1987).

18. Soejatno Kartodirdjo, "Revolution in Surakarta 1945–50: A Case Study of City and Village in the Indonesian Revolution" (PhD diss., Australian National University, 1982), 138–39. It is unfortunate that this dissertation was never published. Its author published at least two articles prior to its completion: Soejatno, "Revolution and Social Tensions in Surakarta 1945–1950," trans. Benedict Anderson, *Indonesia* 17 (April 1974): 99–111; Suyatno, "Feodalisme dan Revolusi di Surakarta 1945–1950," *Prisma* 7 (July 1978).

19. Kartodirdjo, "Revolution in Surakarta 1945–50," 155–57. Siswoyo reports that Lieutenant Colonel Samsudin Musanif, a PKI supporter, was the head of *pepolit* for Sutarto's Division IV. Siswoyo himself worked in the propaganda section of Wikana's office. Siswoyo, *Siswoyo Dalam Pusaran Arus Sejarah Kiri: Memoar Anggota Sekretariat CC PKI* (Bandung: Ultimus, 2015), 31, 35–37.

20. Kartodirdjo, "Revolution in Surakarta 1945–50," 166–68.

21. Kartodirdjo, "Revolution in Surakarta 1945–50," 135.

22. On the negotiations, see Kementerian Penerangan Files, No. 46, ANRI, and the primary source documents reproduced in Pramoedya Ananta Toer et al., eds., *Kronik Revolusi Indonesia*, vol. 4, *1948* (Jakarta: KPG, 2003), 841–47, 850–59, 863–66.

23. Asep Suryaman, "Asep Suryaman alias Hamim dan Jalan Hidupnya," unpublished manuscript (1998).

24. Suryaman, after his release from prison in 1999, wrote several additional essays at my request to elaborate on themes in his memoir. One of the essays is about the Delanggu strike: "Pemogokan Sarekat Buruh Perkebunan Republik Indonesia (Sarbupri) di Delanggu (Klaten), 1 April 1948 Sampai 1 Mei 1948," unpublished typescript (2002).

25. Siswoyo, *Siswoyo Dalam Pusaran Arus*, 40–42. Poeze, *Madiun 1948*, 102–5; George Kahin, *Nationalism and Revolution in Indonesia* (Ithaca, NY: Cornell University Press, 1952), 288.

26. Utami Suryadarma, *Saya, Soeriadi, dan Tanah Air*, ed. Imelda Bachtiar (Jakarta: Yayasan Bung Karno, 2012). Utami Suryadarma, based in Jakarta, was the rector of the Res Publica University and head of the USSR-front organization World Peace Council. One of Utoyo's daughters, Farida, became a celebrated ballerina and actress: Farida Oetoyo, *Saya Farida: Sebuah Autobiografi* (Jakarta: Gramedia, 2014).

27. Bernard Kalb, "Red Mayor in Java Cites Gains, But Opponents Deny Advances," *New York Times*, June 19, 1959.

28. "Konferensi Bakoksi Jogjakarta: Djadikan Seniman Ketoprak Alat Pelaksana Manipol," *Harian Rakjat Minggu*, January 3, 1965, p. 1; Hersri Setiawan, *Aku Eks-Tapol* (Yogyakarta: Galang, 2003), 423–47; J. J. Kusni, *Di Tengah Pergolakan: Turba LEKRA di Klaten* (Yogyakarta: Ombak, 2005); Rhoma Dwi Aria Yuliantri and Muhidin M. Dahlan, eds., *Lekra Tak Membakar Buku: Suara Senyap Lembar Kebudayaan Harian Rakjat 1950–1965* (Yogyakarta: Merakesumba, 2008), 339–53.

29. Lekra, *Laporan Umum Pengurus Pusat LEKRA: Resolusi dan Keputusan Kongres Nasional LEKRA* (1959). This report has been reproduced in Yuliantri and Dahlan, *Lekra Tak Membakar Buku*, 502–36.

30. One may notice that religion is largely a nonissue in both Kahin's *Nationalism and Revolution* and Anderson's *Java in a Time of Revolution*. That is a reflection as much of the political climate of Java in the 1940s as of the biases of the authors.

31. The Diponegoro Kodam covered Yogyakarta as well though that "special administrative zone" was not part of the province of Central Java. I use the term "Central Java" in this chapter to refer to both the province proper and Yogyakarta.

32. Pusat Penerangan Angkatan Darat, *Fakta-fakta Persoalan Sekitar "Gerakan 30 September,"* 282. This 446-page book is a compilation of three monthly reports that the Army Information Office issued on October 5, November 5, and December 5, 1965.

33. Benedict Anderson and Ruth McVey, *A Preliminary Analysis of the October 1, 1965 Coup in Indonesia* (Ithaca, NY: Cornell Southeast Asia Program, Cornell University, 1971), 6.

34. John Roosa, *Pretext for Mass Murder: The September 30th Movement and Suharto's Coup d'État in Indonesia* (Madison: University of Wisconsin Press, 2006).

35. The life history interview was conducted at Pak Bronto's home in Surakarta on December 2, 2012. All the quotes attributed to Bronto are from this interview unless otherwise noted. He had been interviewed by my colleagues in ISSI over a two-day period in 2006 and over a four-day period in 2009. Working with Hersri Setiawan, he has written an essay about his life history: J. Bronto, "Ketika Nakhoda Tidak Satu," in *Kidung untuk Korban: Dari Tutur Sepuluh Narasumber Eks-Tapol Sala*, ed. Hersri Setiawan (Surakarta: Pakorba Sala, 2006).

36. Another old friend of Untung's, Suhardi, recalled that the battalion under Sudigdo's command was known to be full of PKI supporters: "That battalion was

famous in the Boyolali area. It was the only battalion that followed the PKI." "Kisah Pewira Kesayangan Suharto," *Koran Tempo*, October 5, 2009, B3.

37. Captain Suradi Prawiromihardjo led the Movement's troops that took over the RRI station in Jakarta. He was then an officer in the Kodam for Jakarta, Kodam Jaya, with Colonel Latief. He was sentenced to life imprisonment in 1970. "Ex-Kapten Suradi Divonis Pendjara Seumur Hidup," *Kompas*, February 19, 1970.

38. Siswoyo claims that Slamat Riyadi took an oath in early 1949 to join the PKI and that the man who administered the oath was Pak Karto. Siswoyo, *Siswoyo Dalam Pusaran Arus*, 193–94.

39. Siswoyo, *Siswoyo Dalam Pusaran Arus*, 61–62, 67.

40. Siswoyo, *Siswoyo Dalam Pusaran Arus*, 27, 30, 33, 67. A former Politburo member from Surakarta, Rewang, describes "Bung Hadi (Suhadi Bengkring alias Pak Karto)" as the leader of the underground PKI in Surakarta during the Japanese occupation and the head of the committee to reorganize the PKI after independence in 1945. Rewang, *Saya Seorang Revolusioner: Memoar Rewang* (Bandung: Ultimus, 2017), 15.

41. Bronto, oral interview, Surakarta, December 15, 2009.

42. Josef Rabidi refused to be interviewed, despite repeated requests and meetings with him between 2000 and 2012 that involved my colleagues at ISSI as well as myself. He was determined to take the party's secrets to the grave with him. Bronto and Suryaman confirmed that Rabidi had been the Special Bureau agent in Surakarta at the time of the Movement. Rabidi was sentenced to death at a Mahmillub trial in 1967: "Mahmillub Sala Memvonnis Tokoh PKI J. Rabidi Mati," *Sinar Harapan*, June 3, 1967. The sentence was never carried out, and he remained imprisoned at Nusa Kambangan until the end of the Suharto regime.

43. According to army reporting at the time, the officers kidnapped in Surakarta were Lieutenant Colonel Ezy Suharto, Kodim commander; Captain Parman, his chief of staff; and Lieutenant Colonel Ashari (or Azhari), commander of the Sixth Brigade. All three had been released and were back working by October 4. "Ketua FN/Walikota Sala Antek 'G 30 S,'" *Berita Yudha*, October 12, 1965.

44. It is curious that the Suharto regime's official accounts of the Movement do not mention, much less narrate, the kidnapping of the three army commanders in Surakarta: Nugroho Notosusanto and Ismail Saleh, *The Coup Attempt of the "September 30th Movement" in Indonesia* (Jakarta: Pembimbing Masa, 1968), and Sekretariat Negara, *Gerakan 30 September: Pemberontakan Partai Komunis Indonesia* (Jakarta: Sekretariat Negara, 1994), 107–8.

45. Bronto's story is a clear refutation of the thesis in Anderson and McVey's *A Preliminary Analysis*, the so-called Cornell Paper, that Central Javanese soldiers on their own organized the Movement.

46. "Rontoknja Gestapu di Sala," *Angkatan Bersenjata*, October 25, 1965, 2.

47. The army, on October 1, identified three battalions in Surakarta as participants in the Movement: Battalions K, L, and M of the Sixth Brigade. Three days later, it claimed that the battalions were no longer in revolt and that there had been no bloodshed: "we were able to bring under control all the troops that had been involved

by October 4 without any armed conflict." Battalion L was in the process of being "consolidated," and Battalion M was "fully with us." The only remaining problem by October 4 was that two companies of Battalion K were helping the Movement leader from Semarang, Colonel Suherman, find refuge in the Surakarta area. But those two companies returned to their base in Surakara on October 5. Pusat Penerangan Angkatan Darat, *Fakta2 Persoalan Sekitar "Gerakan 30 September,"* 286, 292, 294.

48. David Jenkins and Douglas Kammen, "The Army Para-commando Regiment and the Reign of Terror in Central Java and Bali," in *The Contours of Mass Violence in Indonesia, 1965–68*, ed. D. Kammen and K. McGregor (Singapore: NUS Press, 2012), 78–80.

49. Pusat Penerangan Angkatan Darat, *Fakta2 Persoalan Sekitar "Gerakan 30 September,"* 296.

50. Pusat Penerangan Angkatan Darat, *Fakta2 Persoalan Sekitar "Gerakan 30 September,"* 287.

51. Harold Crouch, *The Army and Politics in Indonesia*, rev. ed. (Ithaca, NY: Cornell University Press, 1988), 84–85.

52. Pusat Penerangan Angkatan Darat, *Fakta2 Persoalan Sekitar "Gerakan 30 September,"* 208, 211. This army source is silent as to the fate of Battalion L.

53. Pusat Penerangan Angkatan Darat, *Fakta2 Persoalan Sekitar "Gerakan 30 September,"* 313. As for Major Iskandar, Bronto claimed that he fled to Jakarta in early October to meet the leaders of the Movement in person and was captured there sometime later.

54. Siswoyo, a member of the Central Committee in 1965, found it odd that Aidit did not remain in Jakarta at the time of such an emergency. Siswoyo, *Siswoyo Dalam Pusaran Arus*, 181.

55. Rewang, oral interview, Surakarta, June 27, 2001.

56. On the workers' strikes in Surakarta and the one report about barricades placed on a road, see Pusat Penerangan Angkatan Darat, *Fakta-fakta Persoalan Sekitar "Gerakan 30 September,"* 204–5, 208.

57. Pusat Penerangan Angkatan Darat, *Fakta-fakta Persoalan Sekitar "Gerakan 30 September,"* 273.

58. Pusat Penerangan Angkatan Darat, *Fakta-fakta Persoalan Sekitar "Gerakan 30 September,"* 214. By implication, Klaten was also included in this area.

59. Pusat Penerangan Angkatan Darat, *Fakta-fakta Persoalan Sekitar "Gerakan 30 September,"* 207, 210, 289.

60. M. Fauzi, ed., *Pulangkan Mereka: Merangkai Ingatan Penghilangan Paksa di Indonesia* (Jakarta: Elsam, 2012), 79–114.

61. John Hughes, *The End of Sukarno* (Singapore: Archipelago Press, 2002), 163.

62. Hughes, *The End of Sukarno*, 162.

63. Air force intelligence agents in Surakarta reported that forty-one people, communists and noncommunists, were killed in clashes in the city and its immediate environs between October 22 and 24. The air force had a base on the western outskirts of the city and provided aerial reconaissance to Sarwo Edhie. It is indicative of how

closely the US embassy was following events that it obtained a copy of the report and archived it. Air Force Intelligence Director, "Ichtisar Situasi Djawa Tengah," October 29, 1965. The document has been posted online by the National Security Archive: https://nsarchive2.gwu.edu//dc.html?doc=4107020-Document-10-Report-from-the-Director-of.

64. Hughes, *The End of Sukarno*, 161.

65. Pusat Penerangan Angkatan Darat, *Fakta-fakta Persoalan Sekitar "Gerakan 30 September,"* 209.

66. Marshall Green, "The Army Takes Hold in Central Java," report to Department of State, November 5, 1966, National Security Archive, Indonesia and East Timor Documentation Project, File 88, 28.

67. Researchers of the Indonesian Insitute of Social History held a daylong discussion with a group of sixty former political prisoners in Surakarta. From this discussion, they were able to gain a general sense of the pattern of the arrests and disappearances. They also conducted oral interviews with forty-six individuals in Surakarta and its immediate environs. Some of their research findings were incorporated into the report on the 1965-66 violence by National Commission on Violence against Women: *Mendengarkan Suara Perempuan Korban Peristiwa 1965* (Jakarta: Komnas Perempuan, 2007). Other findings have been posted online: "Lokasi Penahanan & Interogasi di Solo," http://sejarahsosial.org/kamp_solo/peta-lokasisolo.html.

68. Haryono (pseudonym), oral interview, Surakarta, July 20, 2000.

69. Marniti (pseudonym), oral interview, Surakarta, April 20, 2005.

70. Sunarti (pseudonym), oral interview, Surakarta, July 19, 2000.

71. National Commission on Violence against Women, *Mendengarkan Suara Perempuan Korban Peristiwa 1965*, 70–71.

72. Paini (pseudonym), oral interview, Sukoharjo, July 27, 2005.

73. Sarwo Edhie himself did not take part in it, having left to oversee the murderous work of his subordinates in Bali. "Mengikuti Operasi RPKAD: Pulang Kekandang," *Berita Yudha*, December 29, 1965.

74. Cosmas Batubara, *Sebuah Otobiografi Politik* (Jakarta: Kompas, 2007), 9–11.

75. Soe Hok Gie to Boediono, November 26, 1967. This letter has not been published. I obtained a copy from Stanley Adi Prasetyo. *Tempo* magazine, with Prasetyo's help, has published a booklet about a collection of his letters: Amarzan Lubis et al., *Gie dan Surat-Surat yang Tersembunyi* (Jakarta: KPG, 2016).

76. Firman Lubis, *Jakarta 1960-an: Kenangan Semasa Mahasiswa* (Jakarta: Masup, 2008), 231–33.

Chapter 5. Vanishing Points

1. Jean Couteau, *Museum Puri Lukisan* (Ubud: Yayasan Rathna Warta, 1999), 57.

2. The head of a gamelan troupe in Denpasar expelled six of its members for their affiliation to the PKI. "Sekehe Gong 'Darmabakti' Pemedilan Bersihkan Diri," *Suara Indonesia*, December 9, 1965.

3. On the Indonesian government's sending of artists to perform in foreign countries, see Jennifer Lindsay, "Performing Indonesia Abroad," in *Heirs to World Culture: Being Indonesian, 1950–1965*, ed. Jennifer Lindsay and Maya H. T. Liem (Leiden: KITLV, 2012), 191–222.

4. An important collection of essays on the theme of resistance is primarily about rescuers, people who "conceal the identity of wanted persons and/or help them escape to a safer place." Jacques Semelin et al, eds., *Resisting Genocide: The Multiple Forms of Rescue* (New York: Oxford University Press, 2010), 1. Two of the essays in the collection address a different form of resistance, that of government officials who refuse to follow orders. Raymond Kévorkian discusses the refusal of Ottoman civil servants to enforce deportation orders against Armenians and Scott Strauss discusses Rwandan officials who tried to prevent killings of Tutsis in areas under their control. Resistance by victims is a theme pursued in Benedict Kiernan, *Genocide and Resistance in Southeast Asia: Documentation, Denial, and Justice in Cambodia and East Timor* (New Brunswick, NJ: Transaction, 2008); A. Dirk Moses, ed., *Empire, Colony, Genocide: Conquest, Occupation, and Subaltern Resistance in World History* (New York: Berghahn Books, 2008).

5. Leo Kuper, *The Prevention of Genocide* (New Haven, CT: Yale University Press, 1985). John Heidenrich, *How to Prevent Genocide: A Guide for Policymakers, Scholars, and the Concerned Citizen* (Westport, CT: Praeger, 2001); Samuel Totten, ed., *Last Lectures on the Prevention and Intervention of Genocide* (New York: Routledge, 2018).

6. Soe Hok Gie wrote this article under a pseudonym for a Bandung student newspaper in 1967. It has been republished in Soe Hok Gie, *Zaman Peralihan* (Yogyakarta: Bentang Budaya, 1995), 161–69. An English translation has been published as "About the Mass Killings on the Island of Bali," in *The Indonesian Killings 1965–1966: Studies from Java and Bali*, ed. Robert Cribb (Monash: Monash University Centre of Southeast Asian Studies, 1990), 252–58. Gie's biographer does not believe that he visited Bali in order to write the article. John Maxwell, "Soe Hok-Gie: A Biography of a Young Indonesian Intellectual" (PhD diss., Australian National University, 1997), 233. He may have written it on the basis of discussions with Balinese visiting Jakarta.

7. Hughes's book has been republished as *The End of Sukarno* (Singapore: Archipelago Press, 2002). Clifford Geertz, otherwise known for his profound understanding of both the problems of interpretation and the subtleties of Balinese culture, treated it as an authoritative primary source when asserting that the tens of thousands of Balinese were killed "largely by one another." "Deep Play: Notes on the Balinese Cockfight," *Daedalus* 101, no. 1 (Winter 1972): 37n43.

8. Hughes, *The End of Sukarno*, 184.

9. Horace Sutton, "Indonesia's Night of Terror," *Saturday Evening Post*, February 4, 1967, 25–32.

10. One can compare Sutedja to the PNI leaders Merta and Wedastera Suyasa, about whom brief biographies have been written: Mansur Hidayat, "Biografi Politik I Gusti Putu Merta (1913-1992)" (BA thesis, Udayana University, 1999); Max Lane,

"Wedastera Suyasa in Balinese Politics, 1962–1972: From Charismatic Politics to Socio-Educational Activities" (BA thesis, Sydney University, 1972).

11. Sutedja held the position of Penguasa Pelaksanaan Dwikora Daerah (Pepelrada, Regional Military Authority for the Implementation of Dwikora). Robinson states that Sutedja's appointment as the Pepelrada came in 1961. Geoffrey Robinson, *The Dark Side of Paradise: Political Violence in Bali* (Ithaca, NY: Cornell University Press, 1995), 186. That is incorrect: Sukarno began Dwikora (The Two Commands) in 1964 as part of the Confrontation against Malaysia. The Pepelrada appointments were made in September 1964. Harold Crouch, *The Army and Politics in Indonesia*, rev. ed. (Ithaca, NY: Cornell University Press, 1998), 76.

12. Edward Masters, US Embassy to State Department, "Conflict Erupts in Bali with PNI Opposed to Leftist Governor and PKI," March 23, 1965, National Security Archive, Indonesia and East Timor Documentation Project, File 25, p. 66; Edward Masters, US Embassy to State Department, "Some Aspects of the Army's Relationship with Sukarno and the PKI," August 21, 1965, National Security Archive, Indonesia and East Timor Documentation Project, File 37, p. 32. It is indicative of the close relationship between the US Embassy and the army that Masters obtained the two-hundred-page document containing the transcripts of the speeches at a conference of the army's Kodam commanders held in Jakarta, May 27–29, 1965. Masters devoted a special section of his report on Sjafiudin.

13. "Keputusan Pepelrada Bali dalam Hadapi G-30-S," *Suara Indonesia*, November 1, 1965.

14. Akihisa Matsuno, "The 30 September Movement and Its Aftermath in Bali, October–December 1965," in *The Indonesian Genocide of 1965: Causes, Dynamics and Legacies*, ed. Katherine McGregor, Jess Melvin, and Annie Pohlman (London: Palgrave Macmillan, 2018), 71–88.

15. "DPD PNI Daerah Bali Pak Merta: Bali Seolah-olah Negara Sendiri Jang Terpisah dari Pusat," *Suara Indonesia*, October 29, 1965.

16. "Ditjabut Sementara Idjin Terbit Harian 'Fadjar' dan 'Bali Dwipa,'" *Suara Indonesia*, November 5, 1965.

17. "Brigjen Sjafiudin: Rakjat bersemangat tinggi tumpas habis G-30-S," *Suara Indonesia*, November 11, 1965.

18. "PKI-Partindo Bubarkan Diri," *Suara Indonesia*, October 29, 1965.

19. Sjafiudin ordered the "freezing" of Partindo on December 4, 1965: "Partindo dan Ormas2nja Dibekukan Melibatkan diri dlm G-30-S," *Suara Indonesia*, December 7, 1965.

20. "Tugas Teperda Memeriksa Oknum-Oknum Terlibat G-30-S," *Suara Indonesia*, December 1, 1965.

21. "Instansi/Organisasi Olahraga Dukung Tuntutan Pemetjatan AA Bg. Sutedja," *Suara Indonesia*, December 10, 1965; "Senat Unud Tidak Akui AA Bgs. Sutedja," *Suara Indonesia*, December 12, 1965.

22. "Pernjataan 5 Parpol di Bali: Bubarkan PKI dan Ormas2nja," *Suara Indonesia*, 21 November 1965.

23. "Gab. Seksi DPRD GR Bali Putuskan Tidak Akui A.A.B. Sutedja Ketua DPRDGR," *Suara Indonesia*, December 2, 1965. Sutedja issued a point-by-point denial of the allegation that he was involved in the September 30th Movement: "Djawaban Gubernur Kdh. Bali," *Suara Indonesia*, December 3, 1965, and December 4, 1965.

24. The commissioned biography of Kompiang and his wife contains much valuable information for the historian: I Nyoman Darma Putra, *Pasangan Pionir Pariwisata Bali* (Denpasar: Jagat Press, 2012).

25. "Bersihkan Bali Beach Hotel dari Unsur G-30-S," *Suara Indonesia*, November 11, 1965; "Ditiap Dada Marhaen Berkobar Djiwa Anti Nekolim," *Suara Indonesia*, November 15, 1965; "Petjat Setiap Karyawan Bali Beach Hotel Sanur Pendukung G-30-S," *Suara Indonesia*, November 17, 1965.

26. The most detailed investigation into the Tegalbadeng incident and its aftermath is I Ngurah Suryawan, *Ladang Hitam di Pulau Dewa: Pembantaian Massal di Bali 1965* (Yogyakarta: Galang Press, 2007), 123–243.

27. Ikranagara, "G-30-N di Bali: Catatan Tentang Menjelang Tahun Baru 1966," 2011, http://permalink.gmane.org/gmane.culture.region.indonesia.ppi-india/97081.

28. Ikranagara, "G-30-N di Bali."

29. "Rumah A.A.B. Sutedja di Negara dan 'Ex Pimpinan PKI Hantjur," *Suara Indonesia*, December 4, 1965. Sutedja and his wife were safe in the governor's house in Denpasar at the time.

30. Dhenia had been in police custody since early November. He had been arrested in East Java and then transferred to Bali sometime later. "Dhenia ditangkap di Banyuwangi," *Suara Indonesia*, November 9, 1965.

31. A US Embassy official was told by someone from the Socialist Party that three thousand people were killed in Jembrana and six thousand in the rest of Bali prior to the arrival of the RPKAD. Robert Martens, "Memorandum of Conversation," December 9, 1965, National Security Archive, Indonesia and East Timor Documentation Project, File 55, p. 57. These figures were the products of rumors and are impossible to believe. All the victims, perpetrators, and witnesses I have interviewed have affirmed that there was no large-scale killing in south Bali, the most populous part of the island, prior to the arrival of the RPKAD.

32. Brigadier Generals H. R. Dharsono, Hartono Wirjodiprodjo, and Suharto were, respectively, Assistants III (personnel), IV (logistics), and V (territorial affairs). They had been appointed as assistants to the army commander, Suharto, on October 25, 1965, to replace the generals killed by the September 30th Movement. Soemitro had been appointed Assistant II (operations) on November 3, 1965.

33. "Djenderal2 ke Bali: Masalah Bali Dapat Perhatian Penuh," *Suara Indonesia*, December 10, 1965.

34. A brief report mentioned a plane arriving from Halim Airbase in Jakarta carrying an unspecified number of RPKAD troops: "RPKAD Bantu Penertiban di Bali," *Suara Indonesia*, December 11, 1965.

35. "Panglima Brigdjen Sjafiudin: G-30-S Harus Dipatahkan," *Suara Indonesia*, Desember 10, 1965.

36. "Pangdam XVI/Udayana: Kontrev G-30-S di Bali sebenarnja dapat diatasi hanya dengan Tentara Inf. biasa," *Suara Indonesia*, January 4, 1966.

37. Sukarno issued the letter suspending Sutejda and appointing Merta on December 18, 1965. "Anak Agung Bagus Sutedja Diganti," *Berita Yudha*, December 27, 1965.

38. "Badan Koordinasi Kesatuan Aksi Pengganjangan Kontrev Gestapu," *Suara Indonesia*, December 10, 1965. The head of this organization was Dr. Adnjana Manuaba of the PNI.

39. Team Penerangan Operasi Mental, "Seruan," *Suara Indonesia*, December 11, 1965.

40. "Kendaraan Bermotor Umum jg Telah Diamankan oleh ABRI Supaja Didaftarkan," *Suara Indonesia*, December 10, 1965.

41. "Tindakan ABRI—Massa Rakjat Harus Searah dalam Menumpas G-30-S Sampai Ke Akar-Akarnja," *Suara Indonesia*, December 12, 1965.

42. This document consists of the minutes of a meeting of Bali's PNI leaders on December 22, 1965. Those minutes recount the meeting at Denpasar's Kodim on December 10. The document states that the initiative for the meeting came from the commander of the police in Bali (Pangdak) and was led by Lieutenant Colonel Soekarmen, the commander of the Korem covering Bali. The image of the original handwritten document appears in Mansur Hidayat, "Biografi Politik I Gusti Putu Merta," appendix 3, 116.

43. Mansur Hidayat, "Biografi Politik I Gusti Putu Merta," appendix 3, 116.

44. Soe Hok Gie, "Di Sekitar Peristiwa Pembunuhan Besar-Besaran di Pulau Bali," in Soe Hok Gie, *Zaman Peralihan*, 165.

45. "Dan RPKAD Major Djasmin: Laksanakan dg Konsekwen Adjaran Pembesrev Bung Karno: Di Negara Makmur Komunis Tidak Laku," *Suara Indonesia*, December 20, 1965.

46. "Djangan Bertindak Sendiri2," *Suara Indonesia*, December 24, 1965.

47. Major Matnoer, "Pengertian Tumpas Habis G-30-S Sampai Ke-akar2nja," *Suara Indonesia*, December 23, 1965.

48. "Purwanto Sastroatmodjo SH: Gestapu/PKI Djangan Diberi Kesempatan Hidup Lagi," *Suara Indonesia*, December 20, 1965.

49. I interviewed two Balinese men who managed to finagle travel permits and escape to Java before the slaughter in December. One was the leader of Partindo in Bali: Made Mardiya, oral interview, Denpasar, Bali, August 17, 2000. The other was a midlevel PKI activist: I Made Sutayasa, oral interview, Denpasar, Bali, July 13, 2004. The PNI supporter Ikranegara mentioned the *surat jalan* in his 2011 essay: "G-30-N di Bali."

50. Bhadra, oral interview, Kapal, Bali, January 10, 2001.

51. No trace of it exists today. It was torn down around 1979 after a new prison was opened outside the city in Kerobokan. A shopping center was erected in its place.

52. I Wayan Santa, oral interview, Denpasar, Bali, July 13, 2004.

53. I interviewed a former soldier, Malen, who had been arrested in late 1965 on the charge of being involved in the Movement. He had been a trainer at the army's

training center in Tabanan working under Major Sukarlan. A company of troops at the training center had been waiting on standby on October 1, ready to support the Movement. But they took no action. Malen was arrested on October 7 and held in the Pekambingan prison. He and the other members of his company were passed over as hundreds of prisoners were taken out and executed in late 1965 and early 1966. He was held there without charge until 1978. Malen, oral interview, Tabanan, Bali, August 27, 2000. For more information on the military troops in Bali and the Movement, see Matsuno, "The 30 September Movement and Its Aftermath in Bali."

54. Taran (pseudonym), oral interview, Gianyar, Bali, August 18, 2000.

55. Ni Made Intaran, oral interview, Denpasar, Bali, August 15, 2000.

56. One of Serata's younger brothers, John Ketut Pantja, was an officer in the air force stationed in Makassar. On hearing news of the killing, he returned to Bali and resigned from the air force. He later made a fortune from the Balinese tourism industry and converted to Christianity. The biography that he commissioned of himself discusses his older brother. Nyoman Wijaya, *Biografi Si Penggembala Itik: John Ketut Pantja: Pengalaman dan Pemikiran* (Yogyakarta: Pustaka Pelajar, 2001), 148–51.

57. Ibu Pasek, oral interview, Denpasar, Bali, August 17, 2000.

58. "Mengikuti Operasi RPKAD: Pulang Kekandang," *Berita Yudha*, December 29, 1965.

59. Hughes, *The End of Sukarno*, 190.

60. Ken Conboy, *Kopassus: Inside Indonesia's Special Forces* (Jakarta: Equinox, 2003), 149.

61. Hidayat, "Biografi Politik I Gusti Putu Merta," appendix 3.

62. Notes from an unrecorded interview with Ida Bagus Kompiang, Sanur, Bali, September 2000. Other relatives of his confirmed this information.

63. Ibu Sutedja, oral interview, Jembrana, Bali, August 29, 2000. See also Slamat Trisila, "The Sutedja File: Gubernor Bali Pertama dalam Lipatan Sejarah," *Jurnal Kajian Bali* 3, no. 1 (April 2013).

Chapter 6. Invisible Worlds

1. I am echoing the title of one of the first oral history books about the survivors of the Holocaust: David Boder, *I Did Not Interview the Dead* (Urbana: University of Illinois Press, 1949). An anthropologist doing fieldwork in North Sumatra has described a séance with the spirit of a man who disappeared in 1965–66: Mary Steedly, *Hanging without a Rope: Narrative Experience in Colonial and Postcolonial Karoland* (Princeton, NJ: Princeton University Press, 1994), ch. 8.

2. Robinson mentioned Kapal in a footnote, relaying rumors he had heard: "One of the more notorious killing centers was the village of Kapal, on the road between Denpasar and Tabanan. There is no way of knowing now how many died at Kapal, but it appears that operations continued there for at least two months." Geoffrey Robinson, *The Dark Side of Paradise: Political Violence in Bali* (Ithaca, NY: Cornell University Press, 1995), 301n109. As will be explained later, "operations," meaning

executions, did not continue in Kapal for two months, and Kapal was no more of a "killing center" than any other village in Bali. It was notorious because of the fame of the victims, not the number of victims.

3. How those *puputan* were understood by the people involved and how their meanings have been variously interpreted are questions that can be posed only once it is agreed that something like an event named "a *puputan*" happened. Margaret Wiener has written a fascinating inquiry into the various meanings of the 1906 and 1908 *puputan* for both the Balinese and the Dutch: *Visible and Invisible Realms: Power, Magic, and Colonial Conquests* (Chicago: University of Chicago Press, 1995).

4. John Hughes began this trope, quoting unnamed "Balinese intellectuals" who contended that the victims "were cooperating in the purging of the island": "They had seen the mistake of their Communist affiliation and by dying would be helping cleanse both themselves and the island." He compared the killings to the mass suicides of the early 1900s. Hughes, *The End of Sukarno* (Singapore: Archipelago Press, 2002), 191. In a segment of an NBC hour-long documentary, a Balinese intellectual, perhaps the same one Hughes spoke to, Professor Rata of Udayana University, claimed that the victims in his village begged to be killed. *Indonesia: The Troubled Victory* (New York: NBCUniversal Media, 1967). Horace Sutton, in a particularly presumptuous passage, contended that the Balinese communists, realizing their evilness, "were eager to get out of this life" and be reincarnated as something else. Sutton, "Indonesia's Night of Terror," *Saturday Review*, February 4, 1967, 30.

5. Fred B. Eiseman, *Bali: Sekala & Niskala*, 2 vols. (Rutland, VT: Tuttle, 1990).

6. Tameng Marhaenis means "The Shield of Marhaen." Marhaen was the quasi-fictional character President Sukarno used to represent Indonesia's working poor. Hughes misspelled the name of the militia as Tamin. Hughes, *The End of Sukarno*, 189. His mistake was repeated in Robert Cribb, ed., *The Indonesian Killings of 1965–1966: Studies from Java and Bali* (Monash: Monash University Centre of Southeast Asian Studies, 1990), 241.

7. Poniti interview, August 24, 2000, Kapal, Bali. All subsequent quotes attributed to Poniti are from this interview unless otherwise noted.

8. Robinson, *The Dark Side of Paradise*, 289.

9. The daily newspaper in Denpasar reported that tanks (*panser*) from the army's East Java division had arrived in Bali on December 7. "Panglima Brigdjen Sjafiudin: 'G-30-S' Harus Dipatahkan," *Suara Indonesia*, December 10, 1965.

10. Poniti was in charge of the Tameng, a group of young toughs, in the village, but an older man, Anak Agung Ngurah Perdana, was the head of the PNI in Kapal.

11. Notes from an unrecorded discussion with Poniti, Kapal, Bali, July 30, 2013.

12. Notes from an unrecorded discussion with Putu (pseudonym), Kapal, Bali, August 1, 2013.

13. Notes from an unrecorded discussion with Pan Wayan (pseudonym), Kapal, Bali, August 1, 2013.

14. Notes from an unrecorded discussion with Agung (pseudonym), Sangeh, Bali, July 31, 2013.

15. Poniti claimed that the Kodam commander, Brigadier General Sjafiudin, and the PNI leader, Merta, were present, but I have not been able to confirm their presence. No witness claimed that the RPKAD commander, Major Djasmin, was present.

16. Robinson reports that Dhana became the *bupati* in late 1965, replacing a PKI-affiliated *bupati*. Robinson, *The Dark Side of Paradise*, 268. Dhana's curricula vitae indicates he entered office in June 1965, and notices in the newspaper *Suara Indonesia* reveal he was in office at least by August. The former *bupati*, Anak Agung Gede Agung, who became head of Bali's Information Department, was not affiliated with the PKI.

17. I Wayan Dhana, oral interview, Denpasar, Bali, January 6, 2001.

18. Dhana was referring to a machine gun that uses bullets with a diameter of 12.7 millimeters. Such .50 caliber guns were among the heaviest machine guns available at that time. A Saracen could have been fitted with a .50 caliber machine gun in its turret, though it was usually fitted with a .30 caliber machine gun. None of the other witnesses mentioned firing from the top of the armored personnel carrier. Perhaps the machine guns mounted on these vehicles were taken down and placed on the ground for use by the firing squad.

19. I Made Pugeg, oral interview, Denpasar, Bali, September 3, 2000.

20. The PNI newspaper in Bali mentioned that the deputy commander of the RPKAD sent to the island was First Lieutenant Urip, who was commander of the company of troops called Ben Hur. "RPKAD Turba," *Suara Indonesia*, December 21, 1965. Later he became a captain and was expelled from the RPKAD at some point because of a suspected connection to the PKI dating back to the 1940s. Ken Conboy, *Kopassus: Inside Indonesia's Special Forces* (Jakarta: Equinox, 2003), 154.

21. I Gusti Ketut Reti, oral interview, Denpasar, Bali, January 7, 2001.

22. Bali Oral History Archive, Murdoch University, interview with I Gusti Ketut Reti, Denpasar, Bali, 1996, http://library.murdoch.edu.au/boha/.

23. Multiple witnesses attest to the following PKI leaders as victims of the Kapal massacre: Ktut Kandel, Anom Dada, and Ida Bagus Dupem. The head of a victim's organization in Bali, Wayan Santa, provided me with the names of other men that he believed were killed there: I Gusti Tiaga (a manager at Puger's company, Majapahit), Sutaya (an engineer who worked on the governor's staff), and Cilandek (the head of the PKI-affiliated organization for university students).

24. Horace Sutton, "Indonesia's Night of Terror," *Saturday Evening Post*, February 4, 1967, 27.

25. To list the inaccuracies: (1) His name was Puger, not Buger. (2) The governor, Sutedja, was not a communist. (3) Puger was neither caught nor marched to a cemetery; he had voluntarily put himself in police custody and was transported in an armored personnel carrier to the Kapal cremation ground. (4) He was not fat, as photos of him prove. His killers could not have slashed at him to cut off excess flesh. (6) The number of other men killed was far more than nine.

26. Robinson, *The Dark Side of Paradise*, 299.

27. Dayu Rai, oral interview, Denpasar, Bali, January 11, 2001.

28. The editor of *Fadjar* was I Gusti Made Raka, a young Balinese intellectual who lived in the Kesiman area of Denpasar. He was taken from police custody and killed by Tameng in Denpasar in December 1965. He was the father of Degung Santikarma, who is one of the individuals profiled in the film *40 Years of Silence*. The editor of *Suara Indonesia*, K. Nadha, complained that Puger had poached some of his staff to work at the *Fadjar* office. Bali Oral History Archive, Murdoch University, interview with K. Nadha, Denpasar, Bali, 1996, http://library.murdoch.edu.au/boha/.

29. Made Mardiya was the head of Partindo in Bali. Made Mardiya, oral interview, Denpasar, Bali, August 17, 2000. Oei Tjoe Tat, a member of Sukarno's cabinet, was a leader of Partindo in Jakarta. Oei Tjoe Tat, *Memoar Oei Tjoe Tat: Pembantu Presiden Sukarno*, ed. Pramoedya Ananta Toer and Stanley Adi Prasetyo (Jakarta: Hasta Mitra, 1995), 95–99.

30. The head of the WPC in Jakarta was Utami Suryadarma, who was also the rector of Res Publika University.

31. Hughes, *The End of Sukarno*, 187–88.

32. Robinson, *The Dark Side of Paradise*, 211–17, 247–51.

33. "Bali Mendjadi Tempat KIAPMA," *Suara Indonesia*, October 12, 1965; "KIAPMA Dimulai tg 16 Okt di Djakarta," *Suara Indonesia*, October 14," 1965. The WPC organized the conference.

34. The banning of *Fadjar* was announced on November 3, but the newspaper seems to have already stopped publishing in early October. "Ditjabut Sementara Idjin Terbit: Harian Fadjar dan Bali Dwipa," *Suara Indonesia*, November 5, 1965. The Pugers, along with thirteen others, were made "non-active" in the National Consultative Council on November 15. "Bamunas Daerah Bali Bersihkan Diri," *Suara Indonesia*, November 22, 1965.

35. Jaya Wardhana, oral interview, Batu Bulan, Bali, July 25, 2015. Neither Dayu Rai nor her children could remember the exact date of the attack on their house.

36. Made Mardiya, oral interview, Denpasar, Bali, August 17, 2000.

37. The housing complex was on a narrow dead-end street, Gang Pertani. It was meant to be used by employees of the immigration department but had not yet been inhabited.

38. Raka Suasta, oral interview, Denpasar, Bali, August 18, 2000.

39. Oei Tjoe Tat, *Memoar*, 186.

40. I Wayan Jendra, oral interview, Gianyar, Bali, July 12, 2004.

41. The decision of the Supreme Court case is available online on the court's website: http://putusan.mahkamahagung.go.id/putusan/downloadpdf/5c37d5121fac53f3d088dbd16d0438de/pdf.

42. KOTI Collection, National Archives of the Republic of Indonesia. It should be noted that nothing in the Puger file implicates him in criminal actions or connects him to the PKI.

43. Ida Bagus Kompiang, who knew both men very well, confirmed that the two became rivals in the 1950s after having been close friends in the 1940s. Notes from an unrecorded interview with Ida Bagus Kompiang, Sanur, Bali, September 2000.

Chapter 7. Dead Labor

1. S. W. Kuntjahjo, "Kesan2 Malam Kesenian Buruh," *Harian Rakjat*, May 18, 1963. My account of the Cultural Night is drawn from this article.

2. Another cultural event held in the SBKA hall was an exhibition of Soviet ceramics, paintings, and statues. The PKI's newspaper published a review of the artwork and a photo of the Soviet ambassador opening the exhibition. *Harian Rakjat*, December 1, 1956; "Pameran Sovjet Uni: Seni Sebagai Tontonan Rakjat," *Harian Rakjat*, December 8, 1956.

3. Boejoeng Saleh, "Gerakan Buruh dan Kebudayaan," *Harian Rakjat*, January 10, 1953.

4. Jafar Suryomenggolo, *Organising under the Revolution: Unions and the State in Java, 1945–48* (Singapore: NUS Press, 2015), 127. The SBKA had been squabbling for months with the leadership of the Republic over the provision of rice for railway workers.

5. Suryomenggolo, *Organising under the Revolution*, 98.

6. Tri Ramidjo (1926–2019) made this point in a personal discussion with me in 2009. He grew up with Lukman in the prison camp of Boven Digoel. Lukman invited him to help produce the journal *Bintang Merah* in Jakarta in the early 1950s. He lived with Lukman and other PKI leaders in a rundown house near Pasar Senen. In the 1970s, he was held as a political prisoner on Buru Island. His autobiographical essays are brief and anecdotal: Tri Ramidjo, *Kisah-Kisah Dari Tanah Merah: Cerita Digul, Cerita Buru* (Bandung: Ultimus, 2009).

7. On the history of the railway workers at Manggarai station from the 1910s to 1965, see Razif, "Buruh Kereta Api dan Komunitas Buruh Manggarai," in *Dekolonisasi Buruh Kota dan Pembentukan Bangsa*, ed. Erwiza Erman and Ratna Saptari (Jakarta: Obor, 2013), 91–141.

8. Hilmar Farid, "Indonesia's Original Sin: Mass Killings and Capitalist Expansion, 1965–66," *Inter-Asia Cultural Studies* 6, no. 1 (2005): 9. Farid's essay expresses the view of a social and cultural historian bristling at juridical approaches to history writing. On how these two different approaches might be productively combined, see the essays by Greg Grandin: "History, Motive, Law, Intent: Combining Historical and Legal Methods in Understanding Guatemala's 1981–1983 Genocide," in *The Specter of Genocide: Mass Murder in Historical Perspective*, ed. Robert Gellately and Ben Kiernan (Cambridge: Cambridge University Press, 2003), 339–52; and "Chronicles of Guatemalan Genocide Foretold: Violence, Trauma, and the Limits of Historical Inquiry," *Nepantla* 1, no. 2 (2000): 391–412.

9. On the occasion of the article's tenth anniversary, the journal published a collection of commentaries on it: *Inter-Asia Cultural Studies* 16, no. 2 (2015).

10. David Bourchier, *Illiberal Democracy in Indonesia: The Ideology of the Family State* (London: Routledge, 2014).

11. Jacques Leclerc, "An Ideological Problem of Indonesian Trade Unionism in the 1960s: 'Karyawan' versus 'Buruh,'" *Review of Indonesian and Malaysian Affairs* 6,

no. 1 (1972); Vedi Hadiz, *Workers and the State in New Order Indonesia* (London: Routledge, 1997).

12. Bradley Simpson, *Economists with Guns: Authoritarian Development and U.S.-Indonesia Relations, 1960–1968* (Stanford: Stanford University Press, 2008), chs. 5–8.

13. William Redfern, "Sukarno's Guided Democracy and the Takeover of Foreign Companies in Indonesia in the 1960s" (PhD diss., University of Michigan, 2010), 390–414.

14. Enzo Traverso, *Understanding the Nazi Genocide: Marxism after Auschwitz* (London: Pluto Press, 1999). See also Moishe Postone, "The Holocaust and the Trajectory of the Twentieth Century," in *Catastrophe and Meaning*, ed. M. Postone and E. Santner (Chicago: University of Chicago Press, 2003); Alex Callinicos, "Plumbing the Depths: Marxism and the Holocaust," *Yale Journal of Criticism* 14, no. 2 (2001): 385–414.

15. Writers on genocide have tended not to see capitalism as relevant, even when discussing phenomena that could be easily seen as parts of it, such settler colonialism from the 1500s to the present. Patrick Wolfe, in a widely read article, argued that settler colonialism could be genocidal in some cases, but he did not connect settler colonialism to capitalism: "Settler Colonialism and the Elimination of the Native," *Journal of Genocide Research* 8, no. 4 (2006): 387–409. That connection is made in more recent works, such as Katsuya Hirano, "Thanatopolitics in the Making of Japan's Hokkaido: Settler Colonialism and Primitive Accumulation," *Critical Historical Studies* 2, no. 2 (2015): 191–218.

16. Ooi Jin Bee, *The Petroleum Resources of Indonesia* (Kuala Lumpur: Oxford University Press, 1982), 4. Shell was established in 1907 as a merger of a Dutch oil company operating wells in North Sumatra and East Kalimantan and a British company that could handle the international distribution of the oil. Shell's company within the East Indies (and later Indonesia) was named the Bataafse Petroleum Maatschappij (Batavian Petroleum Company). Stanvac began as the Colonial Netherlands Petroleum Company, a wholly owned subsidiary of the Standard Oil Company of New Jersey, in 1912. A merger with the Standard Oil Company of New York-Vacuum Oil in 1933 led to the new name of Standard-Vacuum Oil Company, abbreviated as Stanvac.

17. Willem Remmelink, ed. and trans., *The Invasion of the Dutch East Indies* (Leiden: Leiden University Press, 2015), 4.

18. Wesley Craven and James Cate, eds., *The Army Air Forces in World War II*, vol. 5 (Chicago: University of Chicago Press, 1953), 107–9.

19. Mestika Zed, *Kepialangan Politik dan Revolusi: Palembang 1900–1949* (Jakarta: LP3ES, 2003), 328–94.

20. Richard McMillan, *The British Occupation of Indonesia, 1945–1946: Britain, the Netherlands and the Indonesian Revolution* (London: Routledge, 2005), 137.

21. Anne-Lot Hoek, "De Verzwegen Moordpartij van Palembang," *Vrij Nederland*, July 26, 2017, https://www.vn.nl/de-verzwegen-moordpartij-van-palembang/.

22. Quoted in Woonkyung Yeo, "Palembang in the 1950s: The Making and Unmaking of a Region" (PhD diss., University of Washington, 2012), 75.

23. Indonesia Project, *Stanvac in Indonesia* (New York: National Planning Association, 1957), 49–50. The Indonesia Project was based at MIT's Center for International Studies. Among the research associates was Guy Pauker, who later studied the Indonesian military.

24. Indonesia Project, *Stanvac in Indonesia*, 51, 54.

25. Audrey Kahin and George Kahin, *Subversion as Foreign Policy: The Eisenhower and Dulles Debacle in Indonesia* (New York: New Press, 1995), 66.

26. Daniel Lev, *The Transition to Guided Democracy: Indonesian Politics 1957–1959* (Ithaca, NY: Cornell Southeast Asian Studies Publications, 1966), 41.

27. The Lampung area, which had many Javanese settlers, was carved out of South Sumatra and made into its own province in 1964. It remained under the authority of Kodam IV based in Palembang. The Bengkulu part of South Sumatra was turned into a province in 1968.

28. Bhaskoro, oral interview, Lampung, February 19, 2001.

29. The leader of Baperki in Palembang, Liem Tjong Hian, was arrested at some point in late 1965. He was a prominent lawyer who had helped establish the province's university in the early 1960s and headed up an association of rubber manufacturers. He survived and, after his release, moved to the safety of the Netherlands, where he became a librarian at Nijmegen University. Leo Suryadinata, *Prominent Indonesian Chinese* (Singapore: ISEAS, 2015), 158.

30. Marshall Green, Telegram to Secretary of State, November 1, 1965. The National Security Archive has posted a scan of this document online: https://nsarchive2.gwu.edu//dc.html?doc=4107019-Document-9-Telegram-1290-from-American-Embassy.

31. "Sebuah Kamp di Tengah Sungai," *Tempo*, October 7, 2012, 100; Truly Hitosoro, "Menapaki Jejak Kekerasan di Pulau Kemaro," *Islam Bergerak*, March 19, 2015, http://islambergerak.com/2015/03/menapaki-jejak-kekerasan-di-pulau-kemaro/; Anwar Putra Bayu, "Di Balik Cerita Sungai Musi," a poem published in Ahmadun Yosi Herfanda et al., eds., *Sungai Isak Perih Menyemak: Antologi Puisi Esai* (Depok: Jurnal Sajak Indonesia, 2014), 35–44; Mochtar Effendy, *Perjuangan Mencari Ridha Tuhan: Catatan Tiga Zaman dari Balik Terali Penjara Rezim Tirani Suharto* (Palembang: AlMukhtar, 2002).

32. Ibu Murtini, oral interview, Lampung, February 17, 2001. Interview by Yayan Wiludiharto. She also spoke to members of YPKP who wrote an account of her imprisonment and published it in a book: Yayasan Tifa, *Saatnya Korban Bicara: Menata Derap Merajut Langkah* (Jakarta: Tifa, 2009). They have posted it online: http://ypkp1965.org/blog/2016/09/07/neraka-di-pulau-kemarau/.

33. Imran Hasibuan and Muhammad Yamin, eds., *Jembatan Kebangsaan: Biografi Politik Taufiq Kiemas* (Jakarta: Q Communication, 2008), 67.

34. Hasibuan and Yamin, *Jembatan Kebangsaan*, 66.

35. Hasibuan and Yamin, *Jembatan Kebangsaan*, 65–66.

36. Sudisman, "Hidup dalam Djuang: Djuang dalam Hidup! Statement Politik Terachir Sudisman Menyongsong Ditembak Mati," typescript in author's possession (October 5, 1968), 2.

37. Ramadhan KH, *Ibnu Sutowo: Saatnya Saya Bercerita!* (Jakarta: National Press Club, 2008), 218. On Ibnu Sutowo's later career, see Hamish McDonald, *Suharto's Indonesia* (Blackburn, Victoria: Fontana Books, 1980), ch. 7. His corruption became world famous in 1976 when he bankrupted the state oil company, Pertamina, precisely at the time when the price of oil was skyrocketing.

38. Ramadhan KH, *Ibnu Sutowo*, 102.

39. J. van Dulm et al., *Geillustreerde Atlas van de Japanse Kampen in Nederlands-Indie, 1942–1945* (Zierikzee: Asia Minor, 2002), 77.

40. This account of Taher's life story is based on his memoir: *Riau Berdarah: Kisah Perjalanan Hidupku* (Jakarta: Hasta Mitra, 2006). I have corresponded with him to clarify certain points.

41. Erwiza Erman has written about the labor relations at the coal mines of Sawahlunto and the intersections between nationalism, communism, and union activism during the colonial period: "Miners, Managers, and the State: A Socio-Political History of the Ombilin Coal-Mines, West Sumatra, 1892–1996" (PhD diss., University of Amsterdam, 1999). Her dissertation has been published in Indonesian: *Membaranya Batubara: Konflik Kelas dan Etnik Ombilin-Sawahlunto, Sumatra Barat, 1892–1996* (Depok: Desantara, 2005).

42. Her grandfather, Mangkudun Sati, is mentioned in Ruth McVey's book *The Rise of Indonesian Communism* (Ithaca, NY: Cornell University Press, 1965), 308, 425, 481.

43. Dewan Nasional SOBSI, "Tentang Kegiatan Ambilalih Perusahaan2 Belanda dalam Perdjuangan Pembebasan Irain Barat," July 21, 1958. The head office in Jakarta sent this sixteen-page document to all the chapters of the union.

44. Kesatuan Aksi Buruh Minjak Sungai Gerong, Pendopo Area, "Proklamasi," March 18, 1965, National Archives of the Republic of Indonesia, R22 240. The statement called for Sukarno to immediately confiscate Stanvac and make it the property of Indonesia.

45. A PKI leader in Jakarta handling Riau matters wrote an analysis of the March actions calling for the nationalization of Caltex. Biro Sumteng [Central Sumatran Bureau], "Soal Aksi Ambil-alih Perusahaan Caltex di Riau," April 5, 1965. I thank Razif for providing me with a photocopy of this document.

46. Neil Sheehan, "Indonesia Seizes Oil Concerns," *New York Times*, March 20, 1965, 1.

47. US Embassy to State Department, "Joint Weeka no. 13," March 26, 1965, National Security Archive, Indonesia and East Timor Documentation Project, File 25, pp. 90–91.

48. The Suharto regime's "White Book" records that nothing happened in Pekanbaru on October 1: Sekretariat Negara, *Gerakan 30 September: Pemberontakan Partai Komunis Indonesia* (Jakarta: Sekretariat Negara, 1994), 113.

49. Taher, *Riau Berdarah*, 139.

50. Taher, *Riau Berdarah*, 139.

51. Audrey Kahin, *Rebellion to Integration: West Sumatra and the Indonesian Polity* (Amsterdam: Amsterdam University Press, 1999), 245–49. Yenny Narni has investigated

the massacres in West Sumatra. She argues that most of the massacres took place in two regencies. Yenny Narni, "Ketika Negeri Adat Bersendi Sarak Merasa Terancam," in *Malam Bencana 1965: Dalam Belitan Krisis Nasional*, vol. 2, *Konflik Lokal*, ed. Taufik Abdullah, Sukri Abdurrachman, and Restu Gunawan (Jakarta: Obor, 2012), 23–50.

52. A meeting between Sukarno and the members of the Panca Tunggal of all provinces was held in Jakarta in early September 1966. Sukarno's address to the conference has been published in Budi Setiyono and Bonnie Triyana, eds., *Revolusi Belum Selesai: Kumpulan Pidato Presiden Sukarno*, vol. 2 (Semarang: MESIASS, 2003), 240–64.

53. Fakhrur Rodzi, "Inilah Cerita Komandan Kopassus Saat Dikudeta Mahasiswa dari Gubernur Riau," *Riau Online*, December 21, 2016.

54. Taher, *Riau Berdarah*, 159.

55. Taher, *Riau Berdarah*, 157–64.

56. Taher, *Riau Berdarah*, 164–65, 168–69. The transcript of Alihamy's trial was published by the Suharto regime: Mahkamah Militer Luar Biasa, *Berkas Berita Atjara Persidangan, Sidang ke-I s/d Sidang ke-XXV dan Putusan Perkara Abdullah Alihamy* (Jakarta: Mahmillub, 1970).

57. *Platt's Oilgram News*, November 8, 1985.

58. Richard Tanter, "The Totalitarian Ambition: Intelligence and Security Agencies in Indonesia," in *State and Civil Society in Indonesia*, ed. Arief Budiman (Clayton: Centre of Southeast Asian Studies, Monash University, 1990); Hadiz, *Workers and the State in New Order Indonesia*, 104–9.

59. On Colonel Poniman's policies in 1966 in West Sumatra, see Kahin, *Rebellion to Integration*, 245–49.

60. Irkham Santosa, *Makmun Murod: Sebagai Prajurit Pejuang* (Jakarta: Dinas Sejarah Angkatan Darat, 2014).

61. Elizabeth Collins describes the ongoing suppression of workers' rights in South Sumatra in the early post-Suharto years, when there was slightly greater freedom for workers to organize: *Indonesia Betrayed: How Development Fails* (Honolulu: University of Hawai'i Press, 2007), 98–115.

Conclusions

1. Harold Crouch, *The Army and Politics in Indonesia*, rev. ed. (Ithaca, NY: Cornell University Press, 1988), 151.

2. Ulf Sundhaussen, *The Road to Power: Indonesia Military Power, 1945–1967* (New York: Oxford University Press, 1982), 178–79.

3. Jess Melvin, *The Army and the Indonesian Genocide: Mechanics of Mass Murder* (London: Routledge, 2018), 138–93.

4. Mokoginta was one of three interregional commanders who stood between the army high command in Jakarta and the Kodams of Sumatra, Kalimantan, and Sulawesi. They did not have command over troops and played a coordinating role. Mokoginta's role was one of advising the Kodam commanders and working with the high command to appoint the Kodam commanders. In effect, Mokoginta was part of the army high command.

5. Yen-ling Tsai and Douglas Kammen, "Anti-communist Violence and the Ethnic Chinese in Medan, North Sumatra," in *The Contours of Mass Violence in Indonesia*, ed. Douglas Kammen and Katherine McGregor (Singapore: NUS Press, 2012), 141.

6. M. Fauzi, ed., *Pulangkan Mereka: Merangkai Ingatan Penghilangan Paksa di Indonesia* (Jakarta: Elsam, 2012), 49–78; Audrey Kahin, *Rebellion to Integration: West Sumatra and the Indonesian Polity* (Amsterdam: Amsterdam University Press, 1999), 243–44; Ann Stoler, *Capitalism and Confrontation in Sumatra's Plantation Belt, 1870–1979*, 2nd ed. (Ann Arbor: University of Michigan Press, 1995).

7. The September 30th Movement had put Rahmat's name on its list of the forty-five-member Revolutionary Council, and the Movement's leaders had recommended him (and two other generals) to Sukarno on October 1 morning to be the temporary caretaker of the army in Yani's absence.

8. "Report from East Java," trans. Benedict Anderson, *Indonesia*, no. 41 (April 1986): 146.

9. Crouch, *The Army and Politics in Indonesia*, 151–52.

10. Rahmat was involved in persuading or forcing Sukarno to issue an order on March 11, 1966, that affirmed Suharto's authority to "restore stability." Suharto used that order as a justification for taking charge of Sukarno's cabinet. The document, which became known as Supersemar, was Suharto's legal basis for staging a coup against the president who issued it.

11. Vannessa Hearman, *Unmarked Graves: Death and Survival in the Anti-Communist Violence in East Java, Indonesia* (Singapore: NUS Press, 2018), 108–10.

12. Harold Crouch, "Indonesian Interviews Two," ANU Open Repository, https://openresearch-repository.anu.edu.au/handle/1885/141110.

13. Hearman, *Unmarked Graves*, 109–12; Siddharth Chandra, "New Findings on the Indonesian Killings of 1965-66," *Journal of Asian Studies* 76, no. 4 (November 2017): 1078.

14. The party was Ikatan Pendukung Kemerdekaan Indonesia (IPKI), founded by General A. H. Nasution.

15. Tsai and Kammen, "Anti-communist Violence and the Ethnic Chinese in Medan, North Sumatra," 138–40.

16. Agus Sunyoto et al., *Banser Berjihad: Menumpas PKI* (Tulungagung: Pesulukan Thoriqoh Agung, 1996), i.

17. Stanley Karnow, "Leaders Deserted Reds in Indonesian Misfire," *Washington Post*, April 18, 1966.

18. Hammer pursues this theme: Mathias Hammer, "The Organization of the Killings and the Interaction between the State and Society in Central Java, 1965," *Journal of Current Southeast Asian Affairs* 32, no. 3 (2013): 37–62.

19. Kammen and Zakaria proposed moving beyond the "long-running debate over the role of the Army and that of civilians" by examining the "provincial responses" of the army officer and civilians to the Army high command's orders to destroy the PKI. Douglas Kammen and Faizah Zakaria, "Detention in Mass Violence," *Critical Asian Studies* 44, no. 3 (2012): 456.

20. Geoffrey Robinson, *The Dark Side of Paradise: Political Violence in Bali* (Ithaca, NY: Cornell University Press, 1995), 286–303; Melvin, *The Army and the Indonesian Genocide*, 162–240; Hearman, *Unmarked Graves*, 68–111.

21. Fathurrahman Zakaria, *Geger Gerakan 30 September 1965: Rakyat NTB Melawan Bahaya Merah*, 2nd ed. (Mataram: Sumurmas, 2001), 110–11.

22. Pipit Rochijat, "Am I PKI or Non-PKI," trans. Benedict Anderson, *Indonesia*, no. 40 (October 1985): 45.

Afterlives

1. An earlier break from the reign of official silence was a 230-page report by the National Commission on Violence against Women, *Mendengarkan Suara Perempuan Korban Peristiwa 1965* (Jakarta: Komnas Perempuan, 2007).

2. The recordings of the proceedings on both days have been posted online: "Simposium Nasional 1965," https://www.youtube.com/watch?v=hIGKzUMzmMY; "Simposium Nasional #2," https://www.youtube.com/watch?v=xlzcCldf61U.

3. Wijoyo's daughter has written thoughtfully about his role in the symposium and her views on it: Putri Lestari, "Ini Kan Buku Komunis? Kisah Cucu Pahlawan Revolusi," *Ingat 65*, April 20, 2016, https://medium.com/ingat-65/ini-kan-buku-komunis-d39a72da473f.

4. Forum Silaturahmi Anak Bangsa, *The Children of War* (Jakarta: Kompas, 2013).

5. Nani Nurrachman Sutojo, *Kenangan Tak Terucap: Saya, Ayah, dan Tragedi 1965* (Jakarta: Kompas, 2013).

6. International People's Tribunal, *Final Report of the International People's Tribunal on Crimes against Humanity in Indonesia 1965* (Bandung: Ultimus, 2017).

7. It is revealing of the army's sense of impunity that Sintong Panjaitan was the officer chosen to deny the reality of the massacres of 1965–66. He was well known for having been responsible for the Santa Cruz massacre in illegally occupied East Timor on November 12, 1991. Army soldiers opened fire into a crowd of people in a manner reminiscent of the Jallianwala Bagh massacre of 1919 in India. Several hundred people were killed in a matter of minutes. Panjaitan was the commander of the Kodam that covered East Timor and was removed from his post soon afterward because of the international outcry. At that time, he claimed, absurdly enough, that his troops were acting in self-defense. He justified the 1991 massacre in the same way that perpetrators have justified the 1965–66 killings: by claiming that it was a time of "kill or be killed." He also minimized the death toll, claiming that only nineteen people were killed. International Commission of Jurists, *Blaming the Victims* (Geneva: ICJ, 1992), 13–14. Because of his experience in the occupied territory, he served as an adviser to the president at the time of the referendum and the scorched-earth operation in 1999. Hamish McDonald et al., *Masters of Terror: Indonesia's Military and Violence in East Timor in 1999* (Canberra: Australia National University, 2002), 147–49.

8. Reports of the mass graves around Pati had already been published: Heyder Affan, "Malam Jahanam di Hutan Jati Jeglong," *BBC Indonesia*, September 29, 2015;

Heyder Affan, "Korban 1965: 'Saya Bertemu Algojo yang Menembak Mati Ayah Saya," *BBC Indonesia*, October 3, 2015.

9. Jeremy Kutner, "A City Turns to Face Indonesia's Murderous Past," *New York Times*, July 13, 2015.

10. On her research and advocacy, see Nurlaela A. K. Lamasitudju, "Rekonsiliasi dan Pernyataan Maaf Pak Wali Kota," in *Luka Bangsa Luka Kita: Pelanggaran HAM Masa Lalu dan Tawaran Rekonsiliasi*, ed. Baskara T. Wardaya (Yogyakarta: Galang Press, 2014), 371–83; Sri Lestari Wahyuningroem, "Working from the Margins: Initiatives for Truth and Reconciliation for Victims of the 1965 Mass Violence in Solo and Palu," in *The Indonesian Genocide of 1965: Causes, Dynamics, and Legacies*, ed. Katherine McGregor, Jess Melvin, and Annie Pohlman (London: Palgrave Macmillan, 2018), 335–56. Lamasitudju also assisted in the writing of a book about the victims of Palu: Putu Oka Sukanta, ed., *Sulawesi Bersaksi* (Jakarta: Lembaga Kreatifitas Kemanusiaan, 2013). There were very few killings in Palu. It was a place of repression without massacre.

11. Puput T. Juniman, "Tragedi 65, Luhut Minta Keluarga Korban Gali Kuburan Massal," *CNN Indonesia*, April 20, 2016.

12. Fabian J. Kuwado, "Jokowi Perintahkan Luhut Cari Kuburan Massal," *Kompas*, April 25, 2016; Jeffrey Hutton, "Indonesia Moves to Investigate Anti-Communist Atrocities," *New York Times*, April 26, 2016.

13. Rakhmatulloh, "Bongkar Kuburan Massal 1965, Luhut Singgung Holocaust Yahudi," *Sindonews*, May 20, 2016; Lalu Rahadian, "Luhut Bentuk Tim Verifikasi Kuburan Massal Korban 1965," *CNN Indonesia*, May 9, 2016.

14. Nabilla Tashandra, "Berbeda dengan Jokowi, Ryamizard Tolak Rencana Bongkar Kuburan Massal Tragedi 1965," *Kompas*, May 13, 2016.

15. Nabilla Tashandra, "Kivlan Zein Sebut PKI Bangkit dan Dipimpin Wahyu Setiaji," *Kompas*, June 1, 2016.

16. For more details of the postsymposium anti-PKI campaign, see "Fobia Hantu Komunisme," *Tempo*, May 16–22, 2016; Geoffrey Robinson, *The Killing Season: A History of the Indonesian Massacres, 1965–66* (Princeton, NJ: Princeton University Press, 2018), 264–91; Saskia Wieringa and Nursyahbani Katjasungkana, *Propaganda and the Genocide in Indonesia: Imagined Evil* (New York: Routledge, 2019), 168–86.

17. Menteri Koordinator Bidang Politik, Hukum dan Keamanan, "Penyelesaian Dugaan Pelanggaran HAM Berat Masa Lalu, Terkait Peristiwa G30S/PKI," press release, October 1, 2016. The printed copies of the press release given to journalists on that day carried a text that is slightly different from the version that the ministry has posted online. I have followed the latter version: https://polkam.go.id/press-release-menteri-koordinator-bidang-politik-hukum-dan-keamanan-tentang-penyelesaian-dugaan-pelanggaran-ham-berat-masa-lalu-terkait-peristiwa-g30spki/.

18. Jean-Paul Sartre, *The Devil and the Good Lord and Two Other Plays*, trans. K. B. Kean (New York: Vintage Books, 1960), 4.

19. A. W. Triyogo, "Survei Wahid Foundation: Komunis dan LGBT Paling Tak Disukai," *Tempo*, January 29, 2018, https://nasional.tempo.co/read/1055349/survei-wahid-foundation-komunis-dan-lgbt-paling-tak-disukai.

20. Marcus Mietzner, *The Politics of Military Reform in Post-Suharto Indonesia: Elite Conflict, Nationalism, and Institutional Resistance* (Washington, DC: East-West Center, 2006), ix.

21. On the irrationalities of the culture of anticommunism, see Ariel Heryanto, "Where Communism Never Dies: Violence, Trauma and Narration in the Last Cold War Capitalist Authoritarian State," *International Journal of Cultural Studies* 2, no. 2 (1999): 147–77.

22. Douglas Kammen, "'Koter Tidak Pernah Mati': The Military's Territorial Structure and the Long Shadow of Authoritarian Rule," in *Menelusuri Akar Otoritarianisme di Indonesia*, ed. B. T. Wardaya (Jakarta: ELSAM 2007), 189–208; "Tim Perumus RUU TNI Sepakat Komando Teritorial Dihapus," *Detik.com*, September 28, 2004; "Komando Teritorial Kuras Uang Negara," *Kompas.com*, June 30, 2010.

23. Agus Wijoyo, *Transformasi TNI Dari Pejuang Kemerdekaan Menuju Tentara Profesional dalam Demokrasi: Pergulatan TNI Mengukuhkan Kepribadian dan Jati Diri* (Jakarta: Center for Strategic International Studies, 2015).

24. Pusat Penerangan TNI (Military Information Center), "Jokowi: Komando Teritorial Tetap Dipertahankan," June 28, 2016, https://tniad.mil.id/2016/06/jokowi-komando-teritorial-tetap-dipertahankan/.

25. "Jokowi Increases Babinsa Income by up to 771%," *Jakarta Post*, June 6, 2018; "Presiden Jokowi Minta Babinsa Jelaskan ke Publik Bahwa Dirinya Tidak Terkait dengan PKI," *BBC Indonesia*, July 17, 2018; M. A. Sapiie and Fabian J. Kuwado, "Pesan Khusus Jokowi bagi Babinsa di Sumatra," *Kompas.com*, December 16, 2018.

26. Rukardi Ahmadi, "Alfatihah Terakhir," *Historia*, September 30, 2015, https://historia.id/politik/articles/alfatihah-terakhir-DAlyj; Rian Adhivira, "Rekonsiliasi Roh ala Mbah Kelik di Plumbon, Semarang," *IndoProgress*, May 24, 2016, https://indoprogress.com/2016/05/rekonsiliasi-roh-ala-mbah-kelik-di-plumbon-semarang/; Martin Eickhoff, Donny Danardono, Tjahjono Rahardjo, and Hotmauli Sidabalok, "The Memory Landscapes of '1965' in Semarang," *Journal of Genocide Research* 19, no. 4 (2017): 530–50.

27. Purwanti Asih Anna Levi, "Dulu Angker, Kini Dikunjungi untuk Cari Keuntungan," *Kompasiana.com*, June 17, 2015, https://www.kompasiana.com/purwanti_asih_anna_levi/54f35ef3745513a22b6c728e/dulu-angker-kini-dikunjungi-untuk-cari-keberuntungan.

28. Blog posting by Yunantyo Adi, "Menelusuri Keluarga Kuburan Massal Plumbon," February 11, 2015, https://yunantyoadi.wordpress.com/2015/02/11/menelusuri-keluarga-kuburan-massal-plumbon-2/.

29. Syahrul Ansyari, "Tangis Keluarga Iringi Penisanan Kuburan Pembantaian 1965," *Viva News*, June 2, 2015; Damar Sinuko, "Kisah Kuburan Massal Korban G30S di Semarang," *CNN Indonesia*, September 25, 2015.

Bibliography

Published Works

Abdullah, Taufik, Sukri Abdurrachman, and Restu Gunawan, eds. *Malam Bencana 1965 Dalam Belitan Krisis Nasional.* Vol. 2, *Konflik Lokal.* Jakarta: Obor, 2012.
Ahmadi, Rukardi. "Ketika Partai Perlu Belajar Sejarah." *Historia*, September 13, 2017. https://historia.id/modern/articles/ketika-partai-perlu-belajar-sejarah-P7xdQ.
Aidit, D. N. *Angkatan Bersenjata dan Penyesuaian Kekuasaan Negara dengan Tugas-Tugas Revolusi; PKI dan Angkatan Darat—SESKOAD II.* Jakarta: Pembaruan, 1964.
Aidit, D. N. *The Indonesian Revolution and the Immediate Tasks of the Communist Party of Indonesia.* Peking: Foreign Language Press, 1964.
Aidit, D. N. "Kembali ke UUD 1945 untuk Perubahan dalam Politik dan Penghidupan!" *Bintang Merah* (July–August 1959): 291–320.
Aidit, D. N. *Kibarkan Tinggi Pandji Revolusi!* Jakarta: Jajasan Pembaruan, 1964.
Aidit, D. N. *PKI dan ALRI.* Jakarta: Jajasan Pembaruan, 1963.
Aidit, D. N. *PKI dan Angkatan Darat (SESKOAD).* Jakarta: Jajasan Pembaruan, 1963.
Aidit, D. N. *PKI dan AURI.* Jakarta: Jajasan Pembaruan, 1963.
Aidit, D. N. *PKI dan Polisi.* Jakarta: Jajasan Pembaruan, 1963.
Aidit, D. N. *Revolusi, Angkatan Bersenjata & Partai Komunis (PKI dan AURI II).* Jakarta: Jajasan Pembaruan, 1964.
Aleida, Martin. "Malam Kelabu." *Horison* 5, no. 2 (February 1970): 36–40.
Alleg, Henri. *The Question.* Translated by John Calder. London: J. Calder, 1958.
Allhoff, Fritz. *Terrorism, Ticking Time-Bombs, and Torture.* Chicago: University of Chicago Press, 2012.
Améry, Jean. *At the Mind's Limits: Contemplations by a Survivor on Auschwitz and Its Realities.* Translated by Sidney Rosenfeld and Stella Rosenfeld. Bloomington: Indiana University Press, 1980.
Amnesty International. *Report on Torture.* London: Amnesty International, 1973.
Anderson, Benedict. "How Did the Generals Die?" *Indonesia* 43 (April 1987): 109–34.

Anderson, Benedict. "Indonesian Nationalism: Today and in the Future." *Indonesia* 67 (April 1999): 1–11.

Anderson, Benedict. *Java in a Time of Revolution: Occupation and Resistance, 1944–1946*. Ithaca, NY: Cornell University Press, 1972.

Anderson, Benedict. Review of Keith Foulcher, *Social Commitment in Literature and the Arts*. *Pacific Affairs* 61, no. 1 (Spring 1988): 196–98.

Anderson, Benedict. "Tentang Pembunuhan Massal '65." Interview with Ben Abel distributed on the Apakabar email list, September 24, 1996.

Anderson, David Charles. "The Military Aspects of the Madiun Affair." *Indonesia* 21 (April 1976): 1–63.

Anderson, Perry. *The Antinomies of Antonio Gramsci*. London: Verso, 2017.

Anderson, Perry. *The H-Word: The Peripeteia of Hegemony*. London: Verso, 2017.

Anwar, Rosihan. *Sukarno, Tentara, PKI: Segitiga Kekuasaan Sebelum Prahara Politik*. Jakarta: Obor, 2006.

Aristotle. *The Art of Rhetoric*. Translated by J. H. Freese. Cambridge, MA: Harvard University Press, 1926.

Aspinall, Edward. "Indonesia: Transformation of Civil Society through Democratic Breakthrough." In *Civil Society and Political Change in Asia: Expanding and Contracting Democratic Space*, edited by Muthiah Alagappa, 61–96. Palo Alto: Stanford University Press, 2004.

Bakri, Syamsul. *Gerakan Komunisme Islam Surakarta 1914–1942*. Yogyakarta: LKiS, 2015.

Ball, Patrick. *Who Did What to Whom? Planning and Implementing a Large Scale Human Rights Data Project*. Washington DC: American Association for the Advancement of Science, 1996.

Batubara, Cosmas. *Cosmas Batubara: Sebuah Otobiografi Politik*. Jakarta: Kompas, 2007.

Bayu, Anwar Putra. "Di Balik Cerita Sungai Musi." In *Sungai Isak Perih Menyemak: Antologi Puisi Esai*, edited by Ahmadun Yosi Herfanda et al., 35–44. Depok: Jurnal Sajak Indonesia, 2014.

Beccaria, Cesare. *On Crimes and Punishments and Other Writings*. Edited by R. Bellamy. Cambridge: Cambridge University Press, 1995.

Benda, Harry, and Ruth McVey, eds. *The Communist Uprisings of 1926–1927 in Indonesia: Key Documents*. Ithaca, NY: Cornell Modern Indonesia Project, 1960.

Boder, David. *I Did Not Interview the Dead*. Urbana: University of Illinois Press, 1949.

Bourchier, David. *Illiberal Democracy in Indonesia: The Ideology of the Family State*. London: Routledge, 2014.

"BPS": Aksi Reaksi. Jakarta, Rakjat, 1965.

Brecher, Bob. *Torture and the Ticking Bomb*. Oxford: Blackwell, 2007.

Bresnan, John. *At Home Abroad: A Memoir of the Ford Foundation in Indonesia 1953–1973*. Singapore: Equinox Publishing, 2006.

Bronto, J. "Ketika Nakhoda Tidak Satu." In *Kidung untuk Korban: Dari Tutur Sepuluh Narasumber Eks-Tapol Sala*, edited by Hersri Setiawan, 14–44. Surakarta: Pakorba Sala, 2006.

Budiardjo, Carmel. *Surviving Indonesia's Gulag: A Western Woman Tells Her Story*. London: Cassell, 1996.

Budiawan. *Mematahkan Pewarisan Ingatan: Wacana Anti-Komunis dan Politik Rekonsiliasi Pasca-Soeharto*. Jakarta: Elsam, 2004.

Budiawan. "Tortured Body, Betrayed Heart: State Violence in an Indonesian Novel by an Ex-Political Prisoner of the '1965 Affair.'" In *Violent Conflicts in Indonesia: Analysis, Representation, Resolution*, edited by Charles Coppel, 242–57. London: Routledge, 2006.

Callinicos, Alex. "Plumbing the Depths: Marxism and the Holocaust." *Yale Journal of Criticism* 14, no. 2 (2001): 385–414.

Chalk, Frank, and Kurt Jonassohn. *The History and Sociology of Genocide: Analyses and Case Studies*. New Haven, CT: Yale University Press, 1990.

Chandler, David. *Voices from S-21: Terror and History in Pol Pot's Secret Prison*. Berkeley: University of California Press, 1999.

Chandra, Elizabeth. "From Sensation to Oblivion: Boven Digoel in Sino-Malay Novels." *Bijdragen tot de Taal-, Land- en Volkenkunde* 169, nos. 2–3 (2013): 244–78.

Chandra, Siddharth. "New Findings on the Indonesian Killings of 1965–66." *Journal of Asian Studies* 76, no. 4 (November 2017): 1059–86.

Clark, Roger. "History of Efforts to Codify Crimes against Humanity: From the Charter of Nuremberg to the Statute of Rome." In *Forging a Convention for Crimes against Humanity*, edited by Leila Nadya Sadat, 8–27. Cambridge: Cambridge University Press, 2011.

Collins, Elizabeth. *Indonesia Betrayed: How Development Fails*. Honolulu: University of Hawai'i Press, 2007.

Comissão de Acolhimento, Verdade, e Reconciliação Timor Leste. *Chega! The Final Report of the Commission for Reception, Truth, and Reconciliation in East Timor*. 5 vols. Jakarta: KPG, 2013.

Conboy, Ken. *Kopassus: Inside Indonesia's Special Forces*. Jakarta: Equinox, 2003.

Courtois, Stéphane, et al. *The Black Book of Communism: Crimes, Terror, Repression*. Translated by J. Murphy and M. Kramer. Cambridge, MA: Harvard University Press, 1999.

Couteau, Jean. *Museum Puri Lukisan*. Ubud: Yayasan Rathna Warta, 1999.

Craven, Wesley, and James Cate, eds. *The Army Air Forces in World War II*. Vol. 5. Chicago: University of Chicago Press, 1953.

Cribb, Robert. "Genocide in Indonesia, 1965–1966." *Journal of Genocide Research* 3, no. 2 (2001): 219–39.

Cribb, Robert. "The Indonesian Marxist Tradition." In *Marxism in Asia*, edited by Colin Mackerras and Nick Knight, 251–72. London: Croom Helm, 1985.

Cribb, Robert, ed. *The Indonesian Killings of 1965–1966: Studies from Java and Bali*. Clayton: Monash University Centre of Southeast Asian Studies, 1990.

Cribb, Robert. "Military Strategy in the Indonesian Revolution: Nasution's Concept of 'Total People's War' in Theory and Practice." *War & Society* 19, no. 2 (2001): 143–54.

Cribb, Robert. "Political Genocides in Postcolonial Asia." In *The Oxford Handbook of Genocide Studies*, edited by Donald Bloxham and A. Dirk Moses, 445–65. New York: Oxford University Press, 2010.

Crouch, Harold. *The Army and Politics in Indonesia*. Rev. ed. Ithaca, NY: Cornell University Press, 1988.

Dake, Antonie. *The Devious Dalang: Sukarno and the So-Called Untung Putsch*. The Hague: Interdoc, 1974.

Dake, Antonie. *In the Spirit of the Red Banteng: Indonesian Communists between Moscow and Peking 1959–1965*. The Hague: Mouton, 1973.

Dake, Antonie. *The Sukarno File, 1965–67: Chronology of a Defeat*. Leiden: Brill, 2006.

Danner, Mark. *Torture and Truth: America, Abu Ghraib and the War on Terror*. New York: New York Review of Books, 2004.

de Certeau, Michel. *Heterologies: Discourse on the Other*. Translated by Brian Massumi. Minneapolis: University of Minnesota Press, 1986.

Department of State. *Indonesia*. Vol. 17 of *Foreign Relations of the United States, 1958–1960*. Washington, DC: US Government Printing Office, 1994.

Department of State. *Indonesia, Malaysia-Singapore, Philippines*. Vol. 26 of *Foreign Relations of the United States, 1964–1968*. Washington, DC: US Government Printing Office, 2001.

Dershowitz, Alan. *Why Terrorism Works*. New Haven, CT: Yale University Press, 2002.

Dewan Pakar DPP. *Peristiwa G30S/PKI: 60 Hari yang Mengguncang Dunia: Mahasiswa Melawan Kiri*. Jakarta: Laskar Ampera Arief Rachman Hakim Angkatan 66, 2016.

Dubois, Lindsey. "Torture and the Construction of an Enemy: The Example of Argentina, 1976–1983." *Dialectical Anthropology* 15, no. 4 (1990): 317–28.

Easter, David. "'Keep the Indonesian Pot Boiling': Western Covert Intervention in Indonesia, October 1965–March 1966." *Cold War History* 5, no. 1 (February 2005): 55–73.

Effendy, Mochtar. *Perjuangan Mencari Ridha Tuhan: Catatan Tiga Zaman dari Balik Terali Penjara Rezim Tirani Suharto*. Palembang: AlMukhtar, 2002.

Egan, Daniel. *The Dialectic of Position and Maneuver: Understanding Gramsci's Military Metaphor*. Leiden: Brill, 2016.

Eickhoff, Martin, Donny Danardono, Tjahjono Rahardjo, and Hotmauli Sidabalok. "The Memory Landscapes of '1965' in Semarang." *Journal of Genocide Research* 19, no. 4 (2017): 530–50.

Eiseman, Fred B. *Bali: Sekala & Niskala*. 2 vols. Rutland, VT: Tuttle, 1990.

Erman, Erwiza. *Membaranya Batubara: Konflik Kelas dan Etnik Ombilin-Sawahlunto, Sumatra Barat, 1892–1996*. Depok: Desantara, 2005.

Erman, Erwiza. "Miners, Managers, and the State: A Socio-Political History of the Ombilin Coal-Mines, West Sumatra, 1892–1996." PhD diss., University of Amsterdam, 1999.

Farid, Hilmar. "Indonesia's Original Sin: Mass Killings and Capitalist Expansion, 1965–66." *Inter-Asia Cultural Studies* 6, no. 1 (2005): 3–16.

Fauzi, M., ed. *Pulangkan Mereka: Merangkai Ingatan Penghilangan Paksa di Indonesia*. Jakarta: Elsam, 2012.

Fealy, Greg, and Katherine McGregor. "Nahdlatul Ulama and the Killings of 1965–66: Religion, Politics, and Remembrance." *Indonesia* 89 (April 2010): 37–60.

Feith, Herbert, and Lance Castles, eds. *Indonesian Political Thinking, 1945–1965*. Ithaca, NY: Cornell University Press, 1970.

Fic, Victor M. *Anatomy of the Jakarta Coup: October 1, 1965*. Delhi: Abhinav, 2004.

Forum Silaturahmi Anak Bangsa. *The Children of War*. Jakarta: Kompas, 2013.

Foucault, Michel. *Discipline and Punish: The Birth of the Prison*. New York: Vintage, 1979.

Foucault, Michel. *Wrong-Doing, Truth-Telling: The Function of Avowal in Justice*. Edited by F. Brion and B. E. Harcourt. Translated by S. W. Sawyer. Chicago: University of Chicago Press, 2014.

Geertz, Clifford. *After the Fact: Two Countries, Four Decades, One Anthropologist*. Cambridge, MA: Harvard University Press, 1996.

Geertz, Clifford. "Deep Play: Notes on the Balinese Cockfight." *Daedalus* 101, no. 1 (Winter 1972): 1–37.

Gerlach, Christian. *Extremely Violent Societies*. Cambridge: Cambridge University Press, 2010.

Gill, Lesley. *The School of the Americas: Military Training and Political Violence in the Americas*. Durham, NC: Duke University Press, 2004.

Ginzburg, Carlo. *Myths, Emblems, Clues*. London: Hutchinson, 1990.

Gramsci, Antonio. *Selections from the Prison Notebooks*. Edited and translated by Quintin Hoare and Geoffrey Nowell Smith. New York: International Publishers, 1971.

Grandin, Greg. "Chronicles of a Guatemalan Genocide Foretold: Violence, Trauma, and the Limits of Historical Inquiry." *Nepantla* 1, no. 2 (2000): 391–412.

Grandin, Greg. "History, Motive, Law, Intent: Combining Historical and Legal Methods in Understanding Guatemala's 1981–1983 Genocide." In *The Specter of Genocide: Mass Murder in Historical Perspective*, edited by Robert Gellately and Ben Kiernan, 339–52. Cambridge: Cambridge University Press, 2003.

Grig, Lucy. "Torture and Truth in Late Antique Martyrology." *Early Medieval Europe* 11, no. 4 (2002): 321–36.

Hadiz, Vedi. *Workers and the State in New Order Indonesia*. London: Routledge, 1997.

Hamba. *Pedoman Operasi Mental*. Jakarta: Jajasan Perdjalanan Hadji, 1966.

Hammer, Mathias. "The Organization of the Killings and the Interaction between the State and Society in Central Java, 1965." *Journal of Current Southeast Asian Affairs* 32, no. 3 (2013): 37–62.

Harff, Barbara. "Genocide and Political Mass Murder: Definitions, Theories, Analyses." In *States and Peoples in Conflict: Transformations of Conflict Studies*, edited by Michael Stohl, Mark Lichbach, and Peter Nils Grabosky, 208–30. New York: Routledge, 2017.

Harff, Barbara. "No Lessons Learned from the Holocaust? Assessing Risks of Genocide and Political Mass Murder since 1955." *American Political Science Review* 97, no. 1 (February 2003): 57–73.

Harff, Barbara, and Ted Gurr. "Toward Empirical Theory of Genocides and Politicides: Identification and Measurement of Cases Since 1945." *International Studies Quarterly* 32, no. 3 (1988): 359–71.

Harsha, Stanley. "An American Library in 1965 Indonesia: From Enlightenment to Torture." *Strategic Review*, March 4, 2019. http://sr.sgpp.ac.id/post/an-american-library-in-1965-indonesia-from-enlightenment-to-torture.

Hasibuan, Imran, and Muhammad Yamin. *Jembatan Kebangsaan: Biografi Politik Taufiq Kiemas*. Jakarta: Q Communication, 2008.

Hearman, Vannessa. "South Blitar and the PKI Bases: Refuge, Resistance and Repression." In *The Contours of Mass Violence in Indonesia, 1965–68*, edited by Douglas Kammen and Katherine McGregor, 182–207. Singapore: NUS Press, 2012.

Hearman, Vannessa. *Unmarked Graves: Death and Survival in the Anti-Communist Violence in East Java, Indonesia*. Singapore: NUS Press, 2018.

Heidenrich, John. *How to Prevent Genocide: A Guide for Policymakers, Scholars, and the Concerned Citizen*. Westport, CT: Praeger, 2001.

Heryanto, Ariel. "Where Communism Never Dies: Violence, Trauma and Narration in the Last Cold War Capitalist Authoritarian State." *International Journal of Cultural Studies* 2, no. 2 (1999): 147–77.

Hill, David. *Journalism and Politics in Indonesia: A Critical Biography of Mochtar Lubis (1922–2004) as Editor and Author*. London: Routledge, 2010.

Hill, David. *The Press in New Order Indonesia*. Jakarta: Equinox Publishing, 2007.

Hindley, Donald. *The Communist Party of Indonesia, 1951–1963*. Berkeley: University of California Press, 1964.

Hinton, Alexander. "Critical Genocide Studies." *Genocide Studies and Prevention* 7, no. 1 (Spring 2012): 4–15.

Hirano, Katsuya. "Thanatopolitics in the Making of Japan's Hokkaido: Settler Colonialism and Primitive Accumulation." *Critical Historical Studies* 2, no. 2 (2015): 191–218.

Hoet, Anne-Lot. "De Verzwegen Moordpartij van Palembang." *Vrij Nederland*, July 26, 2017. https://www.vn.nl/de-verzwegen-moordpartij-van-palembang/.

Horton, William Bradley. "Guy Pauker and US-Indonesia Relationships of the 1950s–1970s." *Journal of Asia Pacific Studies* 29 (October 2017): 85–104.

Hughes, John. *The End of Sukarno*. Singapore: Archipelago Press, 2002.

Hughes, John. *From Paper Boy to Pulitzer: A Newsman's Journey*. Glastonbury, CT: Nebbadoon Press, 2014.

Human Rights Watch. *Aceh at War: Torture, Ill-Treatment and Unfair Trials*. New York: Human Rights Watch, 2004.

Hunter, Helen-Louise. *Sukarno and the Indonesian Coup: The Untold Story*. Westport, CT: Praeger Security International, 2007.

Ignatieff, Michael. "If Torture Works . . ." *Prospect Magazine*, April 2006. https://www.prospectmagazine.co.uk/magazine/iftortureworks.

Ikaning. "Sejarah PKI di Banyuwangi dan Pembantaian Cemethuk 18 Oktober 1965." 2008. https://ikaning.wordpress.com/2008/01/27/sejarah-pki-di-banyuwangi-dan-pembantaian-cemethuk-18-oktober-1965/.

Ikranagara, "G-30-N di Bali: Catatan Tentang Menjelang Tahun Baru 1966." 2011. http://permalink.gmane.org/gmane.culture.region.indonesia.ppi-india/97081.

Indonesia Project, Massachusetts Institute of Technology, Center for International Studies. *Stanvac in Indonesia*. New York: National Planning Association, 1957.

Ingleson, John. *Workers, Unions and Politics: Indonesia in the 1920s and 1930s*. Leiden: Brill, 2014.

International Coalition for Papua. *Human Rights in West Papua 2017*. Wutterpal, Germany: ICP, 2017.

International Commission of Jurists. *Blaming the Victims*. Geneva: ICJ, 1992.

International People's Tribunal. *Final Report of the International People's Tribunal on Crimes against Humanity in Indonesia 1965*. Bandung: Ultimus, 2017.

Ishwara, Helen. *P. K. Ojong, Satu Dari Dua Pendiri Kompas-Gramedia: Hidup Sederhana Berpikir Mulia*. Jakarta: Kompas, 2001.

Jalal, Ayesha. *The State of Martial Rule: The Origins of Pakistan's Political Economy of Defence*. Cambridge: Cambridge University Press, 1990.

Jenkins, David, and Douglas Kammen. "The Army Para-commando Regiment and the Reign of Terror in Central Java and Bali." In *The Contours of Mass Violence in Indonesia, 1965–68*, edited by Douglas Kammen and Katherine McGregor, 75–103. Singapore: NUS Press, 2012.

Kahin, Audrey. "The 1927 Communist Uprising in Sumatra: A Reappraisal." *Indonesia* 62 (October 1996): 19–36.

Kahin, Audrey. *Islam, Nationalism, and Democracy: A Political Biography of Mohammad Natsir*. Singapore: NUS Press, 2012.

Kahin, Audrey. *Rebellion to Integration: West Sumatra and the Indonesian Polity*. Amsterdam: Amsterdam University Press, 1999.

Kahin, Audrey, and George Kahin. *Subversion as Foreign Policy: The Eisenhower and Dulles Debacle in Indonesia*. New York: New Press, 1995.

Kahin, George. *Nationalism and Revolution in Indonesia*. Ithaca, NY: Cornell University Press, 1952.

Kaligis, O. C., and Rum Aly, eds. *Simtom Politik 1965: PKI dalam Perspektif Pembalasan dan Pengampunan*. Jakarta: Kata Hasta Pustaka, 2007.

Kammen, Douglas. "'Koter Tidak Pernah Mati': The Military's Territorial Structure and the Long Shadow of Authoritarian Rule." In *Menelusuri Akar Otoritarianisme di Indonesia*, edited by B. T. Wardaya, 189–208. Jakarta: ELSAM 2007.

Kammen, Douglas, and Katherine McGregor, eds. *The Contours of Mass Violence in Indonesia, 1965–68*. Singapore: NUS Press, 2012.

Kammen, Douglas, and Faizah Zakaria. "Detention in Mass Violence: Policy and Practice in Indonesia, 1965–1968." *Critical Asian Studies* 44, no. 3 (2012): 441–66.

Kartodikromo, Marco. *Pergaulan Orang Buangan di Boven Digoel*. Edited by Koesalah Soebagyo Toer. Jakarta: KPG, 2002.

Kiernan, Benedict. *Genocide and Resistance in Southeast Asia: Documentation, Denial, and Justice in Cambodia and East Timor*. New Brunswick, NJ: Transaction, 2008.

Koespradono, Gantyo. *Kick Andy: Kumpulan Kisah Inspiratif*. Yogyakarta: Benteng, 2008.

Kopkamtib. *Himpunan Surat-Surat Keputusan/Perintah jang Berhubungan dengan Kopkamtib 1965–1969.* Jakarta: Sekretariat Kopkamtib, n.d.

Kuper, Leo. *The Prevention of Genocide.* New Haven, CT: Yale University Press, 1985.

Kusni, J. J. *Di Tengah Pergolakan: Turba LEKRA di Klaten.* Yogyakarta: Ombak, 2005.

Kveder, Dushan. "'Territorial War': The New Concept of Resistance." *Foreign Affairs* 32, no. 1 (October 1953): 91–108.

Laclau, Ernesto. *The Rhetorical Foundations of Society.* London: Verso, 2014.

Laclau, Ernesto, and Chantal Mouffe. *Hegemony and Socialist Strategy: Towards a Radical Democratic Politics.* London: Verso, 1985.

Lamasitudju, Nurlaela A. K. "Rekonsiliasi dan Pernyataan Maaf Pak Wali Kota." In *Luka Bangsa Luka Kita: Pelanggaran HAM Masa Lalu dan Tawaran Rekonsiliasi*, edited by Baskara T. Wardaya. Yogyakarta: Galang Press, 2014.

Langbein, John. *Torture and the Law of Proof: Europe and England in the Ancien Régime.* Chicago: University of Chicago Press, 1997.

Larson, George. *Prelude to Revolution: Palaces and Politics in Surakarta, 1912–1942.* Dordrecht: Foris Publications, 1987.

Latief, Abdul. *Pledoi Kol. A. Latief: Soeharto Terlibat G 30 S.* Jakarta: ISAI, 2000.

Latif, Busjarie. *Manuskrip Sejarah 45 Tahun PKI, 1920–1965.* Bandung: Ultimus, 2014.

Leclerc, Jacques. "An Ideological Problem of Indonesian Trade Unionism in the 1960s: 'Karyawan' versus 'Buruh.'" *Review of Indonesian and Malaysian Affairs* 6, no. 1 (1972): 76–91.

Lembaga Ketahanan Nasional. *Bahan-Bahan Pokok G30S/PKI dan Penghancurannya.* March 1969.

Lenin, V. I. "Terms of Admission into the Comintern." In *Collected Works*, vol. 31, 206–11. Moscow: Progress Publishers, 1965.

Lev, Daniel. *The Transition to Guided Democracy: Indonesian Politics 1957–1959.* Ithaca, NY: Cornell Southeast Asian Studies Publications, 1966.

Liem, Andre. "Perjuangan Bersenjata PKI di Blitar Selatan dan Operasi Trisula." In *Tahun yang Tak Pernah Berakhir: Memahami Pengalaman Korban 65: Esai-Esai Sejarah Lisan*, edited by John Roosa, Ayu Ratih, and Hilmar Farid, 163–200. Jakarta: Elsam, 2004.

Lindsay, Jennifer. "Performing Indonesia Abroad." In *Heirs to World Culture: Being Indonesian, 1950–1965*, edited by Jennifer Lindsay and Maya H. T. Liem, 191–220. Leiden: KITLV, 2012.

Liu, Hong. *China and the Shaping of Indonesia, 1949–1965.* Singapore: NUS Press, 2011.

Lowry, Bob. "Colin East Goes to SESKOAD—in a Year of Living Dangerously, 1964." *Australian Defense Force Journal*, no. 183 (2010): 45–55.

Lowry, Robert. *The Armed Forces of Indonesia.* St. Leonards, New South Wales: Allen and Unwin, 1996.

Luban, David. "Liberalism, Torture, and the Ticking Bomb." In *The Torture Debate in America*, edited by Karen Greenberg, 35–83. Cambridge: Cambridge University Press, 2006.

Lubis, Firman. *Jakarta 1960-an: Kenangan Semasa Mahasiswa*. Jakarta: Masup, 2008.
Luttikhuis, Bart, and A. Dirk Moses, eds. *Colonial Counterinsurgency and Mass Violence: The Dutch Empire in Indonesia*. London: Routledge, 2014.
Luttwak, Edward. *Strategy: The Logic of War and Peace*. Cambridge, MA: Harvard University Press, 2001.
Mahkamah Militer Luar Biasa. "*Gerakan 30 September" Dihadapan Mahmillub, Perkara Njono*. Jakarta: Pusat Pendidikan Kehakiman A.D., 1966.
Maksum, Agus Sunyoto, and A. Zainuddin. *Lubang-Lubang Pembantaian: Petualangan PKI di Madiun*. Jakarta: Grafiti, 1990.
Manafe, Aco. *Teperpu Mengungkap Pengkhianatan PKI Pada Tahun 1965 dan Proses Hukum Bagi Para Pelakunya*. Jakarta: Sinar Harapan, 2007.
Mandan, A. M., ed. *Subchan Z. E., Sang Maestro: Politisi Intelektual dari Kalangan NU Modern*. Jakarta: Pustaka Indonesia Satu, 2001.
Margiyono and Kurniawan Tri Yunanto. *Neraka Rezim Suharto: Misteri Tempat Penyiksaan Orde Baru*. Jakarta: Spasi and VHR Book, 2007.
Matsuno, Akihisa. "The 30 September Movement and Its Aftermath in Bali, October–December 1965." In *The Indonesian Genocide of 1965: Causes, Dynamics and Legacies*, edited by Katherine McGregor, Jess Melvin, and Annie Pohlman, 71–88. London: Palgrave Macmillan, 2018.
McCoy, Alfred W. *A Question of Torture: CIA Interrogation, from the Cold War to the War on Terror*. New York: Metropolitan Books, 2006.
McDaniel, Drew O. *Broadcasting in the Malay World: Radio, Television, and Video in Brunei, Indonesia, Malaysia, and Singapore*. Norwood, NJ: Ablex Publishing, 1994.
McDonald, Hamish. *Suharto's Indonesia*. Blackburn, Victoria: Fontana Books, 1980.
McDonald, Hamish, et al. *Masters of Terror: Indonesia's Military and Violence in East Timor in 1999*. Canberra: Australia National University, 2002.
McGehee, Ralph. "The C.I.A. and the White Paper on El Salvador." *The Nation*, April 11, 1981, 423–25.
McGregor, Katherine. "A Bridge and a Barrier: Islam, Reconciliation, and the 1965 Killings in Indonesia." In *Reconciling Indonesia: Grassroots Agency for Peace*, edited by Birgit Bräuchler, 214–32. London: Routledge, 2009.
McGregor, Katherine. *History in Uniform: Military Ideology and the Construction of Indonesia's Past*. Singapore: Singapore University Press, 2007.
McGregor, Katherine. "Mass Graves and Memories of the 1965 Indonesian Killings." In *The Contours of Mass Violence in Indonesia, 1965–68*, edited by Douglas Kammen and Katherine McGregor, 234–62. Singapore: National University of Singapore Press, 2012.
McGregor, Katherine, Jess Melvin, and Annie Pohlman, eds. *The Indonesian Genocide of 1965: Causes, Dynamics, and Legacies*. London: Palgrave Macmillan, 2018.
McKnight, David. "Work in the Army: Introduction." *Revolutionary History* 8, no. 2 (Summer 2002). https://www.marxists.org/history/etol/revhist/backiss/vol8/no2/comintern.html.

McMillan, Richard. *The British Occupation of Indonesia, 1945–1946: Britain, the Netherlands and the Indonesian Revolution*. London: Routledge, 2005.

McVey, Ruth. *The Rise of Indonesian Communism*. Ithaca, NY: Cornell University Press, 1965.

Melvin, Jess. *The Army and the Indonesian Genocide: Mechanics of Mass Murder*. London: Routledge, 2018.

Mietzner, Marcus. *The Politics of Military Reform in Post-Suharto Indonesia: Elite Conflict, Nationalism, and Institutional Resistance*. Washington, DC: East-West Center, 2006.

Miryanti, Ratih. "Kesaksian Wartawan Antara Atas Tragedi 1965." September 23, 2006. http://langitkata.blogspot.co.id/2011/05/ratih-miryanti-kesaksian-wartawan.html.

Misbach, H. M. *Haji Misbach: Sang Propagandis*. Temanggung: Kendi, 2016.

Moertopo, Ali. *Himpunan Pidato Menteri Penerangan RI 1978–1982: Peningkatan Penerangan yang Berwibawa*. Jakarta: Departemen Penerangan, 1983.

Morgan, Rod. "The Utilitarian Justification of Torture: Denial, Desert, and Disinformation." *Punishment & Society* 2, no. 2 (2000): 181–96.

Mortimer, Rex. *Indonesian Communism under Sukarno: Ideology and Politics, 1959–1965*. Ithaca, NY: Cornell University Press, 1974.

Moses, A. Dirk. ed. *Empire, Colony, Genocide: Conquest, Occupation, and Subaltern Resistance in World History*. New York: Berghahn Books, 2008.

Moses, A. Dirk. "Genocide vs. Security: A False Opposition." *Journal of Genocide Research* 15, no. 4 (2013): 489–94.

Moses, A. Dirk. "Paranoia and Partisanship: Genocide Studies, Holocaust Historiography and the 'Apocalyptic Conjuncture.'" *Historical Journal* 54, no. 2 (June 2011): 553–83.

Mouffe, Chantal. ed. *Gramsci and Marxist Theory*. London: Routledge & Kegan Paul, 1979.

Musso, "Jalan Baru Untuk Republik Indonesia." 1948. https://www.marxists.org/indonesia/indones/1948-JalanBaru.htm.

Najjarine, Karim, and Drew Cottle. "The Department of External Affairs, the ABC and Reporting of the Indonesian Crisis, 1965–66." *Australian Journal of Politics and History* 49, no. 1 (March 2003): 48–60.

Narni, Yenny. "Ketika Negeri Adat Bersendi Sarak Merasa Terancam." In *Malam Bencana 1965 Dalam Belitan Krisis Nasional*, vol. 2, *Konflik Lokal*, edited by Taufik Abdullah, Sukri Abdurrachman, and Restu Gunawan, 23–50. Jakarta: Obor, 2012.

Nasution, A. H. *Tjatatan-Tjatatan Sekitar Politik Militer Indonesia* [Notes on Indonesian Military Politics]. Jakarta: Pembimbing, 1955.

National Commission on Violence against Women: *Mendengarkan Suara Perempuan Korban Peristiwa 1965*. Jakarta: Komnas Perempuan, 2007.

Nersessian, David. *Genocide and Political Groups*. New York: Oxford University Press, 2010.

Neuberg, A. *Armed Insurrection*. Translated by Quintin Hoare. London: New Left Books, 1970.
Noer, Mohammad. *Mengenang dan Menyelusuri Lubang Buaya di Dusun Cemetuk*. Banyuwangi: Public Policy Institute, 2011.
Notosusanto, Nugroho. *The National Struggle and the Armed Forces in Indonesia*. Jakarta: Centre for Armed Forces History, 1975.
Notosusanto, Nugroho, and Ismail Saleh. *The Coup Attempt of the "September 30 Movement" in Indonesia*. Jakarta: Pembimbing Masa, 1968.
Notosutarjo, Akhmad. *Peristiwa Madiun, Tragedi Nasional*. Jakarta: Endang, 1966.
Nursuhud. "Pidato." *Bintang Merah, Nomor Special Jilid II, Dokumen-Dokumen Kongres Nasional Ke-VI, 7–14 September 1959*. Jakarta: Yayasan Pembaruan, 1960.
Oei Hiem Hwie. *Memoar Oei Hiem Hwie*. Surabaya: Wastu Lanas Grafika, 2015.
Oei Tjoe Tut. *Memoar Oei Tjoe Tut: Pembantu Presiden Sukarno*. Edited by Pramoedya Ananta Toer and Stanley Adi Prasetyo. Jakarta: Hasta Mitra, 1995.
Oetoyo, Farida. *Saya Farida: Sebuah Autobiografi*. Jakarta: Gramedia, 2014.
Oka, Putu. *Merajut Harkat*. Yogyakarta: Pustaka Pelajar, 1999.
Ooi Jin Bee. *The Petroleum Resources of Indonesia*. Kuala Lumpur: Oxford University Press, 1982.
Oppenheimer, Joshua, and Michael Uwemedimo. "Show of Force: A Cinema-Séance of Power and Violence in Sumatra's Plantation Belt." *Critical Quarterly* 51, no. 1 (2009): 84–110.
Orr, Kenneth. "Schooling and Village Politics in Central Java in a Time of Turbulence." In *The Indonesian Killings of 1965–1966: Studies from Java and Bali*, edited by Robert Cribb, 177–94. Clayton: Monash University Centre of Southeast Asian Studies, 1990.
Osiel, Mark. "Constructing Subversion in Argentina's Dirty War." *Representations* 75, no. 1 (Summer 2001): 119–58.
Paget, Roger. "Djakarta Newspapers, 1965–1967." *Indonesia* 4 (October 1967): 169–210.
Pauker, Guy. *The Indonesian Doctrine of Territorial Warfare and Territorial Management*. Santa Monica, CA: RAND, 1963.
Peters, Edward. *Torture*. New York: Basil Blackwell, 1985.
Pinardi. *Peristiwa Coup Berdarah P.K.I. September 1948 di Madiun*. Jakarta: Inkopak-Hazera, 1966.
Poesponegoro, M. D., and Nugroho Notosusanto. *Sejarah Nasional Indonesia*. 6th ed. Vol. 6. Jakarta: Balai Pustaka, 1990.
Poeze, Harry. "The Cold War in Indonesia, 1948." *Journal of Southeast Asian Studies* 40, no. 3 (October 2009): 497–517.
Poeze, Harry. "From Foe to Partner to Foe Again: The Strange Alliance of the Dutch Authorities and Digoel Exiles in Australia, 1943–1945." *Indonesia* 94 (October 2012): 57–84.
Poeze, Harry. *Madiun 1948: PKI Bergerak*. Jakarta: KITLV, 2011.
Posner, Richard. "Torture, Terrorism, and Interrogation." In *Torture: A Collection*, edited by Sanford Levinson, 291–98. New York: Oxford University Press, 2004.

Postone, Moishe. "The Holocaust and the Trajectory of the Twentieth Century." In *Catastrophe and Meaning*, edited by M. Postone and E. Santner, 81–114. Chicago: University of Chicago Press, 2003.

Pusat Penerangan Angkatan Darat. *Fakta-fakta Persoalan Sekitar "Gerakan 30 September," Penerbitan Chusus*. Nos. 1–3. Jakarta, October–December 1965.

Pusat Penerangan TNI. "Jokowi: Komando Teritorial Tetap Dipertahankan." June 28, 2016. https://tniad.mil.id/2016/06/jokowi-komando-teritorial-tetap-dipertahankan/.

Putra, I Nyoman Darma. *Pasangan Pionir Pariwisata Bali*. Denpasar: Jagat Press, 2012.

Ramadhan KH. *Ibnu Sutowo: Saatnya Saya Bercerita!* Jakarta: National Press Club, 2008.

Ramidjo, Tri. *Kisah-Kisah Dari Tanah Merah: Cerita Digul, Cerita Buru*. Bandung: Ultimus, 2009.

Ratih, Ayu, et al. "Nyadran di Bengawan Solo." In *Kidung untuk Korban: Dari Tutur Sepuluh Narasumber Eks-Tapol Sala*, edited by Hersri Setiawan, 1–13. Surakarta: Pakorba Sala, 2006.

Razif. "Buruh Kereta Api dan Komunitas Buruh Manggarai." In *Dekolonisasi Buruh Kota dan Pembentukan Bangsa*, edited by Erwiza Erman and Ratna Saptari, 91–141. Jakarta: Obor, 2013.

Rejali, Darius. *Torture and Democracy*. Princeton, NJ: Princeton University Press, 2007.

Reksosamodra, Pranoto. *Catatan Jenderal Pranoto Reksosamodra: Dari RTM Boedi Oetomo Sampai Nirbaya*. Edited by Imelda Bachtiar. Jakarta: Kompas, 2014.

Remmelink, Willem, ed. and trans. *The Invasion of the Dutch East Indies*. Leiden: Leiden University Press, 2015.

"Report from East Java." Translated by Benedict Anderson. *Indonesia* 41 (April 1986): 135–50.

Rewang. *Saya Seorang Revolusioner: Memoar Rewang*. Edited by Joko Waskito. Bandung: Ultimus, 2017.

Robinson, Geoffrey. *The Dark Side of Paradise: Political Violence in Bali*. Ithaca, NY: Cornell University Press, 1995.

Robinson, Geoffrey. *The Killing Season: A History of the Indonesian Massacres*. Princeton, NJ: Princeton University Press, 2018.

Rochijat, Pipit. "Am I PKI or Non-PKI." Translated by Benedict Anderson. *Indonesia* 40 (October 1985): 37–56.

Roosa, John. "Indonesian Communism: The Perils of the Parliamentary Path." In *The Cambridge History of Communism*, vol. 2, edited by Norman Naimark, Silvio Pons, and Sophie Quinn-Judge, 467–90. Cambridge: Cambridge University Press, 2017.

Roosa, John. "Interview with Joshua Oppenheimer." *Rethinking History: The Journal of Theory and Practice* 18, no. 3 (2014): 413–22.

Roosa, John. "President Sukarno and the September 30th Movement." *Critical Asian Studies* 40, no. 1 (March 2008): 143–59.

Roosa, John. *Pretext for Mass Murder: The September 30th Movement and Suharto's Coup d'État in Indonesia*. Madison: University of Wisconsin Press, 2006.

Roosa, John. "The State of Knowledge about an Open Secret: Indonesia's Mass Disappearances of 1965-66." *Journal of Asian Studies* 75, no. 2 (2016): 281-97.

Roosa, John. "Who Knows? Oral History Methods in the Studies of the Massacres of 1965-66 in Indonesia." *Oral History Forum d'histoire orale* 33 (2013): 1-28.

Roth, Kenneth, and Minky Worden, eds. *Torture: Does It Make Us Safer? Is It Ever OK?* New York: New Press, 2005.

Saich, Tony. *The Origins of the First United Front in China: The Role of Sneevliet (Alias Maring)*. 2 vols. Leiden: Brill, 1991.

Said, Lt. Col. Ali, and Lt. Col. Durmawel Ahmad. *Sangkur Adil, Pengupas Fitnah Chianat*. Jakarta: Ethika, 1967.

Sakirman. "Apa Arti Sokongan PKI kepada UUD 1945 dan Demokrasi Terpimpin." *Bintang Merah* (May-June 1960): 194-219; (July-August 1960): 320-40.

Sands, Philippe. *East West Street: On the Origins of "Genocide" and "Crimes against Humanity."* New York: Vintage, 2016.

Santosa, Irkham. *Makmun Murod: Sebagai Prajurit Pejuang*. Jakarta: Dinas Sejarah Angkatan Darat, 2014.

Sanusi, Anwar. "'Front Nasional' yang Diketuai Presiden Sukarno Mulai Bergerak Serempak Ke Luar dan Ke Dalam." *Bintang Merah, Nomor Spesial, Kongres Nasional Ke-VII PKI*. Jakarta: Pembaruan, 1963.

Sarbinatun. "Anggota Lekra Cabang Sala: Laki-Laki Dimanfaatkan Tenaganya, Perempuan Seluruh-Luruhnya." In *Kidung untuk Korban: Dari Tutur Sepuluh Narasumber Eks-Tapol Sala*, edited by Hersri Setiawan, 45-77. Surakarta: Pakorba Sala, 2006.

Sarkar, Sumit. "Orientalism Revisited: Saidian Frameworks in the Writing of Modern Indian History." *Oxford Literary Review* 16, nos. 1-2 (1994): 205-24.

Sartre, Jean-Paul. *The Devil and the Good Lord and Two Other Plays*. Translated by K. B. Kean. New York: Vintage Books, 1960.

Sastrosoewignjo, Soerasto. "You Have Stabbed Us in the Back Again." In *Indonesian Political Thinking, 1945-1965*, edited by Herb Feith and Lance Castles, 373-76. Ithaca, NY: Cornell University Press, 1970.

Scarry, Elaine. *The Body in Pain: The Making and Unmaking of the World*. New York: Oxford University Press, 1987.

Sekretariat Negara, *Gerakan 30 September: Pemberontakan Partai Komunis Indonesia*. Jakarta: Sekretariat Negara, 1994.

Semaoen. "An Early Account of the Independence Movement." Translated by Ruth McVey. *Indonesia* 1 (April 1966): 46-75.

Semaoen. *The Story of Kadirun*. Translated by Ian Campbell et al. Jakarta: Lontar, 2014.

Semelin, Jacques. *Purify and Destroy: The Political Uses of Massacre and Genocide*. New York: Columbia University Press, 2007.

Semelin, Jacques, et al., eds. *Resisting Genocide: The Multiple Forms of Rescue*. New York: Oxford University Press, 2010.

Sen, Krishna. "Death of a Film Legacy: Remembering Indonesia's Bachtiar Siagian."

The Conversation, October 12, 1915. http://theconversation.com/death-of-a-film-legacy-remembering-indonesias-bachtiar-siagian-48444.

Sen, Krishna, and David Hill. *Media and Politics in Indonesia*. Jakarta: Equinox Publishing, 2006.

Setiawan, Hersri. *Aku Eks-Tapol*. Yogyakarta: Galang Press, 2003.

Setiawan, Hersri. *Kamus Gestok*. Yogyakarta: Galang Press, 2003.

Setiyono, Budi, and Bonnie Triyana, eds. *Revolusi Belum Selesai: Kumpulan Pidato Presiden Soekarno 30 September 1965—Pelengkap Nawaksara*. 2 vols. Semarang: MESIASS, 2003.

Sheinin, David. *Consent of the Damned: Ordinary Argentinians in the Dirty War*. Gainesville: University Press of Florida, 2012.

Shiraishi, Takashi. *An Age in Motion: Popular Radicalism in Java, 1912–1916*. Ithaca, NY: Cornell University Press, 1990.

Shiraishi, Takashi. "The Phantom World of Digoel." *Indonesia* 61 (April 1996): 93–118.

Siauw Tiong Djin, ed. *Ureca Berperan dalam Pembangunan Bangsa*. Jakarta: Perkumpulan Res Publica Indonesia, 2014.

Silverblatt, Irene. *Modern Inquisitions: The Colonial Origins of the Civilized World*. Durham, NC: Duke University Press, 2004.

Simpson, Bradley. *Economists with Guns: Authoritarian Development and U.S.-Indonesia Relations, 1960–1968*. Stanford: Stanford University Press, 2008.

Siswoyo. *Siswoyo dalam Pusaran Arus Sejarah Kiri: Memoar Anggota Sekretariat CC PKI*. Edited by Joko Wasito. Bandung: Ultimus, 2015.

Soedarmanta, J. B. *Mempertahankan Cita-Cita, Menjaga Spirit dan Perjuangan: Refleksi 80 Tahun Harry Tjan Silalahi*. Jakarta: Obor, 2014.

Soe Hok Gie. "About the Mass Killings on the Island of Bali." In *The Indonesian Killings of 1965–66: Studies from Java and Bali*, edited by Robert Cribb, 252–58. Clayton: Monash University Centre of Southeast Asian Studies, 1990.

Soe Hok Gie. *Zaman Peralihan*. Yogyakarta: Bentang Budaya, 1995.

Soejatno. "Revolution and Social Tensions in Surakarta 1945–1950." Translated by Benedict Anderson. *Indonesia* 17 (April 1974): 99–111.

Soekarno. *Genta Suara Revolusi Indonesia*. Jakarta: Departemen Penerangan, 1963.

Soekarno. *Jo Sanak, Jo Kadang, Malah Jen Mati Aku Sing Kélangan*. Djakarta: Jajasan Pembaruan, 1959.

Soekarno. *Subur, Subur, Suburlah PKI*. Jakarta: Pembaruan, 1965.

Southwood, Julie, and Patrick Flanagan. *Indonesia: Law, Propaganda and Terror*. London: Zed, 1983.

Steedly, Mary. *Hanging without a Rope: Narrative Experience in Colonial and Postcolonial Karoland*. Princeton, NJ: Princeton University Press, 1994.

Stoler, Ann. *Capitalism and Confrontation in Sumatra's Plantation Belt, 1870–1979*. 2nd ed. Ann Arbor: University of Michigan Press, 1995.

Strassler, Karen. *Refracted Visions: Popular Photography and National Modernity in Java*. Durham, NC: Duke University Press, 2010.

Straus, Scott. *Fundamentals of Genocide and Mass Atrocity Prevention*. Washington, DC: United States Holocaust Memorial Museum, 2016.

Straus, Scott. "What Is the Relationship between Hate Radio and Violence? Rethinking Rwanda's 'Radio Machete.'" *Politics & Society* 35, no. 4 (2007): 609–37.

Subijanto, Rianne. "Enlightenment and the Revolutionary Press in Colonial Indonesia." *International Journal of Communication* 11 (2017): 1357–77.

Subroto, Hendro. *Sintong Panjaitan: Perjalanan Seorang Prajurit Para Komando*. Jakarta: Kompas, 2009.

Sudisman. *Analysis of Responsibility*. Translated by Benedict Anderson. Melbourne: The Works Cooperative, 1975.

Sukanta, Putu Oka, ed. *Sulawesi Bersaksi*. Jakarta: Lembaga Kreatifitas Kemanusiaan, 2013.

Sulastomo. *Hari-Hari yang Panjang: Transisi Orde Lama ke Orde Baru: Sebuah Memoar*. Jakarta: Kompas, 2008.

Sulistyo, Hermawan. *Palu Arit di Ladang Tebu: Sejarah Pembantaian Massal yang Terlupakan*. Jakarta: KPG, 2000.

Sundhaussen, Ulf. *The Road to Power: Indonesian Military Politics, 1945–1967*. New York: Oxford University Press, 1982.

Sunyoto, Agus, et al. *Banser Berjihad: Menumpas PKI*. Tulungagung: Pesulukan Thoriqoh Agung, 1996.

Suparman, H. *Tragedi 1965: Dari Pulau Buru Sampai ke Mekah: Sebuah Catatan Tragedi 1965*. Bandung: Nuansa, 2006.

Suryadarma, Utami. *Saya, Soeriadi, dan Tanah Air*. Edited by Imelda Bachtiar. Jakarta: Yayasan Bung Karno, 2012.

Suryadinata, Leo. *Prominent Indonesian Chinese*. Singapore: ISEAS, 2015.

Suryawan, I Ngurah. *Ladang Hitam di Pulau Dewa: Pembantaian Massal di Bali 1965*. Yogyakarta: Galang Press, 2007.

Suryomenggolo, Jafar. *Organising under the Revolution: Unions and the State in Java, 1945–48*. Singapore: NUS Press, 2015.

Sutojo, Nani Nurrachman. *Kenangan Tak Terucap: Saya, Ayah, dan Tragedi 1965*. Jakarta: Kompas, 2013.

Suyatno. "Feodalisme dan Revolusi di Surakarta 1945–1950." *Prisma* 7 (July 1978).

Swift, Ann. *The Road to Madiun: The Indonesian Communist Uprising of 1948*. Ithaca, NY: Cornell Modern Indonesia Program, 1989.

Taher, Yoseph Tugio. *Riau Berdarah: Kisah Perjalanan Hidupku*. Jakarta: Hasta Mitra, 2006.

Tanter, Richard. "The Totalitarian Ambition: Intelligence and Security Agencies in Indonesia." In *State and Civil Society in Indonesia*, edited by Arief Budiman, 215–88. Clayton: Centre of Southeast Asian Studies, Monash University, 1990.

Taylor, Robert. *The State in Myanmar*. Singapore: NUS Press, 2009.

Thomas, Peter. *The Gramscian Moment: Philosophy, Hegemony, and Marxism*. Leiden: Brill, 2009.

Thompson, Allan, ed. *The Media and the Rwandan Genocide*. London: Pluto Press, 2007.

Timerman, Jacobo. *Prisoner without a Name, Cell without a Number*. Translated by Toby Talbot. New York: Knopf, 1981.
Tjakra-Adisurya, Deny. "Die Exhumierung des Massengrabes in Wonosobo." *Indonesien-Information*, no. 1 (2001). http://www.watchindonesia.org/II_April_2001/Exhumierung.htm.
Toer, Koesalah Soebagyo. *Tanah Merah yang Merah: Sebuah Catatan Sejarah*. Bandung: Ultimus, 2010.
Toer, Prameodya Ananta, ed. *Cerita Dari Digul*. Jakarta: KPG, 2001.
Toer, Pramoedya Ananta. *Haokiau di Indonesia*. Jakarta: Garba Budaya, 1998.
Toer, Pramoedya Ananta et al., eds. *Kronik Revolusi Indonesia*. 5 vols. Jakarta: KPG, 1999–2014.
Totten, Samuel, ed. *Last Lectures on the Prevention and Intervention of Genocide*. New York: Routledge, 2018.
Traverso, Enzo. *Understanding the Nazi Genocide: Marxism after Auschwitz*. London: Pluto Press, 1999.
Trisila, Slamat. "The Sutedja File: Gubernor Bali Pertama dalam Lipatan Sejarah." *Jurnal Kajian Bali* 3, no. 1 (April 2013): 115–38.
Trotsky, Leon. *The History of the Russian Revolution*. Vol. 3. Translated by Max Eastman. New York: Simon and Schuster, 1932.
Tsai, Yen-Ling, and Douglas Kammen. "Anti-communist Violence and the Ethnic Chinese in Medan, North Sumatra." In *The Contours of Mass Violence in Indonesia, 1965–68*, edited by Douglas Kammen and Katherine McGregor, 131–55. Singapore: NUS Press, 2012.
Twining, William, and P. E. Twining. "Bentham on Torture." *Northern Ireland Legal Quarterly* 24, no. 3 (1973): 305–56.
van der Kroef, Justus. *The Communist Party of Indonesia*. Vancouver: University of British Columbia Press, 1965.
van der Kroef, Justus. "Indonesia's Political Prisoners." *Pacific Affairs* 49, no. 4 (Winter 1976–77): 625–47.
van Dulm, J., et al. *Geillustreerde Atlas van de Japanse Kampen in Nederlands-Indie, 1942–1945*. Zierikzee: Asia Minor, 2002.
van Schaack, Beth. "The Crime of Political Genocide: Repairing the Genocide Convention's Blind Spot." *Yale Law Journal* 106, no. 7 (May 1997): 2259–91.
Wahid, Abdul. "Counterrevolution in a Revolutionary Campus: How Did the '1965 Event' Affect an Indonesian Public University?" In *The Indonesian Genocide of 1965: Causes, Dynamics, and Legacies*, edited by Katherine McGregor, Jess Melvin, and Annie Pohlman, 157–78. London: Palgrave Macmillan, 2018.
Wahid, Salahuddin. *Negeri di Balik Kabut Sejarah*. Jakarta: Pustaka Indonesia Satu, 2000.
Wahyuningroem, Sri Lestari. "Working from the Margins: Initiatives for Truth and Reconciliation for Victims of the 1965 Mass Violence in Solo and Palu." In *The Indonesian Genocide of 1965*, edited by Katherine McGregor, Jess Melvin, and Annie Pohlman, 335–56. London: Palgrave Macmillan, 2018.

White, Ben. "Clifford Geertz: Singular Genius of Interpretive Anthropology." *Development and Change* 38, no. 6 (2007): 1187–208.

Wiener, Margaret. *Visible and Invisible Realms: Power, Magic, and Colonial Conquests.* Chicago: University of Chicago Press, 1995.

Wieringa, Saskia. "Persisting Silence: Sexual Slander, Mass Murder, and *The Act of Killing*." *Asian Journal of Women's Studies* 20, no. 3 (2014): 50–76.

Wieringa, Saskia. *Sexual Politics in Indonesia.* New York: Palgrave Macmillan, 2002.

Wieringa, Saskia. "Sexual Slander and the 1965/66 Mass Killings in Indonesia: Political and Methodological Considerations." *Journal of Contemporary Asia* 41, no. 4 (2011): 544–65.

Wieringa, Saskia, and Nursyahbani Katjasungkana. *Propaganda and the Genocide in Indonesia: Imagined Evil.* New York: Routledge, 2019.

Wijaya, Nyoman. *Biografi Si Penggembala Itik: John Ketut Pantja: Pengalaman dan Pemikiran.* Yogyakarta: Pustaka Pelajar, 2001.

Wijoyo, Agus. *Transformasi TNI Dari Pejuang Kemerdekaan Menuju Tentara Profesional dalam Demokrasi: Pergulatan TNI Mengukuhkan Kepribadian dan Jati Diri.* Jakarta: Center for Strategic International Studies, 2015.

Williams, Michael. "Sneevliet and the Birth of Asian Communism." *New Left Review* 123 (September–October 1980): 81–90.

Williams, Michael. *Communism, Religion, and Revolt in Banten.* Athens: Ohio University Center for International Studies, 1990.

Winn, Peter. "The Furies of the Andes: Violence and Terror in the Chilean Revolution and Counterrevolution." In *A Century of Revolution: Insurgent and Counterinsurgent Violence during Latin America's Long Cold War*, edited by Greg Grandin and Gilbert Joseph, 239–75. Durham, NC: Duke University Press, 2010.

Wolfe, Patrick. "Settler Colonialism and the Elimination of the Native." *Journal of Genocide Research* 8, no. 4 (2006): 387–409.

Yayasan Tifa. *Saatnya Korban Bicara: Menata Derap Merajut Langkah.* Jakarta: Tifa, 2009.

Yuliantri, Rhoma Dwi Aria and Muhidin M. Dahlan, eds. *Lekra Tak Membakar Buku: Suara Senyap Lembar Kebudayaan Harian Rakjat 1950–1965.* Yogyakarta: Merakesumba, 2008.

Yusuf, Windu. "Bachtiar Siagian dan Misteri Realisme Sosialis Dalam Film Indonesia." *IndoProgress*, November 5, 2013. https://indoprogress.com/2013/11/bachtiar-siagian-dan-misteri-realisme-sosialis-dalam-film-indonesia/.

Zakaria, Fathurrahman. *Geger Gerakan 30 September 1965: Rakyat NTB Melawan Bahaya Merah.* 2nd ed. Mataram: Sumurmas, 2001.

Zed, Mestika. *Kepialangan Politik dan Revolusi: Palembang 1900–1949.* Jakarta: LP3ES, 2003.

Žižek, Slavoj. "On *The Act of Killing* and the Modern Trend of 'Privatising Public Space.'" *New Statesman*, July 12, 2013.

Žižek, Slavoj. *Event.* London: Penguin, 2014.

Oral Interviews

Unless otherwise noted, I conducted the interviews and recorded them, and the names of the interviewees are their real names. The transcripts and recordings of the recorded interviews are archived at the Institute of Indonesian Social History in Jakarta.

Agung (pseudonym). Sangeh, Bali. July 31, 2013. Unrecorded.
Ahmad (pseudonym). July 28, 2000. Ambarawa, Central Java. Interview by Rinto Tri Hasworo.
Bhadra. Kapal, Bali. January 10, 2001.
Bhaskoro. Lampung. February 19, 2001. Interview by Yayan Wiludiharto.
Bronto. Surakarta, Central Java. December 2, 2012.
Dayu Rai. Denpasar, Bali. January 11, 2001.
Guritno (pseudonym). Bandung, West Java. April 1, 2001.
Haryono. Surakarta, Central Java, July 20, 2000. Interview by Rinto Tri Hasworo.
I Gusti Ketut Reti. Denpasar, Bali. January 7, 2001.
I Made Pugeg. Denpasar, Bali. September 3, 2000.
I Made Sutayasa. Denpasar, Bali. July 13, 2004.
I Wayan Dhana. Denpasar, Bali. January 6, 2001.
I Wayan Jendra. Gianyar, Bali. July 12, 2004.
I Wayan Santa. Denpasar, Bali. July 13, 2004.
Ibu Pasek, oral interview, Denpasar, Bali. August 17, 2000.
Ibu Sutedja, oral interview, Jembrana, Bali. August 29, 2000.
Ida Bagus Kompiang. Sanur, Bali. September 2000. Unrecorded.
Jatiman. Surabaya, East Java. July 16, 2000, and January 2, 2001. Interviews by Cietwo and Asih.
Jaya Wardhana. Batu Bulan, Bali. July 25, 2015.
Joesoef Isak. Jakarta. December 20, 2003.
Kasmin. Rembang, Central Java. September 8, 2000, and July 25, 2001. Interviews by Rinto Trihasworo.
Made Mardiya. Denpasar, Bali. August 17, 2000.
Malen. Tabanan, Bali. August 27, 2000.
Marniti (pseudonym). Surakarta. April 20, 2005. Interview by Erlijna.
Murtini. Lampung. February 17, 2001. Interview by Yayan Wiludiharto.
Ni Made Intaran. Denpasar, Bali. August 15, 2000.
Oei Hay Djoen. Jakarta. January 24, 2002.
Oei Hiem Hwie. Surabaya. July 13, 2000. Interview by Cietwo.
Paini (pseudonym). Sukoharjo, Central Java. July 27, 2005. Interview by Rini Pratsnawati.
Pan Wayan (pseudonym). Kapal, Bali. August 1, 2013. Unrecorded.
Partono. Jakarta. November 13, 2000.
Poniti. Kapal, Bali. August 24, 2000, and July 30, 2013 (unrecorded).
Putu (pseudonym). Kapal, Bali. August 1, 2013. Unrecorded.
Raka Suasta. Denpasar, Bali. August 18, 2000.

Rewang. Solo, Central Java. June 27, 2001.
Ruswanto. Banywangi, East Java. March 21, 2001. Interview by Bambang.
Sukrisno. Jakarta. May 29, 2000. Interview by Rinto Trihasworo.
Sunarti (pseudonym). Surakarta. July 19, 2000. Interview by Rinto Tri Hasworo.
Tan Swie Ling. Jakarta. June 16, 2000, and March 16, 2001.
Taran (pseudonym). Gianyar, Bali. August 18, 2000.
Utomo (pseudonym). Jakarta. November 13, 2000.

Unpublished Documents and Manuscripts

Angkatan Darat, Direktorat Polisi Militer. "Berita Atjara Pemeriksaan Abdul Latief." October 25, 1965.
Biro Sumteng [Central Sumatran Bureau, PKI]. "Soal Aksi Ambil-alih Perusahaan Caltex di Riau." April 5, 1965.
Dewan Nasional SOBSI. "Tentang Kegiatan Ambilalih Perusahaan2 Belanda dalam Perdjuangan Pembebasan Irian Barat." July 21, 1958.
Komando Operasi Pemulihan Keamanan dan Ketertiban, Team Pemeriksa Pusat. "Berita Atjara Pemeriksaan Abdul Latief." December 21, 1965, and December 23, 1965.
Komando Operasi Tertinggi. *Laporan tentang Hasil Fact Finding Commission*. Jakarta, January 10, 1966.
Mahkamah Militer Luar Biasa. *Berkas Perkara Mustafa Sjarif Supardjo*. Jakarta: Mahmillub, 1967.
Mahkamah Militer Luar Biasa. *Berkas Berita Atjara Persidangan, Sidang ke-I s/d Sidang ke-XXV dan Putusan Perkara Abdullah Alihamy*. Jakarta: Mahmillub, 1970.
Munandar, Ashar. Untitled and unpublished manuscript of autobiography, ca. 1990s.
Soepardjan, Adam. "Gerakan Buruh Indonesia pada Prolog, Nalog, dan Epilog G30S/1965." Unpublished typescript, December 17, 2000.
Sudisman. "Hidup dalam Djuang: Djuang dalam Hidup! Statement Politik Terachir Sudisman Menyongsong Ditembak Mati." Unpublished typescript, October 5, 1968.
Suryaatmadja, Tubagus. "Petualangan Politik Seorang Guru Sekolah Rakyat." Unpublished typescript, 2004.
Suryaman, Asep. "Asep Suryaman alias Hamim dan Jalan Hidupnya." Unpublished typescript, January 1, 1998.
Suryaman, Asep. "Pemogokan Sarekat Buruh Perkebunan Republik Indonesia (Sarbupri) di Delanggu (Klaten), 1 April 1948 Sampai 1 Mei 1948." Unpublished typescript, 2002.

Unpublished Dissertations and Theses

Hidayat, Mansur. "Biografi Politik I Gusti Putu Merta (1913–1992)." BA thesis, Udayana University, 1999.
Kartodirdjo, Soejatno. "Revolution in Surakarta 1945–50: A Case Study of City and

Village in the Indonesian Revolution." PhD diss., Australian National University, 1982.
Lane, Max. "Wedastera Suyasa in Balinese Politics, 1962–1972: From Charismatic Politics to Socio-Educational Activities." BA thesis, Sydney University, 1972.
Maiddin, S. H. M. "Microphone Republic: Propaganda and Indoctrination in Guided Democracy Indonesia." PhD diss., University of Sydney, 2016.
Maxwell, John. "Soe Hok-Gie: A Biography of a Young Indonesian Intellectual." PhD diss., Australian National University, 1997.
Purnama, Priya. "Konflik Berdarah di Desa Krangasem Kecamatan Gambiran Kabupaten Banyuwangi (18 Oktober 1965)." BA thesis, Jember University, 2012.
Redfern, William. "Sukarno's Guided Democracy and the Takeover of Foreign Companies in Indonesia in the 1960s." PhD diss., University of Michigan, 2010.
Setiadi, Hilmar Farid. "Rewriting the Nation: Prameodya and the Politics of Decolonization." PhD diss., National University of Singapore, 2014.
Syahyudin, Firman. "Peristiwa Cemetuk Tahun 1965." BA thesis, Jember University, 2009.
Yeo, Woonkyung. "Palembang in the 1950s: The Making and Unmaking of a Region." PhD diss., University of Washington, 2012.

Archival Sources

ANU Open Repository, Harold Crouch documents, https://openresearch-repository.anu.edu.au/handle/1885/141110.
Bali Oral History Archive, Murdoch University, http://library.murdoch.edu.au/boha/.
Kementerian Penerangan Files, National Archives of the Republic of Indonesia.
KOTI Collection, National Archives of the Republic of Indonesia.
National Security Archive, Indonesia and East Timor Documentation Project.

Journals and Media

BBC Indonesia
Bintang Merah
CNN Indonesia
Detik.com
Harian Rakjat
Historia
IndoProgress
Ingat 65
Islam Bergerak
Jakarta Post
Kompas
Koran Tempo
Media Indonesia

Merdeka
New York Times
Platt's Oilgram News
Riau Online
Saturday Evening Post
Saturday Review
Sinar Harapan
Sindonews
Suara Indonesia
Soeara Kita
Tashwirul Afkar
Tempo
Viva News
Washington Post

Films

The Act of Killing. Directed by Joshua Oppenheimer and Anonymous. Austin, TX: Drafthouse Films, 2012.

40 Years of Silence. Directed by Robert Lemelson. Los Angeles: Elemental Productions, 2009.

Indonesia: The Troubled Victory. New York: NBCUniversal Media, 1967.

The Look of Silence. Directed by Joshua Oppenheimer. Austin, TX: Drafthouse Films/Participant Media/Final Cut for Real, 2014.

Shadow Play. Directed by Chris Hilton. Australia: Hilton Cordell/Vagabond Films, 2002.

Index

Abadi, 47
Abdullah, Taufik, 16
Abu Ghraib, 96
Aceh, 17–18, 62, 77, 114, 152, 239, 245–46, 250, 264, 294n83
Achmadi, Major General, 74, 278n72, 280n7
Action Front. *See* KAP-Gestapu
The Act of Killing, 11–12, 262
Adi, Yunantyo, 263–65
Adjie, Ibrahim, 40, 72, 77, 150, 157–58, 235, 244–45
Agung, 188–90
Ahmad, 95–96, 101
Aidit, Dipa Nusantara, 28–33, 43–46, 54–55, 66, 111, 136–37, 213, 276n44, 276n48, 276n54, 299n54
Aidit, Ilham, 256
Aleida, Martin, 118–19
Algeria, 90
Alihamy, Abdullah, 237, 313n56
Alimin, 124, 131
Alleg, Henri, 89
Améry, Jean, 89
Amnesty International, 89, 108
Anderson, Benedict, 78, 81, 99, 129, 273n15, 284n57, 292n39, 298n45
Anderson, Perry, 273n15
Angkatan Bersenjata, 47, 51, 53, 63–65, 71, 75–77

Antara, 48–49, 51–52, 63–64, 74–76, 79, 279n82, 284n58, 285n69, 287n89
anticommunists, 9, 11, 14, 16, 18, 20, 26–27, 29, 30–32, 36, 38–39, 42, 46–49, 51, 55–56, 64, 67, 69, 80–81, 96, 112, 123–24, 126–28, 139, 141, 144, 151, 156, 158–59, 161, 204, 216, 220, 234, 236–38, 240–41, 244–48, 256, 261–63, 265, 272n1, 280n7, 280n9, 288nn105–106
Api, 73–74
Argentina, 27, 89, 93
Aristotle, 90, 292n42
army, Indonesian, 3–4, 6–10, 13–21, 25, 28–31, 33–35, 38–48, 50–84, 86–90, 94–95, 99–109, 111–14, 116, 119–20, 124–25, 128–40, 143–44, 146, 150–53, 155–56, 158–66, 172–74, 176–77, 181, 183–88, 191–93, 195–96, 201, 203–7, 213–16, 219–21, 224–25, 227–28, 230–31, 235, 237–52, 257–66, 269n26, 276n44, 277n57, 277n61, 278n79, 279n82, 280n7, 280–81n9, 281n10, 282n19, 285n64, 286n76, 289n6, 293n69, 298nn43–44, 298n47, 302n12, 304n53, 306n9, 313n4, 315n7; high command of, 8, 16, 20, 30, 40, 47, 50, 120, 128, 150–51, 159, 239, 241–48, 270n38, 313n4, 314n19; regional commanders, 18, 20, 270n38, 313n4; Staff College (SESKOAD) of, 28, 30, 33, 42, 55, 272n1; Territorial Command of, 20, 39–43, 45, 55–56, 60, 62,

army, Indonesian (*continued*) 69, 88, 161, 238–39, 241, 243, 248–49, 259, 262–63, 275n37, 275n44, 303n32; territorial management of, 40, 42; territorial warfare of, 39–40, 42
Asian-African Conference, 59
Atjep, 107
atrocity, 77, 81, 191, 261
Aziz, M. Imam, 26

Bacem Bridge, 116–19
Badan Kerja Sama (BKS), 42, 276n44
Badan Pendukung Sukarnoism (BPS), 47, 277n60
Badan Permusjawaratan Kewarganegaraan Indonesia (Baperki), 66, 223, 287n96, 311n29
Badung regency, 192
Bakorstanas, 238
Bali, 7, 8, 9, 15–16, 20, 22–23, 105, 118, 147, 149–166, 170, 176–208, 239–40, 244–45, 248, 250–51, 300n73, 301n6, 303nn30–31, 306n2, 308n29
Bali Beach Hotel, 157, 177, 198–99
Bali Dwipa, 156
Bandung, 28, 42, 52, 55, 75, 77, 114, 246, 289n6, 294n78, 301n6
Bangli regency, 166
Banser (Barisan Ansor Serbaguna), 10, 249
Banten, 98–99, 123
Banteng Raiders, 104
Banyuwangi, 79
Barisan Tani Indonesia (BTI), 222, 227, 234
Barlian, Lieutenant Colonel, 220
Battle of Agincourt, 250
Batubara, Cosmas, 42, 144
Beccaria, Cesare, 91, 292n42
Bedulu, 150, 178
Beijing, 45, 100, 278n67
Belden, Jack, 131
Belgrade, 59
Bengkulu, 229, 311n27
Benson, George, 42
Bentham, Jeremy, 91
Berita Yudha, 47, 51, 63–65, 70, 72, 75–76, 80
Bhadra, 165–66, 203

Bhaskoro, 100–101, 221–28
Black Book of Communism, 26
Blair Mountain, 216
Bogor, 70, 74
Bonar, 107
Bondowoso, 69
Bonnet, Rudolph, 149
Boven Digoel, 123–24, 142, 232, 296nn15–16, 309n6
Boyolali, 78, 119, 137–38, 298n36
Britain, 32, 64, 107–8, 217–19, 233
British India, 120
Bronto, 128–39, 298n42, 298n45, 299n53
Budiardjo, 107
Budiardjo, Carmel, 106–8
Bumi Sangkuriang, 55
Burma. *See* Myanmar
Buru Island, 104, 108–9, 112, 141, 235, 309n6
bystanders, 15, 62–63, 251, 253, 270n31

Caltex (California Texas Oil Company), 230–37, 312n45
Catholics, 26, 42, 48, 65, 67, 154, 265
Catholic Party, 162
Catur Tunggal, 42, 45
Cemetuk, 79
Central Java, 3, 5, 7, 9, 14, 15, 20, 26, 30, 44, 59, 68–69, 76–78, 94, 97–98, 100–101, 117, 120, 127–29, 135–39, 143–45, 149, 151, 160, 221, 231, 239, 243–44, 247, 249, 257, 260, 266, 269n28, 289n6, 297n31
Central Sumatra, 232, 235, 312n45
Chalid, Idham, 68
Chile, 27
China, 21, 32–33, 35, 39, 69, 100–101, 131, 274n22, 277n57, 278n67, 295n8
Christian Party, 162
CIA (Central Intelligence Agency), 27, 35, 46, 59, 96, 112, 233, 294n76
Ciamis, 68
Cilacap, 68
Cirebon, 73
Civic Action, 42
Cold War, 39, 126, 154, 214
Colombia, 216
Comintern (Communist International), 34, 274n19, 295n8

communism, 5, 34, 42, 49, 120, 122, 123, 128, 130, 206, 214, 216, 263, 312n41
communists, 6, 9, 12, 14, 16, 21, 23–24, 26, 30–31, 33–34, 39, 46, 48–49, 54–56, 60–61, 65, 77–81, 83–84, 87, 101, 107, 113–14, 118–19, 123–25, 127–28, 131, 137, 139, 145, 150, 152, 154–55, 191, 195–98, 200, 205, 207, 216, 224, 232, 240, 259, 262, 274n19, 281n13, 299n63
Conboy, Ken, 176
Confrontation, 36, 100, 134, 189, 200, 233, 235, 302n11
Congo, Anwar, 11–12, 15
Consentrasi Gerakan Mahasiswa Indonesia (CGMI), 231–32, 234
Constitution: of 1945, 32, 35, 41; of 1950, 35, 41
Constitutional Assembly (Konstituante), 35, 128
Corps Polisi Militer (CPM), 98, 100, 110, 135–36, 141, 165–68, 196, 221, 223–28, 234, 238, 279n84, 289n6
Cribb, Robert, 15, 24, 31
Crouch, Harold, 243, 275n37

Dada, Anom, 164, 197, 203, 307n23
Daino, 197
Dake, Antonie C., 112
Darul Islam, 45, 59, 256
Daryatmo, 244
Dasuki, Ahmad, 123–24, 128, 296n15
death toll, 6, 8, 17–18, 169, 239, 247, 269n22, 315n7
Delanggu, 69, 130, 226; strike in, 125, 127, 130, 212, 296n24
Deli River, 11
delusional reality, 20, 61, 243, 262
Denpasar, 156–57, 160, 162–63, 165–67, 170, 172–73, 181, 183–84, 187–88, 190–92, 194, 197–207, 303n29, 304n42, 305n2, 306n9, 308n28; Kesiman neighborhood, 308n28; Panjer neighborhood, 172; Pekambingan neighborhood and prison, 166–68, 173, 305n53; Renon neighborhood, 167; Sanglah neighborhood, 201–3
Dhana, I Wayan, 192–96, 201, 307n16, 307n18
Dharsono, H. S., 159
Dhenia, A. A., 159

Diah, B. M., 47
Digdo Battalion. *See* Sudigdo, Major
Digest of Justinian, 91
disappearances, 4, 8, 15, 26, 142, 170, 173–74
Djasmin, Major, 161–63, 176, 194–96, 207, 307n15
Djawoto, 48–49, 278n67
Djuarsa, 244–46
Djunaedi, H. Mahbub, 52
Dubois, Lindsey, 93
Dupem, Ida Bagus, 189, 197, 307n23
Duta Masyarakat, 52
Dutch colonialism. *See* Netherlands East Indies

East, Colonel, 55
East Java, 7, 9, 10, 15, 22–23, 39, 62, 80–81, 102–03, 107, 114, 126, 144, 155, 160, 164, 210, 239, 243, 246–51, 269n30, 270n31, 270n43, 287n89, 289n6, 292n46, 303n30, 306n9
East Kalimantan, 23, 68, 310n16
East Timor: torture in, 114, 294n83; Santa Cruz massacre in, 315n7
Edhie, Sarwo, 135, 137–39, 143–44, 176, 195, 299n63, 300n73
El Salvador, 216
Eurasians, 81
executioners (*algojo*), 12–14, 150, 177, 203–4, 247, 249, 261

Fact Finding Commission (FFC), 7–9, 11, 20, 202, 257, 268n8
Fadjar, 156, 200–201, 308n28, 308n34
Farid, Hilmar, 214, 272n7
fascism, 31
Fic, Victor, 112
Finland, 206
Flores, 264
Ford Foundation, 4–5, 267n5
Fort Vastenburg, 129
Forum Silaturahmi Anak Bangsa (FSAB), 256, 262
Foucault, Michel, 91, 290n17

Gadjah Mada University, 4–5, 267n2, 267n5
Gandhi, M. K., 58
Garut, 69, 77

Gatak, 143
Gede, I Gusti Nyoman, 147–50, 164, 177–78
Geertz, Clifford, 16, 270n31, 301n7
Geneva Conventions, 252
genocide, 23–26, 54, 62–63, 77, 203, 214–17, 271n51, 310n15; economics of, 214–17, 310n15; political, 24–25, 214–15; prevention of, 151; resistance to, 151, 301n4
Gerakan Wanita Indonesia (Gerwani), 66, 69, 71, 73, 75–76, 79, 100, 113, 128, 141–42, 173, 175, 201, 228, 232, 234
Gerlach, Christian, 16–17
Germany, 229
Gianyar, 150, 196
Goodyear, 216
Gramsci, Antonio, 23, 31–33, 42, 49–50, 272n7, 273nn15–16
Greece, 89–90, 216
Green, Marshall, 8, 59, 224, 280n9
Guantanamo, 96
Guided Democracy, 29–32, 35, 38, 40, 45–49, 53–56, 60, 127, 153–54, 167, 199–200, 236, 239, 244, 274nn23–24, 275n37
Gurr, Ted, 24

Harff, Barbara, 24
Harian Rakjat, 47–49, 51, 64–65
Hartinah, Siti, 146
Hartono, 159
Haryono, 141
Hasan, Amir, 13–15
Hatta, Mohammad, 59, 80–81, 124–26, 211
Hill, David, 46
Himpunan Sarjana Indonesia (HSI), 108
Hinton, Alexander, 25
Hughes, John, 10, 139, 152, 165, 176, 200, 306n4, 306n6
human rights, 21, 26, 93, 108, 214, 252, 254, 256–58, 260, 263–65, 281n10, 294n83
Hunter, Helen-Louise, 112
Hutapea, Oloan, 102–3, 292n46
Hutus, 62

Ibnu Santoro, 3–6
Idris, Fahmi, 144
Ikatan Pemuda Pelajar Indonesia (IPPI), 51, 106, 141, 167–68, 234

Ikatan Pendukung Kemerdekaan Indonesia (IPKI), 162, 314n14
Indies Social Democratic Association (ISDV), 123
Indonesian Film Company (Infico), 85–87, 106–7, 284–85n58
Indonesian National History, 9
Intaran, Ni Made, 170–73
International Conference against Foreign Military Bases, 200
International Convention for the Protection of All Persons from Enforced Disappearance, 26
International Criminal Court, 25
International People's Tribunal (IPT), 256–57
Interrogation Team, 98, 141, 289n3; Central (Tim Pemeriksaan Pusat, Teperpu), 88, 293n59; Regional (Tim Pemeriksaan Daerah, Teperda), 88, 98, 157, 225–26
Isak, Joesoef, 48–50
Iskander, Major, 132–33
Islam Bergerak, 123
Italy, 31, 294n80

Jainsah, 234
Jakarta, 4, 7, 9, 12, 16, 18, 20, 23, 26–27, 30, 40, 42, 46, 50–53, 58, 61, 64–66, 68–70, 73, 77–80, 86–88, 95–102, 106, 108–10, 118, 128–29, 132–39, 143–44, 148, 150–51, 155–56, 159–60, 175, 177, 194–95, 199–200, 206–7, 209–10, 220, 223, 229, 233–34, 236–37, 239–47, 254–57, 263, 267n5, 270n38, 277n57, 279n92, 282n19, 284–85n58, 287n96, 289n1, 289nn5–6, 292n39, 297n26, 298n37, 299nn53–54, 301n6, 302n12, 303n34, 308nn29–30, 309n6, 312n43, 312n45, 313n52, 313n4
Jambi, 225, 229, 238
Japan, 294; invasion of Southeast Asia, 217–18, 231; occupation of Indonesia, 36, 39, 124–25, 130, 165, 211, 215, 217–19, 229–30, 235, 290n10, 298n40
Jatiman, 103–05
Java, 3, 15–16, 22–23, 38, 68, 79, 81, 102–3, 118, 120, 122, 126–27, 144, 156, 160, 164, 177, 193, 217, 221, 226, 232, 235, 237, 265, 276n53, 297n30, 304n49

Java Sea, 117, 146, 217
Jembrana, 151, 158-59, 161, 188, 303n31
Jendra, I Wayan, 202-3

Kalimantan, 134, 313n4
Kalisosok Prison, 103-5
Kampung Kenten, 226
Kandel, Ktut, 164, 181, 197, 207, 307n23
Kapal massacre, 172, 179-208, 305n2, 306n10, 307n23, 307n25
KAP-Gestapu, 64-65
Karanganyar, 138
Karangasem (East Java), 79
Karim Daeng Patombong, 47, 52-53, 66
Kartasuro, 134
Karto, Pak (alias Suhadi Bengkring), 131, 298n38, 298n40
Kartodikromo, Mas Marco, 123, 145
Kasmin, 97-98
Kebayoran Baru (New Kebayoran), 69
Kebayoran Lama (Old Kebayoran), 85, 107-8, 285, 289n1
Kebyar, Mangku, 148-50, 177-78
Kediri, 251
Keimas, Taufik, 228-29
Kemaro Island, 225, 228-29, 240
Kendal, 264
Kesatuan Aksi Mahasiswa Indonesia (KAMI), 144-45, 236
Kesatuan Aksi Pemuda Pelajar Indonesia (KAPPI), 236
Khrushchev, Nikita, 154
Kick Andy, 14
Klaten, 78, 119, 137-38, 299n58
Kodam (Komando Daerah Militer), 40, 55, 155, 216, 241-42, 244-45, 249, 253, 302n12, 313n4; of Aceh, 245-46; of Bali and Eastern Indonesia, 156, 158, 160, 164, 183-84, 189, 193-96, 199, 201, 204-6, 244-45, 248, 307n15, 315n7; of Central Java, 128, 138, 247, 297n31; of East Java, 62, 103, 246-48, 281n14, 292n46; of Jakarta, 52, 177, 298n37; of North Sumatra, 132, 244-46, 248; of South Sumatra, 221, 225, 227-29, 238-40, 244-45, 248, 311n27; of West Java, 52, 157, 244-45; of West and Central Sumatra, 235, 237, 239-40, 244-45, 248

Kodim, 40-41, 55, 249; in Bali, 158, 160, 167, 245; in Denpasar, 162-63, 169, 175; in East Jakarta, 97; in East Java, 246; in Lampung area, 100; in Palu, 258; in Surabaya, 104; in Surakarta, 116, 128, 133, 142, 298n43
Komando Operasi Tertinggi (KOTI), 64, 88, 206
Kompas, 47-48, 51, 64, 277n62
Kompiang, Ida Bagus, 157, 177, 199, 303n24, 308n43
Kopkamtib, 238
Korea, 216
Korem (Komando Resor Militer), 40-41, 55, 246, 249; of Bali, 160, 176, 304n42; of Riau, 235, 239, 244-45; of Surabaya, 105
Krisnayana, 96
Kuomintang, 216
Kuta, 192-93

Lamasitudju, Nurlaela, 257-58, 316n10
Lampung, 100, 221-22, 226-29, 238-39, 311n27
Langbein, John, 91
Latief, Abdul, 109-10, 112, 298n37
Latin America, 42, 90
Laweyan, 127, 139, 141
Leimena, Johannes, 73
Lembaga Kebudayaan Rakjat (Lekra), 48, 73, 86, 95, 106, 113, 127, 134, 142, 209, 232, 234, 273n7, 277n57, 294n78
Lembaga Pertahanan Nasional (Lemhanas), 70-71
Lembang, 114
Lemkin, Raphael, 24, 216
Lev, Daniel, 38
local conflicts paradigm, 16-18, 20-21, 269n30
Lombok, 250
The Look of Silence, 13
Lowry, Robert, 55
lubang, 70
Lubang Buaya, 70-71, 73-76, 79, 83, 113, 255, 259-60
Lubis, Firman, 145
Lubis, Pengulu, 48
Lukman, 30, 66, 111, 137, 309n6
Luttwak, Edward, 120

Madiun, 39, 80–82, 126, 130–31, 288n100, 288n105
Magelang, 94–95, 101
Magetan massacre, 81
Magnis-Suseno, Franz, 26
Mahmillub, 108
Malaya, 36, 211, 217
Malaysia, 36, 45, 61, 64, 100, 134, 155, 189, 200, 233, 235, 237, 302n11
Malik, Adam, 47–48, 278n67
Manado, 69, 223
Manafe, Aco, 113
Manggarai Station, 210–11, 213, 309n7
Marajo, Muhktar Bagindo, 236
Marniti, 141–42
martial law, 41, 48, 51, 274n23, 275n37, 276n44; law for, 252; in Surakarta, 143
Martadinata, 77, 135
Masceti Beach, 150
Masjumi, 35–36, 47, 81–82, 126, 220, 236, 276n53; Hizbullah militia of, 126
mass atrocity, 26, 84
Masters, Edward, 155, 302n12
Mastura, Rudy, 258
Matnoer, Major, 163
Matsuno, Akihisa, 156
McVey, Ruth, 78, 129, 298n45
Medan, 11–13, 17, 77, 216, 246, 261
Megawati Sukarnoputri, 228–29
Melvin, Jess, 17–18, 20–21, 24
Mengwi, 196
mental operation, 40, 61–62, 162–63, 281n14
Merajut Harkat, 106
Merdeka, 47, 49
Merta, I Gusti Putu, 156–57, 161, 184, 304n37, 307n15
Metode Kombinasi Tiga Bentuk Perjuangan (MKTBP), 43–44, 56, 276n46, 276n48, 276n50
military police. *See* Corps Polisi Militer
militias, 10, 100, 124, 126, 130, 141, 150–51, 158, 161–62, 173, 183, 187, 247–49, 306n6
Minas oil field, 231
Misbach, Haji, 123–24, 128, 142, 146
Moertopo, Ali, 49, 243
Mokoginta, Major General A. Y., 77, 216, 239, 246, 248–49, 313n4

Moscow, 232
Moses, A. Dirk, 25
Muhammadiyah, 127, 138
Munandar, Ashar, 108–9, 293n60
Murod, Makmun, 227, 240, 244–45
Murtini, 228, 311n32
Musi River, 217–18, 224–25, 229, 240, 245
Musso, 34
Myanmar, 41, 211, 217

Nahdlatul Ulama (NU), 10, 15, 26, 35, 52, 65, 68, 79, 82, 84, 138, 162, 233, 246–47, 249, 268n17, 281nn12–13, 282n20, 287n89
Nasution, Abdul Haris, 39–40, 42, 47, 53–54, 77, 124, 137, 275n34, 278n76, 314n14
Nasution, Adnan Buyung, 61, 281n10
Nasution, Kaharuddin, 235–37, 239–40, 244–45
Nasution, Noor, 51, 63, 74
National Front, 45, 134, 157, 168, 199, 201, 276n51
nationalization of companies, 215, 233–34, 312n45
National Security Agency (NSA), 46
Nederlandsch-Indische Spoorweg Maatschappij, 211
Negara, 154, 158–59
Nehru, Jawaharlal, 58, 154
Netherlands: recolonization of Indonesia, 11, 29, 34, 36–37, 39, 43, 80–82, 126, 194, 197, 199, 207, 219, 231; West New Guinea dispute, 36, 233
Netherlands East Indies, 39, 58, 120, 122–24, 166, 181, 211, 215, 217–18, 229, 232, 235, 290n10, 295n6, 310n16
Ngalihan massacre, 81–82, 131
Njono, 66, 111, 293n69
Njoto, 30, 49, 66, 111, 137, 277n57
Noer, Arifin C., 113
Non-Aligned Conference, 59
noncommunists, 7, 20, 22, 32–33, 49–50, 63, 69–70, 78–80, 84, 113, 125, 127, 139, 155, 158, 200, 232, 299n63, 306n4
North Sumatra, 7, 9, 11, 13, 15, 22, 68, 77, 132, 214, 244–46, 248–49, 270n43, 305n1, 310n16
Notosusanto, Nugroho, 9, 11, 111–12, 268n14

Nurjanjo, 100–101
Nurmantyo, Gatot, 259
Nusa Dua, 192

Oei Tjoe Tat, 202, 268n8, 308n29
Oey Hay Djoen, 46
oil, 22, 39, 214–15, 217–24, 230–31, 233–34, 237–38, 240, 244, 310n16, 312n37
Oppenheimer, Joshua, 11–14, 22; *The Act of Killing*, 11–12, 262; *The Look of Silence*, 13
Osiel, Mark, 93

Pabrik Pupuk Sriwijaya (PUSRI), 224–25, 227
Padang, 235
Paini, 142–43
Pakis, 101
Pakistan, 41
Palembang, 100, 217–30, 233, 238–40, 245, 311n27, 311n29; Ampera Bridge in, 225–26
Palu, 257–58
Panca Tunggal, 45, 193, 313n52
Panjaitan, Luhut, 256–59
Panjaitan, Sintong, 257–59, 278n71, 315n7
Panuju, Brigadier General, 235, 237, 239, 244–45
Papua, 45, 114, 123, 233, 262, 294n83
Parman, 83
Parmini, Ida Ayu Rai (Dayu Rai), 198, 200–202, 204, 206–7, 308n35
Partai Demokrasi Indonesia-Perjuangan (PDI-P), 182, 228
Partai Indonesia (Partindo), 88, 156–57, 200, 268n8, 304n49, 308n29
Partai Komunis Indonesia (PKI), 3, 4, 6–7, 9–12, 14–15, 17–18, 20–22, 24–36, 38–39, 42–84, 86, 88–90, 92, 94–95, 97–106, 108–16, 119–20, 122–32, 134–46, 149–52, 154–68, 170, 172, 176, 183–87, 189, 191–92, 194–97, 199–200, 203–4, 206–7, 211, 213–16, 221–25, 227–29, 231–52, 254–63, 270n41, 272n7, 273n15, 274n24, 276n48, 276n51, 276n53, 277n57, 277nn60–61, 278n76, 279n93, 281nn13–14, 282n20, 283n35, 288n100, 288n103, 288n106, 292n44, 293n69, 295n9, 295n11, 296n19, 297n36, 298n38, 298n40, 307n16, 307n20, 307n23, 308n42, 309n6, 312n45; Central Committee of, 56, 299n54; Politburo of, 30, 49, 99, 111, 137, 213, 277n57, 298n40; revolt of 1926–27 by, 123–24, 131, 211, 232
Partai Nasional Indonesia (PNI), 31, 35, 52, 68, 82, 94, 119, 127, 138, 141, 143, 149–59, 161–63, 165, 167, 176–77, 182–84, 186–87, 192, 194, 196–97, 199–201, 203–4, 207, 228–29, 233, 245, 247–48, 301n10, 304n38, 304n42, 304n49, 306n10, 307n15, 307n20
Partai Sosialis Indonesia (PSI), 35, 47, 49, 196–97, 303n31
Partono, 108
Pasek, Ibu, 173–76
Pasuma, Benny, 223
Pati, 68, 257, 315n8
Patrice Lumumba University, 232
Pauker, Guy, 42, 275nn43–44, 311n23
Peace Corps, 4
Pearl Harbor, 217
Pedoman, 47
Pekanbaru, 231–32, 234–37, 312n48; An-Nur Mosque of, 235
Pemerintahan Revolusioner Republik Indonesia (PRRI), 34–36, 40, 45–46, 59, 220–21, 233, 235–36, 240, 248, 256, 270n41, 276n53
Pemuda Pancasila, 11, 248–49
Pemuda Rakjat, 66, 68–69, 76–78, 105, 141, 168–69, 231, 276n53, 285n72
Pemuda Sosialis Indonesia (Pesindo), 124
Permesta (Piagam Perjuangan Semesta), 34–35, 40, 45–46
perpetrators, 6, 9–12, 15, 20, 24, 63, 83, 93, 113, 151–52, 181, 185–86, 191, 200, 202, 205, 207, 241, 249–54, 257, 258–59, 261–62, 265, 268n16, 270n31, 303n31, 315n7
Persatuan Buruh Minyak (Perbum), 214, 219, 223–24, 232–38
Persatuan Guru Republik Indonesia (PGRI), 94; Non-Central Faction of, 94
Persatuan Wartawan Indonesia (PWI), 47–48, 52, 279n89
Peru, 91
Philomelo, 60
Pinochet, Augusto, 27
Plaju, 217–18, 223, 227

plantations, 13, 100–101, 120, 125, 209, 214, 216, 231, 246, 248–49
plantation workers, 13, 209, 212, 214, 216, 246
Plantungan, 141
Plumbon, 264–65
Political Manifesto (Manipol), 29, 47, 167
politicide, 24–25, 271n51
Poniman, Colonel, 239
Poniti, I Made, 182–91, 203, 306n10, 307n15
Prabumulih oil fields, 224
Prambanan, 78
Pranoto, General, 55, 57, 59, 280n1
primitive accumulation, 214
prisoners, 32, 84; categorization of, 88, 94, 141, 169, 227, 235, 289n4; killing of, 3–4, 6, 10–13, 19, 21, 80–81, 116–19, 141–43, 145–46, 164–78, 180–198, 202–4, 226–30, 236–52, 260–61, 264–66, 270n41, 292n46, 305n53; political, 3, 18, 23, 86, 89, 100, 107, 124, 140–41, 164, 224, 228–30, 235, 254, 258, 262, 267n1, 296n16, 300n67; torture of, 87, 89–115, 141, 289n6
prisoners of war, 218, 230
Priyono, 67,
Priyono, Ami, 113
Probosutedjo, 113
psychological warfare, 69, 75–76, 113, 158
public killings, 17, 246, 250
Pugeg, I Made, 192, 194–97, 201, 207–8
Puger, I Gde, 181, 185–86, 190–91, 193–94, 197–208, 307n25, 308n28, 308n42
puputan, 181, 306n3
Puri Lukisan, 148
Purwana, Ketut, 195
Putu, 186–87

Rabidi, Joseph, 132, 298n42
radio, 7, 36–38, 57, 60–64, 96, 132–34, 142–43, 220, 224
Radio Malaysia, 61, 64
Radio Republic Indonesia (RRI), 50, 64, 128; Denpasar station of, 201; Surakarta station of, 128
Rahmat, Basuki, 246–47, 314n10
Rai, Ngurah, 181
Raka, I Gusti Putu, 183
Ramelan, Utaryo, 127

Ramelan, Utomo, 127, 134, 138
Ramelan, Utoyo, 127
Ramli, 13
Rand Corporation, 42
Rasjid, Haroen, 123–24, 128, 142, 296n15
Rasjid, Ibu Haroen, 142
Ratyono, Brigadier General, 113
Ray, Arthur, 4
Regent Hotel, 144
Rembang, 98
Resimen Para Komando Angkatan Darat (RPKAD), 134, 137–41, 143–44, 150–52, 160–61, 164, 176, 186, 188–89, 192–97, 203–4, 207, 243, 245, 247–48, 257, 278, 303n31, 303n34, 307n15, 307n20
Res Publica University, 66–67, 297n26
Reti, I Gusti Ketut, 196–97
Rewang, 137, 298n40
Riau, 20, 22, 214–15, 230–40, 244–45, 248, 312n45
Riyadi, Slamat, 131, 298n38
Robinson, Geoffrey, 18, 20, 198, 270n38, 302n11, 305n2, 307n16
Rochijat, Pipit, 251
romusha, 211, 231, 237
Rukun, Adi, 13
Rusiyati, Ibu, 52
Rusli, Sofian, 224–25, 227–28
Ruswanto, 105
Rwandan genocide, 62, 301n4
Ryacudu, Ryamizard, 259

Saba, 150
Sabah, 36
Sacred Pancasila Monument, 76, 113
Sakirman, 30, 111, 293n68
Salatiga, 128
Saleh, Chaerul, 234
Saleh, Ismail, 9, 11, 111–12
Salemba Prison, 110
Santa, I Wayan, 167, 307n23
Santoso, Major, 144
Sanur, 157, 177, 192
Sanusi, Anwar, 65
Saracen, 184
Sarawak, 36
Sarbinatun, 100

Sarekat Buruh Perkebunan Indonesia (Sarbupri), 13, 125, 209
Sarekat Buruh Kereta Api (SBKA), 96, 210–13, 215, 309n2, 309n4
Sarekat Islam, 122–23, 139, 263, 295n10
Sartre, Jean-Paul, 261
Sastroatmodjo, Purwanto, 163–64
Satgas Intel, 86–87, 106–9, 293n54
Sawahlunto, 231, 312n41
Scarry, Elaine, 91–93
Schumacher, E. F., 96
Seda, Frans, 48
Segara Beach Hotel, 199
Segara Village Hotel, 157
Semaoen, 122, 211, 263, 295n9
Semarang, 120, 120, 128–29, 134, 137, 141, 232, 263–66, 295n9, 299n47
Semelin, Jacques, 20, 61, 63
Senayan Stadium, 29, 209, 213
Sentral Organisasi Buruh Seluruh Indonesia (SOBSI), 66, 165, 168–69, 209, 213–15, 224, 233–34, 236
September 30th Movement, 7–10, 14, 23, 25, 50–52, 55, 57, 59–60, 62–65, 68, 70, 75–78, 80, 83–84, 88–89, 94, 96, 100, 108–10, 112–13, 141, 213, 255–56, 259–60, 291n38, 293n59, 303n32, 314n7; in Bali, 155–60, 162–64, 170, 183, 192, 200; in Palembang, 223, 225, 228; in Riau, 234; in Surakarta, 128–37
Serang, 99
Serata, I Wayan, 170–73, 305n56
Setiadi, Hilmar Farid. *See* Farid, Hilmar
Shadow Play, 4–5
Shakespeare, 250
Shell Oil, 217–19, 223–24, 231, 233–34, 310n16
Siagian, Bachtiar, 85–86, 112, 294nn78–79
Sibang, 193
Silalahi, Harry Tjan, 65
Silverblatt, Irene, 91
Simbolon, Maludin, 220
Sinar Djawa, 123
Sinar Hindia, 123
Singapore, 36, 217, 237
Singingi, 231
Sino-Indonesians, 48, 65–66, 81, 122, 139–40, 287n96

Sino-Soviet split, 32
Siswanto, Subrantas, 236–37
Siswomiharjo, Sutoyo, 108, 255
Siswoyo, 56, 131, 277n56, 296n19, 298n38, 299n54
Sitepu, Brigadier General Ulung, 246
Si Tetap, 122
Sixth Brigade, 128–29, 133–36, 298n47
Sjafiudin, Brigadier General, 150, 155–58, 160–61, 184, 195, 201, 244–45, 302n12, 302n19, 307n15
Sjahrir, 197
Sjam, 131
Sjarifoeddin, Amir, 81, 124
Sjumandjaja, 113
Sneevliet, Henk, 122, 211, 295n8
Sobiran, Brigadier General, 246
Socialist Party. *See* Partai Sosialis Indonesia
Soe Hok Gie, 144–45, 152, 301n6
Soejatno, 141
Soekarmen, Lieutenant Colonel, 160, 176, 304n42
Soemanto, Lieutenant, 138
Soemarno, Major General, 7, 73
Soemitro, 159
Soeroto, 51–52
Solo River, 116–19
South Blitar, 102–3, 107, 114, 292n44, 292n46
Southeast Asia Treaty Organization (SEATO), 29, 39
South Sumatra, 20, 22–23, 214–15, 217–38, 240, 244–45, 250, 311n27, 313n61
Spain, 216
Special Bureau (Biro Chusus), 46, 101, 129, 131–34, 277n56, 298n42
Spies, Walter, 148
Sragen, 138, 221
Sri Lanka, 218
Stanvac (Standard-Vacuum Oil Company), 217–21, 224, 231, 233–34, 310n16, 312n44
state of exception, 260
Straus, Scott, 25–26, 63
Suara Indonesia, 157–58, 181, 308n28
Suasta, Raka, 202, 204
Subandrio, 73
Subchan ZE, 65, 247
Subroto, Gatot, 126, 131

Subroto, Ibnu, 50–52, 74–75, 82, 126, 131, 243
Sudigdo, Major, 130–31, 297n36
Sudisman, 49, 55, 99, 102, 229–30
Sugama, Yoga, 243
Sugandhi Kartosubroto, 51–52, 71, 73, 75, 82, 243, 278n76
Suharto, 6, 57–59, 70, 77, 88, 113, 137, 146, 159, 160, 176, 206, 215, 243, 259–60, 267n5, 268n8, 288n106, 298n36, 303n32, 314n10; army, 6, 9, 17–18, 23, 61, 86, 88, 94, 138, 146, 158, 213, 290n10; dictatorship, 3, 144; regime, 9, 12, 16, 70, 79, 88–89, 93, 103, 108, 111–13, 156, 215, 230, 237, 240, 255, 276n48, 277n 64, 288n106, 298n42, 298n44, 312n48, 313n56; years, 47, 76, 194, 238, 262, 313n61
Suharto, Brigadier General, 159, 303n32
Suharto, Lieutenant Colonel Ezy, 298n43
Sukanta, Putu Oka, 106, 292n51
Sukarno, 6–8, 28–31, 35–39, 41–43, 45–50, 52–62, 65–68, 73–75, 77, 80–83, 112–13, 124–27, 132, 135, 137–38, 144, 153–57, 159–61, 167, 189, 197, 199–200, 202, 207, 211, 219, 227–29, 233, 236, 239, 244, 246–47, 260, 268n8, 274n22, 275n39, 278n67, 278n76, 279nn92–93, 280n1, 280n7, 285nn64–65, 302n11, 304n37, 306n6, 312n44, 313n52, 314n7, 314n10
Sukarno, Captain, 136
Sukarnoism, 47
Sukendro, Brigadier General, 73
Sukoharjo, 119, 131, 143
Sulawesi, 23, 40, 257, 269n25, 313n4
Suluh Indonesia, 52
Sumatra, 17, 20, 22, 36, 100, 118, 134, 209, 214, 216, 220–22, 230–33, 235, 237, 239, 246, 248, 270n41, 276n53, 313n4
Sumini, 257
Sunarijadi, 247
Sunarti, 141–42
Sunaryo, Kustinah, 142
Sungai Gerong, 217, 219–20, 224, 227, 230, 233
Supardjo, Brigadier General, 50
Suradi, 130, 298n37
Surakarta, 20, 78, 81, 100, 116–46, 212, 221, 247, 295n4, 295n6, 298n40, 298nn42–44, 298n47, 299n56, 299n63, 300n67; Banjarsari neighborhood in, 141; City Hall of, 140–42; Jagalan neighborhood in, 142; Joint Security Staff of, 138; Kasunanan royal house of, 295n6; Kodim of, 116, 128, 133, 142, 298n43; Mangkunegaran royal house of, 146, 295n6; prison of, 142; Residency of, 22, 120, 124, 126–27, 138, 295n10; Sasono Mulyo detention camp in, 140–42; September 30th Movement in, 128–37
Suryaatmadja, Tubagus, 99–100
Suryadarma, Suryadi, 127
Suryadarma, Utami, 67, 127, 283n36, 297n26, 308n30
Suryaman, Asep, 101–3, 125, 131
Suryasumpeno, 134
Sutarto, Colonel, 124, 126, 296n19
Sutedja, Anak Agung Bagus, 150–51, 154–61, 177, 195, 199–200, 203, 207, 245, 301n10, 302n11, 303n23, 303n29, 307n25
Sutedja, Ibu, 177, 303n29
Sutjipto, Brigadier General, 64–65
Sutojo, Nani Nurrachman, 256
Sutowo, Ibnu, 230, 240, 312n37
Sutton, Horace, 152, 198, 306n4
Suwarto, 42, 55, 246, 272n1
Suyasa, Wedastera, 155, 159
Syukur, Abdul, 189

Taher, Yoseph, 230–32, 234–37
Taiwan, 216
Taman Siswa, 199
Tameng Marheinis, 147, 150–51, 158, 161–62, 171–73, 176, 183, 185–87, 191–92, 194–95, 201, 207, 248, 306n6, 306n10, 308n28
Tampaksiring, 154, 167
Tandjungsari, 69
Tanjung Priok, 69
Tan Swie Ling, 99, 102
Tapol, 108
Taran, 105–6
Tashkent, 207
Tegalbadeng, 158–59, 303n26
Tendean, Lieutenant, 72

Tentara dan Territorium (TT), 39–40, 220
Thayeb, Syarief, 67, 283n35
Timerman, Jacobo, 89
Tito, Josip Broz, 154
Toer, Pramoedya Ananta, 48, 66, 273n7
Topping, Seymour, 83
torture, 11, 20, 85–115; allegations of PKI committing, 70–71, 73, 84, 113; as imposition of a preexisting narrative, 90, 93, 99–102; interrogational, 91–93; liberal theory endorsing, 91; penal, 92; psychological, 96; Scarry's analysis of, 91–93
Tovar, B. Hugh, 59
Traverso, Enzo, 216
Tripp, Jon, 5
Tripp, L. Reed, 5
Trompet Masyarakat, 52
Trotsky, Leon, 34
trucks, 3, 6–7, 11, 19, 104, 136, 140–41, 143, 150, 152, 162, 165, 168–69, 177, 184, 186, 204, 213, 220, 224, 226, 234, 236–37, 239, 245, 247, 249, 251, 264
truth commission, 6, 255
Tutsis, 62

Ubud, 148–50, 154, 177
Udayana University, 163, 205–6, 306n4
Ulpian, 90
Undang-Undang Keadaan Bahaya, 252, 260
United Nations, 24–25, 36, 252
United States, 4, 29, 32, 42, 46, 83, 90, 108, 126–27, 214, 220, 233, 278n76, 290n10, 291n20, 291n25; Air Force of, 218; Navy of, 217
United States consulate in Medan, 17, 216, 246
United States embassy in Jakarta, 8, 42, 59, 61, 155, 224, 278n79, 281n9, 285n64, 300n63, 302n12, 303n31
United States Information Agency, 4
Universal Declaration of Human Rights, 252
University of British Columbia, 4
University of Indonesia, 67
University of Wisconsin–Madison, 3–5
Untung, Lieutenant Colonel, 76, 109, 128, 130–31, 133, 297n36

Urip, 194–95, 307n20
USSR (Union of Soviet Socialist Republics), 21, 26, 28, 33–34, 39, 86, 113, 216, 228, 297n26
Utomo, 114
Uwemedimo, Michael, 14

Vereeniging van Spoor en Tramweg-Personeel (VSTP), 211
victims, 3, 6–7, 9–10, 12, 14–15, 21, 23–24, 26, 48, 51, 62, 67, 75–76, 81, 84, 89, 93, 105, 109, 113, 117–19, 140, 145, 147, 164, 170, 178, 181, 185–89, 198–205, 214, 228, 230, 236–37, 249, 251–66, 287n89, 288n103, 290n10, 301n4, 303n31, 306n2, 306n4, 307n23
Vietnam, 90; Democratic Republic of Vietnam, 26; South Vietnam, 42
violence, 7–9, 12, 15–22, 26, 61–63, 71, 77–81, 83–84, 87, 99, 127, 138, 151–52, 155–56, 159, 162, 171, 174, 176–77, 195, 201, 203, 213–16, 230, 248, 251, 254–55, 261, 273n16, 281n15; atrocious nature of, 21, 261; bureaucratic, 16–18; communal, 16–17, 152; spontaneous, 7–11, 16–18, 20, 152
Violetta, 112

Wahid, Abdurrahman, 26, 84
Wahid, Salahuddin, 84
Wardhana, Jaya, 201
war of maneuver, 31, 50, 55, 274n17
war of position, 31, 46, 49–50, 272n7, 274n17
Warta Bandung, 52
Warta Bhakti (formerly *Sin Po*), 47, 49
Wayan, Pan, 187–89
Wedagama, Dewa Made, 163
West Java, 40, 62, 69, 72, 77, 98, 114, 124, 150, 157–58, 210, 235, 244–45, 289n6
West Kalimantan, 135
West New Guinea (West Papua), 36, 233
West Sumatra, 49–50, 123, 232, 235, 237, 239–40, 244–45, 248, 270n41, 312n41, 313n51, 313n59
West Virginia, 216
Widjanarko, Bambang, 112

Widodo, Joko (Jokowi), 254, 258–59, 262–63
Wijoyo, Agus, 254–55, 257–59, 262–63
Wikana, 124, 126, 296n19
Wiranto, 259–60
Wirka, Badam, 164
Wiwik, 142
Wonogiri, 131, 138
Wonokromo, 105
Wonosobo massacre, 3–7, 15
World Festival of Youth and Students, 206
World Peace Council, 200, 297n26

Yani, Ahmad, 47–48, 54–55, 72–73, 256, 284–85n58, 314n7
Yani, Amelia, 256
Yogyakarta, 3–5, 128–29, 136, 140, 197, 202, 297n31

Zainuddin, 236
Zein, Kivlan, 259
Žižek, Slavoj, 11–12
Zola, Émile, 59
Zulkadry, Adi, 12, 261, 269n21

Critical Human Rights

Memory's Turn: Reckoning with Dictatorship in Brazil
Rebecca J. Atencio

Prisoner of Pinochet: My Year in a Chilean Concentration Camp
Sergio Bitar; translated by Erin Goodman;
  foreword and notes by Peter Winn

Legislating Gender and Sexuality in Africa: Human Rights, Society, and the State
Edited by Lydia Boyd and Emily Burrill

*Bread, Justice, and Liberty: Grassroots Activism and Human Rights
  in Pinochet's Chile*
Alison J. Bruey

*Archiving the Unspeakable: Silence, Memory, and the Photographic Record
  in Cambodia*
Michelle Caswell

Court of Remorse: Inside the International Criminal Tribunal for Rwanda
Thierry Cruvellier; translated by Chari Voss

How Difficult It Is to Be God: Shining Path's Politics of War in Peru, 1980–1999
Carlos Iván Degregori; edited and with an introduction by Steve J. Stern

*Trauma, Taboo, and Truth-Telling: Listening to Silences
  in Postdictatorship Argentina*
Nancy J. Gates-Madsen

From War to Genocide: Criminal Politics in Rwanda, 1990–1994
André Guichaoua; translated by Don E. Webster

*Innocence and Victimhood: Gender, Nation, and Women's Activism
  in Postwar Bosnia-Herzegovina*
Elissa Helms

Inside Rwanda's Gacaca Courts: Seeking Justice after Genocide
Bert Ingelaere

Amending the Past: Europe's Holocaust Commissions and the Right to History
Alexander Karn

Civil Obedience: Complicity and Complacency in Chile since Pinochet
Michael J. Lazzara

Torture and Impunity
Alfred W. McCoy

Elusive Justice: Women, Land Rights, and Colombia's Transition to Peace
Donny Meertens

Conflicted Memory: Military Cultural Interventions and the Human Rights Era in Peru
Cynthia E. Milton

Historical Justice and Memory
Edited by Klaus Neumann and Janna Thompson

The Wars inside Chile's Barracks: Remembering Military Service under Pinochet
Leith Passmore

Buried Histories: The Anticommunist Massacres of 1965–1966 in Indonesia
John Roosa

The Human Rights Paradox: Universality and Its Discontents
Edited by Steve J. Stern and Scott Straus

Human Rights and Transnational Solidarity in Cold War Latin America
Edited by Jessica Stites Mor

Remaking Rwanda: State Building and Human Rights after Mass Violence
Edited by Scott Straus and Lars Waldorf

Beyond Displacement: Campesinos, Refugees, and Collective Action in the Salvadoran Civil War
Molly Todd

The Social Origins of Human Rights: Protesting Political Violence in Colombia's Oil Capital, 1919–2010
Luis van Isschot

The Soviet Union and the Gutting of the UN Genocide Convention
Anton Weiss-Wendt

The Politics of Necessity: Community Organizing and Democracy in South Africa
Elke Zuern

www.ingramcontent.com/pod-product-compliance
Lightning Source LLC
Chambersburg PA
CBHW051047230426
43666CB00012B/2600